Values and Valuables

SOCIETY FOR ECONOMIC ANTHROPOLOGY (SEA) MONOGRAPHS

Deborah Winslow, University of New Hampshire
General Editor, Society for Economic Anthropology

Monographs for the Society for Economic Anthropology contain original essays that explore the connections between economics and social life. Each year's volume focuses on a different theme in economic anthropology. Earlier volumes were published with the University Press of America, Inc. (#1–15, 17), Rowman & Littlefield, Inc. (#16). The monographs are now published jointly by AltaMira Press and the Society for Economic Anthropology (http://nautarch.tamu.edu/anth/sea/).

Current Volumes:

Vol. 1.   Sutti Ortiz, ed., *Economic Anthropology: Topics and Theories.*
Vol. 2.   Sidney M. Greenfield and Arnold Strickon, eds., *Entrepreneurship and Social Change.*
Vol. 3.   Morgan D. Maclachlan, ed., *Household Economies and Their Transformation.*
Vol. 4.   Stuart Plattner, ed., *Market and Marketing.*
Vol. 5.   John W. Bennett and John R. Brown, eds., *Production and Autonomy: Anthropological Studies and Critiques of Development.*
Vol. 6.   Henry J. Rutz and Benjamin S. Orlove, eds., *The Social Economy of Consumption.*
Vol. 7.   Christina Gladwin and Kathleen Truman, eds., *Food and Farm: Current Debates and Policies.*
Vol. 8.   M. Estellie Smith, ed., *Perspectives on the Informal Economy.*
Vol. 9.   Hill Gates and Alice Littlefield, eds., *Marxist Trends in Economic Anthropology.*
Vol. 10.   Sutti Ortiz and Susan Lees, eds., *Understanding Economic Process.*
Vol. 11.   Elizabeth M. Brumfiel, ed., *The Economic Anthropology of the State.*
Vol. 12.   James M. Acheson, ed., *Anthropology and Institutional Economics.*
Vol. 13.   Richard E. Blanton, Peter N. Peregrine, Deborah Winslow, and Thomas D. Hall, eds., *Economic Analysis beyond the Local System.*
Vol. 14.   Robert C. Hunt and Antonio Gilman, eds., *Property in Economic Context.*
Vol. 15.   David B. Small and Nicola Tannenbaum, eds., *At the Interface: The Household and Beyond.*
Vol. 16.   Angelique Haugerud, M. Priscilla Stone, and Peter D. Little, eds., *Commodities and Globalization: Anthropological Perspectives.*
Vol. 17.   Martha W. Rees and Josephine Smart, eds., *Plural Globalities in Multiple Localities: New World Border.*
Vol. 18.   Jean Ensminger, ed., *Theory in Economic Anthropology.*
Vol. 19.   Jeffrey H. Cohen and Norbert Dannhaeuser, eds., *Economic Development: An Anthropological Approach.*
Vol. 20.   Gracia Clark, ed., *Gender at Work in Economic Life.*
Vol. 21.   Cynthia Werner and Duran Bell, eds., *Values and Valuables: From the Sacred to the Symbolic.*

Values and Valuables

From the Sacred to the Symbolic

EDITED BY
CYNTHIA WERNER
AND
DURAN BELL

Published in Cooperation with the
Society for Economic Anthropology

A Division of
ROWMAN & LITTLEFIELD PUBLISHERS, INC.
Walnut Creek • Lanham • New York • Toronto • Oxford

AltaMira Press
A Division of Rowman & Littlefield Publishers, Inc.
1630 North Main Street, #367
Walnut Creek, CA 94596
www.altamirapress.com

Rowman & Littlefield Publishers, Inc.
A wholly owned subsidiary of The Rowman & Littlefield Publishing Group, Inc.
4501 Forbes Boulevard, Suite 200
Lanham, MD 20706

PO Box 317
Oxford
OX2 9RU, UK

British Library Cataloguing in Publication Information Available

Library of Congress Cataloging-in-Publication Data

Values and Valuables: From the Sacred to the Symbolic / edited by Cynthia Werner and Duran Bell.
      p. cm.—(Society for Economic Anthropology (SEA) monographs)
Includes index.
ISBN 0-7591-0544-8 (cloth: alk. paper)—ISBN 0-7591-0545-6 (pbk.: alk. paper)
   1. Economic anthropology. 2. Values—Cross-cultural studies. 3. Material culture—Cross-cultural studies. 4. Exchange—Cross-cultural studies. 5. Saving and investment—Cross-cultural studies. 6. Wealth—Social aspects. I. Werner, Cynthia Ann, 1967– II. Bell, Duran, 1936– III. Series: Society for Economic Anthropology monographs.

GN448.V35 2004
306.3—dc21   2003013698

Printed in the United States of America

♾™ The paper used in this publication meets the minimum requirements of American National Standard for Information Sciences—Permanence of Paper for Printed Library Materials, ANSI/NISO Z39.48-1992.

Contents

FIGURES

TABLES

Acknowledgments

The editors wish to thank a number of individuals who helped make this volume possible. The chapters in this book originate from the annual meeting of the Society for Economic Anthropology (SEA) held in Toronto, Canada, in April 2002. The theme of the conference was "Valuables, Goods, Wealth, and Money." The conference benefited greatly by the participation of Maurice Godelier, who presented the keynote lecture (included in this volume) and provided commentary during a special roundtable session. We would like to thank Professor Godelier for his contribution to the conference and the volume. The conference would not have been possible without the efforts of B. Lynne Milgram, who did a wonderful job as the local arrangements coordinator. We would also like to thank Kathy Gordon, Shadi Eskandani, and David H. Kaye for their conference support. We would like to thank Gavin Alderson Smith and the Department of Anthropology at the University of Toronto for coordinating and cosponsoring the lecture by Professor Godelier. Deborah Winslow, the SEA general editor, provided valuable insights and advice throughout the preparation of this volume. Her influence has certainly made this a stronger book. Thanks also to Rosalie Robertson, our editor at AltaMira, and the anonymous reviewers who provided comments for the volume as a whole, as well as individual chapters. Finally, Cynthia Werner would like to thank the Melbern G. Glasscock Center for Humanities Research at Texas A&M for the valuable time provided by a faculty research leave, and Harriette Andreadis, Brian Harley, and Lori Wright for their valuable insights and support.

Introduction
Values and Valuables: From the Sacred to the Symbolic

Duran Bell and Cynthia Werner

From the earliest days of the discipline, economic anthropologists have been concerned with the material objects that humans produce, consume, accumulate, and exchange. Despite this materialistic bent, economic anthropologists have readily acknowledged that some objects are imbued with either sacred or symbolic qualities whose values can never be reduced to material necessity or monetary equivalent. In some cases, money itself, which is often assumed to be a neutral medium of exchange, is given these additional attributes. In 2002, the Society for Economic Anthropology held a conference to reconsider these ideas in the contemporary world. We invited Professor Maurice Godelier of the École des Hautes Études in Paris, known for his path-breaking theoretical work on sacred objects, to give the keynote address (chapter 1). Forty-four anthropologists from four countries also presented their work on the questions of sacred objects, prestige goods, and monetary instruments. Godelier's latest book, *The Enigma of the Gift,* was a source of inspiration for many participants, especially his concern with things "not given, but kept"—a phenomenon that Godelier has provocatively associated with the sacred. A number of conference participants interrogated the sacred as it appears in various cultures and examined the general category of symbolic things that are kept, not given. Thirteen of the original conference papers have been revised and expanded for this book. Taken together, these chapters provide a wide-ranging overview of the current research on these topics.

This volume is organized around three themes that emerged from the conference. The first part examines the social life of sacred things, including ancestral objects, land, and dreaming stories. The chapters in this section consider the sacred nature of these things and the extent to which sacred objects can or cannot be exchanged or transmitted between individuals. The second part considers the value and power of markets, money, and credit. The chapters in this section consider theoretical models for understanding monetary transactions, consumers' use of money in early capitalist societies (such as colonial Jamaica), competing currencies in colonial societies (including the cowry in West Africa and "guerrilla" currencies in China), and the power of credit among marginalized groups (including Native Americans in the United States and craft traders in the Philippines). The final part examines the ways in which contemporary people bestow symbolic values on some objects (such as family heirlooms, pre-Columbian ceramic replicas, and fashion goods) and how some people (including fashion models and diabetes patients) are valued in monetary and symbolic ways.

THE POWER OF THE SACRED

The chapters in part 1 deal with gifts and other objects that are imbued with sacred qualities and imaginary powers. This is a central concern in Maurice Godelier's work, including his chapter in this book. Since the 1966 publication of *Rationality and Irrationality in Economics,* Godelier has been a leader in the field of economic anthropology. His fieldwork among the Baruya of New Guinea has profoundly influenced his theories in economic anthropology. Characterized as a classless, stateless hunting–horticultural society with extreme gender distinctions, the Baruya were "discovered" by the West in 1951, and they were quickly transformed by market relations, Western colonialism, and Christian missions (Godelier 1986). Although Baruya society has changed in many ways, sacred objects have retained their importance in ritual and economic life. In his most recent book, *The Enigma of the Gift* (1996), Godelier returns to Marcel Mauss's (1990) seminal essay on gift exchange and then directs attention to "things that must be neither sold nor given, but must be kept." Among the Baruya, the things that must be kept are often "sacred objects" (Godelier 1996:108), such as *kwaimatnie,* which are displayed during initiation ceremonies. In chapter 1, Godelier asserts that

> a sacred object is a material object that represents the nonrepresentable, which
> refers men back to the origin of things and attests to the legitimacy of the cos-

mic and social order that replaced the primal time and its events. . . . For those who handle and exhibit them, sacred objects are not symbols. They are experienced and thought of as the real presence of forces that are the source of the powers that reside in them. The sacred object, then, is a "material" synthesis of the imaginary and symbolic components present in the relations that organize real societies.

Here, Godelier's depiction of sacred objects corresponds to Rudolf Otto's foundational discussion on religion, *The Idea of the Holy* (1958), in which he describes the holy as *mysterium tremendum*. From the perspective of Christian theology, the holy is the sacred, which Otto eloquently describes:

> Let us consider the deepest and most fundamental element in all strong and sincerely felt religious emotion. Faith unto salvation, trust, love—all these are there. But over and above these is an element which may also on occasion, quite apart from them, profoundly affect us and occupy the mind with a wellnigh bewildering strength . . . we shall find that we are dealing with something for which there is only one appropriate expression, *mysterium tremendum*. (Otto 1958:12).

For Otto, the holy, or the sacred, is a "wholly other" phenomenon that is simultaneously awesome, fearsome, fascinating, and majestic.

In addition to describing the nature of sacred objects, Godelier raises another point of enormous significance. He suggests a direct correspondence between the sacred object and "the relations that organize real societies." This argument echoes that of Mircea Eliade (1959), who associated powerful gods in "primitive" societies with social relations of domination. Eliade writes from the perspective of a scientific mind that struggles to understand and reach inside the mind of *Homo religiosus*. He associates the sacred with the cosmologies of the primitive and thus presupposes a more rational and profane worldview for modern societies. Of particular interest is Eliade's argument that a strong commitment to a celestial and dominating god is induced by efforts to survive as a culture and as a people, efforts that may reach extremes in exploitative state regimes. In simpler social domains, more proximate gods and symbols will suffice; for example, as gods of fertility, rain, safety. Unfortunately for us, Eliade does not discuss sacred objects as such. Godelier, however, does discuss the relationship between sacred objects and social structure. Among the Baruya, for example, the *kwaimatnie* are bundles of seemingly unspectacular objects upon which enormous significance is placed. The kwaimatnie are the possession of men and are important to *maintaining* the powers and rights that male ancestors have transmitted to men of the moment. Hence, they are not simply symbolic; they also enter the imaginary as a source of power.

How, then, are we to conceive of the sacred in this book? First, a sacred entity must have autonomous powers in the world. It is because of such powers that the sacred can be characterized as the *mysterium tremendum.* For example, ancestors are to be worshipped, not because they were adorable individuals when they lived, but because terrible things will happen in the absence of appropriate ceremonies of appreciation. Perhaps the rains will not arrive, and crops will fail. Perhaps the spirits of the ancestors will become troublesome and cause sickness and confusion. In other words, objects that are sacred have the power to affect contemporary life. Second, the sacred is socially constructed by the socially powerful for important reasons. Sacred objects or beings become factors that reinforce the domination of men over women, of elders over juniors, and of kings over subjects. Peculiar, then, is the transformation of the fearsome and unpredictable Christian God of the slave and feudal periods into the contemporary entity with whom one might have intimate conversations. It is a peculiarity that corresponds to the nonhierarchical structure of capitalist democracies, which allows individuals to experience personal relationships with the sacred.

Since the existence of the sacred resides in the imagination, not in this world, and since it enters as a validation of the social position of individuals, it cannot be "given" in exchange. It can move among individuals only as it devolves within the group for which it provides ethical legitimization. However, the sacred does not monopolize the domain of things not subject to alienation. This point is made most emphatically by Colin Danby (in chapter 4), who cites Godelier's ethnography as evidence. Danby points out that trading relationships between the Baruya (Godelier 1971:61–62) and their neighbors can often be established only with high risk of injury and death. Those who have risked death to provide the tribe with such trading relations are honored in memory and may transmit to their progeny various prerogatives in the continued trading relation. In this case, we find a connection between the domain of exchange (a domain referred to by Sahlins [1972] as "negative reciprocity") and the holding of rights that are kept or shared within a family. Danby argues that even in the trading of salt "keeping, giving, and trading salt must be considered as a whole." The social rank of persons and things may be raised significantly without their gaining the attributes of the sacred.

In chapter 2, the power of the sacred is brought into sharp relief by James A. Egan's discussion of land in Yap, one of the island nations within the Federated States of Micronesia. This is a matrilineal society, in which the fertility of women is the unifying corporate resource. However, for the product of that fertility to gain social location in relation to land, a woman must move onto her husband's land (actually, land to which he is attached). Having been provided the resources of this land, she must demonstrate that she belongs to that long and honored sequence of women whose efforts in ascending generations have provided power to the land. Land in Yap is hierarchically differentiated such that a man has power, or "voice," to the extent that the land that he represents has voice. This power, in turn, is the fantastic consequence of the intersection of production and reproduction by a woman on land that is under the control of her husband's sisters.

> The value of land—and its imaginary power to encode hierarchy while concealing the many social exclusions of the here and now—rests upon the inability of anyone to make such claims. Land transcends individuals. Land transcends generations, linking the living and the dead. Land encodes history. It is this power of land that inspires awe—that makes it numinous—that makes land sacred with or without the gods.

But if land is sacred, it should be kept. And it is, but it is also given. Egan expresses the paradox as keeping-for-giving and (simultaneously) giving-for-keeping. This set of twin contradictions arises from the fact that rights to the use of land (and rights to attach children to land) are yielded to in-marrying women by the sisters of their husbands, who have themselves moved onto other lands for which they attempt to qualify. One of the occasions for the demonstration of merit by a wife has been the *mitmit,* once a ceremony of marriage and now a ceremony of death, to which the female relatives of in-marrying women bring the product of their land. They must *give* (product of land) in order to *keep* (use-rights to land). Those women who yield rights to social positions in land are able to assess the contributions of their brothers' wives to the mitmit and, hence, determine their right to remain on the land.

In this way the women who have departed from the land have given it to others while maintaining a status within it—giving-while-keeping. And if this yielding of access proves to be useful in maintaining the voice of the land, then that which is to be kept is actually strengthened by the giving—giving-for-keeping. In this very competitive society, it is the task of women to gain rights to land whose voice they are obliged to maintain through constant effort. Yet, this voice is to be expressed by men, to be manifested as a *mysterium tremendum* that rationalizes hierarchy in social relations.

These same issues are advanced in a very different context by Françoise Dussart (in chapter 3), who considers the distribution and exchange of "dreaming stories" among the Warlpiri of the central Australian desert. In this case the sacred valuable takes the form of designs or "graphics" that emerge in dreams and the ritual recitation of dreaming stories. We can say that these things are "sacred" because the Warlpiri believe they are directly connected with the spirit world, and the depiction of certain designs and the performance of certain dreams are considered to be powerful and dangerous in a way that is essential to sustaining the productivity of land and people. Warlpiri dreams acquire value when they are incorporated into ritual performances. To ensure the effectiveness of a dreaming performance, several individuals negotiate the proper use of the dream in the performance.

Dream segments are engendered, meaning that kin groups determine whether a particular dream segment is "male" or "female." One of the fascinating sections of Dussart's discussion deals with a particular woman's need for a form of ritual knowledge that is enacted only by men. The woman sought the assistance of her brother, who could provide her a *modified* male shield design. It was only the transformed and modified version of the graphic that entered into exchange, allowing men to continue to keep their own special form of magic. She copied this design and had it painted onto her body while she sang songs. She later rewarded her brother handsomely for use of the graphic. Since her brother resides in a different household, this compensated transfer of sacred materials appears to be an example of giving (exchange). However, it is closer to what Annette Weiner (1992) refers to as "keeping-while-giving." As Dussart explains, "Warlpiri dreams must be exchanged in order to acquire value for their 'owners,' yet dream material that is given to members of the opposite sex must be transformed or modified."

Egan's chapter on ancestral land among the Yap and Dussart's chapter on dreaming stories among the Warlpiri provide exciting examples of sacred things and can be compared to Godelier's case study of sacred objects among the Baruya that are not given in exchange. On the one hand, Egan completely supports Godelier's arguments about sacred objects by suggesting that the use of land—a sacred object with imaginary powers—among the Yap involves both keeping-for-giving and giving-for-keeping. Dussart, on the other hand, provides a counterargument by suggesting that Warlpiri nocturnal dreams "have less to do with giving or keeping and more to do with transforming through transmitting."

MARKETS, MONEY, AND POWER

The second part of this book considers the use of money in markets, the values attributed to money as currency, and the power of money in the form of credit. Comparative studies of money frequently suggest that money is a *neutral* device that facilitates economic activity. Statements suggesting that money is simply a means of exchange and a store of wealth do not consider all the ways in which money is used in society. Although money is not sacred in the sense of possessing *mysterium tremendum*, it is not always a neutral instrument of exchange. The chapters in part 2 examine money as an instrument of exchange, as a valuable that may acquire symbolic value, and as a source of power that may fragment society.

In chapter 4, Colin Danby relates Godelier's views on the relationship between economy and culture to the heterodox subfield of post-Keynesian economics. Using a post-Keynesian approach, Danby challenges the neoclassical view that money can properly be considered a wholly instrumental feature of economic life. While neoclassical economists reduced the human economy of Keynes to the mechanistic neoclassical formulation, post-Keynesian economics is in part an effort to reconnect with the lost brilliance of the Keynesian insight. One should note that Keynes (1936) perceived an economy that was subject to the volatile sentiment of real people. The centerpiece of this model was the "marginal efficiency of capital," a construct arising from the unstable expectations of investors and business firms. Danby says, "To put it a different way, the very coherence of a capitalist economy with active financial markets may depend on the willingness to share representations."

In chapter 5, Georgia L. Fox examines the use of money among early colonists to purchase consumer goods in colonial Jamaica. Port Royal, a thriving Caribbean port city that was destroyed by an earthquake in 1692, was submerged for centuries. The recent excavation of this well-preserved site provides some insight into Caribbean colonial life in the seventeenth century. One of the more interesting finds is a cache of more than twenty thousand used and unused clay pipes. These pipes were mass-produced and affordable products that were probably smoked once and then thrown away. Thus, a community of smokers required thousands of pipes. The quantity of pipes and the presence of luxury goods at Port Royal, combined with the widespread cultivation of tobacco in Jamaica, provide a new perspective for understanding core periphery relations in the seventeenth century. Rather than simply providing raw materials to the British Empire, the colonists at Port Royal were active as both producers and consumers.

From a neoclassical perspective, the state (and hence the money issued by the state) is neutral to the operations of "free market" economies. In his discussion of the French franc and the cowry in West Africa (chapter 6), Mahir Şaul suggests that money, rather than being neutral in colonial situations, can symbolize the domination of one group over another. While tribal economies were depicted as having elders in control of trade and monetary instruments for their own devious purposes, it was claimed that European money implied freedom from such interventions. Hence, the efforts of the French to subdue the cowry and replace it with the French franc can appear to be little more than the advancement of a "civilizing mission."

Cowries were first introduced to Africa by European mercantile traders in earlier centuries. But, as Şaul argues, with the transition from mercantilism to capitalism and colonial exploitation, the cowry became a problem. During an earlier period, the cowry had been traded on the European exchanges; it was readily accepted by local traders and could be used for all economic and fiscal purposes. And most importantly, the cowry eventually proved to be the superior currency, maintaining its value over the course of time while the franc fluctuated in value and depreciated rather disastrously. However, the cowry was initially available in large quantities in the "hoards" of tribal elders. These African elders represented a power center different from the bourgeois state (i.e., the "elders" in Paris). The goal of the metropolis was to reduce African societies to servitude relative to the accumulation of French industrial capital. This role was inconsistent with the persistence of traditional African social structures, justifying the adoption of a "civilizing" mission. The use of moneys with the faces of French people emblazoned on the front was important to this mission. The franc possessed a significance that went beyond its rational economic functions. It was *symbolic* of French culture in its domination of African culture. Indeed, it is readily conceivable that the franc had been revered as a sacred object.

While there has been considerable literature on monetary competitions between colonists and colonized, less attention has been paid to competition within a given national terrain. In chapter 7, Beth E. Notar examines the politics of currency competition in China during the 1920s and 1930s. In the late nineteenth century and the early twentieth century, thousands of different currencies, many issued by foreign colonial banks, provincial banks, and "native banks," were simultaneously in use. Some notes were advertising media, primarily used to attract potential customers, and some notes carried symbolism of the colonial power, such as the notes of a New York bank that pictured "an eagle encompassing the entire world."

The Republic of China entered the fray to bring order to the chaos and to establish the central government as a trustworthy entity. During the 1930s, the Nationalist government tried to establish a currency monopoly, but its efforts failed and a multiplicity of currencies persisted. Mao Zedong's forces developed their own paper money as a way of gaining local resources without alienating the peasantry and as a mode of advertising. Initially, their currencies were strongly Soviet in appearance, featuring the hammer and sickle and pictures of Karl Marx. In areas where Communist and Nationalist forces were in serious competition, the holding of one or the other form of currency could be dangerous and constituted a political act, a fact that strongly establishes money as an item of political symbolism.

In modern economies, currencies still contain important symbolic information about nation–states, yet the importance of paper and coin currency is diminishing as commercial banks implement electronic means to conduct transactions. Commercial banks are often presumed to act as rational profit-maximizing enterprises. Indeed, commercial banking is an extremely sophisticated operation. Yet, there is an overarching value system that guides and constrains behavior. This is so because loans to one sector of the market reduce funds available to other sectors, and the allocation of funds among sectors is sometimes affected by extrinsic social valuations. For example, the creditworthiness of an entire class of applicants may not be calculable by conventional methods, and the social valuation of this class of applicant might affect the inclination of a lending institution to develop appropriate assessing tools. Consequently, in relation to a specific applicant, the lending agent may correctly claim that the costs of assessment are excessive relative to benefits. The disadvantaged sector is likely to be one that is economically and, perhaps, socially marginal—that is, less important to the central forces of capital accumulation.

When classes of applicants who are disadvantaged in the formal sector are able to develop "informal" mechanisms for receiving credit, the official agencies of monetary management may feel threatened. As we have observed in the previous discussion, ruling elites (be they elders of a tribe or elders of a metropolis) demand prerogatives to control the circulation of money. An informal market for credit is not under their control. So, while official forces may not have a great interest in a disadvantaged sector, they are concerned to displace informal lenders whose actions appear to usurp the prerogatives of the formal sector. Such efforts have, in the past, been readily justified by the myth of the usurious moneylender whose existence is alleged to be damaging to his client and to the economy as a whole. Hence, a replacement of the informal by the formal is analogous to the civilizing mission of French colonists in their effort to replace the cowry with the franc.

Formal lenders often find that there are valuable aspects of the informal system that are beyond their imitation (Adams and Fitchett 1992). We have two examples before us of such informal systems. In chapter 8, B. Lynne Milgram examines credit relations among producers, buyers, and retailers of craft objects in the Philippines. In chapter 9, Kathleen Pickering and David Mushinski consider a microbanking operation on the Pine Ridge Indian Reservation in the United States. In both cases the importance of personal familiarity, knowledge of the creditworthiness of specific applicants, and willingness to deal with relatively small loans are distinguishing characteristics of the informal financial systems.

In the Philippines, craft producers often develop a *suki* (patron–client) relation with traders within which credit may be extended with lower risk. Traders pay cash advances to producers, thereby securing a commitment of delivery from the producer while allowing the producer to cover costs of production and (often overlooked) family consumption expenses as well. Particularly surprising is the degree to which traders must yield to the interests of producers, to the extent of forgiving default. Traders may also provide product to retailers on credit, so that the traders face losses from both sides of the transaction. Economic characteristics of the trader's market position deserve additional scrutiny. However, it is difficult to imagine equally effective entrée by the formal sector into these financial arrangements.

The discussion by Pickering and Mushinski of informal banking systems at Pine Ridge suggests that the formal system of banking in the United States effectively excludes Indian reservations. The failure of these institutions to make loans to the people of Pine Ridge is the obverse of the efforts of the French to eliminate trading of the cowry. In effect, it is a refusal to integrate Pine Ridge into the American economy. For these reservations to be integrated into the financial system, bankers must be able to assess the creditworthiness of *individual* borrowers and be able to apply social pressure on those who might otherwise default. However, the dominant society's assumptions about Indian behavior lead to an inordinate suppression of social contact and knowledge about individual capabilities, and this leads to a form of "profiling" that reduces the likelihood of loans to Indians from institutions outside of the reservation.

CONTEMPORARY VALUABLES AND SYMBOLIC VALUES

One can imagine hearing—years ago, and perhaps even today—a minister in a rural southern church ask rhetorically of the parishioners, "What is thunder?" to which a chorus of responses exclaims "God's voice!" Rain, lightning, thunder, and the rays of the sun become imbued with the sacred. Every element of the environment is suffused with wonder, *mysterium tremendum,* and a good measure of danger. But such a world has been lost to many people today. Scientific explanation has leveled and demystified most things, leaving many people searching frantically for the exaltation that arrives in the presence of the sacred. Given the lack of personal recognition of the powers of the "wholly other," there is likely to be a reconceptualization of objects that might once have been considered sacred.

In a world with a decreasing need for a fearsome God, the hugely popular *Antiques Roadshow* on public television often reflects a modern search for proximate and personal sacred objects. With the presentation and (commercial) valorization of heirlooms, individuals seek to infuse daily life more powerfully with elements of the sacred. The selected experts on this program are likely to ascertain the authenticity of the item (proving, for example, that its maker was indeed a highly regarded craftsman in Manchester during the early 1800s). But the crowning moment is the expert's estimate of the item's "auction value." Having made this pronouncement to the brightly beaming owner, the expert will often suggest that the sentimental value of the item might preclude its devolution into commercial exchange. It should be kept!

The chapters in part 3 consider values and valuables in what can be called "contemporary" or "modern" societies. More specifically, these chapters examine material objects that are valued for their symbolic qualities and people who are valued in symbolic and monetary ways. In chapter 10, Eric J. Arnould, Carolyn Folkman Curasi, and Linda L. Price present their research on "inalienable objects," namely, family heirlooms, in middle-class North American households. The authors focus on how certain family possessions are transformed into "objects that should not be given or sold, but kept within the confines of a kinship structure." In this way those items may become emblems of family identity into future generations.

In many societies such transmissions are associated with matrilineal or patrilineal transmissions of wealth in the forms of land and/or animals, much like the inheritance of the family farm in American society. In such cases the history of a herd or of the land carries images of generations past whose efforts have been important to the present prosperity of the group. Today few Americans are able to connect themselves to ancestors and progeny by means of transmissible wealth–assets of this kind. Unable to root their identities in the past and future, they may seek, often in desperation, to locate something emblematic of self that is subject to intergenerational transmission—an emblem that has the potential of achieving the totemic. Some people may refer to these objects as "sacred" objects. However, household items and jewelry are not sacred because they are not invested with the power of the wholly other. Heirlooms do not possess a voice like that of Yapese land, nor do they possess the power of Warlpiri graphics.

The heirlooms discussed by Arnould et al. are concrete items of human manufacture, not animals of the forest or sky like the totems found among aboriginals. Since people of the modern West dominate and often despoil most of the more noble animal species, identification of a family with such beings is unlikely. Much more likely is identification with artifacts of capitalist production. These are the kinds of things that people cherish for their symbolic, rather than their market, value.

Similarly, elegant pre-Columbian ceramics are national treasures not subject to commodification. In chapter 11, Jim Weil describes replicas of pre-Columbian art in Costa Rica as "virtual antiquities" and argues that these valuables should be valued as "authentic" objects rather than "fake" duplicates. These replicas are produced today with similar techniques and designs by the descendants of artisans who produced the originals more than six hundred years ago. In many ways, they are "the real thing." But the ancestors did not pass them down, and they are not kept as heirlooms. Instead, they are sold with other goods in an international ethnic-arts market. Like the heirlooms discussed in chapter 4, these ceramic replicas are not sacred because they do not possess *mysterium tremendum*. These ceramics, however, are given symbolic values by the indigenous artisan communities where they are produced and by the global marketplace where they are consumed. Both producers and consumers believe that the designs on these replicas carry symbolic meanings associated with pre-Columbian peoples. Therefore, these objects are symbols of the symbolic, evoking some of the same sentiments associated with the original ceramics.

In chapter 12, Brian Moeran discusses the values associated with fashion objects and fashion models. His fascinating look at the fashion industry, where the economic value of goods often seems to be excessively high, examines how fashion goods and fashion models are given different kinds of values by different actors within the fashion industry. Fashion clothing is produced by one set of actors, yet its characterization devolves upon others, especially those who produce fashion magazines. It raises questions about "who is bestowing things with what kind of values, when, where, and why." Moeran argues that different categories of actors (photographers, art directors, editors, models, and so on) attribute different kinds of values (technical, social, appreciative, utility) to objects and that these values as a whole "contribute to the total symbolic and commodity exchange values of that object." Fashion models are also valued in different ways. A fashion model does not earn much money for appearing on the cover or in the contents of a fashion magazine, yet this opportunity enhances her value in the commercial side of fashion advertising.

The valuation of people and things is also the subject of chapter 13, in which Melanie Rock examines how Canadian pharmaceutical companies commodify human lives in their marketing strategies for diabetes patients. More specifically, she argues that health insurance companies and drug companies place values on human lives as they make health assessments and determine ways to improve the lives of individuals (by marketing certain products and replacing body parts). It would seem, then, that human lives are symbolically, or at least ideologically, constructed as inalienable, and perhaps sacred, while being always subject to the exploitation of economic interests. These observations suggest that the symbolic significance given to people and things is often under the control of socially dominant categories in society. This parallels the observation that we made earlier with reference to the sacred.

CONCLUSION

Economic anthropologists have always distinguished themselves from economists by placing greater emphasis on the interplay of cultural and economic values in economic life. This book contributes to the literature in economic anthropology by focusing on values and valuables, broadly defined. The chapters are organized along three themes: the power of the sacred; markets, money, and power; and contemporary valuables and symbolic values. Although the chapters deal with a variety of topics, taken together they support several arguments that have been discussed in this introduction. First, as the chapters unanimously suggest, objects with sacred or symbolic qualities are valued quite differently from other objects. Some objects, such as ancestral objects and family heirlooms, are considered to be so valuable that they are kept rather than given or traded. Other objects, such as ceramic replicas and fashion clothing associated with celebrities, are given symbolic values that increase their economic value in the marketplace. Second, as several chapters demonstrate, money itself can acquire symbolic values. In such cases, money does not correspond to textbook assumptions that it is a neutral instrument of exchange. Finally, as many chapters suggest, values and valuables cannot be considered without considering the issue of power. Many chapters demonstrate that the socially powerful often influence the ways in which objects are valued in society; and sacred objects are among those that can be used to reinforce the domination of men over women, of elders over juniors, and of kings over subjects.

REFERENCES

Adams, Dale W., and Delbert A. Fitchett, eds. 1992. *Informal Finance in Low-Income Countries.* Boulder, Colo.: Westview Press.

Eliade, Mircea. 1959. *The Sacred and the Profane: The Nature of Religion.* New York: Harcourt Brace Jovanovich.

Godelier, Maurice. 1971. "'Salt Currency' and the Circulation of Commodities among the Baruya of New Guinea." In *Studies in Economic Anthropology.* George Dalton, ed. Pp. 52–73. *Anthropological Studies* 7. Washington, D.C.: American Anthropological Association.

———. 1986 [1982]. *The Making of Great Men: Male Domination and Power among the New Guinea Baruya.* Rupert Swyer, trans. Cambridge, U.K.: Cambridge University Press.

———. 1999 [1996]. *The Enigma of the Gift.* Nora Scott, trans. Chicago: University of Chicago Press.

Keynes, John Maynard. 1936. *The General Theory of Employment, Interest, and Money.* New York: Harcourt, Brace.

Lévi-Strauss, Claude. 1965 [1915]. *The Raw and the Cooked.* John and Doreen Weightman, trans. New York: Harper & Row.

Mauss, Marcel. 1990 [1925]. *The Gift: The Form and Reason for Exchange in Archaic Societies.* W. D. Halls, trans. New York: W. W. Norton.

Otto, Rudolf. 1958 [1923]. *The Idea of the Holy: An Inquiry into the Non-Rational Factor in the Idea of the Divine and Its Relation to the Rational.* John W. Harvey, trans. New York: Oxford University Press.

Sahlins, Marshall. 1972. *Stone Age Economics.* Chicago: Aldine-Atherton.

Weiner, Annette. 1992. *Inalienable Possessions: The Paradox of Keeping-While-Giving.* Berkeley and Los Angeles: University of California Press.

I

THE POWER OF
THE SACRED

What Mauss Did Not Say: Things You Give, Things You Sell, and Things That Must Be Kept

*Maurice Godelier**

I began my anthropological career teaching economic anthropology in 1962. I had just been made a lecturer under Claude Lévi-Strauss. Before that, however, I had studied philosophy and had been haunted by the question: How can one compare social and economic systems, if such systems exist? At the time, two systems were vying for world domination: the capitalist system and the socialist system, which emerged in Russia in the early twentieth century and had rapidly expanded not only to China but also to Cuba. After receiving my doctorate in philosophy, I had gone into economics and even learned the rudiments of mathematical economics. In reality, I had come to ask myself three questions, which were to be the starting point of my migration to anthropology: On what conditions can economic systems be "compared"? How can one account for their appearance and then disappearance in the course of history? In what way does the Western notion of "economic rationality" enable social systems to be compared?

It was—oddly enough, it may be said—in the hope of finding answers to these questions that I turned to anthropology. For the economists—both the liberal and the Marxist varieties—had what seemed to me too ideological or too narrow a way of formulating these questions, nor was I overly convinced by the historians' accounts of the reasons for the transition from feudalism to capitalism in Europe. It seemed to me that it would be more productive to study the economic systems of contemporary living societies organized

---

*Translated by Nora Scott.

according to social and cultural logics that were fundamentally different from Western logic, even if they were subordinate to the West. It was then that I met Claude Lévi-Strauss. I had just published three articles in the journal *Économie Politique* (Godelier 1960a, 1960b, 1961). These were my first articles on the notion of "structure" in Marx's *Capital,* and I had sent them to Lévi-Strauss, whom I did not know personally at the time. He wrote me a note saying that he had found these texts most interesting and all the more so because, as a young man, before preparing the agrégation in philosophy, he had written an essay on the same topic: "The Logic of Marx's *Capital.*" At the suggestion of Fernand Braudel, I met Lévi-Strauss and explained my desire to become an anthropologist and my reasons. He invited me to join his laboratory at the Collège de France. He joked that I could work "on infrastructures" and do a survey of all the material gathered by anthropologists on the economy of primitive societies.

So it was in 1963 that I began, as almost the only person in France, to explore this field. In the United States, on the other hand, many were already working in this area, disciples of Karl Polanyi, who opposed the "formalists" like R. Firth and Schneider. I began to lay out an anthropology of the systems of production, systems of distribution, and primitive moneys. At the time, Lévi-Strauss had gone back to one of Marx's ideas, that of the existence of so-called structural correspondences that "must" exist between economic, kinship, and religious structures. This was an overarching theoretical view of societies. Today, forty years later, there does not seem to be any structural correspondence between kinship, religion, and the various systems of production that have succeeded each other over time. If such a correspondence exists, I have not seen it demonstrated either in the works of my colleagues or in the field among the Baruya of New Guinea.

To give an example, I of course observed that the Baruya had strategies for saving, not on their working time, which was not a scarce resource, but on the effort expended in clearing primary forest for gardens. In this region of high mountains, they usually chose to cut halfway through the medium- and small-sized trees standing downhill from a forest giant. Then they would cut clear through the trunk of one, which would finish off their work for them by taking down the rest of the trees as it fell. This strategy was typical of certain aspects of their labor process, but it told me nothing about the social relations organizing this labor process. It told me nothing about the social relations by means of which the Baruya control access to land and redistribute it among themselves for horticultural or hunting purposes. Nor did it tell me anything about the division of labor or about the rules the Baruya follow when redistributing the products of their labor. In the field I saw that the social relations that organized the production of their means of subsistence and their means of exchange were in fact their kinship relations and at the same time the political relations that defined the place of each clan within the tribe. This corresponded to the very un-Marxist idea that, depending on the epoch and the society, certain kinds of social relations can operate as relations of production, thus performing, as Marx would say, the twin functions of infrastructure and superstructure.

But what had also struck me about the Baruya was that they produced a salt money that enabled them to obtain a whole series of objects necessary to the organization of their society. The salt was exchanged for the polished stones used to make their adzes, and therefore for means of production. But it was also exchanged for means of destruction: arrows made by their neighbors. Finally, it was exchanged for bird-of-paradise feathers or cowry shells—that is, for the components necessary to the social reproduction of the status of the initiated men. In short, the Baruya's economy was part of a regional economy. Even on this scale, there was no such thing as a purely local economy, and it found in other neighboring societies, within a regional division of production, some of the conditions of its own reproduction. And for this to work, the societies had to exchange. Salt served as an exchange currency and circulated from one group to another as a good. But within the Baruya group itself, salt was never exchanged. It was redistributed as part of the gifts exchanged by kin and affines. This meant that even lineages that did not possess salt-producing lands had salt to exchange [products]. Salt, a gift object for the Baruya, became a commodity that detached itself from the person of its owner and became totally alienated when it entered the goods circuit at the regional economic level.

But material and economic dependence between groups did not explain the internal organization of these groups, what made them a local society, a whole that must reproduce itself as such. In fact I realized that the two aspects of their economy—the organization within the group of the production and distribution of the means of the everyday existence of the lineages and families, and the organization of the exchanges with outside groups—could not explain what made the Baruya society a whole, and a whole that had to be represented and reproduced as such.

What made this society a whole was not its economic relations. It was the system of political and religious dependencies linking all the lineages and clans, and the system that set these dependencies in motion was the system of male and female initiations. It was there, in those practices, a portion of which were addressed to what for us are imaginary realities, that the Baruya affirmed themselves in the eyes of others as a society. But these were not the only practices by which they affirmed themselves; they also affirmed themselves by claiming sovereignty over a territory that they had divided among themselves and that they defended weapons in hand.

My fieldwork had thus brought me face-to-face with commercial forms of exchange, with noncommercial gifts and countergifts, and with sacred objects used in ceremonies and which the Baruya would neither sell nor give to their neighbors. That is why, thirty years later, I have returned, not really to full-blown economic anthropology, but to that privileged domain of analysis we call "exchange." And that is why I have chosen to devote this chapter more generally to why there are some things one sells, others one gives, and yet others that can be neither sold nor given, but which must be kept and transmitted. It is clear that the reasons do not reside in the things themselves. The same object may successively be bought as a commodity, circulated in gift exchange, and ultimately hoarded in a clan treasure as a sacred object and as such withheld for a time from any form of circulation, commercial or noncommercial. Michel Panoff (1969) showed this nicely in his study of the seashells used by the Maenge of southern New Britain.

In exploring this theme, my point of reference can be only one of the great moments in this history, Marcel Mauss's indispensable text, *The Gift* (1990). In a moment I will trace the context in which the essay was written, but first I would like to outline the three reasons that moved me to return to the analysis of these problems and to write a book, *The Enigma of the Gift* (1999). The first is what I discovered in the Baruya society; second, my twenty-year-long dialogue with Annette Weiner and my reading of her *Inalienable Possessions: The Paradox of Keeping-While-Giving* (1992); and finally, the globalization of the Western capitalist system. I will say a few words about each of these contexts.

The Baruya provided me with the example of a society that still practiced gift exchange—the exchange of women, for example—but that did not have potlatch. They also produced a sort of "currency commodity," salt, which they bartered with neighboring tribes for tools, weapons, feathers, and other goods that they did not produce themselves. But salt was never used as money within Baruya society; there it circulated in the form of gifts. Finally, there were the sacred objects, which the Baruya treated with the utmost respect, the *kwaimatnie,* used in the boys' initiation ceremonies and presented as gifts from the gods to their ancestors, gifts that they might not give to other human beings.

Now for Annette Weiner. Our friendship dates back some twenty years to the publication of her *Women of Value, Men of Renown* (1976), which transformed the view we had inherited from Malinowski of the way society worked on Kiriwina. I wrote to her at that time, and she responded with an invitation to come to Austin. Thereafter we regularly exchanged papers and critiques, much to our mutual benefit. It was not only our interpretation of the *kula* that was renovated by her discovery of two notions with which Malinowski was unfamiliar: the notions of *kitoum* and *keda.* It was also, and especially, the fundamental role of women in this society, as she revealed it in her analysis of the notion of *dala,* the substance handed down by the founding female ancestors of the clan, an everlasting substance that circulated through the women and constituted the timeless identity of the clans. This was a dazzling demonstration that a feminist perspective on anthropology brings out the silences, the gaps, the distortions implied by all too often exclusively male observations that are unaware of the consequences this bias entails. But we are indebted to her for more than simply a new interpretation of one particular society. With the publication of her last book, *Inalienable Possessions* (1992), Annette Weiner initiated a reassessment of the whole problem of the interpretation of gift giving. She was the first to propose a different reading of Mauss, to seize upon some of his observations that had hitherto been left unanalyzed by his commentators, foremost among them Claude Lévi-Strauss. Annette Weiner's book triggered my desire to return to my material on the Baruya and to rethink the facts.

But this stimulus would not have sufficed without the third context, that of the Western capitalist societies with their widening gulf between the economy and society, their growing appeals for gifts, for generosity to plug the gaps, the tears in the social fabric. Gift giving is once again becoming a social necessity wherever the economy excludes millions of people, at a time when an earned income has become the general condition for one's material and social existence, where family and community solidarity have shrunk or broken down altogether, and where the individual is isolated within the society by society. Exclusion from the economy quite simply means potential exclusion from society as a whole. In an era in which the idea that "everything is for sale," as the title of Robert Kuttner's book (1997) says, is rapidly gaining worldwide credence, it is urgent that historians and anthropologists begin to reexamine the place of noncommercial relations in market societies and to seek to determine whether there are realities essential to the life of societies that lie beyond the market and that will continue to do so.

These then are the three contexts that meshed and sparked my desire to reexplore the question of gift giving and to reread Mauss. But a rereading of Mauss is not necessarily a return to Mauss, for many of the facts reported in his book have not been analyzed, either by Mauss himself or by his commentators, and many of the questions he raised have gone unanswered, first of all by himself. But perhaps it would be helpful at this point to recall the climate in which Mauss wrote *The Gift*. It was immediately after the end of the First World War, in which Mauss had lost one-half of his friends. As a socialist, he had backed Jaurès, one of the leaders of the European socialist movement, who was assassinated for opposing the war. As a renowned academic, Mauss wrote a column for the popular weekly, *L'Humanité*. Again as a socialist, he had made a postwar visit to Russia, where the communists were building their power structure, and had come back hostile to Bolshevism for two reasons: because the Bolsheviks wanted to construct an economy that bypassed the market, and because they systematically used violence to transform society. But Mauss was most critical, in his essay, of liberalism, and he did not want society to become progressively imprisoned in what he called the "cold reasoning of the merchant, the banker, and the capitalist." In 1921, fifteen years before the Front Populaire swept to victory in France, he drew up a "social–democratic program" in which he called upon the state to provide workers with material assistance and social protection. But he also appealed to the rich and the powerful to demonstrate the kind of self-interested generosity that was practiced by the Melanesian chiefs and the Kwakiutl noblemen, and which had formerly been exercised in Europe by the ancient Celtic and Germanic noblemen. Furthermore, he considered that, even after centuries of Christianity, charity is "still wounding for him who has accepted it." So you see, there seems to be a continuity between our era of global world economy and the era that inspired Mauss.

What did giving mean for Mauss? It is an act that creates a double relationship between donor and recipient. To give is to share of one's own free will what one has or what one is. An obligatory gift is not a gift. A gift freely given brings the giver closer to the receiver. But at the same time, the gift creates a debt, an obligation, for the receiver. Giving does two things at once, then. It both reduces and creates distance between the two parties. It creates a dissymmetry, a hierarchy between giver and receiver. Thus, from the outset, Mauss set out the analytic principle that gift giving cannot be studied in isolation; it is part of a set of relations between individuals and groups that arises from the concatenation of three obligations: the obligation to give, the obligation to accept the gift, and the obligation to reciprocate once one has accepted.

It was because he had defined the giving of a gift as the first link in a chain of acts whose structure must be analyzed as a whole that Lévi-Strauss celebrated Mauss as the precursor of structuralism, that is, as his own forerunner. But only a precursor, for, according to Lévi-Strauss, somewhere in the course of *The Gift*, Mauss had unfortunately lost sight of the methodological principles he had established at the outset and had mistaken for a general scientific explanation of the obligation to reciprocate what was actually a particular indigenous explanation: old Tamati Ranaipiri's account to the anthropologist Elsdon Best of the Maori beliefs concerning the existence of a *hau* (spirit) in the thing given that compelled the receiver to give back the thing or something equivalent. In sum, according to Lévi-Strauss, Mauss had allowed himself to be "mystified" by a subtle and complex indigenous ideology; this was not the first time an anthropologist had fallen into such a trap.

Indeed there was a flaw in Mauss's reasoning, and Lévi-Strauss lost no time in seizing upon it, proposing instead another explanation of the notions of *hau* or *mana,* which he interpreted as "signifiers in their pure state" or "floating signifiers." For Lévi-Strauss, whenever the human mind is confronted with something it cannot explain, it invents empty concepts that directly manifest the unconscious structures of the mind and at the same time attest to the symbolic origin of society. In short, the notions of mana, hau, and *manitou* demonstrate the primacy of language and, on a deeper level, the primacy of the symbolic over the imaginary and the real. For Lévi-Strauss, symbols are ultimately even more real than the reality they symbolize. I think that, if I had to assign primacy, I would say that it is the imaginary that dominates the symbolic rather than the other way around. For sacred objects and valuables are first and foremost objects of belief; their nature is imaginary before it is symbolic because these beliefs concern the nature and the sources of power and wealth, whose content has always been in part imaginary. The shells exchanged for a woman or given to compensate the death of a warrior are symbolic substitutes for human beings, the imaginary equivalents of a life and of life.

But where exactly is the flaw in Mauss's theory? In explaining the first two obligations, that of giving and that of accepting gifts, Mauss had advanced sociological reasons. One is obligated to give because giving creates obligations, and one is obligated to accept because to refuse a gift threatens to create a conflict with the giver. But when he came to the third obligation, that of reciprocating, Mauss offered another type of explanation, one that relied primarily on ideological reason and, in the case at hand, on mystical religious beliefs. What compels the receiver of a gift to reciprocate, he argued, is a force, the action of a "spirit" present in the thing received that compels it to return to its original owner. But the thing itself seems to have a soul as well, and therefore to exist as a person with the power to act on other persons. In short, by espousing these Maori beliefs, Mauss seems to have been trying to indicate that the thing given was not completely alienated, that it remained attached to its owner and was therefore at the same time both inalienable and alienated. How can this duality be explained?

Lévi-Strauss appealed to the unconscious structures of the mind, Mauss to the religious representations of societies. Perhaps the explanation lies in neither but in the fact that the thing given is invested with two legal principles at the same time: an inalienable right of ownership and an alienable right of use. This very interpretation is the one used by the Trobriand Islanders to explain the functioning of their ceremonial exchanges, the famous *kula*, which Mauss analyzed as the Melanesian counterpart of the American Indian potlatch. But Malinowski never discovered this explanation of the kula mechanism, and Mauss could not have known about it. We owe this discovery to Annette Weiner and to Frederick Damon, who began fieldwork in the 1960s in the Trobriand Islands and on Woodlark Island, respectively, two essential points in the kula ring, the set of exchange routes that connects a series of islands and societies in the New Guinea Massif region.

Before going on, I want to repeat that Mauss was not interested in all forms of gift exchange. He was concerned with what he called "total prestations," those exchanges involving whole groups or persons acting as representatives of these groups. Mauss was not interested in the gifts that a friend might make to a friend. Nor was he interested in the (imaginary) gift a god might make of his life in order to save mankind. He was interested in gifts that are socially necessary for producing and reproducing social relationships—kinship relations, ritual relations—in short, a certain number of the social conditions of the existence of the individuals and groups in a given society. As examples of these gifts he cites gifts of women between clans, rites performed by one moiety of a society for the benefit of the other moiety, and so forth. Such prestations he qualifies as "total," a term that he uses to designate two different things: either the fact that gift giving has a *number of dimensions*—economic, political, religious, artistic—and therefore the act condenses many aspects of the society itself; or the fact that, by engendering a constant flow of countergifts, gift exchange mobilizes the wealth and energy of numerous groups and individuals, drawing the whole society into the movement and presenting itself as a mechanism and a moment that are essential to the reproduction of the society as a whole.

But Mauss emphasized something that we have forgotten, that there are two types of total prestation, one of which he called "non-agonistic" and the other "agonistic." However, he says almost nothing about the logic of nonagonistic prestations, and his book privileges the analysis of agonistic gift exchange, which he designated in a general way by a term borrowed from the Chinook language: potlatch.

Yet Mauss clearly indicated (something that is not usually mentioned) that the starting point of his analysis was non-agonistic gift exchange; but this departure point is not to be found in *The Gift*. Rather we find it, for example, in his *Manuel d'ethnographie* (1947). There he cites the examples of the exchange of goods, rituals, names, and so forth between the groups and individuals of the two moieties of dualist societies. He mentions in passing the names of several Australian or North American tribes but without going into the particular logic of these gift exchanges. I will attempt to fill in this gap because, in the course of my fieldwork in New Guinea, I observed the exchange of women between the lineages and clans that make up the Baruya society in which I spent so many years.

The basic principle is familiar: one lineage gives a woman to another lineage, a man gives one of his real or classificatory sisters to another man, who in turn gives him one of his own real or classificatory sisters. To all appearances, these reciprocal gifts should cancel the debt each created. But this is not the case. When a lineage gives a woman to another lineage, it creates a debt in the receiving lineage and finds itself in a relationship of superiority with respect to it. But when the first lineage in turn receives a woman, it now becomes indebted and of inferior status. Finally, at the close of these reciprocal exchanges, each lineage finds itself both superior and inferior to the other. Both are therefore once more on an equal footing, since each is at the same time in a superior and an inferior position with regard to the other. Thus countergifts do not cancel the debts created by gifts. They create new debts that counterbalance the earlier ones. According to this logic, the gifts constantly feed obligations, debts, thereby setting up a flow of services, mutual assistance, and reciprocal obligations of solidarity. These debts are never canceled or extinguished in one fell swoop; instead, they gradually die out over time.

These examples show that to give in turn does not mean to repay, which is hard for a Western mind to grasp. They also show how absurd it would be for a man to give two women for the one he had received. The end result of such non-agonistic gift exchanges is a relatively egalitarian redistribution of the resources available to the groups that make up the society, resources in the form of human beings (women and children), goods, labor, and services. According to this logic, a woman equals a woman, the death of one warrior is compensated by the death of another warrior, and so on. The sphere of equivalencies between objects and subjects, between material wealth and human beings—living or dead—remains restricted. It is no use amassing wealth to get women, or women to accumulate wealth. Accumulating wealth and women does not enhance your name, therefore your influence, and therefore your power. We now see why this type of gift giving in New Guinea is often associated with Great Man societies rather than with Big Man societies. In the latter, as the work of Andrew Strathern, Darryl Feil, and many others has taught us, the fame of a Big Man and his group depends on their continued success in a cycle of competitive ceremonial exchanges like the *moka,* the *tee,* and so forth.

The potlatch (and agonistic gift exchange in general) operates on an entirely different logic. Mauss emphasizes that the potlatch is a veritable "war of wealth" waged for the purpose of winning titles, ranks, and power, in which the spirit of competition dominates that of generosity. We are dealing, as he said, with another type of "economy and moral code dominated by gift-giving." Using descriptions taken from Boas and older Russian and Canadian authors, Mauss shows that potlatches were given to legitimize the transmission of a title that had already been acquired or to obtain the recognition of one's right to acquire it. The potlatch is therefore an exercise in power that entails accumulating massive quantities of valuables and subsistence goods in order to redistribute them in a splurge of ceremonial feasting and competition. At the outset there are several competing clans and their chiefs, but at the finish line there is only one winner, at least until another clan can mount a challenge with an even bigger potlatch. This is no longer the logic of non-agonistic gift exchanges that end in the relatively equal distribution of the resources necessary to the reproduction of the social groups involved. Another difference is that a potlatch debt can be cancelled by a countergift; a debt is canceled when a man gives more than he has received, and the ideal is for a clan ultimately to give so much that no one can reciprocate and it stands alone, unrivaled. Once again we see that debt is an essential component of the logic of gift exchange. And in the potlatch it is the very goal. But as a debt can be canceled by a greater countergift, which in turn creates a new debt, a whirlpool movement is set up that produces a relentless escalation of gifts and countergifts, thereby sucking the entire society into the spiral.

This is a rough outline of Mauss's analysis of the potlatch. However, in his text we find some facts that he did not investigate and that his commentators have not mentioned. For instance, in a footnote he states that the best Kwakiutl coppers, like their greatest titles, "do not go outside of the clans and tribes" and were never entered in potlatch. They were kept in the treasure of the clan, whereas the other coppers—the greater number—that circulated in the potlatches had less value and seemed to "serve as satellites for the first kind." Of all those who commented on this text, only Annette Weiner pointed out the importance of these observations, in her *Inalienable Possessions: The Paradox of Keeping-While-Giving* (1992). This point, which no one else had seen as a problem, in fact altered the whole perspective on those things that could be given or sold, since it introduced the category of things that must neither be sold nor given, but must be kept.

As we have seen, Mauss was trying to understand why a thing that has been given must be returned to the donor or must provoke the return of something equivalent. Already in 1921, while praising the richness of Malinowski's ethnographic material, Mauss regretted that it did not cast much light on the gifts and countergifts exchanged in the kula. He writes:

> Sociologically, it is once again the mixture of things, values, contracts, and men that is so expressed. Unfortunately, our knowledge of the legal rule that governs these transactions is defective. It is either an unconscious rule, imperfectly for- mulated by the Kiriwina people, Malinowski's informants; or, if it is clear for the Trobriand people, it should be the subject of a fresh enquiry. We only possess details. (Mauss 1990:26).

It is not certain that Mauss believed it was clear for the Trobriand people, for he speaks of their confusing categories. But his formulation of the prob- lem was prophetic. The answer, however, came only with new research begun in the 1970s by Weiner, Frederick Damon, Nancy Munn, Jerry Leach, John Liep, and others and conducted in a dozen societies, all of which were part of the kula ring.

Their findings made us realize that the kula that Malinowski described as being practiced on Kiriwina was an exception and not the rule. On Kiriwina only the nobles may engage in kula, and not the commoners, who are thus de- prived of the means of raising their status by success in kula exchanges. This is not the case in other kula-ring societies. But let us look once more at the way kula is conducted. The practice is to send an armband into circulation in the hope of obtaining in exchange a necklace of the same rank, or vice versa. Note that, in this game, it is never the same object or kind of object that takes the place of the object given. It is therefore impossible to argue that a spirit present in the thing compels the receiver of the gift to give it back to the orig- inal owner. Mauss regretted this, writing:

> Malinowski has not found any mythical or other reasons for the direction of this circulation of the *vaygu'a* [i.e., the valuables which circulate in the kula]. It would be very important to discover them. For if there was any reason for the orientation of these objects, so that they tended to return to their point of ori- gin ... the fact would be miraculously identical to the ... the Maori hau. (Mauss 1990:102).

Unfortunately, that is not what was found. Malinowski had missed two key in- digenous concepts that illuminate the kula exchanges and explain why the owner appears to remain present in the object, even after it has been given. These two concepts are *kitoum* and *keda*. A kitoum is something owned by a lineage or even an individual: canoes, shells, stone ax blades, and the like. As kitoum, they can be used by their owners in various contexts and for different purposes. They can be used as compensation for the killing of an enemy, or as bridewealth, to obtain a wife; they can be exchanged for a large canoe, or sold to an American tourist, and so forth. But they can also be launched on a kula exchange path, a keda. Once a necklace is sent along a kula path and has left its owner's hands and comes into the possession of the first recipient, it becomes a *vaygu'a,* an object that can no longer be used for any purpose other than kula exchanges. It continues to belong to the original giver, who can ask the temporary possessor to give it back, thus taking it out of kula. This practically never happens, but the fact that it is theoretically possible clearly indicates the relationship between the owner and original donor and the object he has given. What he ceded when he gave the object is not its ownership but the right to use it for making other gifts. None of those through whose hands the object will pass may use it as a kitoum and thus give it to compensate a killing or to procure a wife. And yet the object given never returns to its original owner, for what comes back in place of a necklace is an armband of equivalent rank, which has been ceded by someone who owned it and wanted to exchange it for a necklace. The armband then travels back along the chain of intermediaries until it finally reaches the necklace owner, who will appropriate it as a kitoum, which closes that particular exchange path (keda).

So there is indeed a legal rule that explains how valuables circulating in gift exchanges can be alienated and still be the inalienable property of their original donor. But what this rule does not explain is why it applies to valuables but not to sacred objects, which are often of the same nature as the valuables: rare shells or very old coppers, for example. And yet, like sacred objects, valuables are endowed with an imaginary value not to be confused with the labor invested in locating or manufacturing them or with their relative rareness. This imaginary value reflects the fact that they can be exchanged for a life, that they are made equivalent to human beings. The time has come, therefore, to cross the line that Mauss did not cross.

But before I take this step, I will conclude my analysis of the potlatch and other forms of agonistic gift exchanges by proposing the following hypothesis, which Mauss did not suggest, namely, that such forms of competition emerge historically only if two sociological and ideological conditions are present and associated. First, marriage must no longer be based primarily on the direct exchange of women; this practice must have yielded to the generalized use of bridewealth, that is, the exchange of wealth for women. And second, some of the positions of power and prestige characteristic of a society, and therefore part of its political field, must be accessible through the redistribution, in the form of ceremonial gift exchanges, of wealth accumulated by the competing groups and individuals. When these two types of social relationships are combined within the same society, it seems that the conditions are present for the emergence of potlatch practices. Moreover, potlatch societies are not as numerous as Mauss imagined. He saw this as a widespread transitional economic system situated between primitive societies practicing non-agonistic gift exchange and market societies. To be sure, today we know of many more examples of ceremonial gift exchange than did Mauss—for example, in New Guinea, Asia, and so forth—but the number is still low and cannot be compared with the much more frequent presence of non-agonistic giving of gifts and countergifts.

This brings us to the things that must not be sold or given but must be kept—for example, sacred objects. Sacred objects are often presented as gifts, but gifts that the gods or the spirits are supposed to have given to the ancestors of men, and which their present-day descendants must keep safely stored away and must neither sell nor give. Consequently they are presented and experienced as an essential component of the identities of the groups and the individuals who have received them into their care. These groups and individuals may use them on their own behalf or for the benefit of all other members of the society. But they can also use them to inflict harm. Sacred objects are thus a source of power within and over society, and, unlike valuables, they are presented as being both inalienable and unalienated.

My fieldwork in New Guinea gave me numerous occasions to see the uses to which a sacred object might be put. Among the Baruya, a certain number of clans own *kwaimatnie*. These are bundles containing objects that are never seen and that are wrapped in strips of red-colored bark, the color of the sun. The Baruya call themselves the "sons of the Sun." The word *kwaimatnie* comes from *kwala* (men) and *nimatnie* (to cause to grow). The kwaimatnie are kept in a secret place in the house of the masters of the boys' initiations. These masters represent the clans responsible for the different stages of the initiation, which takes place over a period of more than ten years, ending with the boys' marriage. At around the age of nine, the boys are torn away from their mothers and the world of women and sequestered in the men's house at the top of the village. There they are introduced to various sacred objects: the flutes, the bull-roarers, and the kwaimatnie. Later they learn that the flutes were originally owned by the women and that an ancestor of the men stole them. These flutes contained, and still contain, the powers women have to make children, even to make them without men. The bull-roarers are said to be objects that the *Yimaka,* the forest spirits, formerly gave an ancestor of the Baruya; they are supposed to contain powers of death: the power to kill game or enemy warriors.

Thus, in the sacred objects, the exclusive property of certain clans that only a few men may touch or handle, are conjoined two types of powers: women's powers, powers of life that the men are supposed (imaginarily) to have expropriated; and men's powers, powers of death and war received directly from the forest spirits. But in the eyes of the Baruya, women still own the powers of which they were dispossessed by men, even if they are no longer able to use them. This is why men must resort to violence to separate the boys from the women's world and initiate them into the secrets of these powers they have appropriated from women. Baruya men justify this expropriation by telling how the first women did not use their powers for the good of society. They killed too much game, for instance, and caused many kinds of disorder. The men had to intervene and dispossess them of their powers so that society and the cosmos might be restored to order.

Finally, a sacred object is a material object that represents the non-representable, which refers men back to the origin of things and attests to the legitimacy of the cosmic and social order that replaced the primal time and its events. A sacred object does not have to be beautiful. A splinter of the "true cross" is not beautiful; it is more than beautiful, it is sublime. A sacred object places man in the presence of the forces that command the invisible order of the world. For those who handle and exhibit them, sacred objects are not symbols. They are experienced and thought of as the real presence of forces that are the source of the powers that reside in them.

The sacred object, then, is a "material" synthesis of the imaginary and symbolic components present in the relations that organize real societies. The interests at stake in the imaginary and in the symbolic always have a real social impact. For instance, when the rites have been performed in the name of their myths, Baruya women are really, and not merely symbolically or imaginarily, dispossessed of landownership, the use of weapons, and access to the gods.

From this standpoint, one might postulate that the monopoly of sacred objects, rites, and other imaginary means of access to the forces which control the cosmos and society must have sociologically and chronologically preceded the development of the various forms of exclusive control of the material conditions of social existence and production of wealth, namely the land and its resources or individuals and their labor. And one might cite the example of the Australian Aboriginal rites for multiplying the living species and the initiated men's monopoly of the sacred objects, the *tjuringas*.

I am not saying that religion is the source of the caste or class relations that have grown up in many parts of the world since Neolithic times. But it does seem to me that religion may have furnished ready-made models for representing and legitimizing the new forms of power in places where certain social groups and their representatives were beginning to raise themselves well above the others and were desirous of legitimizing their place in this now different society by a different origin. Did not the Inka present himself as the son of the Sun? And Pharaoh as a god dwelling among men?

To get to the bottom of the nature of sacred objects, we would need to go even further and understand that they are an ultimate testimonial to the opacity necessary for the production and reproduction of societies. In the sacred object, the men who manufactured it are at once present and absent: they are present but in a form that dissimulates the fact that men themselves are at the origin of the forces that dominate them and that they worship. This is the very same relationship men have with money when it functions as capital, as money that makes money, thereby appearing capable of reproducing itself unaided, of generating money independently of the men who produced it.

It is not true, then, even in highly developed capitalist societies, that "everything is for sale." Let us take the example of the constitution of a Western democracy. It is a fact that votes can be, and frequently are, bought in democratic societies, but it is not yet possible to run down to the supermarket and buy a constitution. Democracy signifies that each person, however rich or poor, of whatever gender or social function, possesses an equal share of political sovereignty. To be sure, a democratic constitution is not a code of law given by God. It is a set of principles that people give to themselves as a means of organizing their life together and that they oblige themselves to respect. A democratic constitution is a common good that, by its very essence, is not the product of market relations but of political relations and negotiation. For this reason, in a democracy, the political power of each person is an inalienable possession.

But let us go a step further. The expansion of the market has its limits, and some of these are absolute. Can one imagine, for instance, a child making a contract with its parents to be born? The very idea is absurd, and its absurdity demonstrates that the first bond among humans, namely birth, is not negotiated between the parties concerned. From its inception, life is established as a gift and a debt, in whatever society this new life may appear.

In conclusion, I would like to present a sort of general hypothesis concerning the conditions of existence and production of human societies. For people not only live in society, like the other primates and social animals, they also produce society in order to live. And it seems to me that, to produce society, three bases and three principles must be combined. There must be certain things that are given, others that are sold or bartered, and still others that must be kept for good. In our societies, buying and selling have become the main activities. Selling means completely separating the thing from the person. Giving means maintaining something of the person in the thing given. And keeping means not separating the thing from the person because in this union resides the affirmation of a historical identity that must be passed on, at least until such time as it can no longer be reproduced. It is because these three operations—selling, giving, and keeping—are not the same that objects in these contexts are presented respectively as alienable and alienated (commodities), as inalienable but alienated (gift objects), and as inalienable and unalienated (sacred objects).

Today the global economy, which encapsulates not only the society of the Baruya but also that of France and many other countries, is no longer a regional globality, as it was in the two or three valleys of New Guinea before the Europeans arrived. It is now a world globality. Local economies are now encapsulated by a single system, the capitalist system, the most highly developed form of market economy. Once again this does not mean that all local culture and forms of social organization are going to be reduced to pale copies of European and American ways of living and thinking. Not everything is for sale, nor will it ever be, and identities continue on through their own transformations. The time has come, it seems to me, to develop a new area of economic anthropology, one that, without claiming to exhaust the complexity of local societies, will explore the new linkages between local and global levels.

REFERENCES

Godelier, Maurice. 1960a. Les structures de la méthode du *Capital* 1. *Economie Politique* 70:35–52.

———. 1960b. Les structures de la méthode du *Capital* 2. *Economie Politique* 71:35–52.

———. 1961. Les structures de la méthode du *Capital* 3. *Economie Politique* 80:49–63.

———. 1999 [1996]. *The Enigma of the Gift.* Nora Scott, trans. Chicago: University of Chicago Press.

Kuttner, Robert. 1997. *Everything for Sale: The Virtues and Limits of Markets.* New York: Alfred A. Knopf.

Mauss, Marcel. 1990 [1925]. *The Gift: The Form and Reason for Exchange in Archaic Societies.* W. D. Halls, trans. New York: W. W. Norton.

———. 1947. *Manuel d'ethnographie.* Paris: Payot.

Panoff, Michel. 1969. *Inter-tribal Relations of the Maenge People of New Britain.* Canberra: Australian National University.

Weiner, Annette. 1976. *Women of Value, Men of Renown: New Perspectives in Trobriand Exchange.* Austin: University of Texas Press.

———. 1992. *Inalienable Possessions: The Paradox of Keeping-While-Giving.* Berkeley and Los Angeles: University of California Press.

2

Keeping-for-Giving and Giving-for-Keeping: Value, Hierarchy, and the Inalienable in Yap

James A. Egan

Maurice Godelier has recently modified Annette Weiner's thesis of "keeping-while-giving" by drawing attention to the simultaneously interdependent and autonomous relationship between alienable and alienable things. "*Keeping-for-giving* and *giving-for-keeping*" is offered as the formula for how people use things of value to create their social worlds. Through discussion of a very unusual ethnographic case, I will show that the complementary processes governing what is and isn't given can also illuminate much about the process of alienation itself and its place in the production of hierarchy. In Yap in the Federated States of Micronesia (FSM), land is *the* item of inalienable wealth that possesses the imaginary power that underscores value, encodes history, and provides the ideological basis for hierarchy. Yet land, too, is transferred between groups—namely, between people of different matriclans in each generation. These transfers, which form the basis of Yapese land tenure, do not occur all at once. Nor do they result in the wholesale and immediate alienation of land from members of one matriclan as it is taken by those of another. Rather, alienation becomes a matter of degree and is realized over a number of generations—and never completely. The reproduction of chiefly authority, land-based stratification, and the political presence of women in Yap all require land to be both given and kept, while other things of value mediate this apparent paradox through their own exchange as forms of gendered wealth. Along the way I will undertake a search for the sacred. Having found it in land, we will see that at the heart of the sacred—and the source of its imaginary power to reproduce hierarchy—are the very tensions between the alienable and the inalienable.

LAND: A BASIS OF HIERARCHY

Of all the many forms of wealth used in Yap, none surpasses land in importance. Land sustains life. Irrigated taro patches, well-tended yam gardens, and
groves of coconut, betel, and breadfruit trees have long provided the people
of this tropical western Micronesian island complex with the means of their
subsistence. Even with active participation in today's heavily U.S.-subsidized
wage economy and widespread consumption of imports, Yapese remain
highly dependent upon locally produced foods (Elymore et al. 1989; Taverner
1990; Egan 1998; Burton, Nero, and Egan 2001). Yet land, for Yapese, is far
more than a vitally important material resource. Land also possesses special
imaginary and symbolic power that makes it a central source of personal
identity and social hierarchy. Individuals are born with ties to fellow members of their respective matriclans, but to become a fully social *person*, each
needs to develop ties to land.

The Yapese sociopolitical hierarchy is imagined to be a hierarchy of land.
Individuals hold no status in and of themselves. Status is instead an essence of
actual parcels of land, with the lands of Yap being differentiated into a complex system of ranked and allied units. Persons are ranked in accordance with
the land that they hold and of which they have become a physical extension.
A man is a chief only because he has become an extension of chiefly land, and
thereby of its powers and privileges. Those over whom he has authority are
those who live upon land over which his land has authority.

A person does not so much "own" land as become a part of it. In this capacity an individual is able to support him- or herself as well as give care to
others. The fundamental relationship of *chitamngin* and *fak*, often glossed as
"father" and "child," describes this relationship and is the general idiom
through which Yapese express all hierarchical relationships (see Schneider
1984). In contrast, a landless individual is effectively a nonperson. In Yapese
parlance, such an individual is a *malethay*, a term denoting a state of having
been severed of ties to land. Such an unfortunate is placed in the position of
having to beg from others for material support. While the malethay has been
stripped of all association to land as punishment for some dishonor, entire
strata of Yapese people in effect have no land of their own and instead live on
the lands of others to whom they owe allegiance. This has long provided the
basis for distinguishing between the two fundamental social classes recognized within the landed hierarchy, the landed *pilung* and the landless *pimil-*

ngay. The pimilngay hold a place within the landed sociopolitical order, but only as "children" of their respective landed overlords, who can call upon them to labor on specific projects, such as burying the overlord's dead, cleaning overlord estate lands, and, formerly, rethatching overlord estate and communal buildings. These distinctions extend into the wage economy and Yap state government bureaucracy, where members of the pimilngay social class are generally excluded from important decision-making positions.

Yapese divide land into estates called *tabinaw.* Each tabinaw has its own taro patches, yam gardens, and groves of coconut, betel, and breadfruit trees. Each may also have its own burial grounds in the highland savannah and fishing grounds upon the tidal flat or reef. Collectively sharing these resources are the estate's residents: a man and his wife, their sons, and their sons' wives and children. The tabinaw also has its place within Yap's landed sociopolitical hierarchy by virtue of the power invested in the soil of its lands. The epicenter of this power is the *def,* the stone platform upon which rests the central dwelling of the estate head. Each def has its own name and rank with respect to other def throughout Yap. Geographically adjacent tabinaw make up the larger landed totality of the Yapese village. Thus, while the people of each estate have their own agricultural resources and burial grounds and identify with their respective def, they also share membership in the village, through which they often act collectively as a political unit. Yapese divide leadership within the village between a number of the village's most prominent tabinaw, each having very clearly defined political functions assigned to its def. Three def in particular hold the most important political functions, and ethnographers have long referred to their respective spokesmen as village "chiefs." Villages are in turn linked to other villages in a series of increasingly inclusive hierarchies of alliances, again all conceived in terms of land and at every level given direction by specific "chiefly" def. Ultimately, all tabinaw of Yap fall into one of three major networks of regional alliances led by three great def that collectively provide leadership across all landed political elements of the Yap island complex.

This landed order operates in close relationship with the Yap State government and the federal government of the Federated States of Micronesia. State senators, the state governor, and representatives to the FSM congress need the support of chiefs, who mobilize village alliance networks to garner votes during elections. The Yap State Constitution, though modeled on that of the

United States, has also established two councils of chiefs as a fourth branch of government (one council made up of chiefs of the Yap island complex, and the other of chiefs of the many neighboring but ethnically distinct coral islands that are also administratively part of Yap State).

The essence of the power of land is *lung,* the voice of authority. Yapese conceive of authority as the right to speak to others, whose right and duty it is to listen. Lung is invested in the soil of land itself, connecting people who live on different lands in chains of authority. People of high land speak to their subordinates of low land, while their subordinates are charged to listen and carry out the directives of the voice. The complex system of intervillage alliances that gives political form to the landed hierarchy operates through the flow of lung. Interconnections between landed units in the broader landed political system follow formal channels of communication called *tha'.* Lung emanates from the highranking def that leads a network of allied villages and flows through these formal channels to carry its message to specific allied lower-ranking def in other villages.

But from where does the power of lung derive? What is the source of the voice of authority? Yapese hold that the power of land is a social product. Its value is the legacy of labor—not in an abstracted form (as is labor power in occidental capitalism), but in a concrete form that is deployed directly in relation to social relationships. Estate ancestors developed the land through their many efforts, transforming it into a material and cultural resource that sustains life. Taro patches have been carefully mulched, channels for irrigated water have been maintained, stone fish traps built, and groves of fruit trees planted. It is through labor that a man or woman becomes part of land and part of the other people who identify with it. Of all products of labor, land has a special place in the Yapese collective imagination. This is so because land does far more than express relationships; it *reifies* them. Labor does more than develop productive resources that are handed down to future generations; the "labor" of estate ancestors has also brought honor to the tabinaw. Through great deeds and self-sacrifice, estate ancestors have earned the special political privileges lodged within the tabinaw def. Tabinaw elders know histories of their land and can recount special tales of predecessors who raised the status of the land by showing bravery in battle or venturing overseas to bring valuables to Yap, or in any way providing aid that established or preserved some lasting feature of the order of Yapese hierarchical relations. These relations become embodied in the land itself.

Greater deeds bring greater status. One history well known throughout Yap concerns the rise of the village of Kanif. Once a pimilngay village of the lowest rank, Kanif was raised to the lofty level of *bulce'* when the hero Thapgnag and his warriors killed a chief of the powerful village of Okaw. The Okaw chief had upset the entire order of Yapese landed relations by taking the life of one of the three great paramount chiefs, effectively placing himself above all other chiefs in Yap. Thapgnag's success thus preserved the balance of power.

LAND MUST BE GIVEN

While land provides people with lung, and hence a place in Yapese hierarchy, those who hold land must *give* it to others. Each generation of people that speaks with the land's voice belongs to a different matriclan, for generation after generation, the voice of the tabinaw def is transferred from people of one matriclan to those of another. There are over thirty matriclans in Yap. Known as *ganong*, Yapese matriclans are exogamous but hold no corporate functions, nor do they have any specified relations with one another. The members of each *ganong* are instead dispersed throughout the Yap island complex. Given the practice of virilocal postnuptial residence, tabinaw daughters leave their natal estates when they marry and bring their respective clans to the estates of their husbands, just as tabinaw sons remain upon the land to take wives of other clans. In this way, the clans of Yap endlessly move from landed estate to landed estate. People of one clan establish themselves as part of a particular estate in one generation, only to pass the estate on to people of other clans in the next generation, even as their own clan progeny have left and found land elsewhere. (See figure 2.1.)

The cultural principle connecting Yapese persons to land is the same principle behind the imaginary power of land; it is *labor* that establishes clan people within the tabinaw. The lung invested in land is an embodiment of the labors of people who once lived on the land and transformed it into a developed cultural and material resource. It is by acknowledging this labor with their own efforts to maintain the productivity and honor of land that the in-marrying wife and her children become part of the tabinaw land. Yapese land tenure is nothing less than the process whereby people of one clan transact the tabinaw with those of another. As much as the wife needs the land, the land needs her and her children if it is to maintain its productivity and place in Yapese hierarchy.

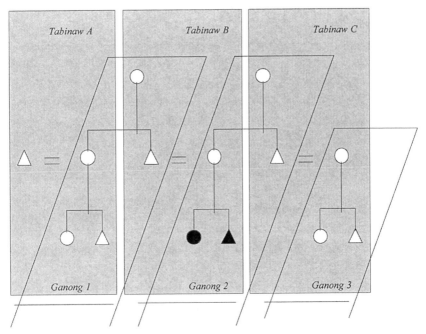

FIGURE 2.1
Ganong (clan group) and tabinaw relations. Cross-sibling set designated as egos and some of their immediate relations to people of other ganong (clan groups) and tabinaw. For purposes of clarity, I have placed individuals within their tabinaw of residence. It must be noted, however, that each married woman is a member of both the tabinaw from which she received her name and that into which she has married.

The wife acknowledges the labor of previous clan people of the estate by first bearing children who will one day speak the land's voice. She is also charged with many of the duties that concern daily household maintenance: preparing food for herself, her children, her husband, and possibly her husband's mother; cleaning and helping keep the tabinaw in presentable order; feeding livestock; and so on. She is also expected to represent the tabinaw in village functions by participating in village dances and contributing her labor to village and municipality projects. Of special importance is her role in agricultural production, especially production of the staple starches that make up the Yapese culinary and exchange category called *ggaan*. She will be given one or more of the tabinaw taro patches for the care of *Cyrtosperma* and, more rarely, *Colocasia* taro. She will also have access to garden land for growing yams, bananas, sweet potatoes, and other produce. Many women also hold wage jobs or run small stores, and their earnings are an important contribution to household income. *Cyrtosperma* taro and yam production are not so labor intensive as to be incompatible with wage work, and women continue to cultivate staple starches. In fact, Yap State has the highest level of consumption of locally produced foods of the four states that make up the Federated States of Micronesia (Taverner 1990; Elymore et al. 1989).

As a newcomer who seeks to become part of land but is as yet not part of it, the young wife is essentially "landless" to the estate people of senior generations. Her position within the tabinaw is low and not infrequently a source of considerable stress. Her every move is scrutinized by the people of clans already established on the land, and her loyalty to the estate and its village is always in question, especially if she has come from another village altogether. It is also not unheard of for wives to suffer abuse from husbands who return from sessions of binge drinking, though mistreatment of wives is much frowned upon in Yap. Still, a woman endures much for the sake of "anchoring" her children (*nga yuluw e bitir*) upon the land, for to leave and return to her natal estate would weaken her own children's claims to tabinaw land and could even leave them utterly landless. A woman who divorces her husband is in fact said to "run away" from her children. This is especially so if she should remarry and thereby direct her labors to land other than that upon which her children live. Her link to children born "of her belly" is not reducible to simple blood ties (see Schneider 1984; Marshall 1999). By severing the ties of labor in the land that bind her children to her, she ceases to be their mother.

The woman's children begin their formal attachment to tabinaw land soon after birth when they are given personal names from the pool of ancestral names associated with the tabinaw def (for this reason children are likely to remain with their fathers in the event of a divorce). It is possible to know where someone is from by knowing the individual's name, though, given virilocal residence, this is truer of men than of women. But the receipt of a name and mother's labor only provide potential. To assume roles of leadership within the tabinaw, the children must also work to make themselves part of the land. Sons help tabinaw elders as workers in estate and village projects and assume chores such as feeding livestock and collecting copra and betel. Pursuant to a man's role in food production, they should provide protein foods (*thumag*) for their parents. Sons fish for parents and/or regularly contribute imported frozen and canned meat purchased with wages. Unmarried daughters are expected to help their mothers with cooking, cleaning, and agricultural production in tabinaw gardens and common household taro patches. They participate in village dances and in regularly scheduled work cleaning and weeding village roadsides and the village center. Should the mother or father operate a small store, daughters are frequently enlisted as sales clerks, putting hours in each week behind the cash register.

While American ethnographers throughout the early postwar period described the tabinaw as being passed from father to son (Schneider 1953, 1962; Mahoney 1958; Lingenfelter 1975), the unit of inheritance is in fact the cross-sibling dyad. The wife's eldest son and daughter will one day come to direct tabinaw affairs. Their respective roles are different but complementary, and each is charged with lung—the voice of authority—needed to enact them (see Smith 1981 and 1983 for a discussion of parallel processes in Palau). To the woman's son fall those tabinaw responsibilities that pertain to the tabinaw def. He will in time replace his aged father in the oversight of all matters concerning his estate's obligations to the broader landed units of which it is a part. He will represent his estate in village councils; he is charged with sending, receiving, or following up all directives of lung made to his def; he will organize the presentation of wealth made by his estate people at funerals, village dances, and other public exchange events. Of course, his mother has only earned him the potential to assume this position; he must first demonstrate his worthiness. An eldest son who fails to participate in the obligations of his estate, and especially one who fails to care for his aged parents, may be bypassed as the voice of the def is transferred to a younger or classificatory brother.

Daughters of the estate leave when they marry and work to earn positions for themselves and their future children in the estates of their husbands, just as their mother had before them. But they too share authority in their natal estate. Sisters are charged with protecting the rights of their brothers—namely, the voice of the land of which they now are part. To this end, sisters as well as brothers are told of the functions and history of the tabinaw def. It is the estate sisters who oversee new clans who come to the estate lands. The sisters keep a close eye on their brothers' wives and their brothers' wives' children. The eldest sister of the tabinaw is formally charged with the distribution of estate taro patches among in-marrying wives. It is also the eldest sister who is formally charged with giving brothers' children their names, thereby establishing their initial link to tabinaw land. Yapese say that a brother's children "belong to the sister." Her brothers are expected to apprise her of all important matters that concern these children, and her right to participate in and even veto decisions regarding them is widely respected.

LAND MUST BE KEPT

While the in-marrying wife and her children attempt to repay the invested labor of the generations that have preceded them, repayment can never be achieved in full. Something is always kept when giving land to people of another clan. Yapese articulate their own form of the paradox of "giving-while-keeping" with the expression *tafedad, tafen be; tafen be, tafedad*. This idiom provided the conceptual core of David Labby's groundbreaking ethnographic work in Yap (1976); he glosses this statement as "our land belongs to someone else; someone else's land belongs to us." To unlock the mysteries of this paradox, as the late Annette Weiner has recently suggested (1992), we must follow the sister.

The place a woman earns in the tabinaw of her husband does not extend to all the people who share her clan totem (*nik*). It does, however, apply to more than her own children. The woman's daughter matures to become an estate sister, and though this sister will come to live on other land (her husband's), it is her voice that speaks with greatest authority with respect to the clan people of the next generation who come to live on the estate land. The sister's authority over her brothers' children is kept by her own children. Her sons and daughters will continue her role as supervisors of the new clans upon the tabinaw in their capacity as *mafen*. *Fen* is a bound morpheme that a number of ethnographers have indicated implies "ownership," leading them to suggest that mafen are in an important sense the true "owners" of estate land (Lingenfelter 1975:52; Labby 1976:36). Following Strathern (1988), I would strongly caution against translations that so powerfully invoke Western property metaphors. As I have noted above, the connection of Yapese persons to land is more a matter of their becoming extensions of land than of owning it. Fen always invokes an association between an individual entity and a physical place that supports or shelters the entity by making the two a single whole, as an enclosure for pigs is called *tafen e babiy*. The merging of land and persons into wholes implied by fen suggests an authoritative relationship between an individual and other persons specifically mediated by the land. Thus the mafen relation links father's sister's children and mother's brother's children in regard to the affairs of an estate. It is a hierarchical relation in which ego accords great respect to father's sister's sons and daughters (who are mafen to his or her estate). At the same time, ego is honored by mother's brother's children, to whose estate ego is mafen.

The supervisory role of the estate mafen holds special power, for the mafen have at their disposal the most powerful of sanctions wielded in Yap: the right to take away the names of mother's brothers' children and entirely strip them of their relation to land. The mafen have no formal claim to estate resources beyond the ritual collection of coconuts from estate lands following the death of a member of the tabinaw. Nor are the mafen ever directly involved in the politics of lung emanating from the tabinaw def. The mafen both live off the lands and direct the political affairs of estates from which they received their own names, or, for female mafen, from the estates into which they have married. Yet as members of the clan group that has given land, they are structurally superordinate to the receivers, the people currently living on the land. They are accorded tremendous respect by their mother's brothers' children, and they are party to all important decisions regarding internal tabinaw affairs. At the same time, it is not unknown for mafen to press their advantage and use land or resources of the estates they oversee, counting on the acquiescence of the estates' current residents (as we shall see shortly).

Mafen represent clan groups that have earned a place in the tabinaw in previous generations. Since a new clan group takes up leadership of the estate each generation, many different clans have a place in the estate's history and can, in theory, make claims upon it. Yapese give special recognition to the three most recent lines, referring to them respectively as *mafen ni be'ech* (new mafen), *mafen ni le'* (coconut shell mafen), and *mafen ni bod* (blackbird mafen). These designations amount to a historical sequence, since any clan group that marries into a tabinaw will eventually pass through each set of relationships. When a woman leaves her natal estate to marry into new land, her children will stand as mafen ni be'ech (new mafen) to the tabinaw from which she received her name. The children of her daughter will become this same estate's mafen ni le' (coconut shell mafen), and the children of her daughter's daughter will in turn be honored as the estate's mafen ni bod (blackbird mafen). (See figure 2.2).

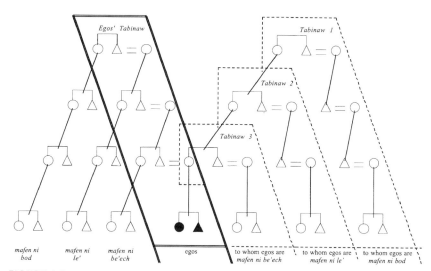

FIGURE 2.2

Mafen relationships. To the left are the three mafen lines to egos' tabinaw; to the right are three tabinaw to whom the egos are mafen.

These three lines of mafen do not speak with equal authority over the affairs of people currently residing upon the tabinaw land. Authority instead diminishes with the passage of each generation, or, in other words, with each step removed from residency upon the land itself. The new mafen line (mafen ni be'ech) speaks with the greatest authority, while the mafen ni le' has less say over current tabinaw people, and the mafen ni bod has the least influence. In fact, affirmation in actual practice of the positions of the latter two lines (mafen ni le' and mafen ni bod) is limited to exchange contexts.

The paradox of "our land belongs to someone else, someone else's land belongs to us" should now be clear. A sibling set that comes to speak for tabinaw land owes respect to its mafen—to people of other clans who are established as part of the land itself, even though they live elsewhere. At the same time, the sibling set stands as mafen to people of other clans who live on land once held by their own clan people. But we also see in the transfer of land between clan groups over the generations a specific, culturally ordered form of alienation. A woman marries into a tabinaw and establishes herself and her children as part of its land. In so doing, she founds a matriline that takes its meaning in reference to this land as mafen. Yet over the generations, the strength of this mafen line's voice wanes. The initial labor invested in the land by the mafen foundress remains and is acknowledged. Her name joins the pool of ancestral names associated with the tabinaw def and may be given to girls born on the land in future generations. But while her labor in the land is inalienable, the voice that it imparts to her clan progeny is not. Even so, alienation is not an all-or-nothing phenomenon; its effects are partial and realized in degree over successive generations. Nor are the issues of keeping-while-giving and inalienability and alienability experienced without tension. It is not unknown for tabinaw mafen to push claims to land, as we see in the following case.

L was an elderly woman widowed after her first husband's death. She remarried, only to divorce her second husband years later, though she had children by both husbands. Following the divorce, L asked her brother for land upon which to build a house, and she lived there for many years. Her brother passed away in time, and his eldest son, C, inherited the voice of the def. On L's death bed, she instructed her brother's son to care for her daughter by her second marriage. This daughter was married to a man with land in a prominent village. Yet after L's death, this daughter and her husband came to live in L's house. This generated much gossip in the village, for the land upon which this home rested, as well as the taro patch beside it, remained part of the broader estate of L's brother, now directed by C. C, however, had nothing to say of the matter. One day L's sons by her first marriage came to the house and ordered the daughter and her husband to leave. The two sons argued that as mafen to this estate, they were so empowered. The daughter and her husband, however, did not go. They *agreed* that they had no right to this home and its land, but they argued that since L had remarried after the death of her first husband (the sons' father), L was no longer the mother of these "sons," and they therefore could not come to the land and speak as its mafen. This prompted further gossip in the village. The daughter now living in L's former house could claim to be mafen to the estate of her mother. This made the matter especially difficult to resolve, and certainly C was in no position to intervene and speak over his father's sister's daughter in matters that concerned the very land of his own def. Yet the older mafen lines remained silent throughout the entire affair, and the issue was still without resolution when I last checked years later.

IS LAND SACRED?

Godelier (1999) has recently reminded us of a fundamental sociological insight: all social orders require the manufacture of consent if they are to be reproduced. To this end he has shown the power of the sacred in establishing consent, where inalienable sacred objects embody the power of the gods, who, as imaginary substitutes for human beings, hide man's role in his own origins. The highly stratified sociopolitical hierarchy of Yap awards great differences in prestige, privilege, and power in accordance with an accident of birth that leaves each person with an identity shaped by gender and position in land. How is consent established in Yap? Why do Yapese, from high to low, appear to accept this order as necessary and beyond reproach?

The answer lies in the underlying structure of Yapese constructs of land and clan. Following Godelier's lead, we might look for a sacred power imagined to lie in land that necessitates keeping it as an inalienable object. And we might begin with origins. Have the great heroes of the past like Thapngag, who led the people of Kanif from the status of lowly pimilngay to the highest ranks of the pilung, become transformed into imaginary beings to achieve these ends? Perhaps. Some of the heroes of legend possessed magical power to cause death and bring typhoons. But by no means are all estate ancestors remembered for supernatural feats. Thapngag did little more than win a battle. Others brought honor to the land by returning home after years of quarrying stone valuables overseas in the islands of Palau. I have even been told the tale of a man who, a hundred years ago, was rewarded by having the status of his own def raised within the village hierarchy for his successful intervention on behalf of the village chief's son. The man spoke German and was able to correct a misunderstanding by German colonial authorities that had led to the son's imprisonment.

But where the origin of landed status is not imagined as a manifestation of the divine, the origins of ganong—the Yapese clan—are closely linked to spiritual beginnings. Each clan has its own history that began with the voyage of a landless female spirit who arrived in Yap as a stranger and who subsequently married a local man whose lands were inherited by her children. Labby (1976) has noted that the totemic clan founder—the nik—gives symbolic support to women's land-seeking role through the association each provides to a specific animal, plant, or force in the natural world. The nik of different clans are often parasitic, each linking its respective people to a fungus, rat, or some other creature that survives by drawing sustenance from something other than that to which it belongs. In the same way, clan women depend upon the estates of their husbands to meet both their own and their children's needs. The ganong of Yap thus move endlessly from estate to estate as each clan daughter continues the odyssey begun by the clan nik.

The fundamental symbolic opposition of male and female has its source in the way that Yapese imagine clan origins, and it is here that we find the underlying imaginary force that provides the basis of Yapese hierarchy. Women are landless and low, while men, as husbands of women, are landed and high. Female is clan; male is land. Female is the raw, uncontrolled power of procreation; male is the established order of hierarchical relations through which female procreative power is harnessed. But men are also the sons of women, who inherit the legacy of mother's labor. Men therefore always owe something to women, that being the labor of their mothers (both in the womb and out) that is their source—and that power is kept by the sister, who brings it to new land.

It is through the tensions implicit within the structural opposition of clan (female) and land (male) in land tenure that Yapese hierarchy is reproduced. This is the tension that makes land both alienable and inalienable. A woman founds a mafen line within the clan by establishing herself and her children in land. Their labor, concretely invested in the land, becomes an inalienable part of estate history. Yet the strength of the mafen line's voice diminishes over the course of successive generations as people of new clans come to speak for the land and the mafen line's members move into positions assessing the accountability of others. Ultimately, the voices of clan line descendants are heard only as the murmurs of village gossip. Yapese land tenure amounts to a process of alienation that proceeds in stages with the passage of each generation and yet never reaches completion. Nor can it ever become absolute if Yapese landed hierarchy is to be reproduced.

The tensions between alienability and inalienability that locate hierarchy in land in ways that put it beyond the practical comprehension of the people who live and breathe it day in and day out are due to a peculiar Yapese logic of accretion. With the passage of each generation, people *make* themselves into persons by attaching themselves to land. Yapese land tenure results in a transfer of the voice of the tabinaw def between people of different matriclans, but the new estate people receive this privilege only by becoming part of a greater whole. When land is given to the in-marrying wife and her children, they have become a part of land—a part of a great legacy of labor to which they contribute but of which even the givers are themselves only a part. It is far too great a claim for any to argue that they alone *are* the land. The value of land—and its imaginary power to encode hierarchy while legitimating the many social exclusions of the here and now—rests upon the inability of anyone to make such claims. Land transcends individuals. Land transcends generations, linking the living and the dead. Land encodes history. It is this power of land that inspires awe—that makes it numinous—that makes land sacred with or without the gods.

GIVING-FOR-KEEPING

As we have seen, the simultaneous alienability and inalienability of land in Yap is not without tensions. Sisters empowered to distribute estate taro patches to in-marrying wives have been known to keep lands for themselves and their daughters. Tabinaw mafen have on occasion seized opportunities to lay claim to the lands they protect. Yet manipulations of this sort are not the rule. This is, in no small part, due to Yapese practices of gifting that mediate the paradox of giving-while-keeping. Ceremonial gifting events provide a forum for people to exercise their voice and publicly proclaim what they keep through what they give.

Yapese have also long used public gifting to accommodate material changes by incorporating new forms of wealth and broadening the range of participants to give expression to new social relations while, at the same time, protecting land as a basis of hierarchy. The most celebrated gifting events practiced in Yap fall into a broad category of ceremonial presentations of wealth called *mitmit*. Mitmit of all kinds have long celebrated the initiation or maintenance of political relations between landed units, be they tabinaw linked by marriage, allied villages, or even entire networks of allied villages. The features of mitmit vary by specific kind and have shifted over the years, though Mauss (1990) would have seen characteristics of agonistic prestation in all; mitmit participants offer items of wealth to each other in the spirit of competition, endeavoring to earn prestige by giving more than they receive.

The past hundred years have witnessed especially remarkable transformations in mitmit as landed hierarchy has faced special challenges from depopulation due to introduced diseases, global trade, colonialism, and emerging capitalist class relations. I cannot discuss these important changes here. I will, however, discuss issues of giving-for-keeping in the context of what has only recently become the most widespread set of ceremonial gifting practices in Yap: funerary prestation. Though Yapese would hesitate to include this very novel set of gifting practices within the category of mitmit, today's funerary prestation closely follows the structure of *m'oy* marriage mitmit that were practiced throughout the twentieth century up until its closing decades (Egan 1998). Funerary ritual, during this same period, occasioned only minor presentations of wealth and lacked the competitive character of marriage exchanges. Over the past thirty years, however, it would appear that Yapese have shifted gifting between tabinaw from the context of marriage to that of death. Yapese funerary prestation continues to mediate the tensions of alienability and inalienability of land through what is given. At the same time, gifting at funerals operates as one point of articulation between the sacred character of land and the new social and economic relations of the wage economy.

Among the many obligations at death that Yapese recognize today, presentation of special forms of wealth to funeral hosts has become primary. The deceased was a member of a particular tabinaw, either as an estate son or as an in-marrying wife, and the many people of the lands associated with its def are collectively the funeral hosts. Very shortly after the deceased has passed away, the hosts (including their respective mafen) will decide on a location for the funeral. Usually this is the homestead compound in which the deceased had resided. The body of the deceased lies in state here for several days before burial, during which time relatives and friends come to pay their last respects. It is the in-laws—the *wecma'*—of the hosting tabinaw who come bringing wealth. The in-laws fall into either of two categories: either they are people of (or supporters of) tabinaw into which the funeral host's sisters have married, or they are people of (or supporters of) the natal tabinaw of the hosting estate's wives. This designation determines what forms of wealth are brought to the funeral.

Husbands of estate sisters and their many supporters provide male-gendered wealth. Protein foodstuffs of the Yapese culinary and exchange category called *thumag* are the principle prestations. This includes fish, either caught by these men or (more likely) purchased at Yap's large government-subsidized fishing venture, as well as cases of tinned meat and tinned fish purchased in local stores. Supporters of the husbands' estates might also bring drinking coconuts and betel. Only at funerals of high chiefs might they bring traditional valuables. If so, they would bring pearl shell valuables (*yar*). People of the natal tabinaw of the funeral host's wives bring female-gendered wealth. Central are staple starchy foods of the *ggaan* category. This consists of baskets of taro, sacks of rice, and, occasionally, bread. Supporters of the funeral host wives also provide textile valuables called *begiy* and occasionally pandanus mats (*chob*).

As each group of guests arrives at the funeral site, its many prestations are publicly paraded and displayed before the entire body of guests assembled. A member of the hosting tabinaw will diligently record in a ledger the kinds and amounts of items brought, along with the name of the guest's figurehead. Notably, the figureheads listed include both men and women. Often more than one name is logged per entry. Totals tabulated from the ledger along with the figureheads' names are periodically read aloud to an attentive audience. Especially large or small levels of prestation are the topic of gossip across Yap for weeks to come. The funeral hosts will later distribute these many items among the guests in accordance with the logic of complementarity in gendered symbolism. Guests who brought taro, rice, and other "female" items will receive a share of the fish and tinned meats. Conversely, those who offered "male" items receive "female" wealth.

The tabinaw of in-laws depend upon many people for support to amass the wealth each needs to present at funerals. Each contribution of estate people to their respective estate's stock of wealth signifies the strength of ties that bind people together as parts of one another and as parts of the tabinaw land. Tabinaw members supply fish, taro, valuables, and other needed items to show their commitment to the estate. Their contributions make visible their claims to tabinaw land and to a place in its landed order. In this connection, the cross-sibling dyad proves critical to the success of funerary gifting, for estate sisters are the greatest sources of support for their natal tabinaw. A man's sister is his *yarif*, a term honoring the sister in her capacity as provider of essential economic assistance. Through her, his estate can draw upon the resources of in-laws, thereby laterally extending the contributors to any given funeral across potentially numerous cross-sibling and spousal chains. When brothers need fish to meet their customary obligations, their principle sources of support are the tabinaw into which their sisters have married.

It must be emphasized that sisters' husbands provide wealth on behalf of their wives, not merely in their own names. This is the case whether the link to the funeral was primary (as when the sister is herself a natal member of the estate hosting the funeral) or secondary (a sister supporting a brother whose own wife hails from the hosting estate). The fish, cases of tinned meat, betel, drinking coconuts, and other items they provide give concrete expression to the place of each sister in the tabinaw from which she received her name. Even though the sister now resides on other land, these many prestations give public affirmation of what she keeps—namely, her voice within her natal tabinaw. Brothers who have failed to recognize their sisters' authority in tabinaw affairs put themselves at great risk. It is within the power of a woman in good standing in the tabinaw into which she has married to instruct her husband not to join her estate people at a funeral. In so doing she can withhold the support of her husband's tabinaw from that of her brothers and bring them grave political embarrassment.

At the same time, the efforts of the sister's husband and his estate supporters are also clearly present in the things given: Reef fish have been caught by the husband, his brothers, and their sons on waters to which they have rights by virtue of their connection to a particular def within a particular village. Coconut and betel have been collected from trees planted generations ago by estate people. Canned fish and meats, cigarettes, and large tuna have been purchased with the wages of other members of the tabinaw. None of this is forgotten when the prestations are brought to the funeral. As much as these many things attest to the voice of the sister in her natal land, they also give concrete affirmation of her place in new land with its own legacy of labor to which she hopes to attach herself.

Brothers are also sources of support for sisters in ceremonial gifting events. When sisters need taro and imported rice to help the estates into which they have married meet their obligations, sisters expect help from brothers' wives. The support of brothers' wives acknowledges the sister and her voice in the land by offering support from the land itself. The taro so provided also publicly attests to the relationship between a brother and his wife. A wife's efforts in this regard amount to nothing less than labor that helps anchor herself and her own children on this land. Moreover, wives who have suffered abuse from husbands may seek help, not from their own brothers, but from husband's sisters. This appeal is made not with words but with things. Expected to provide three baskets of taro for an event, the wife might provide eight, and so raise the alarm.

Just as estate sisters affirm their place within the land through their contributions at public gifting events, so too do the tabinaw mafen serve notice of what they keep. The different lines of mafen offer their support at exchange events like funerals, bringing fish, taro, sacks of rice, and whatever forms of wealth are needed. And just as the contributions offered in the name of an estate sister also contain within them the presence of the people and the land of the tabinaw into which she had married, so too do the things given by mafen manifest the labors of many. Those prestations given by male mafen reveal the work and resources of the tabinaw from which each received his name; those given by the husbands of female mafen on behalf of their wives hold the presence of the wife as well as that of her husband and the people of his estate.

The presence of so many people and their relationships in the things given at funerals indicates a public recognition of their multiple authorship. This is certainly clear to Yapese, who know only too well how to read social relationships into the different stocks of wealth offered at public gifting events. In the case of funerals, multiple authorship might be given recognition in funeral prestation ledgers. In how different a light Yapese gifting stands beside the *moka* of Mount Hagen! Marilyn Strathern (1988) uses the Hagen case to draw our attention to the dangers of importing Western capitalist assumptions of personhood and property into analysis of non-Western systems of wealth. She challenges Lisette Josephides's (1982, 1985) claims that Hagen men have appropriated the pigs produced by their wives through exclusive male control of the ceremonial gifting complex. Strathern notes that alienation of women's labor assumes proprietorship that does not exist in Hagen constructions of persons and their relationship to things. This is so, she argues, because in the sociocultural order of the "gift economy," where persons are partible and things are multiply authored, there is no one-to-one correspondence between things and persons. "Persons," Strathern writes, "simply do not have alienable items, that is, property, at their disposal; they can only dispose of items by enchaining themselves in relations with others" (1988:161). She argues that what occurs in moka is not the conversion of a woman's pigs to a man's pigs, but a *transformation* from something multiply authored—something embodying the identities of numerous producers and the social relations between them— to something with a single source of identity, namely, her husband's prestige with respect to other men.

The point in the Hagen case is well taken, though we must also accept that even the gift economy presupposes other possibilities for the relations between persons and things, as when the very valuables used in gifting are first obtained in barter with outsiders or sale in markets (Godelier 1977). Cash crop production and wage labor introduce additional considerations, so that a multiplicity of forms and meanings governing the circulation of things, as well as recognition of qualitatively different kinds of work, may coexist in the same social formation (Thomas 1991). This is certainly the case in Yap, where over 75 percent of all households in Yap State have some form of regular cash income, and nearly 60 percent have regular income from wages (Taverner 1990). Were we to include only the ethnically Yapese part of the state population and exclude the peoples of the more remote neighboring coral islands, the percentage of households regularly relying on cash income would increase. Of course, the numerous imports that have become standard prestations at funerals must first be purchased with earnings. Even the fresh pelagic fish men contribute to public gifting events are now usually purchased from the Yap Fishing Authority. Elsewhere (Egan 1998) I have also shown that men who do fish frequently sell portions of their catch in local markets. At the same time, taro and yam production is inextricably bound up with the social relations that connect women to land in ways that preclude the sale of these staple starches.

In Yap, presentation of wealth at funerals and mitmit publicly affirms multiple authorship. It is exactly because it does so that exchange of gendered wealth mediates the paradox of giving-while-keeping. Prestations made by estate sisters and tabinaw mafen serve as public reminders that they still keep a voice in estate land even while this land has new residents. The simultaneous presence of the tabinaw into which estate sisters have married or upon which the mafen now live attests to the fact that they have given land over to people of a new clan as their own clan line has moved on.

At the same time, the inclusion of imports in funerary exchange as items of gendered wealth allows success in the wage economy to find expression in the gifting practices that make visible the social ties of land and clan. One both lays claim to positions in land and supports others to whom one has ties of land by using wealth drawn from other kinds of socioeconomic relations. This is, of course, not without its own tensions. The hierarchical relations of land have developed to give order to Yapese material production. As fishing and, especially, taro production become less economically important while households come to depend upon rice and other imported foodstuffs, the landed order may lose its relevance. New structures of local political leadership like elementary-school PTAs, community church organizations, and various kinds of municipality action committees that are better keyed to new resources are already taking over many of the functions of the landed hierarchy. These organizations, as well as the institutions of the state and federal government, give Yapese persons political influence in their own communities in ways that are increasingly coming to reflect their position in the wage economy. It remains to be seen if the landed order can absorb these many challenges.

KEEPING-FOR-GIVING

There is one more piece to the puzzle of keeping-while-giving in the reproduction of Yapese hierarchy. Just as Yapese try to keep their place in land by giving, so do the things given derive their value from what is kept. Land itself is never given as a prestation in mitmit, funerals, or any other gifting event. Yapese often extend the use of idle land to others who wish to build a new house closer to main roads and electrical power lines, or who wish to plant an extra yam garden. But this land is in no way alienated. Borrowed garden land will be "returned" when the garden is harvested. Land borrowed for building a house remains attached to the def of the lender and puts the borrower under his or her authority. Land is almost never transferred between people outside of the process of inheritance between established tabinaw people and in-marrying wives and their children each generation. Yap State law precludes the possibility of sale of land to non–Yap State citizens (though leases may be obtained), and I am unaware of any cases of monetized sale of land between Yapese outside of a set of payments made by the Yap State government to people of tabinaw that years ago had land taken for the Yap airport. Land is kept, and it is because it is kept that other things may circulate.

The most precious classes of items making up that category of wealth known as *machaaf*—traditional Yapese valuables—are also very restricted in their circulation. By law, shell and stone valuables are protected from sale. They are transferred, but only in the context of the politics of the landed political hierarchy. Large mitmit held between villages and village alliance networks continue to be practiced to commemorate special events such as completion of a new village men's meetinghouse. Here at the mitmit, stone and shell valuables are given in strict accordance with the flow of lung, the voice of authority vested in the land. No chief who addresses the body of representatives of the villages assembled at the event can so much as open his mouth without presenting them with a shell valuable. He in fact must plan his words carefully, for he must offer a valuable to each major alliance block present for each major point he makes in his address. It is not he, a simple man, who speaks; it is the voice of the land itself that is heard ringing through the communal meeting hall. The presentation of stone and shell valuables to follow acknowledges special obligations and rights that are lodged within the land. These valuables change hands to affirm the alliances and landed hierarchical relationships that make these many lands parts of a larger unity. And they can do this because they are *substitutes* for the land.

Land is the "gold reserve" of Yap's time-honored sociopolitical hierarchy. As Godelier (1999) has argued more generally of forms of inalienable wealth, land provides the stable source of value that links otherwise unremarkable things to something sacred. While taro and fish are not considered machaaf, Yapese hold these things to be very special forms of wealth. This is so because the taro and fish presented at events like funerals are gifts that substitute for land. But in so saying, we must recognize that every cultural milieu places limits upon the items that can serve as substitutes for the inalienable through gifting. This capacity is never an objective property of the things themselves, certainly no more so than the status of an item as a "commodity" is due to fixed essences (Appadurai 1986; Kopytoff 1986). A large tuna lying in a store freezer does not in any way embody the Yapese cultural relations of land and clan. Only when it is carried high overhead and paraded before the hosts of a funeral by the appropriate in-laws does it do so. Much as Appadurai (1986) has suggested for the commodity, gifts can stand for the sacred only because they have entered a particular state in their social and economic trajectories. Issues of context and specific cultural frameworks that establish the candidacy of an item for such a role require analytical disclosure.

It is the contextualization of taro and fish as gendered wealth in events like mitmit and funerals where they are used as tokens to stake claims to land that transforms them into wealth. Imported rice and tinned meats and fish have also been taken from store shelves and transformed into wealth by making them symbols of the structural relations organizing tabinaw hierarchy. As Roth (2002) has recently shown with respect to Tsimshian potlatching feasts, ceremonially elaborated gifting contexts alter the quantitative–cardinal scale of commodity values to create qualitative–ordinal values appropriate to the gift. A large fish used as a prestation at a funeral, whether purchased or caught, does not represent a sum of money that could just as well have been given in its place, but a specific kind of thing, a class of wealth ranked with respect to other classes of wealth. Moreover, contextualization is effective because the items used as prestations in ceremonially elaborated gifting are able to express the inalienable. The cultural structure of complementarity in Yapese production between male (the husband and son who fishes to provide protein) and female (the wife and mother who labors in taro patch and garden to provide starch) is a necessary basis for the incorporation of taro, fish, and now imports like rice and tinned fish and meat into these special gifting contexts, enabling them to stand as substitutes for land. These many things become *gendered wealth* because Yapese can link them to the ways they imagine the heart of their social world to operate.

In contrast, cash itself cannot easily represent the relations of land and clan that order landed relations between tabinaw and different clan people. Guests at the Yapese funeral also present cash (U.S. dollars) to funeral hosts as a prestation. The cash is given to help offset costs incurred by the hosting tabinaw, such as the deceased's medical bills and other outstanding debts, flowers purchased to decorate the grave site, and the concrete purchased to line the grave and with which to make the grave capstone. Among Yap's heavily Catholic population, cash collected at funerals is also given as a special contribution to the Catholic Church. But cash is kept apart as a qualitatively distinct sort of prestation. Unlike taro and rice, and unlike fish and canned mackerel, cash is not gendered; it is given by all funeral guests, regardless of their relationship to the deceased and his or her tabinaw. Nor is it distributed to specific categories of guests as taro and rice are given to those who provided fish and tinned meats, and vice versa. Cash left over after other funeral costs are covered is usually given to the widow or widower of the deceased or to the deceased's children. I am even aware of a case of a young man who purchased a car with money left from his father's funeral. Cash is presented as "help" (*ayuw*)—a valued display of support for the hosting tabinaw and one that is expected of those with the means to provide it. One can thus translate success in the wage economy into prestige directly through contributions of money, as well as indirectly through purchase of the imports used in funerary prestation. Yet Yapese do not use cash itself to express the underlying cultural relations that organize the reproduction of land as a basis of hierarchy.

While Simmel (1978) and later Bohannan (1955, 1959) once held that money has within it the power to homogenize value and transform multicentric into unicentric economies, we now know that there is no spirit or essence within money itself that brings about this effect (Douglas and Isherwood 1979; Parry and Bloch 1989). Even money has been differentiated into qualitatively different states both in the capitalist West (Belk and Wallendorf 1990) and elsewhere (Shipton 1989; Toren 1989). In Yap, cash has not destroyed qualitative differences between things used in exchange. Yapese keep cash separate from the sacred, not because of the dangers presented by some inherent property of money, but because failing to do so would enable new kinds of economic relations—capitalist class relations—to further undermine the alternative landed basis of sociopolitical relations. Already they are much entangled. Capitalist class relations that produce cash at once find some expression in Yapese gifting even as they are held at distance.

CONCLUSION

Annette Weiner (1992) has mounted an important challenge to the "norm or reciprocity" implicit in so much social theory by drawing attention to the critical role that inalienable possessions play in the creation and reproduction of hierarchy. Lineages, families, and dynasties may enchain themselves with others through exchange, but they also establish difference with others through what they are able to hold back from exchange. Fine mats, shell valuables, crown jewels, and other heirlooms kept over the generations link their owners to sources of power such as ancestors and gods, a role in the production of hierarchy that Weiner has termed *cosmological authentication*. Here Weiner has also shown that women, through their production and control of inalienable things, are directly involved in the practices that impart cosmological authentication.

The analysis of Yapese material presented here stands upon Weiner's shoulders as it also points to additional possibilities beyond keeping. Alienation is not always a threat to hierarchy, but may, under certain circumstances, operate in an interdependent relationship with keeping to reproduce hierarchy. It is with this in mind that Godelier's (1999) recasting of *keeping-while-giving* as the twofold process of keeping-for-giving and giving-for-keeping is so insightful. He returns to Mauss's discussion of *hau* and the spirit of the gift to uncover that which is present in both inalienable things and their many satellites that circulate among persons and groups. This is none other than the sacred—the creative leap of imagination ordered through material relations and practices of exchange—that hides man's role in his own origins. This is the inspiration for the present attempt to demystify the cultural construct of land in Yapese hierarchy.

In Yap, the capacity of land to reify the social and serve as a basis of hierarchy rests upon two things: first, the inalienable association of *persons* and events with land, and second, the protracted separation of *people* and their clan lines from these imaginary constructs of power. The tensions between these two processes—the inalienable and the alienable—produces and legitimates hierarchy in Yap. Land and its many substitutes that circulate as gifts contain within them the tensions between the landless woman and the landed husband. For what is given to the son who stays is kept by the daughter who leaves. In such a world, social status for human beings is always ephemeral. At any moment, the positions of Yapese persons within hierarchy hails from something greater than themselves—something independent of themselves—something sacred.

NOTE

Research for this chapter was conducted during 1991 and 1992 with support from the Wenner-Gren Foundation for Anthropological Research, grant no. 5315. I would like to thank the volume editors, Cynthia Werner and Duran Bell, for organizing an insightful and exciting set of meetings for the Society for Economic Anthropology, out of which this volume has emerged. I would also like to thank Maurice Godelier, whose theoretical insights and endless enthusiasm have provided invaluable inspiration to me and generations of anthropologists. His comments on this chapter, along with those of Cynthia and Duran, have greatly strengthened it, even if I haven't had the good sense to follow all their excellent advice.

REFERENCES

Appadurai, Arjun. 1986. Introduction: Commodities and the Politics of Value. In *The Social Life of Things: Commodities in Cultural Perspective.* Arjun Appadurai, ed. Pp. 3–63. Cambridge, U.K.: Cambridge University Press.

Belk, Russel W., and Melanie Wallendorf. 1990. The Sacred Meanings of Money. *Journal of Economic Psychology* 11(1):35–67.

Bohannan, Paul. 1955. Some Principles of Exchange and Investment among the Tiv. *American Anthropologist* 57(1):60–69.

———. 1959. The Impact of Money on an African Subsistence Economy. *Journal of Economic History* 19(4):491–503.

Burton, Michael, Karen Nero, and James A. Egan. 2001. The Circulation of Children through Households in Yap and Kosrae. *Ethos* 29(3):329–356.

Douglas, Mary, and Baron Isherwood. 1979. *The World of Goods: Towards an Anthropology of Consumption*. London: Allen Lane, Penguin Books.

Egan, James A. 1998. Taro, Fish, and Funerals: Transformations in the Yapese Cultural Topography of Wealth. Ph.D. diss., University of California, Irvine.

Elymore, Jane, Amato Elymore, Jacqui Badcock, and François Bach. 1989. *The 1987/1988 National Nutrition Survey of the Federated States of Micronesia. Summary Report Prepared for the Government and the Department of Human Resources, Federated States of Micronesia*. Kolonia, Pohnpei: Good News Press.

Godelier, Maurice. 1977 [1973]. *Perspectives in Marxist Anthropology*. Robert Brain, trans. Cambridge, U.K.: Cambridge University Press.

———. 1999 [1996]. *The Enigma of the Gift*. Nora Scott, trans. Chicago: University of Chicago Press.

Josephides, Lisette. 1982. *Suppressed and Overt Antagonism: A Study in Aspects of Power and Reciprocity among the Northern Melpa*. Research in Melanesia, Occasional Paper 2. Port Moresby: University of Papua New Guinea.

———. 1985. *The Production of Inequality: Gender and Exchange among the Kewa*. London: Tavistock.

Kopytoff, Igor. 1986. The Cultural Biography of Things. In *The Social Life of Things: Commodities in Cultural Perspective*. Arjun Appadurai, ed. Pp. 64–91. Cambridge, U.K.: Cambridge University Press.

Labby, David. 1976. *The Demystification of Yap: Dialectics of Culture on a Micronesian Island*. Chicago: University of Chicago Press.

Lingenfelter, Sherwood Galen. 1975. *Yap: Political Leadership and Culture Change in an Island Society*. Honolulu: University of Hawai'i Press.

Mahoney, Francis. 1958. Land Tenure Patterns of Yap Island. In *Land Tenure Patterns in the Trust Territory of the Pacific Islands*. John E. deYoung, ed. Pp. 251–287. Office of the High Commissioner, Trust Territory of the Pacific Islands. Guam.

Marshall, Mac. 1999. "Partial Connections": Kinship and Social Organization in Micronesia. In *American Anthropology in Micronesia: An Assessment.* Robert Kiste and Mac Marshall, eds. Pp. 107–144. Honolulu: University of Hawai'i Press.

Mauss, Marcel. 1990 [1925]. *The Gift.* W. D. Halls, trans. New York: W. W. Norton.

Parry, Jonathan, and Maurice Bloch. 1989. Introduction: Money and the Morality of Exchange. In *Money and the Morality of Exchange.* J. Parry and M. Bloch, ed. Pp. 1–32. Cambridge, U.K.: Cambridge University Press.

Roth, Christopher. 2002. Goods, Names, and Selves: Rethinking the Tsimshian Potlatch. *American Ethnologist* 29(1):123–150.

Schneider, David M. 1953. Yap Kinship Terminology and Kin Groups. *American Anthropologist* 55(2):215–236.

———. 1962. Double Descent on Yap. *Journal of the Polynesian Society* 71(1):1–24.

———. 1984. *A Critique of the Study of Kinship.* Ann Arbor: University of Michigan Press.

Shipton, Parker. 1989. *Bitter Money: Cultural Economy and Some African Meanings of Forbidden Commodities.* American Ethnological Society Monograph Series 1. Washington, D.C.: American Ethnological Society.

Simmel, Georg. 1978 [1907]. *The Philosophy of Money.* London: Routledge and Kegan Paul.

Smith, DaVerne. 1981. Palauan Siblingship: A Study in Structural Complementarity. In *Siblingship in Oceania: Studies in the Meaning of Kin Relations.* Mac Marshall, ed. ASAO Monograph 8. Pp. 225–273. Ann Arbor: University of Michigan Press.

———. 1983. *Palauan Social Structure.* New Brunswick, N.J.: Rutgers University Press.

Strathern, Marilyn. 1988. *The Gender of the Gift: Problems with Women and Problems with Society in Melanesia.* Berkeley and Los Angeles: University of California Press.

Taverner, Robert. 1990. *Final Report: Results of the Household Income Expenditure Survey in the Federated States of Micronesia, 1988–1989.* UNDP Project TTP/86/203. New York: United Nations.

Thomas, Nicholas. 1991. *Entangled Objects: Exchange, Material Culture, and Colonialism in the Pacific.* Cambridge, Mass.: Harvard University Press.

Toren, Christina. 1989. Drinking Cash: The Purification of Money through Ceremonial Exchange in Fiji. In *Money and the Morality of Exchange.* Jonathan

Parry and Maurice Bloch, eds. Pp. 142–164. Cambridge, U.K.: Cambridge University Press.

Weiner, Annette. 1992. *Inalienable Possessions: The Paradox of Keeping-While-Giving.* Berkeley and Los Angeles: University of California Press.

3

The Engendering of Ceremonial Knowledge between (and among) Warlpiri Women and Men in the Australian Central Desert

Françoise Dussart

It is a true honor to contribute this chapter to a book focusing on theories of exchange, and in particular on the work of Maurice Godelier. My association with Professor Godelier stretches back more than two decades. I was a student at the time, an undereducated undergraduate studying at the Sorbonne in Paris. A good friend of mine, also a would-be anthropologist, told me about an extraordinary class she was taking at a rival university not far away. She urged me to sneak in and audit the course. So, true to the subversive spirit of the undergraduate, I did exactly that. Hence my introduction to one of the best classes I didn't—at least officially—take. I never found out whether Professor Godelier sanctioned my presence, tolerated it, or simply didn't know that I was surreptitiously attending his lectures. What made the course particularly wonderful was this: I could listen and learn without writing any papers. But now subversion and dereliction have caught up with me. Fate can be postponed but never denied; let this chapter serve as a final assignment for that memorable, career-changing class.

Back then Godelier had yet to publish his monumental *La Production des grands hommes* (1982) (subsequently translated by Cambridge University Press under the title *The Making of Great Men*), but his lectures were already saturated with his insights on matters of ritual and exchange. A few years later, I took Godelier's insights and his book on the Baruya of New Guinea with me to the Warlpiri settlement of Yuendumu,[1] in central Australia, where I cut my teeth as a fieldworker. There, I soon wrestled with a seemingly insurmountable incompatibility: my work focused on women, and Godelier's targeted men. Furthermore, the social structure of the Baruya that Godelier described evince a pervasive—indeed exclamatory—ideology of male hegemony, a gender dominance at odds with the social networks in evidence at Yuendumu. Other profound differences presented themselves in turn. Whereas the Baruya networks of ritual exchange were gender specific, the Warlpiri at Yuendumu seemed to transfer their ceremonial material via networks of kinship that accommodated, indeed reveled in, discrete expressions of cross-gender exchange. Not surprisingly, Godelier's contributions proved stimulating by offering a counterexample to the ritual dynamics I was observing at Yuendumu. I soon broadened my reading on the literature of exchange and came upon the contributions of two of his Melanesianist contemporaries: Marilyn Strathern and Annette Weiner. Whereas Godelier restricted his early research of exchange and rituals to the domain of men, Strathern and Weiner developed correlative theories based on their work among both women and men. Their gender-specific appraisal of the roles of women enriched my own analyses. Particularly potent was Strathern's wise warning—also advanced, albeit less vehemently, by Weiner—against the construction of gender identity in exclusionary, oppositional terms.

Strathern is especially trenchant on the nature of sociality and gender and their relationship to domination. Strathern observes that "men's and women's domains are not socially distinct. Rather, each may act in a same-sex or cross-sex way, in contexts that are always conceptually transient. Time, duration, and sequence are as important to form as they are to the gift" (1988:325). Strathern goes on to offer a trenchant example of a gender-specific scope of action distinguishing women from men. Men of the Highlands, she notes, "enjoy both a collective life and the relations of domestic kinship, whereas women appear confined to the latter" (1988:325). Subverting this general observation with an elegant contradistinction regarding this presumptive dualism, Strathern ends up cautioning against binary formulation. Indeed, she is right; binary conception, whether attached to Highlanders or Warlpiri of Yuendumu, can result in woeful miscalculation. This is why I hesitate to apply conclusions of any Melanesianist to the ritual actions found at Yuendumu. Such comparison must be vigorously modified. Strathern has described a society that privileged spousal connection in the communication of ritual knowledge. Weiner has identified sibling links to be of primary significance. The case of Yuendumu requires both of those seemingly irreconcilable pressures to be acknowledged; the brother–sister and husband–wife axis are both discernible among the Warlpiri at Yuendumu, in the ritual exchanges that take place through a system of negotiations predicated primarily on ties of residential kinship.[2] As I have come to realize, ritual exchange among the Warlpiri women and men of Yuendumu necessitates a view of the ceremonial act that acknowledges a variety of mutually constituted interests but ultimately privileges the bonds of kinship over the ties of gender. The social structures of kin connection serve as a primary motivating force behind ceremonial activity and ritual exchange at Yuendumu, even when that activity appears to be gender specific. Indeed, putatively "male" and "female" ceremonies can incorporate material that has migrated from the ritual sphere of the opposite sex. That material often undergoes change when moving from one sphere to another— a change that further complicates, and enriches, our understanding of Warlpiri ceremonial life.[3] Furthermore, concomitant with this migration there exists a countergesture of payment, in the form of money, blankets, or food, that further nurtures the bonds of kinship. In short, the complex reality of cross-gender exchange offers profound insights into the limits of gender-specific analysis of Warlpiri social engagement and confirms the complementary nature of male and female ritual life at Yuendumu, a settlement that has managed to sustain its egalitarian ethos, tempered by the realities of post-colonial sedentarization.

To accommodate an analysis of how ritual knowledge moves among men and women, I propose to extend the lexical function of the word *gender* by using it as a verb. *To gender* is not the most elegant phrase, but the secondary meanings of the verb form help clarify how Warlpiri men and women often exchange ritual material. As a transitive verb, *to gender*—and the related verb *to engender*—suggests notions of production, creation, and "regeneration."[4] As such, the terms dilute the male–female distinctions that falsely separate the actions of men and women. In the word *engendering* we have a term well suited to the social and ritual transactions among men and women of Yuendumu. And I say "among" rather than the more grammatically correct "between" because the groups in question often act less as "men" and "women" per se than as individuals tethered to a residential kin group. In the nearly twenty years I have conducted fieldwork at Yuendumu (1983–2000), there has been a flourishing exchange of seemingly gender-bound ritual knowledge—an exchange that complicates and entangles the seemingly cloven nature of Warlpiri ceremonial life at Yuendumu. How do the Warlpiri engender ritual knowledge once considered wholly separate by analysts of central Australian Aboriginal cultures? That is to say, how do the men and women of Yuendumu exchange material that might appear, to the outsider, to be restricted to one group or another? There are many contexts in which ritual information can be, and is, transmitted. I have written elsewhere about such exchanges via the production of acrylic canvas representations of the Dreaming for the nonindigenous art market (Dussart 1999, 2000).[5] Here, I will touch on two restricted indigenous settings in which such knowledge is transmitted between and among Warlpiri men and women: nocturnal dreams and ceremonial performance. Accounts of the dynamics of exchange in these two linked domains can be found, more substantially represented, in other works I have published.

NOCTURNAL DREAMS

Nocturnal dreams constitute a principal context in which the Warlpiri cosmology known as the Dreaming or Dreamtime in Aboriginal English and *Jukurrpa* in Warlpiri finds (re)generation and cross-gender exchange.[6] Segments of the Dreaming that emerge during the night—and the ceremonial performances that these segments often trigger—are usually determined during early-morning first analyses overseen by ritual leaders, male and female, often called *yamparru* in Warlpiri. These analyses, often rife with cross-kin-group negotiation, may conclude that the material dreamed at night is male or female, but such distinctions do not prohibit the material from then being incorporated—engendered—in some modified fashion in subsequent ritual activity of the opposite gender. Indeed, much gender-specific ritual knowledge that surfaces in nocturnal dreams often gets exchanged between male and female relatives, a migration of potent knowledge that solidifies residential affiliation and the bonds of kinship. Such exchange is crucial for the invigoration of the ritual life of the settlement, which in turn is a primary source of cosmological nurturance that extends beyond the overtly ceremonial. Most often brothers and husbands pass on ritual material dreamed at night to sisters and wives and vice versa.[7] This engendered material, whether transferred from women to men or from men to women, rarely finds expression in joint ceremonies—that is, events that unite men and women in ritual performances. Instead, it filters into gender-specific ceremonies. The transmission of the modified material tends to follow specific paths, a flow that is more often than not sanctioned by relatives of the opposite sex who are *kirda* (owners) of the Dreaming under negotiation.[8] To repeat the engendered expression of ritual knowledge tends to honor the kinship dynamics that characterize "traditional" ritual connectedness. Here I must state explicitly that Dreaming ritual material transferred is ritual material transformed. As Annette Weiner argues, following Nancy Munn's (1973) and Fred Myers's (1986) works, "the Dreaming constitutes the originating authority for inalienable possessions so that the transmissions of inalienable possessions move between people giving greater security to their transmission" (Weiner 1992:210). Knowledge from the Dreaming that is transmitted between genders is transformed to make possible control of its reenactment. Without sanctioned control, performers cannot reenact the Dreaming, the "inalienable possession" par excellence. An example of the specific nature of this alteration is in order. During one of my stays at Yuendumu, I was able to follow a significant amplification of a segment of a *Ngapa Jukurrpa* (Water Dreaming). A woman dreamed that three mythical female beings—known in Warlpiri as Tiyatiya—were singing and wore ritual body paintings as they danced. The female dreamer told her siblings—male and female ritual performers who were owners of the segment identified by the dreamer herself by the songs she heard in her dream—about her revealing dream. That precipitated several days of intense negotiation between the siblings and other ritual leaders. These talks ultimately resulted in the decision to fold the woman's songs and female designs on the body of the mythical women into the ritual repertoire of male relatives. This engendering demanded that the designs be modified, since the ritual patterns seen in the dream were gender specific and thus could not be ritually reenacted by men unless transformed in the transmission. The transfer was indeed sanctioned by both men and women, but the design adaptations themselves excluded all but the male owners.[9] In the weeks following the transfer cum transformation, the woman who dreamed the segment received five blankets. However, that dividend only represents one moment in the ongoing reciprocity central to patterns of kinship.

Clearly, the broad-stroke description of transformation through transmission forces the Aboriginalist working with the Warlpiri to complicate recent Melanesianist theories of exchange. Weiner's keeping-while-giving (1992) and Godelier's two-pronged response to that aphorism (1999)—the twinned

phrases keeping-for-giving and giving-for-keeping—have limited value for
the analyst of the Central Desert ritual life of Yuendumu. The dynamic nature
of ritual currency—and by "dynamic" I refer not only to the changing foci of
ritual but also to its transformed content—must be privileged when scruti-
nizing Warlpiri ceremonial activity. That is to say, the "giving" of ritual knowledge at Yuendumu modifies "the gift," the very object that is the focus of the
exchange. A correlative to this dynamism must also be mentioned. To "keep"
such material—to prevent knowledge from being transmitted—ultimately
threatens the vitality of that material and with it the strength of its "owners."
That enfeeblement ultimately runs the risk of undermining the cosmology.
Warlpiri ritual knowledge here needs to be understood as a kind of currency,
and, following Weiner's argument, a currency acquires value because it is exchanged (1992).[10] Stated crudely, the Warlpiri pursue a policy of "use it or lose
it" when it comes to matters of ritual exchange. The engendering of ritual
knowledge is elemental to a Warlpiri social identity profoundly tethered to the
sometimes fragile cosmology of the Dreaming.

How does the engendering of nocturnal dreams fit with earlier accounts of
the Warlpiri's gender-specific ritual activity? Although Munn long ago noted
the transfer of ritual material between men and women of Yuendumu via the
intermediary of nightly dreams, she also observed a number of constituent elements of such exchanges that are at odds with the current situation at the
Central Desert settlement. The transfers from men to women that Munn documented in the mid-1950s were exclusively spousal. As I have already suggested, that is no longer the case. It is now quite common for kin to bestow
ownership over dreamed material to members of their kin group other than
their spouses, who are theoretically involved in a *kirda* (owner)/*kurdungurlu*
(manager) relationship according to the rules of preferred marriages.[11] True,
the "reciprocal relationship" of the "marital unit" is still operative, and sometimes even predominant, but it is only one form of engendered knowledge.
Furthermore, it must be reaffirmed that the flow of ritual material can migrate to men—a phenomenon unobserved during Munn's fieldwork—not
only *from* men. It is unclear how much this latter movement has increased
since sedentarization. Ritual leaders who were already actively involved in ritual activities acknowledged that men and women exchanged ritual knowledge
that had emerged in their nocturnal dreams. However, one constant remains,
this constant being the force of kinship among the ritual players. In the con-

text of sedentarized life, kinship strengthens ritual, and ritual strengthens kinship—and both in turn intensify patterns of engendered exchange rarely observed by anthropologists half a century ago.

CEREMONIAL PERFORMANCE

If nocturnal dreams offer the Warlpiri a setting for informal ritual exchange, then the ceremonies themselves—that is, those ritual events that often are prompted by nocturnal dreaming—provide an environment of premeditated and more formally sanctioned cross-gender "business."[12] Clearly, nocturnal dreams and rituals are inextricably linked. Establishing the connections between them enables one to dilate on the motive forces behind the act of social exchange.

Unlike the negotiations surrounding ritual material that is dreamed at night, performed ritual knowledge must be transmitted through formal channels, especially when that material is to be engendered. Cross-gender exchange of material deployed during ceremonies generally begins after the rites of passage in which teens participate. Then, it is common for brothers and sisters to nurture each other by discreetly exchanging gender-specific information linked to the land, thus to the Dreaming and its performance. This assistance is seen as a way of nurturing, protecting, educating, monitoring, and strengthening. Both men and women regularly invoke this last quality when asked about their cross-gendered interventions. As they mature, brothers and sisters generally intensify their commitments to each other and to the Dreamings that they nurture and strengthen in their ritual performances. This support extends beyond the act of performance itself to correlative ritual activities such as visits to sacred sites, meetings with governmental officials, and land rights trials. Perhaps an example of how the Warlpiri engender their ritual knowledge ceremonially is in order. I was once present as an elder male showed his sister, also a senior ceremonial performer, a wooden shield depicting various designs integral to rituals enacted by men alone. This kin-sanctioned revelation carried any number of implicit obligations, both to the Dreaming and to the Dreamer. The man showed his sister the ellipses, dots, and circles on the shield and sang her two songs. To render the design acceptable and helpful to the nurturance of the Dreaming story encoded on her brother's shield, his sister gathered other female ritual performers who were kirda (owners) and kurdungurlu (managers) and transformed the designs of

the shield into designs appropriate for female ritual body paintings. One of
the circles on the shield was transformed into a semicircle on the body painting, and concentric circles had no more than three rings instead of the seven
or eight originally depicted on the shield. The transformed design was painted
on the bodies of two of her sisters (two kirda for the Dreaming exchanged)
and one of her sister-in-law (a kurdungurlu). The participants readily accepted the songs, as they had been already transformed by the woman's
brother to fit the ceremonial enactment of women-only performances. After
some discussion over the body design itself, the female participants sanctioned both songs and body painting for future female-orchestrated ceremonial performance. For his part, the brother who helped engender the design
and songs received money from his sister, as well as the sense of having invig-
orated the Dreaming and his sister's performance of the Dreaming stories they
shared. It is common to exchange ritual knowledge among siblings. The
spousal dynamic is frequently different, often highlighting the giver's managerial (as opposed to proprietary) relationship to the material. Stated suc-
cinctly, the kurdungurlu dynamic is the primary agent of matrimonial
engendering. Significantly, managerial interventions by spouses often impli-
cate Dreamings that are vulnerable—threatened by the absence of the requi-
site number of owners capable of directly nurturing that particular segment
of the cosmology. Wives as often as husbands intervene to replenish threatened material. I have been present when the male manager of a *Pamapardu
Jukurrpa* (Flying Ant Dreaming) taught his wife songs, body paintings, and
choreography to reenact a segment of a Dreaming that she, as the only living
owner, had been unable to perform for some time. With his knowledge, his
wife was able to teach other female kin with whom she shared the responsibilities to perform other Dreamings. These women were not kirda for the Flying Ant Dreaming, but as close kin and longtime partners in ceremonial
reenactment, they assisted her in performing the segment to revivify the
Dreaming, their friend, and her country. To ensure that the knowledge exchanged was appropriately transformed, the husband participated actively in
the first female reenactment of the neglected segment—an unusual occur-
rence. It is rare to see men entering the ground of women-only ceremonies,
however crucial to ensure transformation and thus nurturance.

Reciprocally, I have seen a female ritual leader of a *Yarla Jukurrpa* (Yam
Dreaming) give her husband knowledge that enabled him to adapt, for male

ceremonies, neglected men's segments of that particular Dreaming. The segments had been neglected for over three decades as her husband's kin had been forcibly removed from their traditional lands but had now returned. His wife, on the other hand, had remained and had been able to learn about the segments and exercise her role as manager for the Yam Dreaming neglected segments and associated lands. Subsequently, her husband's female kin, owners of the neglected segments as well, asked her to teach them how to reenact and nurture the Dreaming. At the outset of the first reenactment by women, she received food and money from both her male and female in-laws who were owners of the Yam Dreaming segments.

It must be kept in mind that any act of engendering carries tremendous risk and pressure. No material that migrates from one gender's repertoire to another moves casually, especially when it finds expression ceremonially. Ritual performers of the different kin groups monitor how knowledge moves between men and women. Unauthorized or mishandled transmissions that escape the vigilance of owners and managers can have long-term repercussions on the well-being of the Dreaming and, by implication, the cosmological health of the whole settlement. An example will illustrate the serious implications of impropriety. Fifteen years ago when ritual leaders were getting ready to start their annual initiation ceremonies, ritual material performed by men in men-only ceremonies was one night made unacceptably public by an inebriated man who started to sing and dance in front of women and in particular his mother-in-law, with whom, like all men, he needed to observe a strict rule of total avoidance. The various song verses he sang from the men-only portion of the ceremony associated with circumcision were wholly beyond the purlieu of women and uninitiated males. His singing was loud and clear, and the locus of his misbehavior added to the gravity of the breach. The next morning the transgression was the major topic of discussion among the ritually active men and women of the settlement. Though the specifics of conversations that took place in gender-specific settings differed in explicitness, both the men's and the women's groups spoke of the incident as though anticipating death and preparing for a long period of mourning, as the transgression endangered the well-being of Yuendumu people, the Dreaming sung and its associated sites, and the initiation ceremonies themselves. Several days later, ritual male leaders collectively decided that the initiation ceremonies could not be performed at Yuendumu for two years and that the youth to be initiated would be taken to another settlement to undergo initiation in the interim. At the end of the second year of the ban, a large group of senior Yuendumu men, wishing to reclaim control of the ceremonial arena, campaigned to complete the second set of circumcision events at their own settlement. How to restore the health of the setting generated considerable discussion. To resolve the issue, male ritual performers left the settlement to punish the man who violated the taboo and, over a period of several days and nights, to perform a purification ceremony, a response consistent with the follow-up to death and mourning. The men returned from their trip and announced what they had done. They then performed another set of purification ceremonies, this one intended to be viewed by both men and women as though to release them from a "death" and "mourning" of sorts. This new set incorporated modified elements of the transgressive material that caused all the problems in the first place. In other words, a group of senior men, after a two-year hiatus, engendered the men-only songs that had been made public earlier so that they could be shared with women. The male ritual leaders hoped that this expanded ceremonial context would be seen to nourish the *Jukurrpa* (the Dreaming). While further negotiations took place and initiation ceremonies were once again performed at Yuendumu, women who were kirda owners for the Dreaming associated with the songs the men engendered in their purification ceremonies did use them. Several months later, three women sang the engendered songs and, using acrylic paints on canvas, created designs depicting the actions of the mythical beings evoked in the songs. Acrylic paintings have been very much part of the life of Yuendumu residents since the mid-1980s. These paintings are mainly sold to non-Aborigines; all display stories from the Dreaming that can be told to the uninitiated, and thus the public. The transformation—the engendered transgressed songs—triggered no consternation, since refashioned songs and designs were now controlled by both men and women and performed only in public performances. When I later inquired whether payments had been made to sanction the control of the newly engendered knowledge, women kirda for the Dreaming stories accidentally revealed two years earlier explained that they as well as male kirda had paid the male ritual leaders who had engendered songs and designs and orchestrated the set of public purification ceremonies for the community as a whole.

Exchanges of knowledge formally sanctioned among men and women show how the ritual knowledge among the Warlpiri at Yuendumu is transformed to inhabit different spheres of male and female ritual life. It is only through the performance and circulation of ceremonial currency—ritual knowledge—that the enterprise of ritual is sustained. Circulation augments, rather than diminishes, the value of ritual, a dynamic that offers up a dramatic counterexample to the place of ritual in Melanesian cultures.

CONCLUSION

More than twenty years have passed since I secretly audited Professor Godelier's courses in Paris. My approach to the discipline has evolved substantially since those undergraduate days; then again, so has Godelier's. But if I dig below my research on gender, I can find traces of that early analytic method acquired in the professor's classroom. His elegant formulations on matters of anthropological consequence and his capacity to refine and revise his theoretical suppositions are worthy of emulation even when one's theoretical starting points differ. Likewise, his willingness to fold in, and respond to, other theories is a model I have attempted to embrace in my own work. And indeed, there are traces of Godelier's method in the way I find intellectual sustenance in his Melanesianist contributions, as well as those of his colleagues Marilyn Strathern and the late Annette Weiner. Insights on the spousal dynamic present in ritual exchange stem from work done by one researcher. Insights about sibling exchange have origins in the work of another. But in the end, the engendering of ritual among the Warlpiri of Yuendumu is a sui generis case, with trace elements of other peoples, but an essence that is fundamentally their own. Though cross-gender exchange existed in the early days of sedentarization, it did not manifest itself with the vigor and necessity that are present at the settlement today. There is no question that the pressures of postcolonial settlement life have ratcheted up the level of exchange among men and women. And yet it would be a mistake to assume that this change points to the erosion of ritual integrity. In fact, the increase in cross-gendered activity points to ongoing restructuring and strengthening of another key component of settlement life at Yuendumu—namely, the bonds of kinship. The aphorism that best characterizes Yuendumu Warlpiri-style ritual exchange has less to do with giving or keeping and more to do with *transforming through transmitting.*

Nocturnal dreams and ceremonial activities reveal men and women transacting business among themselves and with each other, and that transaction undermines gender-specific notions of spatially separate dominion. In fact, these cross-gender exchanges of ritual material point to the allegiances of kinship, whereby opposite-gender siblings and spouses, linked to one another residentially, reconfigure dynamic pre- and postsedentarized paths of ownership and responsibility. As do all other exchanges of ritual knowledge, crossgender exchanges of ritual material—whether as a by-product of nocturnal dreams or as a currency negotiated in a ceremonial context—necessitate correlative payments. But it would be wrong to assume that this establishes a dynamic of easy equivalence. It does not. The engendered exchange, whether after nocturnal dreams or prior to ceremonies, is a fluid expression of engagement and commitment that is monitored by those involved in the ritual life of the settlement. The exchange of ritual material between and among women and men—engendering—is a socially transformative act. But perhaps that understates the impact of cross-gender exchange. For the transmission not only changes the social realities of the settlement, it also modifies—and, by modifying, nurtures—Warlpiri cosmology in a way that allows Yuendumu's ceremonial life, and the kinship that sustains it, to live.

NOTES

This work is an outgrowth of an analysis published in Dussart 2000. A draft version of this chapter was presented at the annual conference of the Society for Economic Anthropology in a special session with Maurice Godelier in April 2002 in Toronto. I want to thank Maurice Godelier, Janet Siskind, Duran Bell, and Cynthia Werner for their insightful comments on earlier drafts, but none of them is in any way responsible for any inelegance.

1. Yuendumu is a central Australian desert settlement, governmentally established in 1946, located some 300 kilometers northwest of Alice Springs. The settlement is now owned and run by Warlpiri people. Yuendumu is the largest of five Warlpiri settlements. Of the 1,000 people who reside at Yuendumu, 800 or so are Warlpiri. There are currently about 2,000 Warlpiri who reside mostly in five settlements, all located in the Northern Territory.

2. The now-sedentarized Warlpiri hunters and gatherers who reside at Yuendumu organize themselves into discrete residential units of close kin that I call residential kin groups. These groups are composed of close agnates who may belong to different patrilineal descent groups and their affines; they vary in number between ten and one hundred adults. Given the mobility of the Warlpiri—many move between Yuendumu, various outstations, and other Warlpiri settlements—the size of any kin

group can vary greatly. Less susceptible to fluctuation, but still by no means static, is the number of kin groups in the settlement. Between 1983 and 2000, there were seven kin groups at Yuendumu, of which five were Warlpiri. These five Warlpiri kin groups represent the majority of residents of Yuendumu. Because they possess ownership rights over all the land on which they and other Aboriginal people have been sedentarized, they generally dominate Yuendumu ritual life.

3. Warlpiri ritual, and more specifically the danger the performance of the myths or Dreaming stories generates, is often inventoried at Yuendumu by the use of three value-laden Aboriginal English terms. First, there is that knowledge deemed "cheap" (generally perceived as being without risk and thus usually—though not always—considered public and unrestricted). Then there is knowledge that is "halfway," possessing a performative value dangerous enough to limit participation and observation to the ritually active of both genders (whether in joint ceremonies performed by both men and women or only among women). And finally there is knowledge that is considered "dear"—knowledge so dangerous that it can only be performed by men. These thumbnail translations are true as far as they go. However, at Yuendumu, while that which is dear is always restricted to men, that which is gender specific to men is not always dear. These differences suggest not the relative power of each gender in relation to the other but rather how the value of the ritual material within that gender's ceremonial activity is determined by its ease of distribution. For both men and women, it is the degree to which they control and transmit knowledge in the ceremonial sphere in which they are sanctioned to operate that grants them their authority.

4. See entry for *gender* in the *Compact Oxford English Dictionary.*

5. The terms *Dreaming* and *Dreamtime* are often used in English to refer to the mythical era during which mythical beings shaped the world as Aboriginal people know it today and taught the first human beings how to live. The term used by the Warlpiri is *Jukurrpa.* The land is crisscrossed by Dreaming itineraries, each associated with sites where mythical beings performed marvelous deeds (Dussart 2000).

6. At Yuendumu, the Warlpiri generally recognize four basic distinctions among the dreams they deem to be allied to the *Jukurrpa* (the Dreaming). First, there are those dreams that can be called premonitional visitations. This first category associates the dreamer's spirit with the telling of some nonritual event that has occurred or will occur to a dreamer or a member of the dreamer's residential kin group. No ritual songs—a crucial marker of ceremonial significance—will appear in such dreams. The second category of ceremonially significant dreams takes the form of an

admonition. These dreams caution the dreamer and kin about behavior incompatible with the rules that must be followed by all Warlpiri and that sustain the *Jukurrpa*. The third category of spiritually significant nocturnal activity, and one that carries a specific Warlpiri term, is the *kurruwalpa*. Kurruwalpa dreams are those dreams that identify the conception site and spirit of a soon-to-be-born or newborn child. The dreams of the fourth category are generally described as dreams that have the effect of altering Warlpiri ritual life. These dreams contain "innovative" material—"unknown" mythical narratives, dance steps configured in "novel" ways, designs never seen, and song texts "unheard." Songs are especially potent markers of potential ritual significance. Without a song text, dreamed material cannot be connected to a specific Dreaming. This fourth category is made up of dream material emerging in nocturnal dreams that is reconfigured and redeployed in ritual after a (re)interpretation period. The effect of such retrieval is the reinvigoration of ceremonial activity and the residential kin competition that sustains it (Dussart 2000).

7. See also Poirier 1996.

8. The basic structure of land ownership, and by implication ritual transmission and social organization, are constituted along lines of patrilineal descent. The Warlpiri system of ritual activity, land ownership, and inheritance cleaves individuals into two interrelated patrimoieties. One's patrimoiety is referred to as *kirda*, while the opposite patrimoiety is referred to as *kurdungurlu*. In the most basic sense, a kirda is the "owner" of a Dreaming and its associated sites. An owner must maintain the well-being of the land and its people by reenacting the Dreaming stories associated with that land in ceremonial contexts. While men and women may be identified as kirda for the same segments and sites and share certain versions of the Dreamings associated with that site, there are also segments of that Dreaming that are the exclusive performative province of men or women. The kurdungurlu is a "manager" of a kirda's Dreamings and sites. Reenactment of a Dreaming, in rituals by a kirda, requires the surveillance and advice of a kurdungurlu. The kirda–kurdungurlu relationship is, in theory, reciprocal.

9. I was present during several discussions regarding the transformation of the designs. The songs in this instance were not modified, as their text was "recognized" by both men and women involved in the negotiations as being already modeled as male songs.

10. See Glowczewski 2002, which illustrates the circulation of inalienable objects in northwest and central Australia.

11. See Munn 1973:37; Wild 1975:18.

12. "Business" is an Aboriginal English term often used by the Warlpiri to refer to their ritual activities in general.

REFERENCES

Dussart, Françoise. 1999. What an Aboriginal Acrylic Can Mean: On the Meta-Ritualistic Resonances of a Central Desert Painting. In *Art from the Land*. Howard Morphy and Margo Smith Boles, eds. Pp. 193–218. Charlottesville: University of Virginia.

———. 2000. *The Politics of Ritual in An Aboriginal Settlement: Kinship, Gender, and the Currency of Knowledge*. Washington, D.C.: Smithsonian Institution Press.

Glowczewski, Barbara. 2002. Culture Cult: Ritual Circulation of Inalienable Objects and Appropriation of Cultural Knowledge (Northwest and Central Australia) In *People and Things: Social Mediations in Oceania*. Monique Jeudy-Ballini and Bernard Juillerat, eds. Pp. 265–288. Durham, N.C.: Carolina Academic Press.

Godelier, Maurice. 1982. *La production des grands hommes*. Paris: Fayard.

———. 1986 [1982]. *The Making of Great Men: Male Domination and Power among the New Guinea Baruya*. Rupert Swyer, trans. Cambridge, U.K.: Cambridge University Press.

———. 1999 [1996]. *The Enigma of the Gift*. Nora Scott, trans. Chicago: University of Chicago Press.

Munn, Nancy. 1973. *Walbiri Iconography: Graphic Representation and Cultural Symbolism in a Central Australian Society*. Ithaca, N.Y.: Cornell University Press.

Myers, Fred. 1986. *Pintupi Country, Pintupi Self: Sentiment, Place, and Politics among Western Desert Aborigines*. Washington, D.C.: Smithsonian Institution Press.

Poirier, Sylvie. 1996. *Les jardins du nomade*. Paris: Lit Verlag.

Strathern, Marilyn. 1988. *The Gender of the Gift: Problems with Women and Problems with Society in Melanesia*. Berkeley and Los Angeles: University of California Press.

Weiner, Annette. 1992. *Inalienable Possessions: The Paradox of Keeping-While-Giving*. Berkeley and Los Angeles: University of California Press.

Wild, Stephen. 1975. Walbiri Music and Dance in Their Social and Cultural Nexus. Ph.D. diss., Indiana University.

II

MARKETS, MONEY, AND POWER

4

Conceptions of Capitalism: Godelier and Keynes

Colin Danby

In *The Mental and the Material* (1986) Maurice Godelier speaks of the "active presence of thought at the very heart of our material activities" (1986:18). Godelier has reworked the relationship between economy and culture: rather than thinking of culture and ideology as a system of meanings standing apart from everyday material practice, mystifying or justifying it, he sees them as implicated in material life in a much more fine-grained and active way. Culture is not the top layer of the cake (1986:128) but the leavening throughout it. Making things entails "setting to work mental realities, representations, judgments, principles of thought" (1986:10–11). Godelier (1999) privileges the imaginary over the symbolic, emphasizing the active ability to imagine, to use symbolic resources rather than being used by them.

However, the material activities associated with markets and capitalism appear culturally and socially barren in Godelier's work. His examples of mental activities inside material processes are drawn from noncapitalism. Where capitalism is present, it stands apart from other social institutions like family and community (1986:138, 148–149) and threatens them (1999:2); the threat stems not from any alternative, incompatible, or unpleasant sociality that capitalist workplaces and markets represent, but rather from their complete *lack* of sociality—their alienation, atomism, and anomie. When one works for capitalist firms, "one earns a living as a separate individual" (1999:2) rather than as part of a community; when one buys and sells, one participates in a system of object circulation that is the polar opposite of gift giving, in that it *fails* to create long-term obligations (1999:43, 2002:15). Godelier (1999:43) endorses

Gregory's (1982) stark give–sell split, in which an act of selling leaves "each party . . . once more independent and free of obligations to others."

It is easy to demonstrate the gap between this stark caricature and the observed material life of actual places and times that are commonly described by the terms "capitalist" and "market." Actual markets are complex social institutions (Swedberg 1994), capitalist firms exhibit important internal sociality (Tilly and Tilly 1994), and the notion that capitalism can be understood separate from other social institutions, in particular from gender and race, has been challenged by decades of scholarship (e.g., Hartmann 1976; Hall 1980). It is harder to show that this gap *matters;* it might be argued that Godelier is mainly concerned with noncapitalist phenomena and that his remarks on capitalism and markets should be understood as simple heuristics or gestures of political and moral engagement.

My first argument is that the rhetorical framing that Godelier employs—a framing that opposes a culturally and socially sterile capitalism/commerce to other kinds of material life that are socially and culturally rich—does two kinds of damage. It undoes efforts to avoid modernist prejudgments of the historical and social world, and it reinforces the compartmentalization of social science. This argument is presented in the next section.

My second argument is for a transdisciplinary (Charusheela and Zein-Elabdin in press) approach to the material life of places that are designated "market" and "capitalist." Here I draw on post-Keynesian thought, one of several heterodox schools of economic analysis that may yet help us reintegrate the study of economy with other aspects of our social existence. Two points of theory are important: the post-Keynesian emphasis on the time structure of material life, which gives us a specific way of asking questions about the social embeddedness of economy; and the role of representations and ideas in the ways that large groups or classes of people interact. Here we will see that Godelier's work brings out an important aspect of the thought of John Maynard Keynes.

CAPITALISM AND MODERNITY

Let us take a moment to situate Godelier's work. Economic anthropology has long (a) identified distinct systems or logics by which objects circulate among people and (b) set those distinct systems in relation to one another. The dominant tradition has been to arrange these distinct systems according to a criterion of social density or closeness (Mirowski 1994, 2001; Danby 2002). For several major figures, see table 4.1.[1]

Table 4.1   Theories of Society

	Most Densely Social		*Least Densely Social*
Malinowski	pure gifts	reciprocated gifts	trade
Mauss	total services	gifts	individualistic exchange
Sahlins	generalized reciprocity	balanced reciprocity	negative reciprocity
	(familial pooling)	(gifts)	(trade or theft)
Godelier	keeping	giving	selling

Beyond mere taxonomy, this schema has also functioned as a representation of a theory of society. In this theory, patterns of circulation that *generate* or renew society are placed toward the left side of this continuum, while on the right side we encounter patterns of object circulation that are asocial or even socially corrosive. The core of sociality, in this conception, appears to reside in close kinship and particularly in lineages. But lineages exclude people, by definition. Gifts then play a mediating role between familial closeness on the one side and potentially hostile asociality on the other. By the giving of gifts the socially bonding qualities attributed to close family groups are extended to make a larger society (Sahlins 1972; Gudeman 2001; Godelier this volume).

This framework becomes identifiably modernist when both space and time are mapped onto it, with the modern and West placed at the right side, and the primitive and non-West on the left side.[2] The result is a gemeinschaft-to-gesellschaft story in which close sociality, and the moral qualities attributed to it, first rises as gifting extends social bonds beyond close kin groups and then declines as markets, states, and other modern institutions arise. Space is mapped onto time when the "West" is regarded as close to the end of this history, while the non-West is closer to the beginning. This mapping, which is explicitly present in Sahlins 1972 and Mauss 1990 (Danby 2002), is, I would argue, invoked when Godelier (1999:1–15, 2002:5) suggests that an understanding of Baruya gifting might help address the "widening gap between economy and society" in places like France. Here Godelier juxtaposes

Baruya: Keep . . . Give . . . Sell

and

French: Family . . . Charity . . . Capitalism

in a way that implies an underlying (translocal and transhistorical) framework of this character:

Family (keeping) . . . Community/charity (giving) . . . Capitalism (selling) in which the Baruya can be positioned more to the left (with more of their material life occurring in and through family and community) and the French more to the right. It should be noted that Godelier elsewhere (1999:158) shows himself vividly aware of the dangers of modernist historicization and of any simple mapping of space (West–non-West) onto time (modern–primitive). It is his generalization of the keep-give-sell framework to support a particular political and ethical argument that reproduces the kind of historicism he is anxious to move beyond.

The family–community–market taxonomy also maps a familiar pair of ethical positions (Hirschman 1986). On the right side we can put the liberal, march-of-progress position that celebrates the loosening of old ties and regards Weberian modernity as an attainable ideal. On the left side we can group positions that celebrate family and locality and oppose efforts to homogenize society or culture. Each stance implies—indeed requires—its polar opposite; hence, debates between, for example, "relativists" and "ethnocentrists" occur entirely *within* modernity (Bhabha 1983; Charusheela 2001). To challenge this particular prefabrication of ethical discourse, then, is not to oppose ethical thought in general but rather to open it up to a larger conversation (Charusheela 2000). In other words, to argue that capitalism is socially dense and thick with cultural meaning is not to offer an apology for it. But such an argument does mean that ethical assessments of capitalism must consider the moral qualities of its sociality and culture, rather than assuming that it has none, or that capitalism and markets can be represented as a mere solvent of the sociality and culture present in other institutions like community and kinship.

Modernity, as described above, also underlies a modern–primitive division of the social sciences in which the modern West, with its allegedly distinct spheres of social life, receives the separate attention of political scientists, sociologists, economists, and so forth (with its culture hived off into the humanities), while the primitive world, in which these things are chaotically mingled, is studied by anthropologists. One result of this disciplinary map is that theories of economy become, by definition, formal, universal, and acultural.[3]

THE MENTAL AND THE MATERIAL

Let us return to the Baruya and the activities on the right side of the keep-give-sell framework. In his 1971 "Salt Currency" article, Godelier describes trading by the Baruya with other groups:

Trade routes are opened by daring individuals whose names are passed down in oral history. It was they who ran the risks of first contact with a neighboring tribe and who succeeded in establishing amicable relations with some members of the group as well as sealing a kind of peace pact. Normally, such a pact is passed on from generation to generation and one inherits trade partners from one's father. To give an example of the risks of first contact, about 1942 . . . some Baruya decided to contact the Watchakès. . . . Three men left, accompanied by a woman to prove their peaceful intentions. They received a warm welcome which put them at ease except for one who stood on his guard. This saved him, because a few hours later the three men were rudely attacked by their hosts; he succeeded in escaping, but his two companions were wounded and were later ritually killed and eaten. The woman was married to one of the murderers. The Baruya organized a punitive expedition which failed because the Watchakès had posted watch in the forest. Nevertheless, some time later, the Baruya made a second attempt to create commercial ties with the Watchakès and this time they succeeded. (Godelier 1971:61–62)

While the story has its unpleasant moments it is hardly a description of asociality.[4] It is stylized and shot through with meanings. The sociality described is deeply bivalent, in the sense that a single pattern of interaction contains the possibilities of both violence and peaceable trade.

Note also that particular trading relationships can be passed as an inheritance from father to son—a point that is noteworthy given Godelier's (1999) discussion of father–son transmission of sacred objects in the category of "keeping," in which he shows that keeping is not simply a failure of something to move, not simply an *absence* of circulation, but a way of pinning down social meaning, and that this meaning simultaneously inflects other kinds of circulation. Thus the rightmost category of circulation is tied to the leftmost. Essentially the same point can be seen when we read Godelier's analysis of the circulation of salt by the Baruya, in which the different systems or logics of circulation are far from incompatible with each other; quite the contrary: to grasp Baruya salt production, the complete ensemble of keeping, giving, and trading salt must be considered as a whole. Thus the facts that Baruya trading links are (a) personalized across groups; (b) constructed within a broader, patterned intragroup sociality that contains a set of shared meanings; and (c) passed down the patriline like sacred objects should all lead us to reconsider any notion that trading is essentially asocial and rivalrous.

This ends our critique. We now draw on Godelier's discussion of the "active presence of thought at the very heart of our material activities" (1986:18) and extend it to market activity and capitalism. As we do this, two further points bear emphasis. The first is the intersubjective importance of the "mental realities, representations, judgments, [and] principles of thought" (1986:10–11) that are set to work in material activities. When people collaborate to produce something, or participate in a system by which goods circulate among them, meanings and representations are used and shared. The second point is that while languages and other symbolic resources may be shared and intersubjective experience may be powerful, it is quite possible that different people, and especially different groups of people, apply different and even conflicting meanings to the same material activities (see Godelier 1986:152–153, 164). Men and women, slaveholders and slaves, bosses and workers may participate in the same systems of production and/or circulation and yet imagine them differently. They may imagine different futures. At points of conflict, contending representations of the same material practices may become important. With these two points, we turn to capitalism.

CAPITALISM AND REPRESENTATION

We draw here on the post-Keynesian tradition. For present purposes, the key characteristic of post-Keynesian theory is its interest in the time structure of material life:[5] how are the material processes of production, circulation, and consumption coordinated in and through time? Post-Keynesians point to the real-world importance of *forward* transactions. When I buy bread at the supermarket, that is a *spot* transaction, an instantaneous trade leaving no important further obligation. If payment and delivery of a good or service occur on different dates, I am making a *forward* transaction. Purchases of airplane tickets, college educations, cars, houses, and newspaper subscriptions are forward transactions. Capitalist firms work in dense webs of forward commitments to make and receive goods and services, commitments that cause them to expect cash payments and to promise to make payments at fixed dates. If there is anything that sets capitalist and market economies apart from other forms of economic organization, it is certainly not that they are *less* intricately time-embedded than other sorts of economies.[6]

This points to a different way to ask questions about social embeddedness. Forward transactions entail some kind of sociality linking the transactors, however limited or institution mediated it may be. We can then ask what kinds of social ties or institutions constrain or enable forward transacting of specific types, in particular places and times. An economy in which people make forward commitments to each other is clearly also an economy in which representations matter.

Essential to Keynes's vision is the question of how we think about the future, something of which we cannot have *knowledge* because it does not yet exist. Keynes, who was also a probability theorist, treated probabilistic statements as statements of belief rather than fact (Winslow in press). I suggest that these beliefs have the character of *representations,* with social–cultural characteristics.[7] Discussing decision making under uncertainty, Keynes writes that:

> Knowing that our individual judgment is worthless, we endeavor to fall back on the judgment of the rest of the world which is perhaps better informed. That is, we endeavor to conform with the behavior of the majority or the average. The psychology of a society of individuals each of whom is endeavoring to copy the others leads to what we may strictly term a *conventional* judgment. (Keynes 1937:214)

But this way of proceeding, "being based on so flimsy a foundation,"

> . . . is subject to sudden and violent changes. The practice of calmness and immobility, of certainty and security, suddenly breaks down. New fears and hopes will, without warning, take charge of human conduct. The forces of disillusion may suddenly impose a new conventional basis of valuation. All these pretty, polite techniques, made for a well-paneled Board Room and a nicely regulated market, are liable to collapse. (Keynes 1937:214–215)

Note both the necessity of making and holding representations and the structural or systemic properties of a system of widespread representation holding. The point is even clearer in Keynes's analysis of financial markets (1936:147–164 and passim). The participant in financial markets has to be concerned with what other people believe, and indeed concerned with what others believe others believe, and so forth (1936:156). To put it a different way, the very coherence of a capitalist economy with active financial markets may depend on the willingness to share representations.

Now consider another aspect of Keynes's thought. In a discussion of the effects of inflation, he writes that though a situation of rising prices

> is a source of gain to the business man, it is also a source of opprobrium. To the consumer the business man's exceptional profits appear as the cause (instead of the consequence) of the hated rise in prices. Amidst the rapid fluctuations of his fortunes he himself loses his conservative instincts, and begins to think more of the large gains of the moment than of the lesser, but permanent profits of normal business. . . . With such impulses and so placed, the business man is himself not free from a suppressed uneasiness. In his heart he loses his former self-confidence in his relation to society, in his utility and necessity in the economic scheme. He fears the future of his business and his class, and the less secure he feels his fortune to be the tighter he clings to it. The business man, the prop of society and the builder of the future, to whose activities and rewards there has been accorded, not long ago, an almost religious sanction, he of all men and classes the most respectable, praiseworthy and necessary, with whom interference was not only disastrous but almost impious, was now to suffer sidelong glances, to feel himself suspected and attacked, the victim of unjust and injurious laws—to become, and know himself half-guilty, a profiteer.
>
> No man of spirit will consent to remain poor if he believes his superiors to have gained their goods by lucky gambling. To convert the business man into a profiteer is to strike a blow at capitalism, because it destroys the psychological equilibrium which permits the perpetuance of unequal rewards. The economic doctrine of normal profits, vaguely apprehended by everyone, is a necessary condition for the justification of capitalism. The business man is tolerable so long as his gains can be said to bear some relation to what, roughly and in some sense, his activities have contributed to society. (Keynes 1923:23–24)

Here Keynes argues that something that raises business profits hurts business, and it hurts business by legitimating damaging representations of it. This analysis assumes a society in which different classes form impressions of each other, in which ideas of dignity and desert matter, and in which political struggle occurs in part through contending representations of the same thing.[8]

It is thus not difficult to show that capitalism entails "setting to work mental realities, representations, judgments, principles of thought" (Godelier 1986:10–11), which include alongside representations of nature and humanity itself, representations of the aims, means, stages, and anticipated results of human activities on nature and society—representations which simultaneously organize a sequence of events and legitimize the location and status of agents in society. (Godelier 1986:11)

These representations make capitalism *possible* but also unstable and uncertain. We have sketched only the outlines of an analysis of capitalism and markets in which cultural processes are given their due, and we should again emphasize that post-Keynesianism is only one of several heterodoxies with ideas relevant to this project. But to undertake this effort is to begin reconstructing a nonmodernist social science, one that provincializes and reproblematizes capitalism.

NOTES

For comments I thank Duran Bell, Michael Billig, S. Charusheela, and Cynthia Werner.

1. See Danby 2002 for a more extended discussion of this framework and its development in the work of Malinowski, Mauss, and Sahlins.

2. See Fabian 1983, Chakrabarty 2000, and further discussion and references in Danby 2002.

3. See also Godelier 1972:282 and 1986:198. Unfortunately substantivists conceded the analysis of capitalism to the formalists and confined themselves to a smaller debate over whether formalism could understand noncapitalism. Insights about the cultural life of capitalism from the institutionalist tradition (a source for substantivism) were lost (Neale and Mayhew 1983), and "economic" theory came to mean certain varieties of formalism. Contemporary texts in economic anthropology (e.g., Plattner 1989:6) present a menu of economic theories winnowed to two choices—neoclassical economics and orthodox Marxism—ignoring heterodox traditions.

4. Utter asociality would be something like the "silent trade," which may be an ethnographic chimera (Narotzky 1997:54). If it is chimerical, its persistence as an idea might be explained by its role as placeholder for zero-degree sociality in the larger taxonomy. The neoclassical market model—wordless trade, without merchants—is strikingly similar.

5. See Danby 2002 for a fuller exposition of post-Keynesianism theory as it is relevant to economic anthropology. The canonical survey is Hamouda and Harcourt 1988.

6. Post-Keynesian analysis thus disputes Gregory's (1982) depiction of commerce as not characterized by long-term ties. See also Mirowski 2001:444–446.

7. Ferguson (1988:492) makes a related argument.

8. Compare Godelier 1986:13, 156–164. Keynes draws on an older tradition in political economy, evident in Smith but now thwarted by a compartmentalized social science, which took shared ideas and states of belief very seriously—a markedly superstructural notion of "base." See Winslow (in press) for an examination of some of these aspects of Keynes's thought in a different theoretical framework.

REFERENCES

Bhabha, Homi. 1983. The Other Question. *Screen* 24(6):18–36.

Chakrabarty, Dipesh. 2000. *Provincializing Europe: Postcolonial Thought and Historical Difference.* Princeton, N.J.: Princeton University Press.

Charusheela, S. 2000. On History, Love, and Politics. *Rethinking Marxism* 12(4):45–61.

———. 2001. Women's Choices and the Ethnocentrism/Relativism Dilemma. In *Postmodernism, Economics, and Knowledge.* Stephen Cullenberg, Jack Amariglio, and David Ruccio, eds. Pp. 197–220. London: Routledge.

Charusheela, S., and Eiman Zein-Elabdin. In press. Feminism, Postcolonial Thought, and Economics. In *Feminist Economics Today: Beyond Economic Man.* Marianne Ferber and Julie Nelson eds. Chicago: University of Chicago Press.

Danby, Colin. 2002. The Curse of the Modern: A Post-Keynesian Critique of the Gift–Exchange Dichotomy. In *Research in Economic Anthropology,* vol. 21. Norbert Dannhaeuser and Cynthia Werner, eds. Pp. 13–42. Oxford: Elsevier Science.

Fabian, Johannes. 1983. *Time and the Other: How Anthropology Makes Its Object.* New York: Columbia University Press.

Ferguson, James. 1988.Cultural Exchange: New Developments in the Anthropology of Commodities. *Cultural Anthropology* 3(4):488–513.

Godelier, Maurice. 1971. "Salt Currency" and the Circulation of Commodities among the Baruya of New Guinea. In *Studies in Economic Anthropology.*

Anthropological Studies 7. George Dalton, ed. Pp. 52–73. Washington, D.C.: American Anthropological Association.

———. 1972 [1966]. *Rationality and Irrationality in Economics*. Brian Pearce, trans. New York: Monthly Review Press.

———. 1986 [1984]. *The Mental and the Material*. Martin Thom, trans. New York: Verso.

———. 1999 [1996]. *The Enigma of the Gift*. Nora Scott, trans. Chicago: University of Chicago Press.

Gregory, Chris A. 1982. *Gifts and Commodities*. London: Academic Press.

Gudeman, Stephen. 2001. Postmodern Gifts. In *Postmodernism, Economics, and Knowledge*. Stephen Cullenberg, Jack Amariglio, and David Ruccio, eds. Pp. 459–474. New York: Routledge.

Hall, Stuart. 1980. Race, Articulation, and Societies Structured in Dominance. In *Sociological Theories: Race and Colonialism*. Pp. 305–346. Paris: UNESCO.

Hamouda, O. F., and G. C. Harcourt. 1988. Post-Keynesianism: From Criticism to Coherence? *Bulletin of Economic Research* 40(1):1–33.

Hartmann, Heidi. 1976. Capitalism, Patriarchy, and Job Segregation by Sex. *Signs* 1(3):137–169.

Hirschman, Albert O. 1986. *Rival Views of Market Society and Other Recent Essays*. New York: Viking Penguin.

Keynes, John Maynard. 1923. *A Tract on Monetary Reform*. London: Macmillan.

———. 1936. *The General Theory of Employment, Interest, and Money*. London: Macmillan.

———. 1937. The General Theory of Employment. *Quarterly Journal of Economics* 51(2):209–223.

Malinowski, Bronislaw. 1922. *Argonauts of the Western Pacific*. London: George Routledge and Sons.

Mauss, Marcel. 1990. *The Gift*. W. D. Halls, trans. New York: Routledge.

Mirowski, Philip. 1994. Tit for Tat: Concepts of Exchange, Higgling, and Barter in Two Episodes in the History of Economic Analysis. In *Higgling: Transactors and*

Their Markets in the History of Economics. Neil DeMarchi and Mary S. Morgan, eds. Pp. 313–342. Durham, N.C.: Duke University Press.

———. 2001. Refusing the Gift. In *Postmodernism, Economics, and Knowledge.* Stephen Cullenberg, Jack Amariglio, and David Ruccio, eds. Pp. 431–458. New York: Routledge.

Narotzky, Susana. 1997. *New Directions in Economic Anthropology.* London: Pluto Press.

Neale, Walter, and Anne Mayhew. 1983. Polanyi, Institutional Economics, and Economic Anthropology. In *Economic Anthropology: Topics and Theories.* Society for Economic Anthropology Monographs in Economic Anthropology, vol. 1. Sutti Ortiz, ed. Pp. 11–20. Lanham, Md.: University Press of America.

Plattner, Stuart, ed. 1989. *Economic Anthropology.* Stanford, Calif.: Stanford University Press.

Sahlins, Marshall. 1972. *Stone Age Economics.* Chicago: Aldine-Atherton.

Swedberg, Richard. 1994. Markets as Social Structures. In *The Handbook of Economic Sociology.* Neil J. Smelser and Richard Swedberg, eds. Pp. 255–282. Princeton, N. J.: Princeton University Press.

Tilly, Chris, and Charles Tilly. 1994. Capitalist Work and Labor Markets. In *The Handbook of Economic Sociology.* Neil J. Smelser and Richard Swedberg, eds. Pp. 283–312. Princeton, N. J.: Princeton University Press.

Winslow, Ted. In press. The Foundations of Keynes's Economics. In *Perspectives on the Philosophy of Keynes's Economics: Probability, Uncertainty, and Convention.* Jochen Runde and Sohei Mizuhara, eds. New York: Routledge.

5

Little Tubes of Mighty Power: How Clay Tobacco Pipes from Port Royal, Jamaica, Reflect Socioeconomic Change in Seventeenth-Century English Culture and Society

Georgia L. Fox

In 1692, a devastating earthquake marked the end of England's most thriving port city in the Caribbean, Port Royal, Jamaica. Now submerged, Port Royal left its greatest legacy in the thousands of well-preserved archaeological remains that offer a glimpse into seventeenth-century society and culture. Among the artifacts, more than twenty thousand clay tobacco smoking pipes were recovered from excavations conducted between 1981 and 1990, and their presence tells a story.

Higgins (1999:310) refers to clay pipes as "little tubes of mighty power" because they can be useful in understanding and interpreting the past. Clay pipes, when interpreted within the broader context of Port Royal and seventeenth-century English history, reflect the economic and social transformation of a society emerging from a feudal system to one based on colonization and trade. In this transformation, Port Royal and England's other American colonies figured prominently in England's economic recovery. One of the benefits of colonization was the economic growth derived from raw materials exported from the American colonies, especially tobacco. The colonies not only provided raw materials for export but also required goods from the home country. In this regard, Port Royal, with its relationship to London and then Bristol, England, fits the classic world system paradigm in its trade of tobacco, sugar, and other raw materials in return for consumer goods.

Although the world system model provides an excellent framework for analysis of New World archaeological sites such as Port Royal, it does not take into account certain cultural behaviors that specifically affect the impact of economic outcomes. In this regard, at Port Royal and in England, exposure to consumer and luxury goods provoked a wave of demand that help stimulate preindustrial manufacturing and colonial trade, ultimately contributing to England's economic growth. The aim of this chapter is to demonstrate how artifacts such as clay pipes can reveal other dynamics at play in the changing socioeconomic conditions of seventeenth-century English life.

In the first section, the world system paradigm is discussed in regard to English colonization and trade. Chief among England's trade commodities was tobacco, grown and exported from England's New World colonies, as presented in the second section. Following a brief discussion of Port Royal, early consumerism is addressed in the third section. This consumerism was made possible by a number of factors that allowed for an increase in the purchasing power of English citizens and colonists at Port Royal. Although purchases included necessities, the archaeological and documentary evidence strongly indicates that household spending habits were geared toward the purchase of luxuries in addition to necessities. This behavior is an overall reflection of changing attitudes and social institutions in seventeenth-century English culture and society, which are addressed in the final section of the chapter.

THE WORLD SYSTEM PARADIGM

The seventeenth century has been described as a time of crisis, during which the transition from a feudal to a market economy created a severe economic slump for most of Europe (Frank 1978; Wallerstein 1980). For England, the ascension of Charles II in 1660 and the beginning of the Restoration signaled "the economic exit from medievalism" (Minchinton 1969:11). Part of England's economic recovery derived from overseas colonization and trade, which was accomplished in three ways. First, the emphasis in trade shifted from internal to external markets and sources of supply. Second, imports coming from the New World and the East Indies aided in the growth of a substantial reexport trade. Third, new markets abroad created the demand for a wider range of goods and services from the homeland. These markets included not only the American colonies but also markets in Asia and Africa.

Scholars now generally agree that England's economic renewal was based on "a series of proposals crystallizing into ordinances, proclamations and statutes that formed the dynamic of a new economic policy" (Wilson 1984:61). Economic growth for England was actually a slow process throughout the seventeenth century. In the second half of the sixteenth century, proponents of colonization, such as English clergyman Richard Hakluyt, envisioned colonial trade as a panacea for England's economic woes and proposed ideas about producing desired commodities in English colonies (Parry 1979; Williams 1970). When the American colonies were first settled, imports exceeded exports, making the balance of payments "passive." Yet, under such conditions a growing export trade from the colonies and a healthy reexport trade from Britain's central ports soon facilitated beneficial economic adjustments, which positioned England against its European competitors (Frank 1978).

This transformative process extended to a developing world economy or world system (Braudel 1979; Frank 1978; Wallerstein 1974). In this system, the actors were "participating subeconomies," particularly "the colonized and newly settled regions" (Frank 1978:79). Following Wallerstein's model, newly formed relationships developed between dominant, "core" areas like London and more peripheral areas such as the colonies along the eastern seaboard of North America and in the Caribbean. The colonies would provide raw materials and, in return, would rely on manufactured goods from the mother country. Peripheral areas were divided into two zones, a "middle" zone, a semiurban area containing some of the attributes of the core area, and the larger periphery, a backward area composed of scattered populations. The creation of this *weltwirtschaft* relied on London's economic, social, and political capital. With the exception of Bristol in the late seventeenth century, London had "created and directed England from start to finish" (Braudel 1979:365). The outward flow of goods from London to foreign ports made London the central hub to the growing colonial periphery.

Essentially, this expansion by England and other Western European countries was unique in that it integrated New World economies with European economies, thereby placing the new settlements in a dependent relationship to the centers through specific linkages. In England's case, these consisted of the colonial purchase of English goods and the sole use of English vessels and merchants, thus providing freights, interests, and profits designed to secure state and private profits (Nettles 1933). Colonialism allowed the metropolis to extend its markets for manufactured goods, while the colonies, in turn, supplied raw materials to the metropolis, forming an economic dependency on both sides (King 1990).

The world system paradigm is controversial for a number of reasons, including its Eurocentric bias, which largely ignores the role of indigenous peoples (Abernethy 2000; Thompson 1989). This is especially the case for the Caribbean (Williams 1970). Eric Wolf (1982) has objected to Wallerstein's linking of capitalism to market production, particularly before the advent of a true wage–labor market. For Wolf (1982), capitalism does not occur until the eighteenth century; he regards the period between the 1400s and the early 1700s as mainly a precapitalist phase of mercantile activity.[1]

Others argue that colonization was not central to England's overall economic development (O'Brien 1982). Supporters of this view claim that profits earned in the colonial trade were not sufficient to warrant a significant source of capital, nor did manufactured exports from England spur any major industrial development in core areas like London. In addition, colonial markets for British manufactures were relatively small, only accounting for 20 percent of industrial output, as the home market was greater (McCusker and Menard 1991).

Contrary to this view, colonization did play a major role in European economic revitalization. According to Price (1978), colonial development stimulated England's economy in a number of ways. First, the processing of raw materials from the colonies and the manufacture of goods for export to the colonies employed English workers, utilizing their own resources. Second, colonial demand for goods forced England to find new and innovative ways of dealing with scarce resources that ultimately led to experimentation with "new, cost-reducing technologies" (Price 1978:123). Third, the risky nature of long-distance trade with the colonies initiated important institutional changes involving large sums of capital. These changes included the development of larger merchant firms, more efficient credit arrangements, and more capital and insurers, changes that were ahead of their time (Price 1978). Britain's economic policy could be thus characterized as a blend of private and state interests (Wilson 1984).

Although colonization and the mechanisms of trade were central to developing a robust economy, one factor that has been overlooked in the dynamics of this core peripheral relationship is preindustrial consumerism. From the outset, English colonists were determined to make economic gains to increase their purchasing power, particularly for consumer and luxury goods. To afford such goods, colonists needed a lucrative export commodity. In the early days of colonization, the answer could be found in tobacco. Before the supremacy of sugar, tobacco was the chief agricultural crop that formed the basis for metropolitan–colony relations. The desire for tobacco fueled a reciprocal trade between England and the colonies that helped foster England's early economic development in the seventeenth century, thus setting the stage for England's eventual hegemony in the world system.

THE CASE OF TOBACCO

By the late sixteenth century, tobacco smoking had been adopted with a zeal unprecedented in human history. A New World plant, tobacco was first marketed and supplied by Spain during the second half of the sixteenth century and the early seventeenth century. In reaction to the high duties and restrictions imposed on imported Spanish tobacco, peasants in England, Wales, and the outer islands of Jersey and Guernsey planted tobacco to supplement their incomes.

By 1610, tobacco cultivation in England was well under way, despite a ban imposed by Charles I in an effort to control tobacco production (Farnie 1962). By 1634, tobacco had become a poor man's crop. It provided jobs and cash; for example, tobacco contributed to the growth and prosperity of the English town of Winchcombe until the 1660s, when the Privy Council destroyed tobacco crops in the area. It took about seventy years before the government could eradicate homegrown tobacco in England (Thirsk 1976, 1984). In the end, low tobacco prices from tobacco grown in the English colonies finally curbed home production.

In the English colonies, tobacco was first grown in the Caribbean as part of the early tobacco- and cotton-based agricultural economies (Williams 1970:111). Tobacco was cultivated in Bermuda, Barbados, Saint Kitts, Nevis, Antigua, Montserrat, and Jamaica (Dunn 1973). The bulk of the tobacco trade, however, derived from the Chesapeake, particularly as sugar supplanted tobacco as the chief crop in the Caribbean colonies by the 1660s (Dunn 1973). In opposition to Caribbean tobacco planters, members of the Council of Virginia vehemently protested to the Privy Council about competition from the West Indies. The Chesapeake planters had little to worry about, however, as Caribbean-grown tobacco, especially the notoriously poor-quality Barbados variety that had "an earthy taste" (Williams 1970:111), was inferior to their own tobacco.

For English colonists living in the Chesapeake, tobacco became the chief commodity for export. Exports from Virginia in 1617 alone amounted to about 20,000 pounds, and by 1630, this trade expanded to between 400,000 and 500,000 pounds (Beer 1959; MacInnes 1926). By 1640, the British colonies were producing a total of about 1,250,900 pounds of tobacco, most of it from the Chesapeake (Pagan 1979).

In terms of costs to the consumer, tobacco prices varied during the seventeenth century. Initially, in 1604, to deter smoking and raise revenues, James I increased the import duty on tobacco from 2 pence a pound to 6 shillings, 10 pence on every pound for tobacco imported from Virginia. Cultivation of tobacco in Virginia began by 1607 and was well under way by 1616 (Beer 1948; Farnie 1962; Penn 1901; Thirsk 1984). Royally imposed import duties in combination with the prohibition of imported Spanish tobacco caused the price of tobacco to skyrocket. During the 1620s, however, tobacco prices fluctuated owing to the unpredictability of supplies coming from Spanish America, the West Indies, and the Chesapeake. For Chesapeake farmers, a glutted market beginning in the 1620s ultimately caused tobacco prices to fall and steadily decline, only to slowly rise after the 1680s until the American Revolution (McCusker and Menard 1991; Williams 1970).[2]

For many of the British colonists, tobacco was an ideal crop for new settlement and generating income. It required a short, nine-month growing cycle and could grow in a variety of soils and climates. Although growing tobacco was labor intensive, colonists were willing to maintain the year-round attention that was necessary for a successful crop. This included transplanting tiny seedlings, weeding during growth, topping the plant, harvesting, stalking and stemming, drying, and curing. Once these tasks were completed, the tobacco was tightly packed into hogsheads, large barrels that weighed between four hundred and eight hundred pounds. Because freight rates were based on number rather than weight, hogsheads were packed to the limit, at the expense of damaging the leaves or cracking the barrel staves, which sometimes caused a hogshead to burst during shipment (Breen 1985; Davis 1962; Robert 1967).

For the first half of the seventeenth century, London merchants dominated the tobacco trade. Because London was a major port city, its merchants had the necessary capital to oversee trade activities. London was also the favored port of the Crown, and, consequently, from 1624 through 1638, all imports of tobacco were restricted to London (MacInnes 1926; Pagan 1979). London

Port Book figures for 1620 indicate that tobacco rated eighth in the list of the city's imports. The leading imports included textile materials, groceries, timber, and wine (Minchinton 1969). By 1633 tobacco ranked fifth, and by 1640, it was the number one import in London (Williams 1955). Imported quantities rose from 173,372 pounds in 1620 to 1.25 million pounds in 1640 to approximately 7 million pounds in 1662 and 9 million pounds in 1668–1669 (Davis 1954; Minchinton 1969). By the late 1680s, the English were consuming 13 million pounds of tobacco and reexporting 25 million pounds to Europe (Davis 1954). For 1686 alone, tobacco imported from the colonies accounted for 68 percent of the total value of raw materials shipped from the colonies (Zahedieh 1994). Until the large-scale production of sugar overtook it, tobacco remained the most remunerative crop in British America.

PORT ROYAL AND CLAY PIPES

What is the material evidence that cultivation and use of tobacco was widespread? The answer lies in the spectacular number of clay pipes that have been found at various New World archaeological sites during the last sixty years. At present, Port Royal has one of the most extensive and documented clay pipe collections from the New World. During ten years of excavation, 21,575 clay pipes were recovered at Port Royal. Although the exact amounts are currently unavailable, sizable collections numbering in the thousands were also recovered from Martin's Hundred and Flowerdew Hundred in colonial Virginia (Noël Hume 1982; Deetz 1993). The seventeenth-century "Pipe Wreck," located at Monte Cristi, Dominican Republic, yielded 25,000 Dutch clay pipes from just one shipwreck (Hall 1996). In addition, 50,000 pipes were found at colonial Jamestown (Cotter 1994). The impressive numbers of clay pipes excavated at these sites indicate both the ubiquity of the clay tobacco pipe and the popularity of tobacco smoking.

As Britain's foremost port in the Caribbean, Port Royal fits the standard core periphery model of world system theory, with London, then Bristol, acting as the metropolitan core. Almost by accident, Port Royal was founded in May 1655 following an aborted attempt by William Penn and Robert Venables to capture Hispaniola from the Spanish in 1654. To maintain honor and placate Oliver Cromwell, Penn and Venables then sailed to nearby Jamaica, where they captured the poorly defended island from the Spanish. The capture of Port Royal turned out to be fortunate, however, as the spot was ideal for settlement with its deepwater harbor, safe anchorage, and flat topography. Following fortification, Port Royal grew quickly, providing an advantageous locale for merchants, sea captains, and craftspeople to settle. Between 1655 and 1692, Port Royal was the fastest-growing colony settled by the English in the New World, and it became the most economically important port in the Americas (Hamilton 1992).

By 1692, Port Royal had between 6,500 and 7,000 inhabitants, an estimated two thousand buildings on fifty-one acres, and a busy port that possibly cleared between 150 and 200 vessels a year (Hamilton 1992; Pawson and Buisseret 1975; Zahedieh 1986). Built on a town plan modeled after London, Port Royal represented a society infused with imported luxury goods and one that mimicked its London counterpart. Unfortunately, shortly before noon on June 7, 1692, Port Royal's glory days ended as a devastating earthquake shook the town to "a heap of rubbish"; the earthquake was followed by a tidal wave. Combined, the earthquake and inundation of water killed more than four thousand people and reduced the town from fifty-one to twenty-five acres (*Gentleman's Magazine* 1750:212; Pawson and Buisseret 1975).

The result was a buried archaeological site that was well preserved in situ in a kind of "Pompeii effect." Although a number of excavations were attempted, the first systematic excavation was conducted and directed by D. L. Hamilton of the Nautical Archaeology Program of the Department of Anthropology at Texas A&M University, in conjunction with the Institute of Nautical Archaeology and the Jamaica National Trust Commission, then the Jamaican National Heritage Trust. Hamilton's excavations were conducted from 1981 to 1990, focusing on the commercial heart of the city at the intersection of Queen and Lime Streets (Hamilton 1991).

During ten years of fieldwork, eight discrete buildings were excavated, revealing an assemblage that was exhilarating in both its breadth and its scope. In addition to clay pipes, thousands of wine bottles were discovered, as well as a formidable collection of pewter utensils and dishes, high-end Chinese porcelain, fine glassware, and other objects, providing a glimpse into the material life of this once thriving port.

The documentary evidence also substantiates the presence of these consumer and luxury goods in the archaeological record at Port Royal. For example, clay pipes can be traced through the Port Books of the Office of the Exchequer, Series E/190, which include handwritten entries of goods being shipped from English ports to their destinations for both London and Bristol. Among the items more commonly listed in the inventories were clay pipes, often shipped in barrels by the gross (144 pipes). Barrels were often packed with several gross of pipes that were either contained in small boxes or loosely packed in the barrels and insulated with straw or other packing materials to prevent breakage. Itemized port records for 1682 and 1694–1695 for Bristol reveal the vast quantities of clay pipes being shipped to England's overseas colonies by Bristol pipemakers such as Llewellin Evans. For example, eighteen shipments of clay pipes from Bristol to Jamaica in 1682 totaled 405 gross, or 58,320 pipes, and twenty-six shipments from Bristol to Jamaica in 1694–1695 amounted to 3,778 gross, or 544,032 pipes (Office of the Exchequer 1682, 1694–1695). Given that probably not all shipments were recorded, these amounts may be lower than actual receipts at the port. Such large shipment figures support the archaeological evidence.

In addition to the Port Records, the Jamaica Probate Inventories, which are essentially lists of deceased individuals' property at the time of death, complement the findings from the Bristol Port Book entries and the archaeological record. The most helpful probate records were those of Port Royal's merchants and sea captains who were engaged in overseas trade. As with the port books, the numbers of pipes for these individuals totaled in the thousands. For example, 80 gross, or 11,520 pipes, were recorded in the probate inventory of Port Royal merchant Michael Baker (Jamaica Public Archives 1693: V3/F 602–606). For Port Royal merchant Joseph Brown (Jamaica Public Archives 1686: V2/F202), six barrels of 158 gross, or 22,752 pipes were listed, but even more impressive was the 258.5 gross of pipes (37,224 pipes) packed in twelve chests in the inventory of ship Captain Nicholas Verbraack (Jamaica Public Archives 1685:V2/F110–112).

THE RISE OF CONSUMERISM

The artifacts, combined with the documentary evidence from the English Port Records and Jamaica Probate Inventories for Port Royal, clearly indicate a port city steeped in consumerism. In this regard, the evidence from Port Royal often parallels finds from other New World archaeological sites, indicating that an early "consumer revolution" was taking place between 1650 and 1750 (Johnson 1999). These findings have thus caused some scholars to reevaluate the world system paradigm, particularly as it relates to archaeological research.

Although highly relevant and applicable to historical archaeology, the world system model is also limited with respect to patterns of consumption, which have largely been ignored by world system and dependency theorists.

The result is now a shift from previous "top-down" models that regarded the Industrial Revolution as the true beginning of capitalism to a more complex, "bottom-up" preindustrial consumer model that takes into account the cultural preferences and actions of consumers, both at home and in the colonies (Johnson 1999). Advocates of the pre-industrial consumerism model include Thirsk (1978), Weatherill (1988), Shammas (1990), and McCracken (1990).

The consumers discussed in this context specifically refer to "middle-range" members of English society, who chiefly made their living either as farmers or as wage earners living in smaller towns or more urban areas, both at home and in the colonies. These groups comprised mostly farmers, husbandmen, craftsmen, shopkeepers, and merchants. In this regard, these consumers do not make up a socioeconomic continuum from preindustrial societies to those of the capitalist industrial era. Rather, they represent a body of workers who, early on, demonstrated a form of consumer behavior in terms of limited spending habits and changing tastes as they were exposed to new commodities both in England and in Port Royal. It is precisely this early consumerism that has been overlooked in modern world system theory. Recent developments in colonial economic history and historical archaeological research in social class, consumer behavior, and capitalism suggest a definable shift in consumer behavior as early as the mid-seventeenth century, but certainly not on the scale of industrial and postindustrial consumers.

Given these defining characteristics, what makes this earlier consumerism significant is the *desire* of middle-range members of English society for consumer and luxury goods, which played an important role in sustaining core periphery relationships. From the earliest days of English colonization, settlers demanded goods that far exceeded the basic requirements for survival, such that they "were prepared to devote some or all of their labor to producing export commodities whose sale paid for imported goods" (Abernethy 2000:61). In this regard, colonists constituted a "transplanted private sector" that even Hakluyt and Carlisle recognized as a colonial market for British manufactures, which would pour "into a country larger than all Europe" (Abernethy 2000; Beer 1959:72).

CONSUMERISM AND ITS RELATION TO THE CHANGING ECONOMY

One of the key questions arising from preindustrial consumer research is: How were middle-range members of English society able to afford consumer and luxury goods both in the colonies and in England? At present, there are several possible explanations. First, as mentioned previously, the economy was changing slowly over the seventeenth century, allowing for fluctuations in consumer prices. During this time, it also appears that small-scale preindustrial manufactures helped fuel the economy and provided extra income for family households (Holderness 1976; Coward 1992; Woodward 1994). Coinciding with these developments were changes in the urban landscape that directly affected middle-range spending behavior. A closer look reveals the interconnectedness of these developments and the dynamics involved in this budding consumerism.

Changing Prices and Urbanization

Although consumer prices fluctuated rather widely during the seventeenth century, there was a general tendency for prices to decline, thereby affecting the spending habits of wage earners. As goods became more available, they also became more affordable, especially perishable goods or groceries (Shammas 1990). These items included pepper, sugar products, and caffeine drinks, which often appear in the various Port Book entries for London, Bristol, and other port towns, as well as probate inventories for the period. For the first time, it was possible for more people to enjoy pleasures they were previously denied, including smoking tobacco. In England, farmers, craftsmen, shopkeepers, and others slowly began to thrive in the economic upswing, finding new outlets for both their earning and their spending potential. In Port Royal, the combination of the availability of consumer and luxury goods and an ample flow of cash from trade, smuggling, and agricultural pursuits also provided such opportunities for English settlers.

The availability of more affordable goods also coincided with the influx of workers into urban areas such as London, Bristol, and Port Royal. Members of this new workforce had little time to prepare their own food, so any extra pocket change might go toward purchasing already prepared items, including meals in taverns. As a result, middle-range wage earners in towns and cities became more dependent on the market for their "bread and beer" (Mintz 1985:165). Contemporary accounts support these developments as

London tradesmen spent "most of their money . . . every Week in the Neigh-boorhood in Strong-Drink, several sorts of Flesh, Bread, Butter, Cheese, Sugar, Spice, Spanish Fruit and in Cloathing, which caused a quick Circulation in all Business" (Tryon 1699:17). In Port Royal, it was common for merchants and other workers to take their midday meals in taverns and eating establishments.

The expanding workforce and the demand for perishable and nonperishable goods also coincided with what Peter Borsay terms an "urban renaissance," in which towns became the "engines of the commercial system, pumping goods to and fro along the arteries of trade" (1989:viii, 23). The proliferation of retail shops in England by 1640 and in Port Royal supports these developments and the growing reliance on new sources for more affordable staples and imported luxury goods (Davis 1966; Patten 1978; Shammas 1990). Englishman John Taylor was especially struck by the "large shops and comodious store houses" he observed on his visit to Port Royal in 1688 (1688:252). Some of the most common shops were of the grocers, apothecaries, and tobacconists (Shammas 1990). In fact, the profusion of tobacco retailers caused antitobacconist Barnabe Rich (1937:537) to complain that tobacco was sold in "every Taverne, Inne, and Alehouse, as either Wine, Ale, or Beare; and for Apothecaries Shops, Grosers Shops, Chandler Shops, they are (almost) never without company, that from morning till night are still taking of Tobacco."

Wages and Preindustrial Manufacturing

Along with an increase in the number of urban workers, retail shops, and periods of lower prices, rising incomes may also have affected seventeenth-century consumer behavior among the middle-range members of society. The most likely source of improved incomes was preindustrial manufacturing. Generally, English manufacturing consisted of two types: first, the larger-scale processing and production of raw materials into goods such as glass, paper, textiles, and bricks; and second, the smaller cottage industries (Holderness 1976). These small-scale manufactures probably improved the household income and therefore affected the spending habits of the middle-range households.

A 1994 study of seventeenth-century households in Northern England suggests that many families took on extra work to offset a period of rising prices while trying to maximize their total income (Woodward 1994). This is especially true for middle-range members of English society who supplemented their household incomes by taking on additional craft specialties and/or cottage industries. By taking on additional work, some of these families were eventually able to produce extra pocket money that enabled them to make small purchases of affordable goods and small luxury items. In fact, this extra income "made all the difference between a precarious existence and a modicum of comfort" (Thirsk 1978).

Whether as supplemental income to farming or husbandry, or as the sole source of income, the small-scale production of goods in English villages and towns often provided a livelihood for single households and introduced many alternative sources of work into rural communities (Holderness 1976; Shammas 1990; Thirsk 1978). Oftentimes these small family work units required little fixed capital and were labor intensive, unlike the large production units of the Industrial Revolution (Clarkson 1972). In addition to members of the immediate family, a few journeymen or apprentices may have been included in the work unit, especially if a trade was involved that required guild membership, such as pipemaking (Coward 1992).

Small craft industries included stocking-knitting, buttonmaking, pinmaking, bookbinding, distilling, and the production of such items as ribbon and lace, linen, starch, candles, soap, ale, and clocks (Arnold 1977; Patten 1978; Thirsk 1978). Chief among these small-scale industries was clay pipe manufacturing, an industry that was "more dirty than laborious, and but moderately profitable" (Campbell 1747:326). Families involved in pipemaking could set up a simple kiln in their backyard or adjacent to their house and produce as many as eight thousand pipes per week. One such family was Llewellin Evans and his sons of Bristol, who were quite successful in supplying the colonial market with clay pipes. Most of the Port Royal pipes that have makers' marks can be traced to Bristol pipemakers such as the Evans family (Fox 1999). Work by Walker (1977) and more recently Peacey's (1996) research on pipe kiln sites testify to the emergence of family-owned and -run clay pipe kilns in Bristol and other English towns during the seventeenth and eighteenth centuries. Manufactured, used, and discarded in a relatively short period of time, clay pipes were possibly one of the first disposable commodities, thus assuring a steady livelihood for pipemakers, especially those involved in the colonial trade.

NEW TRENDS IN SOCIAL INSTITUTIONS

Although family household incomes may have benefitted from such cottage industries as pipemaking, other factors also contributed to a growing consumerism and England's economic growth. The Nobel Prize–winning economist Robert Lucas notes that when economic circumstances change, people's behavior tends to change, not necessarily in predictable ways (Lucas 1972, 1981). Although Lucas is referring to human expectations in relation to changing economic policy, his argument can be applied to assessing shifts in trends or fads dependent on the vagaries of human nature. A good example of this is evident in another form of consumer behavior in mid-seventeenth-century English society, namely, a more outward social behavior occurring in the public sphere.

Jürgen Habermas (1989:25) maintains that the transformation of English culture in the seventeenth century developed in public places where people came "together to form a public, [and] readied themselves to compel public authority to legitimate itself before public opinion." The public forum was embodied in institutions such as coffeehouses, taverns, and clubs, where conversation helped shape and instruct morals, attitudes, and manners (Habermas 1989).

Although public drinking houses were nothing new in England, their popularity as social outlets increased significantly over the course of the seventeenth century. For instance, in 1577, over seventeen thousand drinking establishments, most of them alehouses, in thirty counties were recorded, (Clark 1983:2, 14). By 1628, however, Londoners such as Richard Rawldige complained about the proliferation of alehouses, for "every street [is] replenished with them" (Clark 1983:39). By mid-century, there were over fifty thousand alehouses in England, or one for every one hundred inhabitants (Reay 1985).

Coffeehouses also became popular meeting places. At coffeehouses, customers could gossip, have intellectual discussions, read, or relax quietly. Like England, Port Royal probably had its share of coffeehouses. The Jamaica probate inventory of Charles Booker (Jamaica Public Archives 1688:V3/F112–113) includes entries for "nine Coffe dishes; 12 Cofee Plates; 12 pounds of Coffe Berreys; [and] coffe Potts," thus suggesting a commercial use for these items, such as a coffeehouse.

Perhaps of all drinking establishments none was more central to English life at home and abroad than the tavern. In his essay *Micro-cosmographie*, John

Earle (1980:33) preferred the tavern to the alehouse because it "is a degree, or . . . a pair of stayres above an Alehouse. . . . [I]t is the busie mans recreation, the idle mans businesse, the melancholy mans Sanctuary, the strangers welcome, the Innes a Courtmans entertainment, the Scholers kindness, and the Citizens courtesie."

Port Royal, like England, had its share of taverns, prompting one observer to note that "there is not now resident upon this place ten men to every house that selleth strong liquors" (Burns 1954:329). During his visit to Port Royal, Ned Ward (1933:16) noted how the people took "pleasure in drinking" to the point of shameless debauchery and offensive behavior that made Port Royal the "very Sodom of the Universe." In fact, for many of Port Royal's citizens, tavern life signified their daily routine. Port Royal as well could boast its fair share of assorted drinking establishments.

Although drinking was the main activity, the proliferation of public places was aided and abetted by tobacco as well as other "drug foods" such as coffee, sugar, and chocolate, which offered the opportunity to experience new sensations and stimuli within a socially acceptable context such as a coffeehouse or tavern (Mintz 1985, 1996). Idling hours away in a tavern with smoke and drink was a chief recreation for many, allowed for the exchange of ideas, and reinforced social identities. Entertainment could include, but was not limited to, card games, dancing, and singing (Clark 1983:68, 155; Spink 1992:9–13). Taverns also played host to political discussions and the maintenance of political alliances. For example, to protect their interests, wealthy Caribbean sugar planters living in England often formed lobbies. One such group, known as the Jamaica and Guinea Coffee House, met regularly in a London tavern to discuss political strategy to influence royal policy, at which they were quite successful (Williams 1970).

Generally, taverns at Port Royal, like their English counterparts, allowed for these types of activities, partly because of their general layout. Most taverns contained several rooms in addition to storage areas and sometimes a second story. Taverns typically included the standard wooden tables and chairs, candles, serving pots, tableware, sometimes pewter, a pair of shove-halfpenny game boards, and an area stocked with wine and spirits (Davis 1966). Common items in the storage area, or "cellar," would include liquor, clay pipes, candles, and other provisions. A substantial array of artifacts of this type was recovered from a possible tavern (Room 4) at Port Royal, including the remains

of over sixty wine bottles. Many of these bottles were found still corked and
containing liquid. Also discovered were a wooden table, a stool found crushed
under a brick wall, a Bellarmine jug, coarse red earthenware sherds, and the remains of two wooden barrels that possibly contained wine (Hamilton 1984).
The artifacts also complement the probate inventories of six Port Royal tavern
keepers as well as the archaeological record. Leshikar-Denton (1988) observed
that pewter dishes, cutlery, and tankards, as well as saucers, salt cellars, por-
ringers, and other items related to serving food, made up a significant part of
the inventories.

CONCLUSION

Valuables, goods, wealth, and money are essential components to understanding socioeconomic change, and their impact on such change can be gleaned
from the archaeological record in something as simple and ubiquitous as a
clay smoking pipe. As an artifact, the clay smoking pipe reflects the popularity of smoking and tobacco use. In the world system paradigm, tobacco as raw
product was traded by Chesapeake and Caribbean colonies for money and
goods exported from the core centers of London and Bristol. Tobacco smoking also signaled a preindustrial consumerism, a factor that has been overlooked by the world system model as having affected England's overall
economic recovery.

This early consumer behavior is supported in part by the archaeological evidence at Port Royal in the form of pewter, Chinese porcelain, clay pipes, and
hundreds of other objects, as well as in probate inventories and port records
for both England and Jamaica. Early consumer behavior was also stimulated
by changing prices and a growing urbanization that included the proliferation
of shops that exposed consumers to new goods and luxuries. Changes in
spending habits were also facilitated by preindustrial cottage industries such
as pipemaking, which supplemented family household incomes and allowed
for the purchase of new commodities.

The sizable number of clay pipes recovered at Port Royal affirms the popularity of smoking in the seventeenth century. In addition to smoking, other
changes in personal dietary habits are reflected in the demand for sugar, coffee, chocolate, and tea. These dietary changes point to another important social development, namely, the transition from private to more public forms of
socializing in such institutions as the tavern, which proliferated both at home

and in the colonies. In these places men, and possibly women, could drink and smoke freely on a daily basis.

As mass-produced objects in an early consumer culture, clay pipes were affordable throwaway objects that were shipped and sold by the thousands in the taverns and wine shops of Port Royal and other colonial settlements, possibly making them the first disposable commodity.

Finally, as archaeological objects, clay pipes embody the more ephemeral moments of life in the pleasurable, and sometimes forbidden, acts of smoking and drinking, but they also provide a window into seventeenth-century English society, both at Port Royal and in England. Peering through this window, we see a society emerging from former economic constraints, at a time when the opportunity to purchase new goods helped provide the impetus for social change and economic growth that would eventually propel England onto the world stage.

NOTES

1. For a good discussion of some of the major criticisms of world system theory, see Sanderson 1999.

2. Prices for colonial tobacco, however, cannot be firmly established because of local differences and the difficulties of converting colonial currencies into modern equivalents (McCusker and Menard 1991).

REFERENCES

Abernethy, David B. 2000. *The Dynamics of Global Dominance: European Overseas Empires, 1415–1980.* New Haven, Conn.: Yale University Press.

Arnold, C. J. 1977. The Tobacco Pipe Industry: An Economic Study. In *Pottery and Early Commerce.* D. P. S. Peacock, ed. Pp. 313–336. London: Academic Press.

Beer, George L. 1948. *The Commercial Policy of England.* New York: Peter Smith.

———. 1959 [1908]. *The Origins of the British Colonial System 1578–1660.* Gloucester, Mass.: Peter Smith.

Borsay, Peter. 1989. *The English Urban Renaissance: Culture and Society in the Provincial Town 1660–1770.* Oxford: Clarendon Press.

Braudel, Fernand. 1979. *The Structures of Everyday Life: The Limits of the Possible,* vol. 1. New York: Harper & Row.

Breen, T. H. 1985. *Tobacco Culture: The Mentality of the Great Tidewater Planters on the Eve of Revolution*. Princeton, N.J.: Princeton University Press.

Burns, Alan. 1954. *History of the British West Indies*. London: George Allen & Unwin.

Campbell, R. 1747. *The London Tradesman*. London: T. Gardner. Sterling Evans Library, Texas A&M University, College Station, Texas. Microfilm.

Clark, Peter. 1983. *The English Alehouse: A Social History 1200–1830*. London: Longman.

Clarkson, Leslie A. 1972. *The Pre-Industrial Economy in England, 1500-1750*. New York: Schocken Books.

Cotter, John L. 1994. *Archaeological Excavations at Jamestown, Virginia*. Archaeological Society of Virginia. Washington D.C.: Special Publication No. 32. U.S. Department of the Interior. National Park Service.

Coward, Barry. 1992. *The Stuart Age: A History of England, 1603–1714*. 2d ed. London: Longman.

Davis, Dorothy. 1966. *Fairs, Shops, and Supermarkets: A History of English Shopping*. Toronto: University of Toronto Press.

Davis, Ralph. 1954. English Foreign Trade, 1660–1700. *Economic History Review,* 2d ser. 7:150–166.

———. 1962. English Foreign Trade, 1700–1774. *Economic History Review,* 2d ser. 15:285–303.

Deetz, James. 1993. *Flowerdew Hundred: The Archaeology of a Virginia Plantation, 1619–1864*. Charlottesville: University Press of Virginia.

Dunn, Richard S. 1973. *Sugar and Slaves: The Rise of the Planter Class in the English West Indies, 1624–1713*. New York: W. W. Norton.

Earle, John. 1980 [1628]. *Micro-cosmographie*. West Orange, N.J.: Albert Saifer.

Farnie, Douglas A. 1962. The Commercial Empire of the Atlantic, 1607–1783. *Economic History Review*. 2d ser., 15:205–218.

Fox, Georgia L. 1999. *The Kaolin Clay Tobacco Pipe Collection from Port Royal, Jamaica*, vol.15: *The Archaeology of the Clay Tobacco Pipe*. Peter Davey, ed. BAR International Series 809. Oxford: British Archaeological Reports.

Frank, Andre Gunder. 1978. *World Accumulation, 1492–1789*. New York: Monthly Review Press.

Gentleman's Magazine. 1750. Dreadful Earthquake at Jamaica. *Gentleman's Magazine,* 20:212–215.

Habermas, Jürgen. 1989. *The Structural Transformation of the Public Sphere: An Inquiry into a Category of Bourgeois Society.* Cambridge, Mass.: MIT Press.

Hall, Jerome H. 1996. A Seventeenth-Century Northern European Merchant Shipwreck in Monte Cristi Bay, Dominican Republic. Ph.D. diss., Texas A&M University.

Hamilton, Donny L. 1984. Preliminary Report on the Archaeological Investigations of the Submerged Remains of Port Royal, Jamaica, 1981–1982. *International Journal of Nautical Archaeology and Underwater Exploration* 13:11–25.

———. 1991. A Decade of Excavations at Port Royal, Jamaica. In *Underwater Archaeology Proceedings from the Society for Historical Archaeology Conference.* John D. Broadwater, ed. Pp. 90–94. Richmond, Va.: Society for Historical Archaeology.

———. 1992. Simon Benning, Pewterer of Port Royal. In *Text-Aided Archaeology.* Barbara. J. Little, ed. Pp. 39–53. Boca Raton, Fla.: CRC Press.

Higgins, David A. 1999. Little Tubes of Mighty Power: A Review of British Clay Tobacco Pipe Studies. In *Old and New Worlds.* Geoff Egan and Ronn L. Michael, eds. Pp. 310–320. Oxford: Oxbow Books.

Holderness, B. A. 1976. *Pre-Industrial England: Economy and Society 1500–1750.* London: J. M. Dent & Sons.

Jamaica Public Archives. 1679–1686. *Probate Inventories,* vol. 2. Nautical Archaeology Program, Port Royal Project, Texas A&M University, College Station. Microfilm.

———. 1686–1694. *Probate Inventories,* vol. 3. Nautical Archaeology Program, Port Royal Project, Texas A&M University, College Station. Microfilm.

Johnson, Matthew. 1999. Historical, Archaeology, Capitalism. In *Historical Archaeologies of Capitalism.* Mark P. Leone and Parker B. Potter, eds. Pp. 219–232. New York: Kluwer Academic.

King, Anthony D. 1990. *Urbanism, Colonialism, and the World Economy.* London: Routledge.

Leshikar-Denton, Margaret E. 1988. Seventeenth-Century Taverns of Port Royal, Jamaica. Paper, Department of Anthropology, Texas A&M University.

Lucas, Robert E. 1972. Expectations and the Neutrality of Money. *Journal of Economic Theory* 4(2):103–124.

———. 1981. *Studies in Business-Cycle Theory.* Cambridge, Mass.: MIT Press.

MacInnes, Charles M. 1926. *The Early English Tobacco Trade.* London: Kegan Paul.

McCracken, Grant. 1990. *Culture and Consumption: New Approaches to the Symbolic Character of Consumer Goods and Activities.* Bloomington: Indiana University Press.

McCusker, John. J., and Russell R. Menard. 1991. *The Economy of British America, 1607–1789.* Institute of Early American History and Culture. Chapel Hill: University of North Carolina Press.

Minchinton, Walter E., ed. 1969. Introduction. In *The Growth of English Trade in the Seventeenth and Eighteenth Centuries,* Walter Minchinton, ed. Pp. 1–63. London: Methuen.

Mintz, Sidney W. 1985. *Sweetness and Power: The Place of Sugar in Modern History.* New York: Viking.

———. 1996. *Tasting Food, Tasting Freedom.* Boston: Beacon Press.

Nettles, Curtis P. 1933. The Place of Markets in the Old Colonial System. *New England Quarterly* 6:509–510.

Noël Hume, Ivor. 1982. *Martin's Hundred.* New York: Alfred A. Knopf.

O'Brien, Patrick. 1982. European Economic Development: The Contribution of the Periphery. *Economic History Review,* 2d ser. 35:1–18.

Office of the Exchequer. 1682. *London and Bristol Port Books, Series E/190.* Department of Anthropology, Texas A&M University, College Station, Texas. Microfilm.

———. 1694–1695. *London and Bristol Port Books, Series E/190.* Department of Anthropology, Texas A&M University, College Station, Texas. Microfilm.

Pagan, J. R. 1979. Growth of the Tobacco Trade Between London and Virginia, 1614–40. *Guildhall Studies in London History* 3:248–262.

Parry, John H. 1979. Introduction: The English in the New World. In *The Westward Enterprise: English Activities in Ireland, the Atlantic, and America 1480–1650.* Kenneth R. Andrews, Nicholas P. Canny, and Paul E. H. Hair, eds. Pp. 1–16. Detroit: Wayne State University Press.

Patten, John. 1978. *English Towns: 1500–1700.* Kent, England: William Dawson & Sons.

Pawson, Michael, and David Buisseret. 1975. *Port Royal, Jamaica.* Oxford: Oxford University Press.

Peacey, Allan A. 1996. *The Archaeology of the Clay Tobacco Pipe,* vol. 14: *The Development of the Clay Tobacco Pipe Kiln in the British Isles.* Peter Davey, ed. BAR International Series 246. Oxford: British Archaeological Reports.

Penn, W. A. 1901. *The Soverane Herbe: A History of Tobacco.* London: Grant Richards.

Price, Jacob M. 1978. Colonial Trade and British Economic Development, 1660–1775. *Lex et Scientia: The International Journal of Law and Science* 14:101–126.

Reay, Barry. 1985. Introduction: Popular Culture in Early Modern England. In *Popular Culture in Seventeenth-Century England.* Barry Reay, ed. Pp. 1–30. New York: St. Martin's.

Rich, Barnabe. 1937 [1615]. The Honestie of This Age. In *Tobacco: Its History Illustrated by the Books, Manuscripts, and Engravings in the Library of George Arents, Jr.,* vol. 1. Pp. 537–538. New York: Rosenbach.

Robert, Joseph C. 1967. *The Story of Tobacco in America.* Chapel Hill: University of North Carolina Press.

Sanderson, Stephen K. 1999. *Social Transformations: A General Theory of Historical Development.* New York: Rowman & Littlefield.

Shammas, Carole. 1990. *The Pre-industrial Consumer in England and America.* Oxford: Clarendon Press.

Spink, Ian. 1992. Music and Society. In *The Seventeenth Century.* Ian Spink, ed. Pp. 1–65. Oxford: Blackwell Publishers.

Taylor, John. 1688. *Multum in Parvo or Parvum in Multo, or The Historie of his Life and Travels in America.* Transcription on file, Department of Anthropology, Texas A&M University, College Station, Texas.

Thirsk, Joan. 1976. Seventeenth-Century Agriculture and Social Change. In *Seventeenth-Century England: Society in an Age of Revolution.* Paul S. Seaver, ed. Pp. 71–110. New York: New Viewpoints.

———. 1978. *Economic Policy and Projects: The Development of a Consumer Society in Early Modern England.* Oxford: Clarendon Press.

———. 1984. *The Rural Economy of England.* London: Hambledon Press.

Thompson, Richard H. 1989. *Theories of Ethnicity: A Critical Appraisal.* New York: Greenwood.

Tryon, Thomas. 1699. *England's Grandeur and Way to Get Wealth, or, Promotion of Trade Made Easy and Lands Advanced.* London: Harrow & G. Conyers.

Walker, Ian C. 1977. *Clay Tobacco Pipes with Particular Reference to the Bristol Industry.* 4 vols. Ottawa, Canada: History and Archaeology Series, Parks Canada.

Wallerstein, Immanuel. 1974. *The Modern World System.* New York: Academic Press.

———. 1980. *The Modern World System 2. Mercantilism and the Consolidation of the European World-Economy, 1600–1750.* New York: Academic Press.

Ward, Edward. 1933. *Five Travel Scripts Commonly Attributed to Edward Ward.* New York: Columbia University Press.

Weatherill, Lorna. 1988. *Consumer Behavior and Material Culture in Britain, 1660–1760.* London: Routledge.

Williams, Eric. 1970. *From Columbus to Castro: The History of the Caribbean 1492–1969.* New York: Harper & Row.

Williams, N. 1955. The London Port Books. *Transactions of the London and Middlesex Archaeological Society* 18:13–26.

Wilson, Charles. 1984. *England's Apprenticeship, 1603–1763.* 2d ed. London: Longman.

Wolf, Eric R. 1982. *Europe and the People without History.* Berkeley and Los Angeles: University of California Press.

Woodward, Donald. 1994. The Determination of Wage Rates in the Early Modern North of England. *Economic History Review* 47:22–43.

Zahedieh, Nuala. 1986. Trade, Plunder, and Economic Development in Early English Jamaica, 1655–1689. *Economic History Review* 39:205–222.

———. 1994. London and the Colonial Consumer in the Late Seventeenth Century. *Economic History Review* 47:239–261.

6

The Dominance of the Cowry Relative to the Franc in West Africa

Mahir Şaul

The disappearance of the precolonial currencies of West Africa and introduction of colonial currencies has been discussed in economic anthropology within the framework of a contrast. The older moneys are assumed to be "special purpose" whereas the coins and bills introduced by colonial governments in the early twentieth century are considered "general purpose." This chapter introduces a sharply inverted situation, which is more characteristic of what happened in many parts of the West African interior following its European occupation in the 1890s.

In two brief but influential papers Paul Bohannan (1955, 1959) tied the notion of special-purpose money to the idea that there were discrete "spheres of exchange" in African economic life. The precolonial moneys could purchase only certain goods, introducing incommensurability between different values and safeguarding the stability of the old system. The introduction of European moneys that could be exchanged against everything was a blow that dealt death to precolonial society. Economic historians (Latham 1971; Dorward 1976) severely criticized these views for their historical inaccuracy about the Tiv, but I am here more concerned with the assumptions underlying the analysis that have been uncritically projected to other African situations by anthropologists. The devastating "impact of [colonial] money" on economies with distinct spheres of exchange appears to come about outside the will of the local people. Colonial currencies were apparently totally new kinds of objects that are nonetheless presumed to have held an irresistible attraction for the local population.

This reasoning is questionable. Why should a people be attached to one type of money for a long period of time and then so uncontrollably drawn to another type? Can a money have inherent characteristics that are unconnected to the economic objectives of a people? Can the discussion of money be so isolated from power relations, those within the local society and those between the colonial government and the population? Recent historical studies indicate that, contrary to these assumptions, colonial populations often rejected the new colonial moneys and transformed the colonial economy in ways unanticipated by its overlords.

This chapter goes one step further by exploring the reasons for the colonial officials to impose new currencies in the West Volta region of West Africa, a desire that should not be taken for granted, and, more importantly, the reasons for some segments of the local population to reject these colonial currencies for approximately five decades, up to the 1940s. The case is extraordinary in its own right, and the following analysis aims to add to the recent discussions by Kopytoff (1986), Bloch and Parry (1989), and Guyer (1995), which need to be taken up in detail elsewhere. The boundary between those who were for and those who were against cowry shell currency in the West Volta region was not neatly drawn between expatriate and native, and I make the case that greater attention should be paid to political relations to understand the sources of the opposition to the new moneys.

THE PRECOLONIAL ECONOMY OF THE VOLTA REGION

The Sudanic region of West Africa possessed in the nineteenth century a vast network of trade and markets involving professional merchants and dependent in part on a monetary system based on cowries and gold. It spanned different ecological zones, from the equatorial forest in the south to the Sahel on the fringes of the Sahara in the north. We are particularly concerned in this chapter with the portion of this region situated between the Bani and the Volta (Muhun) Rivers. The lowest tier of the trade network consisted of itinerant operators, who carried their loads on their heads, or on donkeys, as they crisscrossed the paths leading from one merchant colony to another. Prices could change suddenly as a result of shortages due to climate or other factors affecting supply (Monteil 1895:60). The major commodities were kola nuts of the forest region, which were taken north, and desert salt bars and smoked fish from the Niger River, which were taken south.[1] The region of Bobo-Dioulasso also produced quality cotton cloth and iron, which was mostly destined for the south, either raw or as forged tools. Caravans also moved to the south cattle, sheep, and shea oil.

In important market towns the highest-value goods changed hands not in the marketplace but in the houses around it. At one end was the exchange of horses or imported firearms for slaves. This trade concerned only a very small number of military men and largely took the form of barter transactions initiated with letters of offer circulated to the few possible distant partners by couriers. In this "epistolary commerce," slaves often served as the unit of account as well as the medium of exchange, and quoted rates fluctuated widely with the intensity of armed confrontations. Although gold dust and European silver coins also circulated, they were scarce. Cattle, for example, could be directly exchanged for iron goods (Sundström 1974:70). Cowry shells were characteristic of lower values and dominated the marketplaces where women generally retailed food and men traders broke bulk to retail imported commodities. One could also express the value of more expensive goods in cowries, and slaves were frequently purchased with shells.

Imports from Europe made up a very small percentage of this trade. In 1888, Gustave Binger estimated that imports from Europe accounted for only about one-twelfth of the value of the trade between the towns of Kong and Bobo-Dioulasso (1892:375). A sporadic market existed in imported luxuries such as paper, Arabic manuscripts, fancy cloths, and other exotic goods, all of which were ultimately financed by the sale of captives.

When looked at as a regional phenomenon, what is distinctive about this economy is not the presence of impediments to convertibility resulting in something like spheres but the patchy character of trade life. The mesh of commerce engulfed the entire zone, but trading activity was not evenly distributed. The footpaths busy with the traffic of trader and donkey caravans bypassed communities that seemed isolated from trade. Even the important trade protagonists took part in this activity in peculiar ways. It was not only that land was not exchanged and wage labor was almost nonexistent, but the staple food grains also did not enter the market as wholesale commodities (except for the anomaly of a few cities such as Timbuktu on the fringes of the Sahara, where grain had to be supplied by camel transport). Even the major military leaders who had large numbers of dependents and soldiers and the Muslim clerics who had large crowds to feed ran basically self-provisioning households dependent on the labor of captives, who were settled in separate farm hamlets. Although the West Volta region was a production center for exported fine textiles and a transit point for the wool blankets brought from the Masina area to its north, most villagers in their daily lives either went naked or wore crude loin covers made of fresh leaves. Villagers did not consume the kola nuts that passed in transit to supply the Muslim cities in the Sahel.

The farmers did engage in some exchange, but much of it was conducted using no money. Bobo women, for example, exchanged the peanuts and earth peas they produced in their personal parcels for cooking pots (whereas the large jars used for brewing beer were purchased by matrilineal elders). In many villages the leading families had their own dependent specialist black-smith groups who were in a long-term relationship of solidarity and supplied metal and forged tools in return for food-grain contributions. Thus the provision of tools within the local area remained separate from the regional trade in iron. Village women obtained dried fish or other condiments in exchange for handfuls of grain or craft products, but those, too, were most often bartered rather than sold for money. Trading was a specialty of particular, often diasporic, communities that today are regarded as ethnicities (Zara, Jula). Women of these commercial groups went to villages and exchanged fish, shea oil, grains, firewood, and fermented locust beans, engaging in multiple loops of barter to bulk the commodities that eventually ended up in the longer-distance regional trade conducted with cowries. In situations of food shortage, a regional market in grain could emerge and prices could skyrocket (in December 1888 Binger observed in Senufo country the doubling of prices within two weeks [Binger 1892:215]), but heads of household in the 1880s were wary of selling much grain openly to avoid being victimized by military groups that roamed around and engaged in banditry. Bobo villagers did not collect tolls from the caravans that had safe passage from Watara warlords, although they harassed them with difficult-to-comply-with ritual interdictions to squeeze out fines from them.[2]

This picture of contrast gives only part of the story. The communities of farmers were not as thoroughly insulated from trade as the account so far would imply. An "inner interface" existed between the farm groups and the translocal trade conducted by market specialists. It was constituted by an oligarchy of elders, the senior men heading the groupings of households that are often indicated by names such as "house" or "entrance" in local languages, or—in the southern part of the Volta region where double descent is common—by the men and women elders of matrilineages. These people controlled access to currency and to the goods with which it could be acquired, imposing a kind of communalism within their sector that deprived the individual members of the ability to participate in the marketplace. For one thing, the elders made sure that marriage was tightly regulated within closed circuits of endogamy and delayed exchange and could not be interfered with by way of transfers of accumulated wealth objects, a setup that even the parallel efforts of the colonial nouveaux riches (salaried employees) and Roman Catholic missionaries could not modify until the end of the colonial period (Şaul 1989).

The elders organized the activities that led to sales that brought the cowries. In the southern Bobo country, matrilineally related women came together in large teams to collect shea nuts and produce oil for sale as well as for their own use. The proceeds were kept in a fund of the descent group. Village groups also participated in raids in alliance with regional military leaders, who in reciprocity gave them gifts from among the captives or herds captured as booty. The elders appropriated these and thus turned these resources into property of their matrilineal group. In the villages a market existed for sorghum beer, the principal way of converting grain surpluses into cash. The money was spent on ceremonies such as funerals, for divination, or for the purchase of medicine to cure a member. Senior men had the privilege of also spending some of the money on beer and special foods prepared in the market. But most of the cowry money was hoarded. Out of the accumulated funds payments were made for the purchase of firearms, livestock, and the special goods that filled the matrilineal treasure baskets.

Little of the early ethnography of the Volta region reveals full awareness of these links of elder men with the market. Firearms (muzzle-loaded muskets), for example, became totally integrated in village life during the nineteenth century, transformed hunting and agriculture, and were given a central place in ceremonies such as funeral commemorations. Although cloth was minimally used in daily life, leaders of house groups purchased fabric and dresses for display on ceremonial occasions (Tauxier 1912:43–44). In the southern Bobo country, matrilineal treasure baskets included important quantities of blankets, wraparound cloths, and men's costumes. A French missionary was filled with wonder to discover a deceased elder seated on the mortuary rostrum, "his back against the wall of his room, dressed in magnificent fineries, hat, multicolored blankets, etc., a fly-whisk made of cowries placed on his shoulder" (the diary of the Mission of Tounouma, entry for September 20, 1930, Rome, Archives of the White Fathers).

Matrilineages, or patrifilially formed house groups accumulated huge sums of cowries. How cowries became the focus of this hoarding obsession is an interesting historical puzzle that requires further study (see Iroko 1987:480–553 for a discussion). In any case, these hoards played a crucial role in colonial money matters, as we will see.

The use of cowries by junior members of village communities was under the strict control of their elders. Cowries were needed to pay for medicines and divination, and were used in burials and memorial funerals. Fines that the villages imposed on younger members were also paid in cowries. For all these purposes young men and women were dependent on their men and women elders, who controlled the funds. The income that heads of household could obtain by personal activities such as hunting or the production of honey was siphoned off into the common funds by obligatory contributions. Firearms and other objects of great value, and sometimes even farm tools, were purchased by matrilineal and patrilineal group elders, who granted them to others for temporary use. Thus, although the farm communities participated in the regional trade, supplying some of the primary materials that sustained it and creating an insatiable demand for cowries, their links to it were highly regulated to prevent individuals from taking part in exchange.

COWRIES IN THE WEST VOLTA

The cowry shells (mollusks of the species *Cypraea moneta* and *C. annulus*) were brought to West Africa from the Indian Ocean by European merchants. In the precolonial centuries they were one of the international commodities traded on the Amsterdam and London exchanges and destined primarily for the West African trade. Hogendorn and Johnson (1986) provide an exhaustive history of the large volume of shells brought to West Africa and of the cycles of inflation these imports caused, on the basis of European and African coastal records. In their movement to the interior the shells crossed several linguistic and cultural borders. In a vast zone cowry shells coexisted not only with gold dust and imported silver coins but also with salt bars, brass rods, and manillas (horseshoe-shaped heavy brass bracelets), locally produced iron and cloth currencies, beads, and other means of payment. There were areas and pockets that did not accept the cowry currency, but it prevailed in the merchant networks that animated the reticulum of trade roads and footpaths covering the region within the large bend of the Niger River. This region has always included several distinct sociopolitical zones, and the Volta basin in particular was the stage for a highly unstable pattern of strongmen and village alliances (Şaul 1998). When a monetary instrument is transacted across such a broad region that is outside the purview of any single political authority, the regularities that stand behind the value it communicates cannot be easily traced to a source.

The cowries were brought to Africa as commodities, and their flow via commerce followed in part the logic of commodity moneys. Hogendorn and Gemery (1988) remind us that every single cowry shell was unloaded in West Africa in exchange for some export good and thus was fully paid for before it entered the region's trade circuits. In that sense the cowries were a real-resource money (as opposed to fiat money, or to representative money like the bills that only stand for an asset such as gold). As inflation struck the cowries in the coastal region following the immoderate volumes introduced, it became less and less profitable to transport cowries inland. By the end of the nineteenth century it seems that the flow of new cowries to the Volta region was reduced to an insignificant trickle. Then, like the proverbial cigarettes that turned into currency in prisoners' camps, their exchange value became dissociated from their cost and dependent on the demand for them (under a ceiling constituted by the cost of introducing new shells). What is special about the case in the Volta region, however, is that this demand was mostly created by the desire to add to descent-group hoards and the number of ostentatious ceremonial objects. At the point at which the colonial administration established itself at the end of the nineteenth century, the volume of cowries that changed hands in sale transactions in the Volta region must have been like the tip of the iceberg compared to the huge volumes that were piled away in the dark rooms of the compounds belonging to the senior men and women of descent groups.

The administration, by forcing its own money upon the population, created multiple currencies. West Africans were not unfamiliar with this situation. But the request that people stop using the cowries as money was new, and it meant asking them to give up the real resource value contained in the shells. People like the money changers, who got very busy during tax payment time, benefitted from the double-money economy. Elders resisted for their own reasons. Market women preferred to maintain capital stock in both kinds of money, and other sectors of the population simply refused because they considered the coins and bills a nuisance. Not all people in the emergent colonial society, however, could dismiss French money as a token of the new authority that could be confined to relations with the administration, and the tension that resulted from that situation generated a different kind of interest for colonial rulers.

THE POLITICAL ECONOMY OF COLONIAL INSTALLATION

Even before the regime was consolidated in the interior parts of Western Sudan, the French colonial government banned the importation of cowry shells, as did the British government in its own territories (see Leduc 1965 for a history). But it did not oppose the shells' circulation as money, which would have been impossible, given that the regional economy ran with them and local people did not have colonial currency. A stock of colonial money, however, slowly started to be constituted in the newly defined provinces as the administration and colonial employees made expenditures and French firms opened stations to buy produce for export and to sell a few imported consumer goods.

The still continuing conquest had thrown the local economy in turmoil (to put it mildly). An important change was the emergence of a new set of actors and the disappearance or mutation of an old one. The new set was colonial employees. The number of nonproducers probably did not increase with colonial occupation, but their nature, compared to the period before, changed. Prior to the conquest the nonproducers were military leaders, the soldiers in their armies, merchants and traders, and Islamic clerics and some of their dependents, categories with some degree of overlap. These were the people who created the demand for the imported fancy goods and supplied the most important means to pay for them, including the horses–slaves–firearms circuit. This market vanished with some of its agents transferring to the colonial employees category with different characteristics. The result was the drying up of fancy imports—the chinaware of Europe, the sophisticated outfits of the Islamic civilization, the knotted carpets and manuscripts of the Middle East and other kinds of expensive curiosities—an event that the descendants of the people of this stratum still today think of as a loss of splendor in their land.

The new class with purchasing power, colonial employees, included the soldiers of the colonial army, guards, interpreters, clerks, eventually teachers, and colonial chiefs, including some of the precolonial military personnel who allied themselves with the French. The new luxury goods, mostly textiles and liquor, were supplied by the European firms' outposts. Another important difference was that many of these new elite people did not produce food but had to buy it, or if they still produced food, they were no longer self-sufficient in it. For example, the old military leaders who became canton chiefs maintained many armed men, as before, as well as crowded households, but the economy of captives had received a blow, and instead of their extensive farms of the past they had to find new forms of revenue. The salaried personnel were largely dependent on the market (soldiers and guards were married or encumbered with dependents of similar sorts). The new colonial towns became nuclei of a wholesale food market (Şaul 1986) and small-scale food industries such as the production of sorghum beer, mead, and butchered meat. In 1888 the explorer Binger had estimated that the two villages and three satellite settlements that eventually became Bobo-Dioulasso had a total population of 5,000. With a military camp, province headquarters, and a school, the population rose to 8,554 according to the 1915 census and 11,000 according to the 1925 census.

The major innovation of the colonial regime was the head tax. Although this was the name it carried from the very beginning, this tax was never collected from individuals. It was levied on the basis of largely imaginary census figures for entire communities, which in turn divided the burden among their constituent units by various means, and it was paid by heads of large households or of kinship groups for junior members under them. The administration was only interested in total revenue and the political symbolism of paying the tax; the entire issue of the distribution of the burden was left to local bodies. This led to cruel rivalry among village dignitaries and house heads to secure the favor of the new powers and thus reduce the share of their own constituencies.

The tax rate was 0.75F per adult man and woman at the turn of the century; it went up to 0.80F in 1909, to 1F and 1.25F in 1911, to 2F in 1915, and to 2.50F in 1920. Initially these taxes were not collected in the colonial money in which they were levied. In 1899 and 1900 the entire revenue was collected in kind. After 1902, as the war of conquest subsided, total revenue strongly increased, and in 1903 payments in colonial currency caught up in value with payments in kind. For the following three years in-kind payments remained at the level of about one-third of total revenue. For the French, "in kind" included cowries. A law of January 1907 prohibited local administrations from accepting taxes in cowries, which meant the end of "in-kind" bookkeeping entries, although there was at least one case the following year in which the Bobo-Dioulasso treasury had to accept cowries and then spend them (1908 second-quarter report).

The growth in tax revenue (6.5 times higher in 1920 than in 1904) was more than twice the increase in the tax rate, because the size of the collection depended on political (or more accurately, military) factors, such as the number of subdued villages, and not on the nominal rate or the population size. In addition to the head tax, the administration collected market taxes (also assessed and paid in cowries in the first decade of the century), fees to issue passes, judicial fines, and firearm taxes; individuals could also purchase the labor they owed to the government for public work projects by paying an additional tax.

Where were these cowries coming from? Most of them came out of the hoards managed by the senior men and women in the villages. The elders paid in shells the tax of the dependent members of their group, with no hope of ever getting them back. The administration kept a separate, local budget in cowry shells and spent this in-kind revenue mostly in the city, to buy provisions and other necessities such as wood or building materials, or to pay the daily workers who were hired to do odd jobs. Thus, through the portion of the tax collected in cowries and spent locally, the administration became responsible for bringing out a large volume of cowry shells from the hoards in the villages, and then threw this amount at the developing consumer market in the city.

The dynamics of the situation did not substantially change after the prohibition of 1907, although it is difficult to document it with as much precision. Starting in 1908, official bookkeeping recorded the revenue exclusively in colonial currency, but this does not mean that all taxpayers actually paid it in that money. Until the 1920s, tax collection was far from a peaceful exercise. A good proportion of the revenue was obtained by intimidation or force during the dry-season police rounds to the villages that could be subdued. The rounds took the form of unannounced raids on weaker communities. In these raids, herds, flocks, or any goods of value that could be carried away were seized and the loot was taken to regional markets. Thus converted into colonial money, the amount was entered in the books as tax payment. Among the goods that were seized were large amounts of cowrie shells. Thus the shells continued to be forced out of the village hoards and injected in the market.

By more peaceful means, taxes continued to motivate the flow of cowries to the market after 1907. Many elders facing an impossible tax assessment for their large group to pay in the month of January found no other solution than taking cowries from the treasure houses to money changers to convert them into the needed coins. It gives an idea of the size of the treasures that had been constituted in the villages in the previous two centuries that all these payments did not exhaust the cowry stocks until well into the 1940s. Oral interviews in the area of Bobo-Dioulasso indicate that in those years changing cowries was still a normal way to pay taxes. In the Samo area of the province of Dedougou to the north, Hubbell (1997) also discovered that villagers were often more able and more willing to take out cowries to pay taxes than to sell grain or animals.

One reason for this preference was that economies were achieved by converting the cowries rather than making a sale. The franc depreciated continuously, while the cowry preserved its value or appreciated. The reasons for the great loss of value of the franc are multiple; there was inflation in France in the interwar period, the franc lost value internationally against the British pound, and a large volume of colonial money was introduced in the provinces of the Volta region, as I will discuss below. The result was that despite the threefold increase in the per capita tax rate between 1900 and 1920, the cowry equivalent of the tax rate was actually lower at the end of the period than in the beginning (Boutillier 1993). The prices of the export products that were the alternatives to earn the money to pay taxes had not kept up with this increase.

These conversions from cowry to colonial francs brought to prominence a key figure of early colonial economic life: the money changer. Recollections and literary references reveal the very strong yearly up-and-down cycle in the exchange rate of cowries to francs and the ubiquitous presence of money changers, who made large profits (for a rare ethnographic description, see Labouret 1931), although it is hard to come by reliable time-series data on the exchange rates. The activities of money changers are referred to in the distant areas of the provinces of Gaoua, Bobo-Dioulasso, and Dedougou. Cowries lost value in January, tax payment time when the colonial coins were at a premium, and gained it back again after the tax payments were over, when the offer of cowries from villagers dried up.

The coincidence of two occurrences—the growth of the consumer market due to the emergence of a group of colonial employees, and the abundant supply of cowries to the same market by the policy of taxation—proved providential, if totally unplanned. Especially in the early phase of this period, colonial money was very scarce in the province of Bobo-Dioulasso and would not have allowed for the local commercial expansion that occurred. Credit transactions are common between customer and seller, but the difficulties in collecting debts from consumers (in contradistinction to transactions among traders themselves) make this a highly risky strategy that tends to snuff out any retailing operation that has to rely on it in a major way. Besides, the debts cannot be "cashed in" to make expenses before the original party pays them off, and therefore they remain a dead end in terms of money creation. The fledgling colonial consumer market would have stifled without the injection of substantial amounts of cowries from village treasures. The colonial administrators combated "the cowry economy" partly because they saw it as a rival to what the Europeans fantasized as a progressive colonial economy based on metal coins. Yet, not only were the cowries a heritage of the centuries-long connection to European commerce, but the very cowry transactions that the Europeans condemned and tried to eradicate were part of the real colonial economy that they were unwittingly easing into existence.

The efflorescence of trade in this colonial economy can be followed in the fiscal records. Most traders were women, generally belonging to the commercial communities previously mentioned. In 1907, forty-five women bought licenses to sell sorghum beer in the town of Bobo-Dioulasso. The market fees these women paid totaled 2,700F. This sum was larger than the fees paid by the registered African male merchants and the eight French companies established in the city combined. Although it is possible that the fee structure made these women pay taxes at a higher rate than the comparison group, there can be little doubt that they were a significant presence in the business life of the city and that large profits accrued to them. These women were, by the nature of their activity, conducting their affairs from a fixed point in the city. Other ambulatory women were bringing grain and other produce from the villages following the previous pattern of barter, petty trade, and bulking. At this point in time, the dendritic structure that brought the grain to the cities and came to be typically dominated by major (male) merchants had not yet emerged, and the only other source of food grain in the city was farmers from nearby villages who brought some surplus grain to sell. One can surmise that much of the sorghum for brewing was also brought to the city in the same manner, but these small movements of trade are hard to follow because they were not captured by the authorities and taxed. In 1919, a year of commercial crisis, the license fees paid by the brewers and women vendors of Bobo-Dioulasso had grown to 7,320 francs, more than three times the amount paid by the French companies in the city.

Colonial officials put most of the blame on women traders for refusing to accept colonial money and for perpetuating the cowry economy. What were the reasons for this "obstinate refusal"? At one level there were practical reasons for rejecting the colonial currency. The coins were unfamiliar to these trade specialists who had developed many mental and practical skills to calculate value with the older instruments and could not handle with the same confidence the new money. This is a common difficulty in periods of monetary transition. Even in the (relatively speaking, much less drastic) moves in Europe from old to new francs, or most recently from the national moneys to the Euro, people find it hard to adjust to the new arithmetic and for years carry out their old habits of value assessment which forces them to resort to complicated mental operations of conversion. The colonial coins also did not lend themselves to the conventions for counting and storage that had been developed for the shells. The centime piece, for example, was too light and was easy to drop or misplace. The paper bills had all these defects in a more exaggerated manner and traders showed strong aversion to accept them. These moneys were also not accepted by the villagers who would neither make them part of their hoards nor use them in ceremonies as substitutes. Thus, to use colonial money as part of their working capital, the traders had to maintain two separate accounts and use the services of money changers more frequently, with all the risks and costs that this involved.

Some authors have also pointed out that there was a direct political awareness in the stance of the African populations that opposed the replacement of cowries with colonial money. By that time cowries were exclusively associated with African civilization (as they are still today). Of Cameroon it has been written:

> The attachment to the cowry and the refusal to adopt the money of the White man was a way of defending the independence and sovereignty that they possessed before the [colonial] conquest. They had the feeling that the demonetization of the cowries was a way to cut them off from a significant symbol of their history and of their culture, in favor of the franc, an anonymous money. (F. Iroko, quoted by Boutillier 1993:254)

This political awareness intermeshed with another and more technically economic stance, articulated in the complaints of people who provisioned themselves in local markets. These complaints were an important motivation for the administrators to take certain measures against the prevalence of cowries in the market.

THE CONTEST OF POWER THROUGH MONEY

Colonial employees, especially the civilians who had to live primarily on their salaries, were the most vocal in complaining about the practices of market vendors. The supply of food was chronically unreliable and the price was always very high. When the franc lost value because large amounts of colonial currency had entered the province, or because of longer-term secular trends, the difficulties of the salary earners turned into crisis. The administration addressed the complaints but generally failed to find a longer-term remedy. Often the administrative action consisted of provisioning the employees by buying foodstuffs using political authority.

Food prices evolved differently in cowries and in colonial currency, as did the exchange rate of cowries to francs. In the long term, as the franc became more available during the opening decade of the twentieth century, it first appreciated against the cowry; thereafter it started to decline in value, at various speeds but without ever totally stopping. The major reason for the falling value of the franc was the return home of soldiers who had been demobilized from the colonial army, with their allotments. After World War I, to the abundance of money created by soldiers returning to the province were added complications from the fact that they had been paid in bills, which the general population loathed much more than the coins.

The introduction of a large number of bank notes with the payment of the allotments had the effect of limiting even further the number of commercial operations. The Bobo farmer keeps his grain and does not bring it to the market; thus he avoids being paid in paper money, for which he has great aversion, which time only will overcome. . . .

The abundance of money has resulted in a large increase in the cost of living. The native employees have tremendous difficulties in buying what they need for their families. The administrator will try in the coming months to supply the guards with the millet they need for their subsistence. (ANCI, Bobo-Dioulasso, 1919, first quarter report, commercial bulletin)

In the 1920s the situation was exacerbated by the steady loss of value of the French franc against the British pound. Cowries were easier to convert than francs to the British colonial currency used in the neighboring Gold Coast. This facilitated the import of European goods from across the border but also helped the pound-to-franc exchange rate directly affect the cowry equivalency of the franc. The cowry emerged as the steady currency that maintained its value not only in terms of the price of locally grown food but in terms of the price of imported goods sold in the stores. Demand for the shells grew for savings. Money holders responded by keeping the cowries and spending the francs, which made the downward movement of the French franc in the colony even more precipitous than its international devaluation. In 1920 the value of the 5F piece went down to 3,000 cowries (which incidentally is roughly equal to the value calculated by Binger in 1888). The face value of silver coins fell below their metal value, and they disappeared and were converted into jewelry. The banknotes, if they were accepted at all, went at 50 percent of their face value.[3] This was also the case in the Leo residency of the neighboring province (Duperray 1984:225).

Inhabitants of villages were largely insulated from the grain price movement expressed in coins because they purchased little food in general, and none with coins. The long-term movement of exchange rates worked in their favor if they converted cowries to pay the taxes (although they suffered from the cyclical loss of value of the cowry at tax payment time). Many households preferred to find the cash they needed for the taxes by selling rubber latex that the junior members collected from the wild Landolphia vines, the principal commodity exported to Europe in the first decade of the twentieth century.

It appears that market vendors also systematically charged higher prices (in terms of the nominal cowry-to-franc exchange rate) to the employees of the administration, who had to buy with colonial money. Such discrimination is easily achieved when two categories of buyers can be clearly distinguished, even without collusion on the part of the vendors or an oligopoly structure. In the Volta region the existence of the two monetary media used by different kinds of people facilitated the distinction. The employees of the administration found it hard to convert their revenue into cowries because the shells were not easy to come by at advantageous rates outside of the market.[4] Although cowries are no longer used as money, they are still needed as ritual objects in the western part of Burkina Faso, and different cowry exchange rates still occur today in the villages. In most villages around Bobo-Dioulasso and the Tagwa plateau, cowries change hands in a closed circuit against the Communauté financière africaine (CFA) franc, at a fraction of the price charged for them elsewhere. Musicians, blacksmiths, or other recipients of cowries keep the shells and sell them back, at a privileged rate of exchange that is valid only among covillagers, to villagers who want to use them again at another occasion. Because cowries cost much more elsewhere, a person who introduces new cowries to the village is given great honors. Somda (1993) describes in the Dagara villages of southern Burkina Faso two exchange rates for cowries, one four times higher than the other, valid in different contexts.[5]

The perception that food prices were lower in cowries than in colonial francs led to bitter recriminations by the salaried personnel of the administration. They incited the administrators against the market traders and the franc–cowry duality. Especially when the franc lost value because of an inflow of currency into the province, the charges that necessities cost less in cowries became very insistent, even though in those moments the personnel had effectively lost salary income because of inflation in the franc, and it was not necessary to invoke pricing discrimination against them to explain their hardship.

THE RESPONSES OF THE ADMINISTRATION

To explain the reasons for the administration to replace the cowries, many commentators invoked the "inconveniences" of using the cowries, which appeared quickly to the authorities during the first decade of their use. These inconveniences included the time spent counting them and the lack of precision that came with it, the difficulty of transporting them due to their weight, and the problem of stocking them (Boutillier 1993:250). Ofonagoro (1979:640), writing about southern Nigeria, criticizes Marion Johnson for putting too much emphasis on such practical difficulties and proposes that a deeper reason for the British government's opposition to the old currencies lay in the desire to open the indigenous economies and facilitate trade with Britain. Boutillier also mentions that the integration of the population in a colonial economy motivated the policies. He adds another consideration in the French case: the fear that with the demonetization of cowries in much of the rest of colonial Africa the shells would come in a rush to flood the areas that continued to use them, such as the French territories of the Volta (Boutillier 1993:251).

One should distinguish here a few strands of these economic arguments. Cowries were not used everywhere in French West Africa, and it is clear that continuing to use them in some places created problems of flexibility for the overall budget in colonial finances. However, this problem was not as insurmountable as it seems, because the budgets of the provinces in the Volta region were quite small and local expenditures more than absorbed the cowries that were collected in these places. One desire of the French administration was to put a stop to, or at least reduce, the inherited pattern of north–south trade with the Gold Coast and divert it in favor of the French colony of Ivory Coast. But for many years in the colony of Ivory Coast the coastal zone and the northern part were cut off from each other by the Baule opposition in the middle, and the north–south integration became a reasonable aim only after the suppression of the Baule resistance and the conquest of their territory around 1913. That the cowry currency was facilitating the maintenance of the undesirable trade with the northern Gold Coast was only a vague second-order thought in the mind of the administrators.

In the French territories of the interior, the interests of the civilian and military bureaucracy and those of the expatriate trades groups were not identical, and the idea that trade integration was an aim in the suppression of the cowries needs to be restated with this knowledge in mind. The administrators did express an abstract desire to see exports to France grow, but until the constitution of Upper Volta as a separate colony in 1919 they took few concrete steps in that direction. In the province headquarters, the representatives of French firms appeared as a small irritation to the commandants, rather than as allies. The local administration was against the issuing of concessions for the establishment of commercial plantations and was later unfavorable to the recruitment of labor for the plantations in the Ivory Coast. The merchant houses, on their side, objected to the in-kind tax collection because they found that the collection of wild rubber as tax deprived them of their market share for exports. The influence of the headquarters of these commercial houses in France over the Ministry of Colonies was important in the suppression of in-kind tax collection in 1907. Between the merchant-house representatives and the province administrators a cold cordiality was more characteristic than warm ties and frequent exchange of ideas.

One of the irritations for administrators in the Volta region was, as a matter of fact, the trade houses' complicity in continuing to do business with cowries, thus ignoring the official pronouncements against doing so.

> It is necessary that the [French] merchants choose to use this [colonial] money rather than the system of cowries, but unfortunately their goodwill runs up against the refusal of the natives who want any money, even the cowries, instead of the centimes. (ANCI, Bobo-Dioulasso, 1908, fourth quarter)

As European merchants had done in the centuries before, the factories of the French houses had found that in these provinces they could more easily purchase the export commodities that they sought and sell the goods that they offered by using the cowry shells rather than fighting them. The French administrators felt sabotaged and betrayed. What is clear is that the administrative moves in Bobo-Dioulasso against the cowry shells were in no way undertaken under pressure from French merchant houses (see Naanen 1993 for the parallel case in southern Nigeria).

What were some other reasons for administrative moves against the shells then? Reading the periodic reports of the province, one is left with the impression that a psychological factor was at least partly at play. The administrators felt that the cowry was the symbol of a primitive lifestyle that stood in the way of their desire to transform local society. In the locals' refusal to abandon the shells the administrators saw an affront to their vision of the world and their authority. The rejection of French coins by women vendors in the marketplace especially wounded their pride as Frenchmen and threatened their understanding of the meaning of the colonial conquest. Here was a concrete example of the rejection of the civilizing mission and the hollowness of the narrative of superior civilization altogether.

Another, more practical consideration was the colonial employees' constant complaints that they had a hard time provisioning themselves. These complaints forced the administrators to find solutions without delay and added considerably to the pressure of their quotidian work. The evanescent market was also so far out of their reach that it was not easy to solve the problems raised without having recourse to coercive measures, which were costly and politically risky.

The abolition of in-kind tax collection in 1907 had come from the government general, part of a colony-wide move inspired by a variety of considerations and decided in the context of a growing sense of control in the newly occupied territories, opening the way to tighter administration. It was not only aimed at abolishing the cowry but also forced the administrations in the Volta region to take measures to stop the monetary use of the cowries. To that end, the government proposed the use of coins of small enough value to become substitutes to the cowry shells. The centerpiece of the effort was a new copper coin worth 1 centime. It had been introduced in 1898 specifically for the colonies (it was rarely used in metropolitan France) and continued to be minted until 1920 (see Krause and Mishler 1995). The population found this, and the similar 2 centime piece, too light and completely rejected it. To discover ways to gain acceptance of these coins became a "constant preoccupation" of province administrations.

Indeed, during 1908 and 1909 it was the central task that the administration of Bobo-Dioulasso assigned itself. Trying to unburden itself of the stock of centime pieces that had been sent to the province, the administration used the pieces to pay porters and make purchases. Administrators went on tours to villages and lectured on the virtues of using these coins, to no effect. The centime pieces that had been put into circulation immediately returned to the treasury, because the locals made all the payments to the administration in these light coins until they rid themselves of them. In response, in 1908 the administration declared that it would not accept the centime coins back unless they were only a small proportion of the payment, which had to be made using other coins first. Thus the centime pieces were turned from being special purpose to having almost no purpose at all. Realizing that this was probably not a brilliant piece of economic policy, the administration reversed itself in

1909 and declared that it would take all the centime pieces without limit. This time it quickly ended up with a much larger number of centime pieces than it had issued; it was discovered that traders were collecting the detested coins in the neighboring province of Sikasso and bringing them for redemption to Bobo-Dioulasso. The commandant's effort to coordinate his policy with that of neighboring provinces failed, and the treasury was forced to stop its free-acceptance policy. The attempt to replace the cowries with the centime pieces ended in recognition of complete failure.

After this, in 1914 the government general introduced new coins worth 5 centimes (locally called *shu* from French "sou") and 10 centimes (called *pomporo* or *koporo*). They had a larger diameter and a hole in the middle so that they could be strung like some other currency objects used in other parts of the colonial empire (in the Volta region, when used as currency, the cowries were never strung but were always paid and counted in loose form). In response to an esthetic preference sensed among the locals for the British coins, these new French coins had been made to look like them, and near the border with the Gold Coast traders indiscriminately mixed the coins of the British and French authorities. These coins met with greater success than the centime among the population. But contrary to the expectations of the administrators, higher-value denominations were even more popular. The *tanka* (50 centime piece) and the *tama* (1F piece) were also accepted. Most appreciated of all was the *dorome* (5F piece), which had emerged in the early 1900s as the money of the wild rubber trade to become the best coin with which to pay the head tax, a "token of payment," the supreme coupon of the colonial regime. Behind these idiosyncratic quirks of valuation lay the rejection of the administration's program of shifting the economy from cowries to francs. The colonial money was confined to the short circuit of export sales, payment of the head tax, and soldiers' allotments, leaving a large field exclusively to the cowry.

The modifications brought to the face value of the money by the strong local preference for some of the coins and not for others created problems for European commerce as well as for the administration. Merchant houses found that they were hindered in their purchases if they did not possess the right combination of coins. The situation led the administrator to desperation:

> The 5 F piece is more and more appreciated. The 2 F piece, on the other hand, is not desired; the natives always show repugnance to accept it. With the 1 F

piece they feel that they are cheated. They prefer the English piece of 2 shillings much better, because it is larger and in their mind is a closer equivalent of the value of two 1 F pieces. The shilling and the double shilling is found in fairly large quantities in the hands of the natives. . . . Of course, this money is not accepted by our treasurers. The *sou* coins are accepted without difficulty, but each time the natives make a payment to us they have a tendency to immediately return them. (ANCI, Bobo-Dioulasso, 1908, Financial Report, fourth quarter)

"The ideal would be to suppress the cowries completely," continues the report. "How can we do it? I think we should proceed in a radical fashion, and for this we need the help of the [French] commerce." This help was not forthcoming, and for many years the coins continued to be strictly tied to taxes. In 1908, out of the 129,241F of fiscal revenue of the province treasury, 126,290 was paid in 5F coins (98 percent). The dorome (5F) remains to this day the basis of money accounting in Jula and all the other languages of the Volta region.

A drastic measure to undermine the cowry was undertaken in Bobo-Dioulasso in 1917. For that one year the administration accepted the cowries for tax payments, in order to destroy them and thus make the shells so scarce as to render their use as money impossible. There is no record of how many cowries were collected in that year. If we assume that tax revenue in 1917 was comparable to that of 1916, their value would have come close to 400,000F. Huge piles were made of the collected shells in the headquarters, and they were burned before perplexed onlookers, to make lime and use as whitewash. Subsequent events indicate that the measure failed to achieve its main objective. The value of the cowry against the franc rose very sharply following the inflation that struck European currencies after the end of World War I, and there can be little doubt that the destruction of a large volume of shells in 1917 helped this rise; it ultimately strengthened the position of the cowry by confirming the population's confidence in it, without making the shells too scarce.

In 1925 the colonial government published a new version of the Code d'Indigénat, the special penal code that applied to subjects of the colonies. It reduced the number of offenses punishable by administrative authority to half of what it was in the previous list. The refusal to accept French currency in the marketplace, however, remained an offense punishable without trial.[6]

The cowries continued to be used in market transactions in the Bobo province until the 1940s. After World War II and in an atmosphere of political ferment that eventually led to independence, cowries disappeared from the marketplaces of the province. The young generation was now quite proficient in the use of the coins and bills, and the conviction spread that colonial money was in for good. People who had large stocks of cowries turned them out, and in the flooded market the value of cowries went down for a brief period. The monetary adventure of the cowry had come to an end. I believe that this end was ultimately prepared by the growth of trade in the region and the growing proportion of goods imported from Europe, coupled with a tremendous increase in the volume of colonial currency, which together made the cowry shells finally a comparatively scarce and inconvenient commercial medium. So the shells finally succumbed, if not to the "authority" of the colonial regime then to the economic changes that it brought. But in the fifty years of survival, they had served their partisans well. They protected the local economy from inflation and the erratic impact on prices of fluctuating volumes of European-issued money, and they helped squeeze some value from the relatively affluent local group of salaried employees, perhaps even by facilitating double-pricing practices that discriminated against them.

The demonetization of the cowries did not proceed uniformly. While they stopped being transactional currency in Bobo-Dioulasso, in the neighboring province of Gaoua and in northern Ghana, the Dagari-Lobi populations continued to use the cowries for trade well into the 1970s. In the late 1950s two-thirds of all market transactions in the Gaoua province were made with cowries; 90 percent of the trade in food, as produce or in prepared form, was conducted using cowries (Boutillier 1993:251). The explanation for this longer preservation of the monetary function of the cowries among the Dagari-Lobi partly lies in the troubled final two decades of the nineteenth century. This area had then become the base of operation for Zaberma merchant-warrior leaders who, in the heightened generalized insecurity made worse by conflict between many powerful rivals and presaging the French colonial occupation, turned it into an entrepôt for their captives. A large volume of cowries was brought into this area by people who came to purchase or ransom these captives (Tauxier 1912:140–141). This beginning and the fact that the area was far from colonial centers and less affected by the growing colonial trade, as well as less subjected to taxation, together made the shells not lose their utility in the Gaoua province, as they had done in the Bobo province, for another thirty years.

The continued use of the shells as money in Gaoua, while they were being turned out from monetary use in Bobo, created the conditions for arbitrage. A strong commercial movement followed. Jula traders collected the cowries in the Bobo province at the low prices to which they had fallen and, with the newly available trucks, took them to the Gaoua province to buy produce, especially the export product shea oil, cattle, and gold produced locally by households. A report of the police station in Bobo-Dioulasso reveals that in the single month of September 1946 this commerce involved ten metric tons of cowry shells (Somda 1993:242). The inflow made the shells even more plentiful in the province and further extended their life as a medium of exchange. In more recent years the Gaoua province served as a reservoir of cowry shells for other places. People from all over the region started to come to Diebougou or to the other major markets, seeking cowries for purchase.

This was because the other uses of cowry shells did not come to an end when they stopped serving as currency. Their use as ritual objects and as payment on specific ceremonial occasions continued unmodified. They remained in great demand for these particular purposes. During the 1970s and 1980s a nominal exchange rate of 20 cowries to 5 CFA francs became set and was quoted unchanged despite the growing volume of CFA francs, inflation, and the diminution in the number of cowries due to attrition and losses during ritual use. This standard rate in fact undervalued the cowry shells; people preferred to keep them, and, outside the privileged transaction within communities of the type mentioned above, the cowry disappeared from exchange altogether. It became an extremely precious commodity. The value of cowries continued to rise in recent years, putting pressure on, and in the end causing the collapse of the standard quoted rate. It reached alarming levels for the village elders who are responsible for organizing the ceremonies. Some observers bemoan the lot of the West Africans who lost the "real resource" value of the cowries when the shells stopped functioning as money. But the price of the shells kept rising after demonetization, except for the brief reversal at the transition point. This trend accelerated in recent years. As Boutillier notes (1993:261), in the long run those who kept their cowries were the winners; they did better not only than the people who saved in francs (for example, in post office accounts) but also than those who saved in gold. Between 1900 and

1960 the French franc (of which the CFA franc until the 1996 devaluation remained just a version with a different face) lost its value 750 times while the cowry appreciated.

NOTES

1. Caillé 1968 provides the earliest window by a European on this trade.

2. The great historian Yves Person (1975) described the active pan-regional trade networks superimposed over a landscape of self-provisioning communities as a "capitalistic sector," an expression he adopted from Maxim Rodinson, who coined it for the medieval Islamic world, with the double purpose of contrasting it to capitalism as such and also drawing attention to the developed state of profit-oriented commerce.

3. Rapport d'Ensemble sur la Situation de la Colonie de la Haute Volta, December 31, 1920, ANCI 5 EE 1(1).

4. Similarly, Douglas describes among the Lele of the Congo three exchange rates for raffia, the highest being charged to outsiders who had to buy it with Belgian francs (1967:145). Ofonagoro (1979:628) observed that in northern Nigerian markets Europeans were charged higher prices than locals. A double price structure can also be maintained by other means. A linguist working in Gaoua (Showalter 2001:173) was told by a local interlocutor that the Kaan were charged systematically higher prices in the marketplace and for that reason he chose to interact with vendors in Jula to hide the fact that he was a Kaan.

5. Of course, it is not necessary to have two moneys to maintain two sets of prices for different people. In recent times, for example, Goldin (1985:195) reports K'iche' vegetable vendors selling at higher prices to American expatriates than to locals. It is also a common observation in various parts of the world that tourists are made to pay higher prices than locals.

6. The text of this code, which includes fifteen items, is given in Spittler (1981:200–201) in its French original.

REFERENCES

Archives Nationales de la Côte d'Ivoire (ANCI). 1898–1940. Monthly and quarterly reports of the province (*cercle*) of Bobo-Dioulasso, 1898–1940: 5 EE 1(1); and 5 EE 1(2). Archived material, Abidjan, Côte d'Ivoire.

Binger, Louis Gustave. 1892. *Du Niger au golfe de Guinée par le pays de Kong et le Mossi (1887–1889).* Paris: Hachette.

Bloch, Maurice, and Jonathan Parry. 1989. Introduction: Money and the Morality of Exchange. In *Money and the Morality of Exchange.* M. Bloch and J. Parry, eds. Pp. 1–32. Cambridge, U.K.: Cambridge University Press.

Bohannan, Paul. 1955. Some Principles of Exchange and Investment among the Tiv. *American Anthropologist* 57(1):60–70.

———. 1959. The Impact of Money on an African Subsistence Economy. *Journal of Economic History* 19:491–503.

Boutillier, Jean-Louis. 1993. Les cauris en tant que monnaie dans le sud-ouest de Burkina Faso au vingtième siècle. In *Images d'Afrique et Sciences sociales: Les pays lobi, birifor et dagara.* M. Fiéloux, J. Lombard, and J.-M. Kambou-Ferrand, eds. Pp. 249–261. Paris: ORSTOM (Institut Français de Recherche Scientifique pour le Développement en Coopération).

Caillé, René. 1968 [1830]. *Travels through Central Africa to Timbuctoo and across the Great Desert to Morocco,* vol. 1. London: Frank Cass & Co.

Dorward, D. C. 1976. Precolonial Tiv Trade and Cloth Currency. *International Journal of African Historical Studies* 9(4):576–591.

Douglas, Mary. 1967. Primitive Rationing: A Study in Controlled Exchange. In *Themes in Economic Anthropology.* R. Firth, ed. Pp. 119–141. London: Tavistock.

Duperray, Anne-Marie. 1984. *Les Gourounsi de Haute-Volta.* Wiesbaden: Franz Steiner Verlag.

Goldin, Liliana. 1985. Organizing the World through the Market: A Symbolic Analysis of Markets and Exchange in the Western Highlands of Guatemala (Mesoamerica). Ph.D. diss., SUNY Albany.

Guyer, Jane. 1995. Introduction: The Currency Interface and Its Dynamics. In *Money Matters: Instability, Values, and Social Payments in the Modern History of West African Communities.* J. Guyer, ed. Pp. 1–33. Portsmouth: Heinemann; London: James Currey.

Hogendorn, Jan S., and H. A. Gemery. 1988. Continuity in West African Monetary History? An Outline of Monetary Development. *African Economic History* 17:127–146.

Hogendorn, Jon, and Marion Johnson. 1986. *The Shell Money of the Slave Trade.* Cambridge, U.K.: Cambridge University Press.

Hubbell, Andrew Frederick. 1997. Patronage and Predation: A Social History of Colonial Chieftaincies in a Chiefless Region—Souroudgou (Burkina Faso) 1850–1946. Ph. D. diss., Stanford University.

Iroko, A. Félix. 1987. Les cauris en Afrique Occidentale du dixième au vingtième siècle. Doctorat d'Etat diss., 2 vols., Université de Paris 1, Panthéon—Sorbonne.

Kopytoff, Igor. 1986. The Cultural Life of Things: Commoditization as Process. In *The Social Life of Things.* A. Appadurai, ed. Pp. 64–91. Cambridge, U.K.: Cambridge University Press.

Krause, C. L., and C. Mishler; C. R. Bruce II, ed. 1995. *Standard Catalog of World Coins.* 23rd ed. Iola, Wisc.: Krause Publications.

Labouret, Henri. 1931. *Les tribus du rameaux lobi.* Paris: Institut d'Ethnologie.

Latham, A. J. H. 1971. Currency, Credit, and Capitalism on the Cross River in the Pre-Colonial Era. *Journal of African History* 12(4):599–605.

Leduc, Michel. 1965. *Les institutions monétaires africaines: Pays francophones.* Paris: A. Pedone.

Monteil, Parfait-Louis. 1895. *De Saint-Louis à Tripoli par le Lac Chad.* Paris: Alcan.

Naanen, Ben. 1993. Economy within an Economy: The Manilla Currency, Exchange Rate Instability, and Social Conditions in South-eastern Nigeria. *Journal of African History* 34:425–446.

Ofonagoro, Walter I. 1979. From Traditional to British Currency in Southern Nigeria: Analysis of a Currency Revolution, 1880–1948. *Journal of Economic History* 39(3):623–654.

Person, Yves. 1975. *Samori: Une révolution Jula,* vol. 1. Dakar: IFAN (Institut Fondamental d'Afrique Noire).

Şaul, Mahir. 1986. Development of the Grain Market and Merchants in Burkina Faso. *Journal of Modern African Studies* 24(1):127–153.

———. 1989. Corporate Authority, Exchange, and Personal Opposition in Bobo Marriages. *American Ethnologist* 16(1):57–74.

———. 1998. The War Houses of the Watara in West Africa. *International Journal of African Historical Studies* 31(3):537–570.

Showalter, Stuart. 2001. *The Same but Different.* Dallas, Tex.: SIL (Summer Institute of Linguistics) publication.

Somda, Nurukyor M. C. 1993. Les cauris du pays lobi. In *Images d'Afrique et sciences sociales: Les pays lobi, birifor et dagara.* M. Fiéloux, J. Lombard, and J.-M. Kambou-Ferrand, eds. Pp. 232–246. Paris: ORSTOM (Institut Français de Recherche Scientifique pour le Développement en Coopération).

Sundström, Lars. 1974. *The Exchange Economy of Pre-colonial Tropical Africa.* London: C. Hurst.

Spittler, Gerd. 1981. *Verwaltung in einem afrikanischer Bauernstaat: Das koloniale Französisch-Westafrika.* Freiburg: Atlantis Verlag.

Tauxier, Louis. 1912. *Le noir du Soudan.* Paris: Emile Larose.

7

Ties That Dissolve and Bind: Competing Currencies, Prestige, and Politics in Early Twentieth-Century China

Beth E. Notar

In October 2000, a senior Chinese official, Wen Tiejun, chief economist of the People's Bank of China research center, traveled to Ithaca, New York, to investigate a local currency system called "Ithaca HOURS."[1] Started by Paul Glover in 1991, Ithaca HOURS became a flourishing independent currency with over two thousand participants and served as a model for other independent currency systems across the United States.[2]

There existed a certain irony in having a chief economist of the national People's Bank of China come to investigate an alternative currency system in the United States. The roots of the People's Bank had been in Communist army print shops that had printed guerrilla currencies in the 1930s and 1940s in opposition to the currencies and policies of centralized state banks. Whereas money for the Chinese "revolutionary masses" had once been issued in opposition to state money, "People's Money" (*renminbi*) was now China's state money; and the United States was the site of an alternative currency movement.

The current local currencies issued in the United States and the previously issued Chinese Communist guerrilla currencies printed in the 1930s and 1940s have been fundamentally different. The local currencies are now being issued as *complementary currencies,* not intended to completely replace the national currency. They circulate in unbounded local areas in conjunction with the state-sponsored currency. The Communist guerrilla currencies, on the other hand, were *competing currencies* issued in the context of civil war. As I will show below, they were "territorial currencies" (see Helleiner 2003) that circulated in circumscribed, enforced areas.

While fundamentally different, the two types of currency share some similar features. Both have been independently produced and distributed in opposition to state currencies, and both have been intended to stimulate local economic development. Moreover, both have been used to create either a sense of community, in the case of local currencies (Witt 1998; see also Swann and Witt 1995), or, in the case of guerrilla currencies, a sense of identification with the revolutionary cause.

This latter goal—creating an alternative group identification through currency—seems surprising given that money has often been described as a force of social dissolution. This raises a series of questions: What role does money play in political and social group formation? How are social, political, and economic boundaries maintained or transgressed by money? How is money used as a form of control or resistance? In these processes, what does it matter that money is a symbolic object?

This chapter attempts a preliminary investigation of these questions by turning to China in the 1920s to 1940s when thousands of different currencies circulated simultaneously. As Gilbert and Helleiner have pointed out: "Studies of the historical relationship between nation-states and national currencies, and of alternatives to national currencies . . . can help us to interpret contemporary monetary transformations" (Gilbert and Helleiner 1999:2). This chapter suggests that in early twentieth-century China, different currencies marked different communities of users who were distinguished socioeconomically and politically. Contrary to Anthony Giddens's statement that money "as symbolic tokens . . . can be 'passed around' without regard to the specific characteristics of individuals or groups that handle [it] at any particular juncture" (Giddens 1990:22), money marked difficult and sometimes dangerous socioeconomic and political boundaries. Competing social, economic, and political groups issued and used different currencies, visually marking them as having a certain prestige or politics.

PERSPECTIVES ON MONEY

Following Hart (1986) and Von Glahn (1996:15–18), this chapter broadly defines money and currency as that which can serve at least one of the following four functions: as a means of exchange, a measure of value, a store of value, or a mode of payment to the state. Money has served an additional, fifth function, that of a form of communication between issuing groups and users (see Hewitt 1994, 1995, 1999; Gilbert 1999; Unwin and Hewitt 2001; Foster 2002; Helleiner 2003; Notar 1996, in press). Moreover, money may take different forms: commodity money, nominal money (or money of account), or fiduciary money ("fiat" or "token" money) (Von Glahn 1996:19–23). Different types of money may have different functions and meanings; and the same type of money may have different uses and meanings in different contexts and at different times (Von Glahn 1996:10; Bloch and Parry 1996). Here I focus on money in object form (as opposed to ledger form), for it is in object form that the dual aspect of money as both commodity and symbolic token (Hart 1986) can be most readily observed. As Parker Shipton has pointed out, "symbolics and economics need not, and should not be discrete topics" (Shipton 1997:169). I would add to this that symbolics, economics, and politics are not discrete, for, as will be illustrated below, money is a political as well as an economic and symbolic object.

Anthropologists have long drawn attention to the symbolic aspects of precapitalist currencies (see Parry and Bloch's classic volume 1996). Yet, as C. A. Gregory has urged, anthropologists need to take more seriously the symbolic meaning of contemporary currency (Gregory 1997:250). Moreover, while much attention has been paid to the linguistic and ritual symbolism of money (Parry and Bloch 1996; Barber 1995), anthropologists have often neglected its visual symbolism (one recent example that examines visual symbolism is Foster 2002), leaving this analysis so far to others (see Hewitt 1994, 1995, 1999; Wang 1995; Gilbert 1999; Unwin and Hewitt 2001; Helleiner 2003). Paying attention to the visual aspects of currency in China reveals new communication functions of money and ways that money was geared to certain currency communities.

Ever since Paul Bohannan's classic essay about the impact of colonial currency on Tiv spheres of exchange (Bohannan 1997), anthropologists have been interested in what Frederick Errington and Deborah Gewertz aptly term "dueling currencies" (Errington and Gewertz 1995:49). In exploring these dueling currencies, Melanesianists have been particularly effective at illustrating the ways in which, in the face of colonial and national currency consolidation, shell currencies have remained vital means of exchange, symbols of cultural identity, and markers of ritual spaces (e.g., Errington and Gewertz 1995; Akin 1999; Robbins and Akin 1999; Foster 2002; for a comprehensive discussion from the Nigerian context, see Ekejiuba 1995). However, anthropological attention has focused primarily on the colonial/colonized (what used to be called the "modern" and "primitive") and national/"native" currency oppositions. More attention needs to be paid to other dueling currencies at the transnational, national, and local levels. Some fruitful investigations have started to emerge in this area. Anthropologists have just begun to investigate local currency movements (see Maurer 2000; Hart 2001), "dollarization" (Meisch 2002), and reactions to the euro (Peebles 2002). Some work has been conducted in the sphere of competition between national and transnational currencies, for example, Virginia Dominguez's (1990) work on shekels and dollars in Israel, which reveals that a national currency is not necessarily a unified or general-purpose money. Alaina Lemon's exploration of dollars and rubles in Russia illustrates that "state-issued currencies mark movement not only across national borders, but into and out of social spaces" (Lemon 1998:39). This connection between currency and social space played an important role in China, as will be seen below.

Anthropologists still need to pay more attention to the meanings of money and "whole transactional systems" (Bloch and Parry 1996:23) in contexts of warfare (see Gamburd 2002 and Kwon 2002 for forays into this field). Below, I examine currency in China during the 1920s to 1940s, a time of great social, political, and economic tumult shaped by colonization, dynastic end, nation-building, war with Japan, and civil war. While particularly interesting research has recently emerged on the development of national currencies and their role in fostering "social consensus" and "social integration" (Gilbert 1999:42; see also Unwin and Hewitt 2001:1026; Helleiner 2003), this chapter focuses on the role of currencies in maintaining socioeconomically distinct groups and fomenting political resistance. I will first examine privately issued currencies and currency communities of socioeconomic distinction, and then turn to analyze state-issued national currencies versus Communist-issued guerrilla currencies as currency communities of political opposition.

COLONIAL CURRENCY COMPETITION

Altogether, thousands of currencies circulated in China in the late nineteenth and early twentieth centuries. This phenomenon of competing "modern moneys" was not unique to China. In the United States, up until the creation of the Federal Reserve System in 1913 and the circulation of national notes, numerous state and private banks issued their own currencies. The United

States first started to nationalize the currency in 1863, but only the Northern, not the Southern Confederate states, adhered to this policy (see Helleiner 2003:34–35; Slabaugh 2000). In seventeenth- to mid-nineteenth-century Tokugawa Japan, hundreds of different kinds of *hansatsu*, feudal clan notes, circulated simultaneously. They were not replaced by a national currency until the Meiji government did so in 1872 (Maruyama 1999). We often forget that the creation of "One Nation/One Money" systems (Cohen 1998) is largely a nineteenth- and early twentieth-century phenomenon (Helleiner 2003). As Richard Von Glahn has reminded us for the case of China, "What often has been labeled a degenerated and chaotic monetary system actually was the result of the profusion of market monies in the absence of a strong and effective monetary authority" (Von Glahn 1996:257).

The proliferation of private currencies in early twentieth-century China reflected the competing economic and political interests of the time. The last dynasty, the Qing, had collapsed in 1911 after decades of internal rebellion and colonial aggression. Since the Opium Wars with the British in the 1840s, European, American, and Japanese colonial powers had negotiated unequal trading treaties and increasingly carved out minicolonies known as "treaty ports." These treaty ports served as points of entry for expanding colonial economic interests. Foreign trading firms such as Jardine, Matheson and Company began by importing opium grown in British India in exchange for Chinese silver and then expanded into textile production, taking advantage of what they perceived to be the "'cheap, plentiful, submissive, capable labour'" versus the "'dictating and exacting labor'" of Britain (quoted in Honig 1986:16).

To facilitate financing of the opium and cotton trade, foreign banks soon followed the foreign traders. In the 1870s, the functions of these foreign banks expanded to making loans to the imperial Qing government to repay indemnities charged by the colonial powers after their military conquests, and in the 1890s, to financing foreign railway and industrial construction. Between 1848 and 1934, over one hundred foreign or joint Sino-foreign banks opened in China. Not all of these banks continued in operation, but while they were in operation, they each issued their own currency in different units of account: pounds, francs, dollars, guilders, and yen (see Tamagna 1942:24–34).

In the context of competing colonial banks and currencies, the imagery on money took on the communication function of advertising. Writing in 1926,

Frederic E. Lee, a former American economic consul based in China, stated that "the notes of American banks in China are *mainly* for advertising purposes, and at times, such as the time of the run on the Asia Bank at Tientsin, following the Banque Industrielle fiasco, they proved to be expensive and dangerous methods of advertising" (Lee 1982:103; emphasis added). Although it seems Lee was writing somewhat satirically, banknotes could serve as a kind of promotional coupon through which to advertise a bank to potential customers, namely, wealthy foreign and Chinese clients. The danger of printing banknotes without sufficient reserves, however, was that if trust in the bank diminished, a bank run might occur, and the bank would be required to redeem the notes for silver. A bank run might then force a bank into bankruptcy, which is what happened to the Banque Industrielle. However, not all foreign banks in China operated this precariously or faced this fate (see Tamagna 1942).

Overall, the imagery on these colonial currencies represented ideals of power and hegemony. For example, the 1909 notes of the International Banking Corporation (based in New York) showed an eagle perched above two globes, one showing the Americas, the other showing Eurasia and Africa. The image captured the idea of the United States's commercial hegemony (the eagle) encompassing the entire world. (See figure 7.1.)

COURTESY OF THE AMERICAN NUMISMATIC SOCIETY, NEW YORK. PHOTO BY BETH E. NOTAR.

FIGURE 7.1
A 1909 note of the International Banking Corporation illustrated symbolic U.S. hegemony.

A five-piastre note issued by the Banque de l'Indochine, whose notes circulated in southwest China along the Kunming–Hanoi railway line, illustrated a twist on Orientalism. On one side, a French woman wields the spear of power; on the other side, an Indochinese woman gently holds a flower of peace. She stands in front of temple ruins, the decay of a former civilization. (See figure 7.2.) As Virginia Hewitt has observed for colonial banknotes in other contexts, the bodies of white women often served as allegorical figures of colonial paternalism (Hewitt 1994, 1995).

Colonial banks were not the only ones to issue their own paper currencies. Provincial banks and thousands of "native banks" issued notes (for illustrations see Wu 1998; Wang 1995). Dr. Frank Tamagna, foreign economist at the Federal Reserve Bank of New York, in an "inquiry" conducted on banking in China under the auspices of the Institute of Pacific Relations, observed that: "Owing to their low face value, these [native bank] notes circulated mostly among the poorest classes of the population and their depreciation caused great distress among the people" (Tamagna 1942:69). In addition to the native banks, "cash shops," a step up from pawnshops, issued low-denomination "copper notes in all places and at all times the public was willing to take them, notwithstanding official prohibitions" (Tamagna 1942:84).

In a large treaty-port city, such as Shanghai or Canton, several hundred different currencies issued by colonial banks, government mints, native banks, and cash shops could circulate simultaneously. In a smaller town in the interior, a dozen currencies might cocirculate. Hoping to provide a guide for the American businessman interested in doing business in China in the 1920s, Frederic E. Lee documented a staggering array of currencies. He recorded that before the Nationalist revolution and fall of the Qing dynasty in 1911, the measure of value, measure of weight, and unit of account was the "tael" (*liang* in Mandarin). Yet, there existed multiple definitions of what constituted a tael (this is analogous to saying that there were different meanings of what constituted an "ounce"). The government alone recognized three: the customs tael (for foreign traders), the treasury tael (for transactions within and with the government), and the tribute tael (for major transactions of rice and silk). In addition to these three, Lee noted, "Every important commercial center in China has . . . its 6, 10, 12, or 20 local taels" (Lee 1982:15). Fees, taxes, and prices of expensive or bulk commodities would be quoted in taels; however,

FIGURE 7.2
Two sides of a five-piastre Banque de l'Indochine note showed a feminine twist on Orientalism.

payment could be made through a number of different currencies: gold coins; silver bullion (calculated not only by its weight but also by the fineness of silver); silver trade dollars (Spanish, Mexican, Peruvian, Bolivian, Chilean, American, French, British, Japanese); Indian rupees; different provincial silver dollars; currencies issued by warlords (in metal and paper); colonial, government, native bank and cash shop paper notes; and strings of copper cash called *tiao* (the number of copper cash per *tiao* also varied by region). Prices and payments for small transactions would be quoted in copper cash and paid in loose copper cash; loose token coins in copper and silver whose value was determined less by their face value than by their metallic content, metallic fineness, and weight (see Lee 1982:8–42); and copper cash notes. A price might be renegotiated depending on the means of payment. For example, Lee noted that if he paid chair bearers (who carried elites through city streets in sedan chairs) in copper cash notes, they requested 10 percent more than if he paid them in copper cash (Lee 1982:11). (In the mid- to late 1920s, a basic male laborer could earn 80–120 copper cash per day [Lee 1982:9]—a pittance, but more than a female factory worker, for example, in a match factory, who could earn 40–100 copper cash per day for twelve hours of work [Fang 1980:50]. In 1926, 1,800 copper cash was equivalent to one silver dollar, and 3,600 to one gold dollar. In theory, 1,000 copper cash was the equivalent of 1 tael of silver, but this varied widely from place to place, with a range of 160 in northwestern Lanzhou to 980 in southwestern Yunnan (Lee 1982:8–9)

The extent to which any one currency could be used for a transaction would depend on the reputation of a particular currency-issuing institution, the extent to which a currency was deemed authentic, the size of the transaction, the distance the currency had to travel before payment was made, the type of commodity purchased, the time of year of the payment, the place of payment, and the socioeconomic status of the parties involved. The higher the reputation of an issuing institution, the wider the geographic space in which a currency circulated. Some currencies, called "street notes" (*jie tiezi*), may have only circulated along a single street of merchants (Wang 1995:94–95). Similar currencies existed in seventeenth-century London and eighteenth-century Mexico City (Helleiner 2003:24).

The greater the authenticity of the currency in one's possession, the lower the payment one could negotiate. Silver bullion, some silver coins, and paper notes were "chopped" (i.e., stamped) by assayers and assessors who guaranteed their authenticity, sometimes falsely. Native banks employed *"shroffs,"* assistants whose job it was at the end of the day to test the silver coins received that day and separate them "into spurious, debased, chopped, and standard pieces" (Lee 1982:69).

In deciding which currency to use, the size of the transaction and place of payment had to be considered. Paper notes were the lightest to transport, but they might not be accepted outside a certain street, city, or region. Silver was the most highly valued merchant currency, but some provinces had export embargoes to try to stop silver drains. Strings of copper cash were the most accessible but the heaviest and most expensive to transport. Yet, to convert copper cash to silver would mean losing money on an unprofitable exchange rate (see Lee 1982). The time of year of payment was also a factor. Merchants would try to avoid transporting copper or silver before the sorghum harvest, when tall stalks next to the road could easily conceal bandits (Lee 1982:56).

Socioeconomic status acutely determined the type of currency to which an individual had access. The higher one's socioeconomic status, the greater the likelihood of coming into contact with silver or colonial banknotes. A higher-status person would use copper cash to pay laborers and workers, but a lower-status person would rarely, if ever, use silver. The lower a person's status, the greater the likelihood of using only small copper cash or cash shop copper notes. While both a high-status and a low-status person could use paper currency, the currencies would be of different types of issue. C. A. Gregory notes a similar phenomenon in colonial Australia, where "the native-born children of white settlers were called 'currency' lads and lasses" according to the promissory notes they used and were "seen as inferior to the British-born who were 'sterling' characters" according to their use of government-backed bills of exchange (Gregory 1997:259). Gilbert and Helleiner have identified a "tiered monetary order" of "two classes" (1999:3) as part of prenational–currency systems; however, such a tiered order has continued under some systems. For example, Lemon (1998:41) describes a "currency apartheid" that existed between dollar users and ruble users in 1990s Russia. Currently in the United States, lower-income individuals tend to pay with food stamps and cash, and higher-income individuals with checks and debit and credit cards (Weatherford 1997:230). Credit cards are further status-distinguished by the symbolic names "gold" and "platinum." Gregory's formulation that different currencies can operate as different "standards of value" that reflect "a struggle for prestige" (Gregory 1997:253) fits well to these types of tiered currency systems.

This situation of different currency use according to differing socioeconomic status is not the same as Bohannan's "spheres of exchange" in which the focus is on *what* can be exchanged for *what*. Instead, the focus here is on *who* has access to *which* means of exchange and payment. In other words, using a particular kind of currency identifies one as a particular kind of socioeconomic being. This is my first challenge to Giddens's claim that currencies circulate without regard to those who handle them at any particular juncture.

CREATING A NATIONAL CURRENCY

In the decades after the fall of the Qing dynasty in 1911, the new Nationalist government of the Republic of China attempted to establish a unified national currency system. Over the past few years, scholars have begun to examine the role of money in nation-building projects. Drawing inspiration from Benedict Anderson's (1991) identification of "print capitalism" (he suggested in the form of novels and newspapers) as key to creating a sense of a national "imagined community" among strangers, scholars have suggested that paper money has been an important—and analytically neglected—medium through which governments have attempted to foster identification with a national community (see Euraque 1996; Gilbert 1999; Gilbert and Helleiner 1999; Unwin and Hewitt 2001; Foster 2002; Helleiner 2003; Notar 1996, in press). As a "mundane instrument" (Foster 2002:53) of the state, money is perhaps the prototypical form of the everyday "banal nationalism" that Michael Billig (1995) identifies.

In his path-breaking discussion of money and national identity, Eric Helleiner asks: if money, as theorists such as Karl Marx and Georg Simmel have described, "undermines social context and tradition, how could it be linked to the sense of collectivity and common history that underlie national identities?" (Helleiner 2003:119). The seeds of an answer to Helleiner's question are anticipated in the writings of Marx, Simmel, and Giddens themselves. Marx asked of money, "Cannot it not dissolve and bind all ties?" (Marx 1978:104). Similarly, Simmel stated that "precisely because it destroys so many other kinds of relationships between people . . . money establishes relationships between elements that otherwise would have no connection whatsoever" (Simmel 1990:346). While Giddens views money as "disembedding" personal local ties, he suggests that it subsequently extends other relationships "across indefinite spans of time-space" (Giddens 1990:21). In other words, money can be used to create new kinds of extended group identification. As Joshua Roth has pointed out in a different context, "communities exist not only as imagined solidarities, but also as exchange relationships in different degrees of tension with each other" (Roth 2002:116).

Helleiner has identified three key measures that are necessary for a government to establish a national currency: (1) "produce high-quality, uniform, and difficult-to-counterfeit coins and notes in mass quantities," (2) eliminate "subnational monetary standards and coinages," and (3) create "large-scale, state-managed 'fiduciary' coinages" (Helleiner 2003:32–33). The Nationalist government undertook each of these three steps; however, as will be seen below, they were thwarted in their attempts to establish a national currency monopoly.

In March 1933, the Nationalist government promulgated a new coinage law. The former unit of account, the tael (*liang*), was to be abandoned in favor of the Chinese dollar, the *yuan*. Under the supervision of Robert Grant, former director of the U.S. Mint, three Chinese experts who had spent time training in the United States, and an American minting technician, the new Shanghai mint began producing high-quality silver dollars with the head of national founding father Sun Yat-sen (Sun Zhongshan) on one side and a fishing junk "shown against rays of the sun with three gulls flying overhead" on the other. The detail of the design was intended to prevent counterfeiting, but for some, the sun's rays evoked the Japanese imperial flag, and the gulls the Japanese planes that had bombed Shanghai in 1932. The design was changed (Young 1971:184–187).

In November 1935, the government attempted a national currency monopoly, decreeing that only the currency of three state banks—the Central Bank of China, the Bank of China, and the Bank of Communications—would count as legal tender, or *fabi* (two years later, the currency of the fourth bank, the Farmer's Bank of China was also recognized). Furthermore, the government decreed that all other currencies would be removed from circulation, including all silver in circulation, which would be nationalized (Tamagna 1942:142–143), and that the Shanghai mint would begin producing low-denomination fiduciary (token) nickel coins (Young 1971:253).

As Helleiner (2003) and others have also identified (see Euraque 1996; Gilbert 1999; Unwin and Hewitt 2001; Notar in press), the imagery on new

national currencies has prominently displayed certain national ideals. Four
main visual themes ran through the new Nationalist government money: authority, authenticity, modernity, and historical identity. The main image on
the Bank of China and Central Bank currencies between 1935 and 1948 was
the portrait of Sun Yat-sen. While images of rulers had long graced currency
of the Greco-Roman world, the image of a ruler—or, as on U.S. currency, deceased statesmen—was a new phenomenon to Chinese currency, dating only
to the late nineteenth century. Sun's portrait served as a new type of political
icon, a metonym for Nationalist government authority and ideals of nation-
hood. (See figure 7.3.)

Although images of rulers were new on Chinese currency, images of money
as icons were not. Paper money had first been invented in the Middle Kingdom in the eleventh century by merchants who sought alternatives to strings
of heavy iron coins. These merchants issued private money called *jiaozi* (ex-
changeables) on mulberry paper (Editorial Boards 1983:49). Some of the earliest surviving paper money from the thirteenth century references these
strings of cash at the top, illustrating that this piece of paper was indeed
money (see Von Glahn 1996:59). This associated authenticity of metallic
money had figured prominently in twentieth-century provincial and private
bank notes (see Pick 1996:188, 200) and continued to do so in the republican
state currencies. For example, on a note from the Central Bank of China (see

FIGURE 7.3
A 1936 note from the Central Bank of China used metallic money icons and Sun Yatsen's
portrait to establish authority.

figure 7.3), ancient Chinese coins provide a frame as well as a faint background. As paper money became increasingly worthless in "inflationary spirals" (Chang 1958) currency issues were dubbed "silver yuan" and "gold yuan" to further remind citizens that this paper was in fact money.

A third theme that coursed through the notes of the republican state banks was that of modernity. In particular the notes of the Bank of Communications highlighted modern technology. Trains pull into stations, steamships up to docks; electric cable cars move through city streets while electric towers traverse the land. (See figure 7.4.)

While the notes of the state banks illustrated modernity, they seemingly contradictorily invoked ancient Chinese civilization with images of ancient coins and bronze ritual vessels. (See figure 7.3.) However, illustrating "links between the past, present and future" (Gilbert 1999:42) has been a familiar theme, not only of new national currencies (Gilbert 1999; Unwin and Hewitt 2001:1023) but also of the overall symbolism of nation-building projects in general, which juxtapose "cultural traditions and modern economy" (Foster 2002:48). Like other "invented traditions" of the nation that would "use history as a legitimator of action and cement of group action" (Hobsbawm 1983:12), the images on Chinese national notes evoked a past to which all China's new citizens should claim heritage. Founding father Sun Yat-sen had

FIGURE 7.4
A Bank of Communications note produced by the American Bank Note Company, New York, portrayed modernity.

imagined China as a new national empire that would combine the great unity, nationalism, and modernity of the United States with the great power and glory of former empires in China (see Sun 1918).

While the Republican state sought a currency *distribution* monopoly, it did not seek a currency *production* monopoly. Much of the national paper currency was engraved and printed overseas by foreign banknote companies such as Thomas De La Rue of London and the American Bank Note Company of New York. For example, it was the famous American engraver Robert Savage (1868–1943), head of the picture engraving department at American Banknote Company, who engraved the portrait of Sun Yat-sen for the Central Bank of China (Hessler 1993:253–260). This international production of national currencies as a commodity deserves an in-depth investigation in itself.[3]

While the Nationalist government tried valiantly to establish a stable national currency monopoly, it was thwarted by world economic events, military invasion, and civil war. Global economic events and U.S. policy had prompted a severe silver drain from China that precipitated the government's nationalization of silver. Japanese military invasion threatened the coastal economy, and both the Japanese army and Communist revolutionaries issued competing currencies.

Faced with the Great Depression, deflation, and an election year in 1934, U.S. president Franklin D. Roosevelt had placated the "silver senators" who urged the U.S. Treasury to purchase silver from China at above-market prices. The senators, led by Sen. Key Pittman of Nevada, were from silver-producing states that would benefit from a rise in the price of silver, but they couched their proposal as one that would "restore the purchasing power of the Orient," since the value of silver was low relative to that of gold. Despite concern expressed by Chinese officials, bankers, and U.S. economic advisers in China, the United States adopted the Silver Purchase Act of 1934. The price of silver per fine ounce jumped from US$0.24 in July 1933 to over US$0.81 in 1935. This created a silver drain from China to the United States, leading to an economic crisis compounded by lack of banking regulation. With dwindling silver reserves, credit contracted. Moneylenders and banks called in loans, which led to bankruptcy, business failures, and factory closures, which in turn led to high unemployment and dispossession. Some banks, without sufficient silver reserves, failed (Young 1971:188–237). After the Nationalist government nationalized silver in November 1935, it then negotiated to sell silver to the

United States at a lower rate of US$0.45 in exchange for gold (Young 1971:239–257).

External threats to Chinese national self-determination came not only from U.S. manipulation of silver market prices but also from Japanese military invasion. After defeating the Qing dynasty in a battle over the Korean peninsula in 1894–1895, Japan had claimed the peninsula and the island of Taiwan as colonies. In 1931, Japan had conquered resource-rich Manchuria, north of Beijing, and by December 1937 had launched an all-out land and air attack against central and coastal China (Snow 1939 [1938]:17–20). Part of this attack included "currency warfare" (Chang 1958: 21): printing colonial currencies that resembled national currencies (see Pick 1996), prohibiting the use of national currencies, and punishing any Chinese caught with a non-Japanese-issued currency (Spence 1990:453).

The internal threat to the Nationalist republic's economic and political stability came primarily from the Chinese Communists. Originally, from 1925 to 1927, the Nationalists and the Communists had united to defeat the numerous warlords who filled the power vacuum after the collapse of the Qing dynasty. Yet, after jointly defeating the warlords, the Nationalists began a bloody purge of the Communists. Starting on April 12, 1927, thousands of suspected Communist sympathizers—intellectuals, students, workers, and peasants—were arrested and executed (Snow 1939 [1938]:47–48; Spence 1990:353–354). Survivors fled from Shanghai and other urban areas to the countryside where they established Communist "soviets" (*suweiai*) and base areas (*genzhudi*). From these base areas the Communists issued guerrilla currencies that, ironically, came to play an important role as "print capitalism" (Anderson 1991) in building the new Communist nation.

GUERRILLA CURRENCIES

The Communist survivors of the 1927 purge faced a double dilemma. First, how could they finance their guerrilla armies without alienating the peasant population? And second, how could they draw more recruits to their revolutionary cause? Paper money addressed both of these problems for it provided an inexpensive means of extracting resources (they were "paying" peasants for goods instead of looting them), while concurrently spreading the message of revolution. Money became both a political and economic weapon.

After fleeing to the countryside, future leader of China Mao Zedong addressed the economic catch-22 in which the Communists found themselves:

> The shortage of necessities and cash has become a very big problem for the army and the people inside the white [Nationalist] encirclement. . . . The Red Army has to fight the enemy and to provision itself at one and the same time. It even lacks funds to pay the daily food allowance of five cents per person. (quoted in Schran 1976:49).

The Communist Red Army solved this dilemma through two primary means. The first was to confiscate money, goods, and property from households that the army identified as "landlords" or "gentry" (Schran 1976:56). The second was to print its own currency.

When the Sixth Congress of the Chinese Communist Party met in Moscow in the summer of 1928, their Comintern-prepared resolution for revolutionary economic development included establishing banks and a "unified monetary system" (Schran 1976:50). The pragmatics of funding a revolution overcame any ideological concern with money itself. (Lenin, in an interview with Bertrand Russell, had once "laughed over the exchange the peasant is compelled to make, of food for paper" in the form of Soviet paper currency [in Vaillant and Richards 1985:222–223]). The Chinese Communists justified issuing guerrilla currency by describing it as a patriotic act, a form of "currency struggle" (*huobi douzheng*) that was essential to the overall political and economic struggle (see *Zhongguo geming genzhudi huobi*, hereafter abbreviated *ZGGH* 1982:185). For example, in 1941, when Mao Zedong met comrade Shang Boheng, master engraver of the Communist Shaanxi-Gansu-Ningxia Border Area Bank's Guanghua Printing workshop, at a play, he called out: "'Hero! Hero!' . . . 'Everything rests on you few [printing] comrades to grasp financial power in this border region.'" (Wei and Guo 1994:37).

There were three main stages of guerrilla currency production. The first stage, that of "Soviet base areas" (*suweiai* or *genzhudi*), was from 1928 to 1935 as the Communists struggled to survive continuous Nationalist attacks. The second stage, of "border areas" (*bianqu*), lasted from 1936 to 1945 when Nationalists and Communists were nominally united to fight Japan, but the Communist guerrillas issued their own "resistance currencies" (*kangbi*). The third stage, "liberated areas" (*jiefangqu*), was from 1946 to 1949, as the Communists and Nationalists once again engaged in all-out civil war (*ZGGH* 1982).

Here I focus on the first stage, when Communist survivors of the Nationalist purge attempted to establish Soviet base areas in rural, often mountainous regions. Upon reaching a potential base area, Communist cadres and soldiers confiscated the property, possessions, money, and grain of wealthy inhabitants. They distributed grain and land to peasants in the area and used the rest for their own supplies and reserves (Li 1991:25). A subsequent step was to print their own money, called "Soviet notes" (*Su piao*) or "Soviet currency" (*Su bi*) (*ZGGH* 1982).

Despite the fact that the Communists had relocated to the rural areas, they still had not relocated their ideology. The early guerrilla currency was dominated by a distinctly Russian Soviet and industrial emphasis: images of Marx, Lenin, and Stalin, hammers and sickles, workers and factories, all occupied the money. (See figures 7.5 and 7.6.) It is difficult to know how farmers reacted to the imposition of, and imagery on, these guerrilla currencies. Future oral history research might prove productive in this area.

In some base areas the Communists used simple woodblock prints as currency. In other areas the production of the currency was a highly developed process. For example, in the Chuan-Shaan base area of northern Sichuan and southern Shaanxi provinces, the Communists captured three currency-printing factories and mints of former warlords. They consolidated these in Tongjiang county and "welcomed" the two hundred former technicians and workers. To print cloth and paper currency (as well as newspapers, pamphlets, and documents) they set up eight lithographic presses that were run by thirty workers. To produce coins, over two hundred people worked in a mint, overseen by security guards who checked entry passes and examined workers before they left the premises. To avoid charges of theft, printing workers were paid in coin, and mint workers were paid in paper. Between December 1933 and October 1935, the Chuan-Shaan base area produced 2 million yuan worth of cloth and paper currency, 500,000 yuan worth of silver coins, and 300,000 yuan worth of copper coins (Li 1991:24–26, 33).

Party cadres and soldiers took the lead by first accepting and then distributing the guerrilla currency. Distribution stations were set up where people were encouraged to exchange their old currency for new. Finally, base area banks gave out low-interest or no-interest loans in the new currency (Li 1991:33).

FIGURE 7.5
Early Communist guerrilla currencies reflected Soviet ideals. Lenin stands below a hammer and sickle with the slogans "Workers of the World Unite!" and "Resolutely Defend Red Areas!"

全世界無產階級聯合起來
川陝省蘇維埃政府工農銀行
叁串
一九三三年

FIGURE 7.6
A power fist appears on a Sichuan-Shaanxi Soviet Government Worker and Peasants Bank three-guan cloth note from 1933.

Contemporary mainland sources tend to describe the process of currency conversion as a smooth one. However, future research might examine what kinds of problems the Communists faced in convincing people to accept the new base area currencies—did this differ by location, ethnicity, gender, occupation, or age? What problems did people in base areas face if they tried to travel or trade outside?

Because the base areas were surrounded and blockaded by Nationalist troops, like "red" islands within a "white" sea, currency necessarily took on a territorial character. Helleiner has argued that the "existence of a nation-state and 'industrial' money had to be present for territorial currencies to emerge" (Helleiner 2003:6). The Communists were in opposition to a nation-state and for the most part did not have access to industrial standard production, yet their currencies were territorial in that they circulated within delimited and enforced areas (see Sack 1986:21–22). The currencies themselves symbolically communicated the political distinctions between red- and white-held territories.

The Communists strictly controlled currency circulation within a base area by preventing the circulation of other currencies (*ZGGH* 1982:185). When journalist Edgar Snow entered the Yan'an base area in 1936, he attempted to pay Mr. Liu, chief of the Poor People's League, for his room and board. Liu responded: "'your money is no good. . . . Haven't you any Soviet money?' When I responded in the negative, he counted out a dollar's worth of Soviet paper notes. 'Here—you will need this on the road'" (Snow 1939:31).Liu spoke like a proper host to Edgar Snow, but he literally meant that Snow's outside money was "no good" in the base area. Not only Nationalist and foreign currency was prohibited from circulation, so too were the currencies of other base areas (*ZGGH* 1982). Because base areas were widely dispersed and currency production was localized, the cadres of one base area had little way of identifying the currency of other base areas so as to guard against counterfeiting.

On the one hand, Communist cadres regarded those caught counterfeiting guerrilla currency (*weizao Subi de ren*) as traitors and counterrevolutionaries. For instance, a merchant caught in Tongjiang county was paraded through the streets wearing a tall hat and with a wooden sign hung around his neck (Li 1991:35) (punishments that later became common during the 1966–1976 Cultural Revolution). Some counterfeiters were even executed (Yu 1983:41–43). On the other hand, the Communists actively produced "imitation" (*fangzhi de*) Nationalist coin currencies that they smuggled into white areas to purchase critically needed supplies (Li 1991:35; see Bower 1995 for other examples of the use of counterfeit currencies in wartime).

Snow observed that Chinese peasants in the heart of the base areas "bore no resentment towards my Red companions . . . freely offered for sale what edibles they had, and accepted Soviet money without hesitation" (Snow 1939:60). Yet, at "the borders [between red- and white-held areas], peasants often refused Soviet money" (Snow 1939:223). Indeed, as Communist base areas fell before Nationalist offensives, peasants were left holding red money that became worthless and dangerous overnight (Yu 1983:42). Dangerous, because the currency a person used marked the individual as a particular kind of political person. This is my second challenge to Giddens's claim that currencies are issued and circulate without regard for those who handle them. To handle a particular kind of currency can be a highly political act. As C. A. Gregory has pointed out, "money is never neutral" (Gregory 1997:248).

CONCLUSION

Giddens's claim that money "as symbolic tokens . . . can be 'passed around' without regard to the specific characteristics of individuals or groups that handle [it] at any particular juncture" (1990:22) may hold true within a currency community but not between currency communities. In contexts where complementary or competing currencies cocirculate, the characteristics of groups and individuals who handle money at any historical moment cannot be overlooked.

The case of China in the 1920s and early 1930s, when thousands of currencies circulated simultaneously, illustrates that different currencies circulated among different communities of users. A hierarchy of currencies, from silver and colonial banknotes to cash shop notes, reveals that the type of currency to which a person had access acutely reflected his or her socioeconomic status within the society.

In their nation-building efforts, the Nationalist government of the Republic of China attempted to erase competing currencies and currency distinctions and instead create a national, unified currency system. The new national currencies visually projected ideals of authority, authenticity, modernity, and historical identity to promote identification with the larger imagined community of the nation. Because of external and internal warfare, however, the

Nationalists were unsuccessful in maintaining a unified currency system, and competing currencies continued to circulate.

For the Chinese Communists, money became a means of political and economic struggle against the Nationalists. To finance the revolution (in addition to confiscating supplies from landlords, merchants, and wealthy households), they printed their own guerrilla currencies to "purchase" supplies instead of looting from poorer households. But these currencies did more than help finance revolutionary activity. The imagery on the guerrilla currencies served an additional function of communicating a revolutionary message to a largely illiterate rural population.

The currencies further offered a means of territorial control over their revolutionary base areas. To maintain territorial currency control, the Communists enforced use of a guerrilla currency within a base area. Using Nationalist or colonial currency in a base area was considered a treasonous act that risked punishment or even death. Different currencies clearly identified groups and individuals as particular kinds of political beings.

In China in the 1920s and 1930s, money functioned as a means of control and resistance, a marker of socioeconomic distinction, a means for fostering national identification, and an instrument of political differentiation. These understandings from China might be useful for investigating contemporary contexts of competing currencies and instability, for example, the use of money in national consolidation efforts in Afghanistan ("Money to Burn" 2002:37) and Iraq, or the use of rebel money in the civil war in Sudan ("A Dog's Dinar," 2002:68).

This chapter has drawn on published histories, reports, accounts, and interviews in Chinese and English. However, problems exist with relying on published sources, for they tend to provide mainly elite perspectives on events. Several unanswered questions remain; for example: How did groups and individuals negotiate the different currencies in circulation? Which currencies might someone use for what types of exchange or payment? Since different currencies politically marked people and places, how did travelers and traders negotiate currency zones? Who designed the symbolic imagery of the currencies, and how did they choose their designs? How did different groups of people view and understand these currencies in relation to their own social, political, and economic status? Answers to these questions might be discovered through future oral history interviews and archival research and could provide useful comparative material for understanding the current processes of currency competition and consolidation in the world.

NOTES

I received valuable questions after presentations of some of this material at the Society for Economic Anthropology's Twenty-second Annual Meeting on the topic "Valuables, Goods, Wealth, and Money" in Toronto, Canada, April 19–20, 2002; and at a Trinity College Center for Teaching and Research spring 2002 lunch lecture. My Trinity colleagues Frederick Errington, Dario Euraque, Jane Nadel-Klein, and Jim Trostle have offered insightful comments; Dean Stephen Peterson provided much-welcomed financial support for conference travel and publication; and Duran Bell, Michelle Bigenho, Julie Hemment, Robert Hunt, Joshua Roth, Cynthia Werner, and Barbara Yngvesson have provided much welcomed suggestions for revision. Gene Hessler, Mark Tomasko, and Terry Bodenhorn provided encouragement and suggestions on an earlier incarnation of this chapter. This chapter has further benefited enormously from the comments of four anonymous reviewers. Susan Witt of the E. F. Schumacher Society gave historical background on the local currency movement in the United States. Michael Bates of the American Numismatic Society guided my initial inquiry and allowed me access to the society's collection. Virginia Hewitt and Helen Wang suggested important readings and allowed me access to the British Museum Chinese currency collection. Thank you all. Any errors remain my own.

1. See Glover 2001.

2. Many local currencies or "scrips" were issued in the United States during the Great Depression, when banks closed and people lost trust in the federal dollar. The earliest of the postdepression currencies was Constants, created in Exeter, New Hampshire, in 1972 by economist Ralph Borsodi and Robert Swann, later president of the E. F. Schumacher Society, a society dedicated to promoting local economic development (Swann and Witt 1995). Constants lasted only one year, but Swann later helped to create "Deli Dollars" in western Massachusetts in 1989 to help finance Frank Torotriello's delicatessen (Witt 1998). Paul Glover started Ithaca HOURS after he heard a radio interview about Deli Dollars (Swann and Witt 1995) and spent a week at the E. F. Schumacher Society (Witt, telephone interview, August 23, 2002). William Maurer of the University of California, Irvine has begun an ethnography of Ithaca HOURS (see Maurer 2000). There are now nearly twenty local currency systems operating in the United States (see www.schumachersociety.org for a list). Similar systems such as LETS (Local Exchange Trading Systems) operate in Canada

and England, and SEL (Systèmes d'échange local) operate in France (Hart 2001:279–283).

3. Virginia Hewitt has commenced work in this area, looking at the British production of banknotes in the colonies. See Hewitt 1999. See also Bloom 1983.

REFERENCES

Akin, David. 1999. Cash and Shell Money in Kwaio, Solomon Islands. In *Money and Modernity: State and Local Currencies in Melanesia.* David Akin and Joel Robbins, eds. Pp. 103–130. Pittsburgh, Pa.: University of Pittsburgh Press.

Anderson, Benedict. 1991 [1983]. *Imagined Communities: Reflections on the Origin and Spread of Nationalism.* Rev. ed. London: Verso.

Barber, Karin. 1995. Money, Self-Realization, and the Person in Yoruba Texts. In *Money Matters: Instability, Values, and Social Payments in the Modern History of West African Communities.* Jane I. Guyer, ed. Pp. 205–224. Portsmouth, N.H.: Heinemann.

Billig, Michael. 1995. *Banal Nationalism.* London: Sage.

Bloch, Maurice, and Jonathan Parry. 1996 [1989]. Introduction: Money and the Morality of Exchange. In *Money and the Morality of Exchange.* Jonathan Parry and Maurice Bloch, eds. Pp. 1–32. Cambridge, U.K.: Cambridge University Press.

Bloom, Murray Teigh. 1983. *The Brotherhood of Money: The Secret World of Bank Note Printers.* Port Clinton, Ohio: BNR Press.

Bohannan, Paul. 1997 [1955]. Some Principles of Exchange and Investment among the Tiv. In *Perspectives on Africa.* Roy Richard Grinker and Christopher B. Steiner, eds. Pp. 119–198. Oxford: Blackwell.

Bower, Peter. 1995. Economic Warfare: Banknote Forgery as a Deliberate Weapon. In *The Banker's Art: Studies in Paper Money.* Virginia Hewitt, ed. Pp. 46–50. London: British Museum Press.

Chang, Kia-ngau. 1958. *The Inflationary Spiral: The Experience in China, 1939–1950.* Cambridge, Mass.: MIT Press.

Cohen, Benjamin J. 1998. *The Geography of Money.* Ithaca, N.Y.: Cornell University Press.

A Dog's Dinar: A Currency Split in a Split Country. 2002. *Economist.* December 14:68.

Dominguez, Virginia. 1990. Representing Value and the Value of Representation: A Different Look at Money. *Cultural Anthropology* 5(1):16–44.

Editorial Boards. 1983. *A History of Chinese Currency, Sixteenth Century BC–Twentieth Century AD.* Hong Kong: Xinhua (New China) Publishing House.

Ekejiuba, Felicia. 1995. Currency Instability and Social Payments among the Igbo of Eastern Nigeria, 1890–1990. In *Money Matters: Instability, Values, and Social Payments in the Modern History of West African Communities.* Jane I. Guyer, ed. Pp. 133–161. Portsmouth, N.H.: Heinemann.

Errington, Frederick K., and Deborah B. Gewertz. 1995. *Articulating Change in the "Last Unknown."* Boulder, Colo.: Westview.

Euraque, Dario. 1996. La creación de la moneda nacional y el encalve bananero en la costa caribe caribeña de Honduras: ¿En busca de una identidad étnico-racial? *Yaxkin, Revista del Instituto Hondureño de Antropología e Historia* 14(1–2):138–150.

Fang Fu-An. 1980 [1931]. *Chinese Labour.* New York: Garland.

Feuerwerker, Albert. 1995. *The Chinese Economy, 1870–1949.* Ann Arbor: Center for Chinese Studies, University of Michigan.

Foster, Robert J. 2002. *Materializing the Nation: Commodities, Consumption, and Media in Papua New Guinea.* Bloomington: Indiana University Press.

Gamburd, Michele. 2002. The Economics of Enlisting: Currency, Corruption, and Sri Lanka's Ethnic Conflict. Paper presented at the Annual Meeting of the American Anthropological Association, New Orleans, November 21.

Giddens, Anthony. 1990. *The Consequences of Modernity.* Stanford, Calif.: Stanford University Press.

Gilbert, Emily. 1999. Forging a National Currency: Money, State-making and Nation-building in Canada. In *Nation-States and Money: The Past, Present and Future of National Currencies.* Emily Gilbert and Eric Helleiner, eds. Pp. 25–46. London: Routledge.

Gilbert, Emily, and Eric Helleiner. 1999. Introduction—Nation-States and Money: Historical Contexts, Interdisciplinary Perspectives. In *Nation-States and Money: The Past, Present, and Future of National Currencies.* Emily Gilbert and Eric Helleiner, eds. Pp. 1–21. London: Routledge.

Glover, Paul. 2001. Chinese Government Studies Ithaca Hours. January. Electronic document, www.lightlink.com/hours/ithacahours/archive/0101.html; accessed July 16, 2003.

Gregory, C. A. 1997. *Savage Money: The Anthropology and Politics of Commodity Exchange*. Amsterdam: Harwood Academic.

Hart, Keith. 1986. Heads or Tails? Two Sides of the Coin. *Man* 21(4):637–656.

———. 2001. *Money in an Unequal World: Keith Hart and His Memory Bank*. New York: Texere.

Helleiner, Eric. 2003. *The Making of National Money: Territorial Currencies in Historical Perspective*. Ithaca, N.Y.: Cornell University Press.

Hessler, Gene. 1993. *The Engraver's Line: An Encyclopedia of Paper Money and Postage Stamp Art*. Port Clinton, Ohio: BNR Press.

Hewitt, Virginia. 1994. *Beauty and the Banknote*. London: British Museum Press.

———. 1995. Introduction. In *The Banker's Art: Studies in Paper Money*. Virginia Hewitt, ed. Pp. 9–11. London: British Museum Press.

———. 1999. A Distant View: Imagery and Imagination in the Paper Currency of the British Empire, 1800–1960. In *Nation-States and Money: The Past, Present, and Future of National Currencies*. Emily Gilbert and Eric Helleiner, eds. Pp. 97–116. London: Routledge.

Hobsbawm, Eric. 1983. Introduction: Inventing Traditions. In *The Invention of Tradition*. Eric Hobsbawm and Terence Ranger, eds. Pp. 1–14. Cambridge, U.K.: Cambridge University Press.

Honig, Emily. 1986. *Sisters and Strangers: Women in the Shanghai Cotton Mills, 1919–1949*. Stanford, Calif.: Stanford University Press.

Kwon, Heonik. 2002. The Dollarization of Vietnamese Ghost Money. Paper presented at the Annual Meeting of the American Anthropological Association, New Orleans, November 21.

Lee, Frederic E. 1982 [1926]. *Currency, Banking, and Finance in China*. New York: Garland.

Lemon, Alaina. 1998. "Your Eyes Are Green like Dollars": Counterfeit Cash, National Substance, and Currency Apartheid in 1990s Russia. *Cultural Anthropology* 13(1):22–55.

Li Qinglan. 1991. Chuan-Shaan genzhudi huobi lunlue. (A brief discussion of the currency of the Sichuan-Shaanxi Base Area). *Zhongguo qianbi* (China numismatics) 32(1):24–35.

Maruyama, Makoto. 1999. Local Currencies in Pre-Industrial Japan. In *Nation-States and Money: The Past, Present, and Future of National Currencies.* Emily Gilbert and Eric Helleiner, eds. Pp. 68–81. London: Routledge.

Marx, Karl. 1978. Economic and Philosophic Manuscripts of 1844. In *The Marx-Engels Reader.* 2d ed. Robert C. Tucker, ed. Pp. 66–125. New York: W. W. Norton.

Maurer, William. 2000. Alternative Globalizations: Community and Conflict in New Cultures of Finance, National Science Foundation Grant Proposal. *Political and Legal Anthropology Review* 23(1):155–172.

McElderry, Andrea Lee. 1976. *Shanghai Old-Style Banks (Ch'ien-Chuang) 1800–1935.* Ann Arbor: Center for Chinese Studies, University of Michigan.

Meisch, Lynn A. 2002. Sellout or Salvation? Responses to Dollarization in Ecuador. Paper presented at the Annual Meeting of the American Anthropological Association, New Orleans, November 21.

Money to Burn: The Country Gets a New Currency. 2002. *Economist.* December 14:37.

Notar, Beth E. 1996. From Class Cash to Multicultural Money: Socialist Imperialism and Nationality Fetishism in the PRC. Paper presented at the Annual Meeting of the American Anthropological Association, San Francisco, November 21.

———. In press. Viewing Currency "Chaos." In *Defining Modernity.* Terry Bodenhorn, ed. Pp. 123–149. Ann Arbor: Center for Chinese Studies, University of Michigan.

Parry, Jonathan, and Maurice Bloch. 1996 [1989]. *Money and the Morality of Exchange.* Cambridge, U.K.: Cambridge University Press.

Peebles, Gustav. 2002. Black, White, and Grey Markets: Currencies and Moral Schemas at the Swedish-Danish Border. Paper presented at the Annual Meeting of the American Anthropological Association, New Orleans, November 21.

Pick, Albert. 1996. *Standard Catalog of World Paper Money, General Issues to 1960.* Vol. 2, 8th ed. Colin R. Bruce II and Neil Shafer, eds. Iola, Wisc.: Krause Publications.

Rawski, Thomas G. 1989. *Economic Growth in Prewar China.* Berkeley and Los Angeles: University of California Press.

Robbins, Joel, and David Akin. 1999. An Introduction of Melanesian Currencies: Agency, Identity, and Social Reproduction. In *Money and Modernity: State and Local Currencies in Melanesia.* David Akin and Joel Robbins, eds. Pp. 1–40. Pittsburgh, Pa.: University of Pittsburgh Press.

Roth, Joshua Hotaka. 2002. *Brokered Homeland: Japanese Brazilian Migrants in Japan.* Ithaca, N.Y.: Cornell University Press.

Sack, Robert David. 1986. *Human Territoriality: Its Theory and History.* Cambridge, U.K.: Cambridge University Press.

Schran, Peter. 1976. *Guerrilla Economy: The Development of the Shensi-Kansu-Ninghsia Border Region, 1937–1945.* Albany: State University of New York Press.

Sheehan, Brett George. 1997. *The Currency of Legitimation: Banks, Bank Money, and State–Society Relations in Tianjin, China, 1916–1938.* Ph.D. diss., University of California, Berkeley.

Shipton, Parker. 1997. Bitter Money: Forbidden Exchange in East Africa. In *Perspectives on Africa.* Roy Richard Grinker and Christopher B. Steiner, eds. Pp. 163–189. Oxford: Blackwell.

Simmel, Georg. 1990 [1900]. *The Philosophy of Money.* David Risby, ed. London: Routledge.

Slabaugh, Arlie R. 2000. *Confederate States Paper Money.* 10th ed. Iola, Wisc.: Krause Publications.

Snow, Edgar. 1939 [1938]. *Red Star over China.* New York: Garden City.

Spence, Jonathan. 1990. *The Search for Modern China.* New York: W. W. Norton.

Swann, Robert, and Susan Witt. 1995. Local Currencies: Catalysts for Sustainable Regional Economies. Electronic document, http://www.schumachersociety.org, accessed April 5, 2003.

Sun Yat-sen. 1918. *Memoirs of a Chinese Revolutionary: A Programme of National Reconstruction for China.* London: Hurchinson.

Tamagna, Frank M. 1942. *Banking and Finance in China.* New York: Institute of Pacific Relations.

Unwin, T., and V. Hewitt. 2001. Banknotes and National Identity in Central and Eastern Europe. *Political Geography* 20(8):1005–1028.

Vaillant, Janet B., and John Richards II, eds. 1985. *From Russia to USSR: A Narrative and Documentary History.* New York: Longman.

Von Glahn, Richard. 1996. *Fountain of Fortune: Money and Monetary Policy in China, 1000–1700.* Berkeley and Los Angeles: University of California Press.

Wang, Helen. 1995. Late Qing Paper Money from Dianshizhai and other Printing Houses in Shanghai, 1905–1912. In *The Banker's Art: Studies in Paper Money.* Virginia Hewitt, ed. Pp. 94–117. London: British Museum Press.

Weatherford, Jack. 1997. *The History of Money: From Sandstone to Cyberspace.* New York: Crown.

Wei Xiewu and Guo Cuiyun. 1994. Yinchao gongren huainian Mao zhuxi (Currency printing workers remember Chairman Mao). *Zhongguo qianbi* (China numismatics) 44(1):37.

Witt, Susan. 1998. Printing Money, Making Change: The Future of Local Currencies. *Orion Afield* 2(4):18–22.

Wu Chouzhong. 1998. Zhongguo zhibi yanjiu. (Research on Chinese paper money). Shanghai: Shanghai guji chubanshe.

Young, Arthur N. 1971. *China's Nation-Building Effort, 1927–1937: The Financial and Economic Record.* Stanford, Calif.: Stanford University, Hoover Institution Press.

Yu Tao. 1983. Tudi geming shiqi genjudi de huobi liutong. (The circulation of currency in the guerrilla bases during the agrarian revolution period). *Zhongguo qianbi* (China numismatics) 1 (January–February):41–43.

Zhongguo renmin yinhang jinrong yanjiusuo (People's Bank of China Finance Research Center) and Caizhengbu caizheng kexue yanjiusuo (Ministry of Public Finance, Public Finance Science Research Center) (ZGGH). 1982. *Zhongguo geming genzhudi huobi.* (Currency of China's revolutionary base areas). Beijing: Wenwu chubanshe.

8

Crafts, Gifts, and Capital: Negotiating Credit and Exchange in the Northern Philippines

B. Lynne Milgram

In the northern Philippines, as in rural regions worldwide, the commoditization of artisan production continues to expand as the world market for craft objects grows. Improved transportation and communication systems enable once physically remote artisan groups to reach ever wider regional and currently global markets. With such transformations in local economies come transformations in the avenues through which artisans and traders refashion social and economic relationships to craft the most mutually beneficial forums for trade. A key component in this negotiation continues to revolve around access to informal credit.

Much of the scholarship on informal credit in rural economies and in the Philippines in particular, tends to treat as mutually exclusive the spheres of borrowing and lending that it identifies. On the one hand, studies conducted by many economists see households as discrete reproductive units with credit and loan activities primarily directed toward "consumption smoothing" (e.g., Lund 1996; Udry 1990). Analyses such as these maintain that informal borrowing and lending occur within small established personal networks, "not anonymous market exchange" (Lund 1996:2). While part of this argument is indeed the case, such studies cast household and individual activities largely within a model that hinges on sharp divisions between "domestic" and "public" spheres or between "family" and "economy."

On the other hand, the business relations between producers and traders in which both partners develop favored relationships with one another has also been well documented in different regional contexts (e.g., Anderson 1969;

Dannhaeuser 1983; Davis 1973; Rutten 1993). Such a *suki* relationship, as it is termed in the Philippines, is a regular trade arrangement that involves trust and reciprocal favors such as advances of production credit and favorable prices by traders in return for a steady supply of goods from producers. The aim is to reduce risk in an unpredictable economic environment.

I suggest, however, that in separating the so-called productive and reproductive spheres, these analyses neglect the integral linkages between both of these access-to-informal-credit arenas. This has become more evident since the 1990s with the devaluation of the Philippine peso and the sharp rise in the cost of basic commodities. With such shifting economic conditions, I found that artisan families commonly seek informal loans beyond the close-knit circle of family and friends. To pay for consumption needs, they request credit from their business *sukis* and, in some cases, from traders to whom they are selling goods for the first time.

Artisans may also default on their credit advances from their regular traders, often spending this money on their family's household expenses such as education and health care. My findings reveal then that both patron–client and interhousehold credit relationships as previously documented cannot be simply regarded as enduring constants. Rather, in the northern Philippines, such credit and exchange arrangements emerge as a heterogeneous combination of negotiations that are "only ever partially fixed and always under subversion" (Gibson-Graham 1996:15).

In this chapter I explore the multiple dimensions of informal credit relations in the northern Philippines by highlighting the channels through which handicraft traders currently refashion trade relations with craft producers. I argue here for understanding such negotiations in terms of a "middle ground" as proposed by ethnohistorian Richard White (1991). In this model, when two groups with different behavioral, and I add economic, environments meet, they need to establish common cultural scripts in order to achieve effective social action. This can occur through the creation of a middle ground in which both parties formulate parameters of exchange in which one group's expectations or aims do not totally overshadow the other's. I extend White's model from its roots in different cultural groups, First Nations and European colonizers, to include members of different class-based groups, namely, artisans and traders. Although the economic differential between these two may, in some instances, be small, nevertheless, traders more often have access to capital sufficient to establish such locally meaningful distinctions; and producers aspire to enter the latter's profession because it is an avenue to social power and prestige that does not require the same amount of manual work (see Platteau and Abraham 1987:479). Indeed, Lynn Stephen (1996:388) describes textile merchants and artisans in Oaxaca, Mexico, as "class-based occupational groups."

To craft such a middle ground, artisans and traders negotiate a "new set of common conventions" that govern "suitable ways of acting" but frequently do not involve an alteration of core concepts (White 1991:50–52). Members of both groups are bound through their own interests to gain cooperation from each other but lack the power to do so through force. As producers and traders jostle to attain the best conditions for business, as well as basic survival, the middle-ground rituals become more or less stable through their repeated reenactment. This results in the creation of new cultural forms that are nevertheless subject to "rival interpretations" and "imperfect reproductions" (White 1991:50–53, 333–334).

To pursue this argument with regard to exchange relations in the Philippine Cordillera, I first review some of the relevant literature on informal credit activities in Southeast Asia, and in the Philippines, in particular. I then outline the organization of the handicraft trade in Ifugao Province with a specific focus on the role of women, and I use two case studies to highlight some of the avenues through which traders and producers negotiate the changing circumstances of informal credit.

(RE)SITUATING INFORMAL CREDIT

The literature on informal credit relations between producers and traders in rural economies can be problematic, as it largely posits credit within a relationship marked by dependence between provider and receiver and either as a "helping hand" or a "Trojan horse" (Rutten 1991:109). In the former, the positive side of credit frees rural producers from traditional bonds and enables them to participate in the market (see also Milgram 2001b). In this light, Hill (1986:83–84) argues that the expansion of credit in commoditizing economies should be viewed not as a "submission to rapacious creditors" but as a sign of "an active economy." More often, however, in such economies informal credit is cast as a Trojan horse. By extending credit, merchants lure subsistence producers into capitalist market production, and in the process small producers become victims of unequal exchange and surplus extraction, processes that eat away at their independence (Fegan 1981). As Rosanne Rutten (1991:109–110) points out, adherents of the first view tend to portray credit relations in terms of "choice," "participation," "leverage," and "opportunity," while proponents of the second view tend, instead, to use terms such as "debt," "merchant control," and "subordination" and to write about producers as being "tied to merchants" (Cook 1982:390, 1993; see also Fegan 1981, 1989).

Studies of the handicraft industry tend to adopt a negative view of informal credit. Artisans' indebtedness is generally taken as a symptom of merchant control and even as a disguised form of artisan wage dependency. In instances where artisans receive advances in cash or in raw materials, some authors argue, "the artisans have become, in effect, wage-workers for the entrepreneur" (Littlefield 1979:476; Ehlers 1990, 1993), and the payment received by the direct producer for his or her products may be considered "as a *de facto* inferior wage" (Cook 1982:391).

In the rural Philippines, as in similar agrarian communities, credit relations between traders and producers, including artisans, revolve around the advance system (see Fegan 1989; Rutten 1991). Traders pay producers in cash or in-kind partly in advance, thereby laying a claim to products, while producers use advance payments to cover production and, as I want to argue later, also subsistence costs. Producers obtain cash to cover their daily needs until they complete the project and receive final payment. Entrepreneurs generally tend to use the advance system to introduce and expand the cultivation of commercial crops (Esguerra and Meyer 1992) and the manufacture of market products among small-scale producers (Lamberte 1992; Rutten 1993). In this arrangement, traders attain large production volumes without having to purchase land or establish factories.[1]

While some studies see the advance system as a calculated means of control and exploitation imposed on producers by entrepreneurs (e.g., Fegan 1981), others argue that under some conditions the advance system can be imposed by producers (e.g., Rutten 1991, 1993). To understand the complexities of the terrain on which the terms of such exchanges are continually contested, however, we need to consider the relative bargaining power of both parties and how each party teases out opportunities to leverage optimum results.

Rosanne Rutten (1993), for example, documents informal credit relations among traders and weavers of rattan hats and sleeping mats in Aklan Province, central Philippines. She (1993:186) argues that, in general, the bargaining power of weavers increased rather than declined as traders extended more credit and linked weavers to broader markets with the growth of the industry, especially after 1950 and during the "export period" of the mid-1970s when village buyers engaged in fierce competition for artisans' products (Rutten 1993:163–187).

With the decline of the export period frenzy, village-based agents not engaged in local-to-national sales of hats and mats have not been able to force weavers to pay their outstanding debts, although some artisans admit they still feel obligated to repay their advances. Currently, Aklan weavers can choose the form of credit they prefer, cash or raw materials, and buyers most often come to them to fill their orders. Rutten (1993:116) cautions, however, that although traders depend on weavers to supply them with products, the latter, on the whole, are the weaker part in the trade relationship as they are the poorest and most in need of money. She argues, then, that the commercial expansion of the hat and mat industry has yielded a complex set of credit relations that differentially benefit different players at different times (see also Narotsky and Moreno 2002), and that increased credit to artisans should be viewed as an element of their potential bargaining power rather than as a sign of an increased subjection to trader control.

In their study of rural fishers in Kerala, India, Platteau and Abraham (1987), like Rutten, argue that in such communities credit plays multiple roles that cannot be adequately analyzed in terms of a single monolithic model hinging on a production–reproduction divide. They demonstrate how informal credit transactions serve the function of reducing risk in agrarian/fisher societies as they perform in insurance-motivated credit exchanges. The authors' identification of "credit as an output-securing device," one of three credit-access spheres, recalls Rutten's analysis and most applicably captures the Philippine context in which credit functions as a "market-tying loan" (Platteau and Abraham 1987:479) to secure products, especially in times of fierce competition, and, more broadly, to secure regularity in economic and social relations where formal contracts are nonexistent.[2]

Indeed, as in the Philippines, such interlinkages of credit and marketing relations differentially advantage different parties. Aside from easy access to long-term capital finance, Kerala fishers benefit from this arrangement, as interest on loans is strictly proportional to the size and value of the fish catch—no fish means no interest is due. Thus, fishers are protected from accumulating large unpaid debts to merchants through mounting interest charges and, in addition, may receive consumption loans when pressing needs arise (Platteau and Abraham 1987:482). The drawback is that fishers may be forced to accept a purchase price below the competitive level that the free play of market forces would have spontaneously set (Platteau and Abraham 1987:480).[3]

The pervasiveness of such multiplicity in informal credit relations is also noted by Mario Lamberte (1992) in his work on the footwear industry in the lowland urban Philippines. Footwear manufacturers, much like Cordillera craft traders, occupy an intermediary position between producers and buyers. To reduce strain on their limited capital, small manufacturers take inputs from suppliers on credit while providing trade credit to customers who often take thirty to sixty days to pay for their goods. If repayment is due to input suppliers during this time, manufacturers obtain other sources of funds to pay these obligations (e.g., banks, moneylenders, friends) (Lamberte 1992:136–137). Manufacturers may also organize a "tie-in" arrangement with input suppliers who are also wholesalers. Much like the situation noted by Platteau and Abraham (1987), under this arrangement, the input supplier provides trade credit to the manufacturer on the condition that the latter sells his or her goods back to the supplier at a pre-agreed price, thus repaying the debt.

Although these studies highlight the key roles such personalized credit relationships perform in trade for both borrowers and lenders, they primarily focus on credit advanced solely for production. They do not address the fact that many production loans are, in fact, often used for consumption purposes or that traders engage in other informal gifting arrangements (e.g., redistributive feasting) that do not formally figure into the credit advance system and from which the financial expectation of return is vaguely timed.

As artisans in the northern Philippines find it more difficult to sustain their livelihoods, they increasingly ask traders for loans for consumption as well as for capital production when the market for crafts is strong.[4] Such consumption loans, rather than circulating within the close-knit arena of interhousehold lending, more frequently originate in relations established through market exchange. A key to traders' success in extending such informal credit, then, lies in their selection of trustworthy associates and in negotiating terms of repayment that can be realized by artisans in a craft market.

Esguerra and Meyer (1992:162), and Onchan (1992:106) for example, in their studies of informal credit among rural farmers in the lowland Philippines and Thailand, respectively, argue that with the commercialization of agriculture (move to yield-increasing rice technology) exchange relations have expanded beyond the circle of friends and relatives as more money was needed for inputs. Credit transactions continue within "highly personalized" and village-based social networks (Esguerra and Meyer 1992:157), but both traders and producers have developed new dimensions of exchange to meet expanding needs. For example, traders facilitate credit transactions and re-payments in informal markets through channels such as "collateral substi-tutes" (e.g., pawning of cultivated land, required sale of output) and "informal lender specialization," a system in which lenders advance credit to specific borrowers for specific purposes (Esguerra and Meyer 1992:157, 159).[5]

Onchan (1992:106) similarly notes that in rural Thailand, although most informal lending is still done among fellow villagers who know each other well, since the 1980s the importance of relatives, friends, and landlords as the dominant informal lenders has, in fact, declined. With commoditization, ex-change circles from which to source consumption credit are widening to in-clude common rural businesses such as rice trading and milling and selling dry goods (1992:108). Such findings, as noted, sharply call into question stud-ies that continue to see informal credit solely as "consumption-smoothing" loans negotiated between close neighbors and relatives (e.g., Lund 1996) and that neglect to consider the fluidity between money used for production and that used for consumption, a situation clearly evidenced in other research (e.g., Karim 1995).[6] I suggest then that in the northern Philippines, the cur-rent shifts in access to informal credit blur any boundaries between inter-household and patron–client lending to make visible the multiplicity in such lending and borrowing negotiations.

The resultant situation is one in which informal credit options are increas-ing with the advent of global capital, and the terms of such exchanges do not neatly fall into either a negative or a positive camp. This recrafting of the ad-vance system between artisans and traders to include generalized gifting and consumption loans materializes a new middle ground of negotiation in the craft industry. Artisans and traders innovate new solutions to shared challenges that result, in most cases, in the creation of mutually satisfactory rituals of exchange based on "parallels and congruencies" (White 1991:50–53). Because a defining feature of the middle ground is that neither artisans nor traders can attain their goals by means of force, a typical strategy is for each group to "justify their own rules in terms of what they perceive to be the practices of the other," or to "appeal to the values of others in order to manipulate them" (White 1991:82, 330). Thus traders respect the special needs of artisans, as they themselves experience similar situations, and to this end contribute cash or in-kind donations to special occasion celebrations, while producers may gift extra items to buyers in a gesture of good faith toward the latter's often slim profit margin. The middle ground emerges then as a realm of ongoing invention that, through repeated performance, becomes convention (White 1991:53).

BANAUE, IFUGAO, NORTHERN PHILIPPINES, AND THE CRAFT TRADE
The Setting

Ifugao Province is situated in the Gran Cordillera Central Mountain Range, which extends through much of northern Luzon. The main economic activity here, as throughout the Cordillera, is subsistence wet-rice cultivation carried out in irrigated pond fields; in many areas the high elevation (1,500 m.) and cool climate limit cultivation to one rice crop per year. With no mixed agricultural production base and little agricultural surplus for sale, most families sustain themselves throughout the year by combining cultivation with nonagricultural income-generating work such as producing crafts, working in the tourist service industry, or operating grocery stores. The increase in tourism since the 1970s means that crafts, formerly made for local use and regional trade, are increasingly targeted for commercial sale, especially during the busiest part of the tourist season, from December to May. This situation is particularly the case in Banaue, one of Ifugao's main craft-producing centers.

Both men and women engage in extrahousehold income-generating activities. While men more commonly work in jobs such as contract wage labor (road repairs), both men and women operate stores and work in craft production, but women predominate as craft traders. The region's socioeconomic systems of bilateral kinship and inheritance, ambilocal residence, and primogeniture (inheritance based on seniority, not gender) mean that women own

land and inherited wealth and have ready access to different economic opportunities. Most women are prominent in the management of household finances and hold power in this sphere by controlling the allocation of
household cash resources. Men, however, assume most public positions in
politics and in religious office, and although men participate in domestic
tasks, women still assume the bulk of child care and domestic responsibilities
(Kwiatkowski 1998; Milgram 2001a). Throughout the Cordillera, moreover, it
is important to consider the differences among women. Depending upon factors such as social class (landed elite, tenant, or landless) and education, some
women may have more of an advantage than others to gain prestige and increase income through their involvement in new craft spheres.

Female craft traders, in particular, have eclectically built on these indigenous socioeconomic systems, adapting certain ideas and techniques from external market relations and actively resisting others to create a complex sphere
of craft practice. Since the 1970s, the growth in tourism in provinces such as
Ifugao, along with the government's "export-oriented" policies, has opened
the way for the commoditization of rural crafts and, in turn, for women's varied engagement in the craft trade (Aguilar and Miralao 1984:6–7; Milgram
2000; Pineda-Ofreneo 1982).

Organization of the Craft Trade

Building on their history of trading weavings for goods not locally available, female traders now also sell wood carvings and have emerged as the region's foremost craft marketers (Barton 1919).[7] They operate as the main
risk-taking entrepreneurs, developing new business opportunities with the
rise in tourism and the popularity of collecting "indigenous folk art." In multifaceted exchange activities they reconfigure cultural community expectations
and external market forces to fashion a middle ground for trade.

While women are the primary weavers and men dominate in wood carving, some female artisans have started to carve small versions of the most
popular types of wood products (Milgram 1999). Drawing on a regional ideology that supports the interchangeability of gendered tasks, especially within
the household, female artisans and traders have been able to easily engage in
making and selling wood carvings, crafts previously the prerogative of men.
Neither the type of crafts produced nor their trade is gender specific. Although women dominate the trade in weavings, both men and women buy

and sell wood carvings. However, the market for handwoven textiles sold as yardage or sewn into a variety of functional items tends to be more limited to regional-to-national tourist shops while the market for wood carvings has made the leap from local to international. Thus, wood carving is the more profitable handicraft trade and often imparts a degree of prestige to the women marketing this craft. Marketing handicrafts, especially wood carvings, has the potential to become an important basis for local accumulation, which can, in turn, be transformed into other forms of social capital.

In Banaue, as throughout Ifugao, the production and trade of weavings and wood carvings is too small to support an intervening level of intermediaries. These crafts remain low-technology, household-based enterprises controlled by independent artisans and marketers. As there is "no ideological restraint on economic upward mobility" (Rutten 1993:138; see also Hilhorst 2001), the ease of entry into relevant trade channels means that female artisans, in particular, can move into trading if suitable opportunities arise.

At any one time in the Banaue town center there are approximately fifteen handicraft stores whose sales of handwoven and carved products are targeted to the local tourist trade and to buyers purchasing for their own craft businesses in other parts of the Philippines. In addition, approximately ten to fifteen craft traders work from their homes and do not maintain retail outlets. The following discussion focuses on the local-to-international trading practices of these small-scale town and household-based traders in Banaue, Ifugao.

Female handicraft marketers assume responsibility for all financial business matters and thus are the pivot in the cash flow, negotiating a middle ground of practice between urban buyers on the one hand and rural artisans on the other. They issue cash and in-kind advances to artisans, and when required, they negotiate their own loans for both business and personal purposes with local moneylenders or banking cooperatives in much the same sort of negotiation documented by Lamberte (1992) in Philippine footwear manufacturing. They communicate with buyers in Manila and Baguio City, negotiating the terms of purchase orders, delivery dates, and extensions as well as traveling to urban centers to follow up on orders and payments.

As the linchpin in the handicraft industry, they obtain their stock directly from local artisans and, in turn, sell directly to urban buyers with no intervening brokers. On the buying side, faced with the collection of goods from artisans who live, not together in villages, but individually scattered over a wide area near their rice fields, traders continually negotiate the amount and nature of the advances they give to artisans to enable them to gain more control over the artisans' products. Often traders take pieces from artisans on consignment. This opportunity to obtain consigned goods enables traders to participate in trade when they are short of capital. However, at the time goods are consigned, traders may offer producers, in return, livestock such as a chicken or a duck, which can provide a special meal. Through such gestures, I suggest that traders attempt to extend the time they have to pay producers for their goods while re-inforcing artisans' sense of obligation to deliver their products to traders. On the retail end of the trade chain, traders sell their products through their shops, if they have a local retail outlet, or independently to their own network of urban buyers in Baguio City and Manila craft stores.

Most traders do not obtain advances from their urban buyers but bear the responsibility for transporting their goods to regional or national markets and for negotiating all payments and contracts. In most instances, Banaue traders respond to specific orders from their buyers in Baguio City and Manila and must formulate strategies to cope with the fluctuating demand. With hand-woven products, there is a definite seasonality to the orders with the slow season corresponding to the rainy and nontourist season from mid-May to December. Generally, the traders dealing in textiles make the trip to Baguio City every month-and-a-half just to keep in contact with their buyers. Only a few of the larger traders who have retail space and ready cash are able to stock weavings and carvings at this time of low demand.

Positioned between the demands and expectations of urban buyers and those of rural artisans, traders' businesses are vulnerable to interruptions in their cash flow that may arise from problems with either group. Within the framework of informal credit ties, the marketing of handicrafts then remains very much a process in which the negotiating skills of traders are essential for their business success. Building on their mediation skills and mobility between rural and urban spheres and between different local contexts of activities within and outside the household, female traders in particular negotiate a middle ground of craft practice.

NEGOTIATING THE MIDDLE GROUND

Within an uncertain economic climate and fluctuating demand for crafts, ne-gotiating a mutual understanding through a suki relationship, however tenuous, is marketers' first priority to ensure business sustainability. The suki relationship, a form of personalized relations, is marked by "subjective values and extralegal sanctions which encourage individuals to meet obligations to others" (Davis 1973:211). As James Anderson (1969:642, 648) argues, "economic personalism" is so important to Philippine entrepreneurs because it is only by forming "personal networks of obligatory relationships that they can overcome the barriers posed by a lack of trust and a weakness of institutional credit facilities" such as the absence of written contracts. Women in particular operationalize the suki bond by continuing, as they have always done, to adapt, reinterpret, and transform their skills in reproductive activities to their business practices. By developing suki relations with producers, traders can, in theory, give credit with less risk and be somewhat more certain of the volume of supply of commodities.

As White (1991:52–53) argues, in this regard, traders justify their own actions in terms of what they perceive to be producers' needs. They may act for interests anchored in their own group, but they convince artisans that some mutual action, such as delayed payments for goods, is fair and legitimate. Any congruence between these forums, no matter how tenuous, can be put to work and can take on a life of its own if it is accepted by both sides. Such "conventions do not have to be true to be effective any more than legal precedents do"; they only have to be accepted (White 1991:53).

Yet, the tension between artisans either accepting or rejecting such conventions emerges, in some instances, when artisans default on their credit advances for production and shift allegiances. As one longtime Ifugao trader explains, "You can't even depend on your relatives anymore." This situation has prompted traders to offer credit for consumption formerly more common to interhousehold lending, as noted by Lund (1996). Broadening suki relations to encompass consumption as well as production loans means understanding the variability in middle-ground transactions that may shift the balance of power between producers and traders, clearly disputing the steamroller model of capitalist and now global market forces.

Female handicraft traders in Banaue continue to develop personalized tactics to address the current weaknesses in the suki bond. To reduce the risk of loan default, they nurture their survival networks by developing new personal ties; by activating existing relations of kinship, neighborhood, and community; and by instilling a sense of personal obligation on the part of producers. At ritual occasions, for example, it is customary for neighboring and kin-based households to offer gifts to the host, in-kind or in cash in accordance with their economic status. It is important to note, however, that one does not reciprocate with an item of equal value. Such equitable exchanges signify to the receiver that the giver wishes to terminate the relationship. Rather, one gives more or less than the original gift one had received, signifying the desire to continue the friendship. As one person explains: "If my relative or neighbor brings a chicken to my *baki* (ritual) when I had donated a duck to his celebration, that means he must come again." Traders abide by this customary practice of interhousehold exchange, as indeed they also participate in this practice locally. But because traders will more often give producers a larger gift than they might have received earlier, such gestures may, in fact, take on a further dimension of obligating artisans to supply the latter with craft products (see also Scaglion 1996).[8]

Female traders confirm that to maintain the loyalty of their producers when demand for products is strong, they must explore every avenue as nurturers to fulfill artisans' requests for help. Artisans most often request cash to pay for medical expenses or for sacrificial animals that are required for the numerous life-passage rituals, in addition to advances for raw materials. In their efforts to foster a middle ground, traders put no time limit on when artisans must repay these advances, and indeed, no interest is due. Thus, depending upon the strength of the trader–artisan bond, artisans have access to interest-free loans for unlimited periods of time. Although traders gain the loyalty of the producers, they must bear the financial burden of having their capital tied up for long periods of time in outstanding loans that do not accumulate interest. In turn, when traders obtain loans from a third party to supply producers' needs, the interest due on these loans is yet another drain on the traders' resources. In instances where artisans betray their allegiances, traders explain that they cannot bear a grudge for long and, indeed, will approach artisans who have defaulted if their services are required for a particular order. Many traders feel that reemploying such artisans is the only way to recoup their investment, and thus they must build this loss of bargaining power into their new business model.

Negotiations between traders and producers thus involve a pattern of behavior that Rosanne Rutten (1993:148) perceptively describes as "wooing and flattering." Such performance in trade relationships is shaped by the specific conditions of Ifugao's handicraft industry. In times of high demand, for example, products may not be available because artisans migrate to find work or choose cultivation over craft production such as during the harvest season from June to August. Because of the seasonal fluctuation in the demand for crafts, moreover, neither traders nor artisans hold secure positions; thus their relationship takes on a seesawlike arrangement. While traders want to foster allegiances with producers to ensure their claim on the latter's products when needed, they also want to reduce risk by minimizing outlay to artisans when demand is low. At the same time, because rural traders cannot always control the prices they receive from urban buyers, their vulnerability prevents them from passing on benefits to producers in any consistent manner (see Milgram 2001b). "Groveling and cajoling" (Rutten 1993:148) then are very much the norm, as traders try to wrest carvings and weavings from artisans and convince them to honor their credit advances. Indeed, the threat that artisans might sell their products to another trader contributes to constraining traders' opportunism (see also Russell 1987).

To encourage artisans' timely delivery of products when she requires stock, for example, Mary Cugog,[9] a trader, ensures that selected producers, and especially those not in her village, are included in family and community redistributive feasting. In 2001, for example, Mary held extensive celebrations both in the church and in her village to celebrate her daughter's marriage. Chickens and pigs were killed, and ample rice was cooked to feed the guests. This is an opportune time for artisans to enjoy generous meals and to receive portions of meat and vegetables to take home to family members. Artisans' reactions to these generous in-kind gifts vary. While some admit that they feel compelled to give Mary the first choice of their craft products, others explain that she is simply fulfilling her community or family obligations. In such negotiations, female traders in particular demonstrate that the distinctions between domestic and nondomestic work are not so easily discerned. As Wazir Karim (1995:28) notes of Southeast Asian women's work in general: "So-called domestic activities are often part of a continuous chain of productive enterprises linked to a women's need [and ability] to obtain independent sources of income."

I suggest, then, that by employing such actions, traders like Mary Cugog exercise powerful managerial and control techniques to maximize their economic transactions. To understand the power shifts resulting from such credit ties means reconsidering how different players' interests, operating in multiple sites, contribute to reformulating the emergent middle ground of exchange. The following two case studies particularize the channels through which traders fashion the parameters of informal credit relations in everyday life and in formal relations.

ALTERNATIVE ACCESS TO TRADING CRAFTS
Manufacturing Weavings

The seasonal demand for woven products means that textile traders enter into individual arrangements with artisans that build on and extend the suki relationship; this ensures them a steady supply of weavings during the busy period but partially exempts them from buying all of the artisans' weavings when demand is low. Leslie Kayan, a former weaver and thirty-three-year-old mother of three children, gave up weaving to start her sewing business in 1993. As her husband, Steven, was unemployed, she taught him how to sew, and he regularly helps in the business. Following Leslie's designs, Steven does the cutting and initial basting of the pieces, while Leslie does the final sewing. Leslie also assumes responsibility for the financial side of the business as she travels to Baguio City with the orders, samples the new products to her urban buyers, and negotiates the payments. She works with three weavers regularly and five when demand is strong. She advances cash or food to the artisans as required and promises to pay them the fair market price for their weavings as well as to buy as much of their work as she can afford when demand is low (June to November). In return, weavers promise to bring her everything they weave during the busy season although they may be approached by other buyers.

During the busy part of the tourist season from mid-February through May, competition for woven runners is particularly fierce, and traders may find themselves confronting one another over a weaver's loom. Some of Banaue's female craft store owners who buy and sew weavings for the local tourist trade do not wait for weavers to bring their products to the market. When traders need weavings, they personally trek into the villages with ready cash, laying claim to whatever finished pieces they can find. Sewers from the same village then are often in competition, not only with one another, but also periodically with town shop owners. Thus, it is imperative for local village traders like Leslie to negotiate a middle-ground arrangement with artisans that can provide the traders with the leverage they need to purchase the most suitable products while minimizing the strain on their resources.

In 1998, Leslie formulated a tactic to further formalize her trade arrangement with weavers. In the past she had complained that if she gives advances to weavers, she risks losing control over the quality of the product, as some weavers sacrifice quality for speed. She then feels compelled to accept these lower-quality weavings to meet her deadline with urban buyers. To enhance her competitive edge, Leslie currently designs her own line of functional products. Her storage shelf of neatly aligned woven cotton table runners (30 cm $\times$ 150 cm) attests to her good design sense and unique color combinations. She matches patterns and colors to the composition of her products and instructs artisans how to weave to her specifications. She advances her self-selected yarns to the weavers and, in a piecework arrangement, deducts the cost of the yarn from the value of the weavings delivered. Although artisans are paid only for their labor, Leslie has earned a reputation for always paying the market price for the runners promptly upon delivery, and she often includes an in-kind bonus of chickens or vegetables from her household garden. Some weavers explain that since they often lack the capital to buy their own yarn, Leslie's arrangement facilitates an optional avenue to earn cash, especially when child care demands preclude extrahousehold work. On the other hand, Leslie also makes a profit on the yarn, as she buys it wholesale but advances it to the weavers at the retail price.

Still, some weavers do not deliver the orders they have promised. Because Leslie buys and combines very distinctive yarn colors, it is easy for her to tell when one of her weavers has taken an advance of yarn but then sold the weavings to another trader who may have appeared on the weaver's doorstep with cash in hand. Leslie calculates that one kilogram of yarn yields four runners. Thus, when a weaver who receives this standard one-kilo advance delivers only two woven runners, Leslie knows that the weaver has sold the other pieces to another trader. Some weavers have returned to Leslie with runners woven from yarns other than those they have received from her, and Leslie has accepted these as the only way to retrieve her investment.

Leslie must also nurture ties with her urban buyers. To encourage her buyers' prompt payment and repeat business, she gives, as a gift, samples of her new products in which her buyers have expressed interest. If these samples sell well, she explains, she has a better chance of receiving new orders. Similarly, if the buyer does not bargain with her to reduce the amount of the final payment, Leslie makes a symbolic gesture of good faith by rounding off the total due to make a small deduction. To maintain a buyer's favor, Leslie has agreed, on different occasions, to take back and repair woven vests that were damaged by rodents. Since the vests had been sold months earlier than the requests for repairs, the damage was clearly not her responsibility, but she felt that to refuse such requests would ultimately alienate this buyer and cost her future orders.

Collecting Wood Carvings

The expansion of the wood-carving industry has also meant that new opportunities in marketing have emerged, not only for established traders seeking to expand their businesses with urban buyers, but also for those with less access to capital who nevertheless seek an entry into the craft market. Women have created and filled an intervening niche in the marketing of wood carvings by assuming the positions of "stockers" or "collectors." These fledgling traders live in or near villages noted for wood carving and may also operate grocery stores or work in the tourist service industry to augment this new income. They work from their shop-front homes, which are usually accessible by road to the Banaue market. This accessibility makes it easier for artisans and buyers who need to deliver, pick up, and transport large numbers of carvings. As their capital permits, they purchase rough, unfinished carvings from local artisans and store the carvings in or around their houses. Their clients are primarily the local wood-carving entrepreneurs, men and women, who periodically need additional stock to complete orders when their own deliveries fall short.

Since the early 1990s, with much of the wood-carving business being funneled directly to Manila, more urban buyers from Baguio City's large wood-finishing industry have been personally making the ten-to-twelve-hour drive to Banaue to supplement their local production. They travel between cities once or twice a month in the busy season in December and from mid-February to May and irregularly when demand slows down between June and November. Some of these collectors try to concentrate on particular items such as "native" Ifugao spoon sets or different sizes of "rice gods," items that are always in demand. In so doing, they become known for their specialized stock. The main problem for collectors occurs when they cannot secure the types of items that buyers require. In purchasing alternatives, they risk that these carvings may not be accepted. Reselling the substitute items in the local Banaue town market, where the demand for rough carvings fluctuates, often means realizing a profit lower than they expected.

Jane Magastino, one of Banaue's busiest wood-carving entrepreneurs, has developed an informal trade relationship with a number of collectors, the majority of whom are women. Most of Jane's junior traders had no capital to begin marketing and approached her with the idea of working for her in this capacity. They secured capital advances of 1,000 to 5,000 pesos (US$40–$125),[10] a portion of which Jane deducts upon each delivery until the balance is paid. At the local level, collectors negotiate with their personal network of artisan neighbors, visiting carvers regularly to claim their products. The women who collect for Jane, in fact, make only a small profit in this business. They most often pay in cash upon the receipt of the carvings since their limited capital prevents them from making substantial advances, and they add only a minimal markup to items, from 5 to 15 pesos per piece. Once or twice a month, they deliver orders whose value equals the amount of their capital, collecting a small profit of approximately 10 to 15 percent. However small this income, their access to Jane's informal credit enables these collectors to earn additional money when, as noted with weavers, child care and domestic responsibilities preclude more full-time employment away from home.

Jane confirms that in this arrangement she is actually paying more for her carvings than if artisans delivered products to her directly. But she explains that this action, this new middle ground in the craft trade, is her way of helping these women earn a living, and in effect, laying the groundwork for future business opportunities while earning her social capital within the community for her efforts. In the future, Jane may choose to transform her social standing into an income-generating opportunity, such as lowering the prices she pays for goods.[11]

Yet, with access to such opportunities, one of these women, Susan Lagun, 35, has been able to take her business a step further. After three years of collecting carvings, she approached Jane for a loan to purchase her own sanding machine. Susan is repaying the loan through deductions made from her deliveries and through her labor sanding rough carvings. Although she is required to give priority to Jane's sanding orders, in 1998 Susan was able to accept work from two other Banaue traders and pocket this income directly.

In addition, instead of simply collecting carvings and forwarding them to Jane as rough products, Susan sands selected items as time permits, and, in so doing, adds an additional markup per piece for her labor.

Although the income of the women who collect and stock carvings is limited, they have succeeded in securing a toehold in the craft industry with little personal investment outside of their time; through further negotiations with more established traders they endeavor to build on this niche position. Through this intermediary level of collecting and selling carvings, women have been able to forge a new middle ground in the craft trade that enables them to maintain their independence and, in some instances, assume producer–trader status.

Addressing similar issues, Villia Jefremovas (1985) and Susan Russell (1983) examine the changing economic practices in the weaving and knitting industries in other Cordillera provinces. They illustrate that different businesswomen operationalize multiple dimensions of rural kinship and community networks as well as capitalist market practice to benefit both their enterprises and their personal positions within the community. Successful Cordillera traders have maintained their operations through channels similar to those Leslie and Jane pursue. They recruit labor on the basis of kin and community ties and represent themselves as generous benefactors, distributing goods and sponsoring lavish feasts. Indeed, through these repeated performances, such gifting and feasts have emerged as new cultural conventions much like the seasonal bonus.

CONCLUSION

While the market for Philippine crafts is indeed expanding, producers and traders continue to negotiate the terms of informal credit in efforts to mitigate the ongoing uncertainties of this industry. Fluctuations in the supply of, and demand for, craft products may result from producers' irregular access to raw materials, delayed payments from buyers at all levels, or the seasonal and changing trends in tourist markets. In response to these variable conditions, individuals tend to develop informal solidarity mechanisms to ensure their mutual survival (see also Fafchamps 1992). Such reciprocal insurance can take different forms such as facilitating access to credit, land, labor, or food. In Ifugao's craft industry, solidarity as a form of mutual insurance between producers and traders emerges in the suki relationship, whose terms are negotiated across a middle ground. The persistence of economic uncertainties, however, means that the character of this middle ground is being continually refashioned "through varied, fragmentary, polymorphous arrangements of social relations of production . . . [and] . . . life production or reproduction" (Narotsky 1997:210). What results then is a reconfigured arena of exchange between producers and traders that includes generalized gifting and consumption loans as well as credit for production negotiated across market and community spheres.

Both producers and traders make small economic and cultural concessions to accommodate the other as neither holds total control over the conditions of production, exchange, and consumption. In times of strong demand for crafts, competition is fierce among traders for both producers and buyers. In the course of this struggle, each party might bargain away a proportion of its respective advantages. In some instances, producers may jeopardize their suki relationship for short-term gains by selling to one trader products commissioned by another; and traders may indeed exploit producers, in situations for example, when they continue to pay artisans low prices although they are receiving higher payments from urban buyers. In the latter case, traders' frequent trips to urban markets equip them with the knowledge of current prices, thus facilitating this advantage. At the same time, however, rural traders themselves are vulnerable to the business practices of their urban buyers who may delay or discount their payments, interrupting the traders' cash flow. Thus, traders and producers both make efforts to maintain long-term, congenial relations, in some form, as insurance for those periods when demand for crafts is low. At these times, producers often need credit from traders for their consumption needs, while traders need assurances from artisans that their products will be forthcoming when orders resume. Indeed, as the net income of many small traders is only marginally more than that of producers, few traders can afford not to participate in this mutual solidarity system and thus continue to negotiate with artisans on its reconfiguration.

In such circumstances, however, traders tend to emerge in a more advantageous position than do producers, although class-based differences among traders account for variations in this advantage. Because traders are often from the landed class, they have the capital needed to establish their businesses and are better positioned to accumulate wealth (cash, livestock, land) and command the labor and allegiance of kin and community members. This relative advantage could potentially threaten the system of mutual insurance, but limits on wealth accumulation emerge as self-imposed constraints, in most cases, due to the customary practice of wealth redistribution and the community belief in one's "right to subsistence" (Fafchamps 1992:160).

Redistributive feasting, access to credit, and periodic gifting of in-kind items from traders to producers were cultural expectations previously confined to the landed elite. The current emergence of these practices as new conventions increasingly expected of the newly rich, such as those who have made money from their work in crafts, suggests a multileveled reciprocity much like the situation for informal interhousehold lending noted by Lund (1996). The expectation for traders to sponsor feasts and extend consumption credit preserves insurance for less well-off producers and thus the community good, while their ability to help others in need becomes a source of prestige and potential for social mobility. Female traders, in particular, most effectively operationalize these channels as they draw on a flexible range of productive-reproductive activities from a varied range of capital, labor, and community resources that come under their control (see also Karim 1995:28).

On one level, lavish expenditures and prodigal assistance to the poor may be instruments to wrest producers away from their sukis or to obligate producers to traders, but in the process artisans benefit and traders' accumulated wealth, to a degree, is kept in check. Indeed, Narotzky and Moreno (2002:283), in problematizing the concept of reciprocity to reveal its "dark side," argue that analyses must consider the recurrent articulation of both negative and positive interacting forces in "giving, receiving, and taking." They (2002:282–283) identify the tension between "beneficent and maleficent processes" that simultaneously create solidarity and differentiation, manifesting a sense of mutual communality in some parts of the social fabric and individual self-interest in others. The coexistence and interdependence of both agents emerge in the Philippine cases in the middle-ground negotiations that differentially advantage producers and traders at different times.

In the northern Philippines, then, the complexity of the terrain of artisan–trader credit transactions manifests how "the actual accomplishment of rule . . . [or business, is] worked out in the contingent and compromised space of cultural intimacy" (Li 1999:295). It makes visible the channels through which traders actively negotiate shifting power differentials with artisans and buyers across rural-to-urban spheres to reconfigure the middle-ground parameters of credit and exchange, and in so doing, carve a space in the global craft trade.

NOTES

Field research for this paper was conducted over several periods from 1994 to 1995, for seven months in 1998, and for two-and-a-half months in 2000 and 2001. Financial support for this research was provided by the Social Sciences and Humanities Research Council of Canada, Doctoral Fellowship, Postdoctoral Fellowship and Standard Research Grant. In the Philippines, I am affiliated with the Cordillera Studies Center (CSC), University of the Philippines, Baguio, Baguio City. I thank my colleagues at CSC for their generous support of my research. I also wish to thank the volume editors and anonymous reviewers for their thoughtful comments on this paper. To the residents of Banaue, Ifugao, I owe a debt of gratitude.

1. Rutten (1991, 1993) and Fegan (1989) outline similar advance system arrangements between traders and artisans and between landowners and rice cultivators, respectively, in the lowland Philippines. The advance system may also develop into the outgrower system in agriculture (Russell 1987) or the putting-out system in crafts (Pineda-Ofreneo 1982; Aguilar and Miralao 1984). For further discussion of such credit arrangements, see also Floro and Yotopoulos 1991 and Ghate 1992.

2. Platteau and Abraham (1987:461–462) argue that lenders may have different motivations when they give credit to villagers in rural areas, and to this end they identify two other spheres of credit used as advances between fishermen and traders/middlemen. These include the "classical explanation" and the "default" hypothesis.

3. Repayment terms for loans to Kerala fishermen are similar to those used in Philippine crafts. In Kerala, merchant-creditors do not normally insist on the repayment of the loan principal. Indeed, unless the owner-borrower is a poor performer, lenders have an interest in prolonging the credit-cum-marketing relation to keep control of fish catches through credit obligations. Thus, middlemen and merchants try to prevent owner-fishermen from totally repaying their outstanding debts to keep them financially tied to these lenders (Platteau and Abraham 1987:467).

4. Lacking conventional collateral such as land or cash and often the degree of literacy required to complete bank application forms, many artisans do not have access to loans from the formal banking sector or from regional banking

cooperatives. The main sources of funds for such artisans, as for rural residents generally, are relatives, who may not charge interest, or local moneylenders, who customarily charge 10 percent interest per month. Moneylenders are usually local businesspeople or government employees, men and women. Thus the option of securing interest-free loans from traders emerges as artisans' preferred choice (see also Milgram 1999).

5. Informal lenders may use various forms of collateral substitutes. For the farmer-lender who extends consumption loans to landless laborers (Lund 1996), the objective may be to elicit the optimal effort from workers or to secure casual laborers during periods of peak labor demand. As Onchan (1992) points out, for some traders, acquiring the farmer-borrower's marketable surplus at harvest time is clearly the main motivation for lending. For lenders employing the pawning contract, the object is to reap the gains from farming that modern technology and tenurial reform have provided. In all cases, "collateral substitutes" help enforce loan repayment and serve as screening devices through which borrowers are chosen. Lenders may tend to specialize in giving funds to certain classes of borrowers according to the collateral substitute they use (Onchan 1992).

6. Onchan (1992:113–114) found, moreover, that farmers' attitudes toward informal lenders were generally positive; credit is easy, quick, and flexible, with negotiable repayment terms. However, as in Rutten's (1993) findings, credit also has negative connotations. Onchan (1992:114) finds that the main complaints are about the high interest rates.

7. Parts of this section draw on and expand material published in Milgram 2001a.

8. As Scaglion (1996) argues in his work on exchange and reciprocity in Papua New Guinea, certain individuals (e.g., chiefs) accumulate and distribute goods with generosity in order to gain greater local prestige and claim products from supporters. Thus, the dividing line between generalized reciprocity or gifting and extortion is often a blurred one. In Scaglion's case, as in the Philippines, the success of such initiatives depends upon whether these prominent individuals can convince producers of the mutual benefit of this middle-ground arrangement.

9. All personal names of individuals are pseudonyms.

10. In 2000 the exchange rate was US$1 = 38–40 Philippine pesos; in 2001 the exchange rate was US$1 = 42–45 Philippine pesos.

11. Bourdieu (1980:191–210), quoted in Narotsky and Moreno 2002:286–287), argues that the transformation of economic capital into social capital enables

social reproduction of systems of inequality and dominance by disguising material interests and legitimizing relationships of economic dependence and exploitation.

REFERENCES

Aguilar, Filomeno V., and Virginia A. Miralao. 1984. *Handicrafts, Development, and Dilemmas over Definition (The Philippines as a Case in Point).* Handicraft Project Paper Series 1. Manila: Ramon Magsaysay Award Foundation.

Anderson, James N. 1969. Buy-and-Sell and Economic Personalism: Foundations for Philippine Entrepreneurship. *Asian Survey* 9(9):641–668.

Barton, Roy Franklin. 1919. Ifugao Economics. *University of California Publications in American Archaeology and Ethnology* 15(1):385–446.

Bourdieu, Pierre. 1980. *Le sens pratique.* Paris: Les Editions de Minuit.

Cook, Scott. 1982. *Zapotec Stoneworkers: The Dynamics of Rural Simple Commodity Production in Modern Mexican Capitalism.* New York: University Press of America.

———. 1993. Craft Commodity Production, Market Diversity, and Different Rewards in Mexican Capitalism Today. In *Crafts in the World Market: The Impact of Global Exchange on Middle American Artisans.* June Nash, ed. Pp. 59–84. Albany: State University of New York Press.

Dannhaeuser, Norbett. 1983. *Contemporary Trade Strategies in the Philippines: A Study in Marketing Anthropology.* New Brunswick, N.J.: Rutgers University Press.

Davis, William G. 1973. *Social Relations in a Philippine Market: Self-Interest and Subjectivity.* Berkeley and Los Angeles: University of California Press.

Ehlers, Tracy Bachrach. 1990. *Silent Looms.* Boulder, Colo.: Westview.

———. 1993. Belts, Business, and Bloomingdale's: An Alternative Model for Guatemalan Artisan Development. In *Crafts in the World Market: The Impact of Global Exchange on Middle American Artisans.* June Nash, ed. Pp. 181–198. Albany: State University of New York Press.

Esguerra, Emmanuel F., and Richard Meyer. 1992. Collateral Substitutes in Rural Informal Financial Markets in the Philippines. In *Informal Finance in Low-Income Countries.* Dale W. Adams and Delbert A. Fitchett, eds. Pp. 149–164. Boulder, Colo.: Westview.

Fafchamps, Marcel. 1992. Solidarity Networks in Preindustrial Societies: Rational Peasants with a Moral Economy. *Economic Development and Cultural Change* 47(1):147–174.

Fegan, Brian. 1981. *Rent-Capitalism in the Philippines.* Quezon City: Third World Studies Center, University of the Philippines, Diliman.

———. 1989. Accumulation on the Basis of an Unprofitable Crop. In *Agrarian Transformations: Local Processes and the State in Southeast Asia.* Gillian Hart, Andrew Turton, and Benjamin White, eds. Pp. 159–178. Berkeley and Los Angeles: University of California Press.

Floro, Sagrario, and Pan A. Yotopoulos. 1991. *Informal Credit Markets and the New Institutional Economics: The Case of Philippine Agriculture.* Boulder, Colo.: Westview.

Ghate, Prabhu. 1992. *Informal Finance: Some Findings from Asia.* Manila: Oxford University Press for the Asian Development Bank.

Gibson-Graham, J. K. 1996. *The End of Capitalism (as We Knew It): A Feminist Critique of Political Economy.* Oxford: Blackwell.

Hilhorst, Dorothea. 2001. Village Experts and Development Discourse: "Progress" in a Philippine Igorot Village. *Human Organization* 60(4):401–413.

Hill, P. 1986. *Development Economics on Trial: The Anthropological Case for a Prosecution.* Cambridge, U.K.: Cambridge University Press.

Jefremovas, Villia. 1985. Exploitation and Resistance: Kinship and Community Ties in Northern Luzon. In *Contemporary and Historical Perspectives in Southeast Asia.* Alice B. Chen, ed. Pp. 273–290. Ottawa: University of Ottawa Press.

Karim, Wazir Jahan. 1995. Introduction: Genderising Anthropology in Southeast Asia. In *"Male" and "Female" in Developing Southeast Asia.* Wazir Jahan Karim, ed. Pp. 11–34. Oxford: Berg.

Kwiatkowski, Lynn M. 1998. *Struggling with Development: The Politics of Hunger and Gender in the Philippines.* Boulder, Colo.: Westview.

Lamberte, Mario. 1992. Informal Finance in the Philippines' Footwear Industry. In *Informal Finance in Low-Income Countries.* Dale W. Adams and Delbert A. Fitchett, eds. Pp. 133–148. Boulder, Colo.: Westview.

Li, Tania Murray. 1999. Compromising Power: Development, Culture, and Rule in Indonesia. *Cultural Anthropology* 14(3):295–322.

Littlefield, Alice. 1979. The Expansion of Capitalist Relations of Production in Mexican Crafts. *Journal of Peasant Studies* 6(4):471–488.

Lund, Susan M. 1996. *Credit and Risk-Sharing in the Philippine Uplands.* Los Baños, Philippines: International Rice Research Institute, Social Science Division Discussion Paper 3/96.

Milgram, B. Lynne. 1999. Crafts, Cultivation, and Household Economies: Women's Work and Positions in Ifugao Northern Philippines. In *Research in Economic Anthropology,* vol. 20. Barry Isaac, ed., Pp. 221–261. Stamford, Conn.: JAI Press.

———. 2000. Reorganizing Textile Production for the Global Market: Women's Craft Cooperatives in Ifugao, Upland Philippines. In *Artisans and Cooperatives: Developing Alternative Trade for the Global Economy.* Kimberly M. Grimes and B. Lynne Milgram, eds. Pp. 107–207. Tucson: University of Arizona Press.

———. 2001a. Situating Handicraft Market Women in Ifugao, Upland Philippines: A Case for Multiplicity. In *Women Traders in Cross-Cultural Perspective: Mediating Identities, Marketing Wares.* Linda J. Seligmann, ed. Pp. 129–159. Stanford, Calif.: Stanford University Press.

———. 2001b. Operationalizing Microfinance: Women and Craftwork in Ifugao, Upland Philippines. *Human Organization* 60(3):212–224.

Narotsky, Susana. 1997. *New Directions in Economic Anthropology.* London: Pluto Press.

Narotsky, Susana, and Paz Moreno. 2002. Reciprocity's Dark Side: Negative Reciprocity, Morality, and Social Reproduction. *Anthropological Theory* 2(3):281–305.

Onchan, Tongroj. 1992. Informal Rural Finance in Thailand. In *Informal Finance in Low-Income Countries.* Dale W. Adams and Delbert A. Fitchett, eds. Pp. 103–118. Boulder, Colo.: Westview.

Pineda-Ofreneo, R. 1982. Philippine Domestic Outwork: Subcontracting for Export-Oriented Industries. *Journal of Contemporary Asia* 12(3):281–293.

Platteau, J. P., and A. Abraham. 1987. An Inquiry into Quasi-Credit Contracts: The Role of Reciprocal Credit and Interlinked Deals in a Small-Scale Fishing Community. *Journal of Development Studies* 23(4):461–490.

Russell, Susan D. 1983. Entrepreneurs, Ethnic Rhetorics, and Economic Integration in Benguet Province, Highland Luzon, Philippines. Ph.D. diss., University of Illinois at Urbana-Champaign.

————. 1987. Middlemen and Moneylending: Relations of Exchange in a Highland Philippine Economy. *Journal of Anthropological Research* 43(2):139–161.

Rutten, Rosanne. 1991. Interpreting Philippine Credit Relations. *The Netherlands' Journal of Social Sciences* 27(2):108–117.

————. 1993. *Artisans and Entrepreneurs in the Rural Philippines: Making a Living and Gaining Wealth in Two Commercialized Crafts.* Quezon City, Philippines: New Day Publishers.

Scaglion, Richard. 1996. Chiefly Models in Papua New Guinea. *Contemporary Pacific* 8(1):1–31.

Stephen, Lynn. 1996 [1991]. Export Markets and Their Effects on Indigenous Craft Production: The Case of the Weavers of Teotitlan del Valle, Mexico. In *Textile Traditions of Mesoamerica and the Andes: An Anthology.* Margot Blum Schevill, Janet Catherine Berlo, and Edward B. Dwyer, eds. Pp. 381–402. Austin: University of Texas Press.

Udry, Christopher. 1990. Credit Markets in Northern Nigeria: Credit as Insurance in a Rural Economy. *World Bank Economic Review* 4(3):251–271.

White, Richard. 1991. *The Middle Ground: Indians, Empires, and Republics in the Great Lakes Region, 1650–1815.* Cambridge, U.K.: Cambridge University Press.

9

Locating the Cultural Context of Credit: Institutional Alternatives on the Pine Ridge Indian Reservation

Kathleen Pickering and David Mushinski

In recent years, academics from various disciplines have recognized the importance of local cultural and social institutions to the functioning of credit markets in developing areas. When formal market lenders, such as banks, will not lend to individuals entering home-based enterprise activity, informal institutions outside strict market control may provide alternative access to credit (Besley 1995). These nonmarket institutions use social and cultural information to determine appropriate credit recipients otherwise rejected by formal market lenders.

This chapter focuses on formal and informal lending institutions on the Pine Ridge Indian Reservation, located in a remote region of southwest South Dakota. Lakota people have retained a culturally distinct community within the reservation boundaries since these lands were retained by treaty in the 1860s, centered around family-based social units called *tiyospayes* (Pickering 2000). The reservation is surrounded by border towns where white homesteading settlers generated their own social and economic practices tied to mainstream commodity markets, with extensive appropriations of Lakota natural resources but limited connections to Lakota people (Wagoner 2002). The reservation has long been known for high rates of poverty and low levels of market economic activity, although extensive informal-sector economic activity is undertaken by Lakota home-based entrepreneurs (Pickering 2000; Sherman 1988). Formal market lending is virtually absent on the reservation.

By combining economic theory and anthropological analysis, it is possible to identify and contrast the cultural knowledge and social relationships required to receive credit through various institutional alternatives, including formal banking institutions, informal community-based lending, and nonprofit institutions deliberately introduced to expand credit access in developing areas. This chapter compares border-town banks, family-based tiyospayes, and the Lakota Fund, a nonprofit community-based development financial institution on the reservation, with respect to the opportunities and constraints each provides in terms of credit access and the modes of cultural knowledge employed in, and meaningful social relationships required for, their provision of credit.

REVIEW OF PERTINENT ANTHROPOLOGICAL AND ECONOMIC THEORY

Economic anthropology has a long history of exploring how social and cultural relationships affect economic transactions and create economic incentives (Malinowski 1984; Mauss 1967; Radcliffe-Brown 1965; Nash 1967; Halperin 1998). Following on the work of Karl Polanyi (1957), scholars across the social sciences have explored how socially embedded relationships and institutions work to facilitate economic transactions and outcomes (Granovetter 1973; Halperin 1988; Mingione 2000; Stiglitz 2000). Social relationships are critical to interpreting how both formal and informal social institutions function (Mingione 1996; Stiglitz 2000:64; Woolcock 2001:194, 1998:162).

Economic analysis also highlights the importance of social relationships and institutions to the functioning of financial markets. Neoclassical economic analyses of financial transactions start by considering the characteristics of lending contracts in perfectly competitive markets because those markets achieve efficient outcomes. Perfectly competitive markets are present when, among other factors, all parties have all information pertinent to the transaction (perfect information is present) and there are no costs associated with the transaction. In perfectly competitive markets no loan applications are rejected because everyone who is willing to borrow at existing lending terms obtains a loan. Furthermore, since a lender can—without cost—observe all outcomes (or states) realized by a borrower, the lender will offer a "state-contingent contract" that ties the amount that the borrower has to repay to the state realized by the borrower (Freixas and Rochet 1998). Under a state-contingent contract, when a bad outcome occurs, the borrower may pay little, if anything, to the lender, while the entrepreneur may pay the lender more when she experiences a good outcome.

State-contingent loan contracts are not observed in formal credit markets. This absence of state-contingent contracts may be explained by the presence of market imperfections including asymmetric information (which arises when one party to a transaction has information not possessed by another party to the transaction) and the presence of costs of negotiation, monitoring, and enforcement of loan repayment. Informational asymmetries have been identified as reasons for lenders rejecting loan applications (Besanko and Thakor 1987) and lenders adding collateral requirements to lending agreements (Bester 1987). Ultimately, market imperfections may produce rationing in formal credit markets, with its attendant inefficiencies (see, e.g., Stiglitz and Weiss 1981; Carter 1988).[1]

In the context of developing areas, economists have responded to possible rationing in formal credit markets by looking to informal credit markets and considering the extent to which local social and cultural institutions and relationships mitigate the market imperfections that give rise to the formal credit market rationing. If informal credit markets remedy formal credit market rationing, there are no inefficiencies to mitigate.[2] Udry (1990), for example, found that informal credit markets in several villages in Northern Nigeria mitigated formal credit market rationing. After noting the virtual absence of credit from formal markets, Udry observed that the type of state-contingent contract predicted by perfectly competitive credit markets was present in these informal markets. He attributed the presence of these contracts to the informational environments arising out of the social and cultural relationships in the villages.

When informal credit markets do not remedy formal credit market inefficiencies, some economists try to identify nonmarket institutions that may be introduced in those communities to alleviate market imperfections (see Hoff and Stiglitz 1990:249). Some have focused on the importance of social and cultural factors to the success of nonmarket institutions introduced to fill gaps in access to credit left by formal markets (Guinnane 1994; Pickering and Mushinski 2001). In analyzing Grameen Bank–type credit groups, Stiglitz (1990:353) observed that the credit groups' success may be due to their use of "the local knowledge of members of the group" in creating incentives for group members to monitor each other. Besley and Coate (1995) showed how the use of social collateral by the Grameen Bank credit group structure improved loan repayment rates. Mushinski (1999) observed that, in making lending decisions, credit unions may possess informational advantages over banks through their use of knowledge available only to people who live in a small community.

In both instances, analyses of informal credit markets depend on local-level anthropological data about social and cultural institutions and relationships within a community. Knowledge of a community's social and cultural relationships provides important insights into the informational flows in that community and interactions between community members, which, in turn, provide insights into the efficiency and functioning of informal financial markets in the community.

ALTERNATIVE SOURCES OF CREDIT ON THE PINE RIDGE RESERVATION

The Pine Ridge Reservation has presented a special challenge to economic development. It encompasses the county that had the highest rate of poverty in the 1980 and 1990 U.S. Decennial Censuses. It suffers from persistently high levels of unemployment, ranging between 70 percent and 90 percent, according to Bureau of Indian Affairs estimates, and low levels of human capital.[3] The largest source of employment is a combination of federal, state, and tribal government jobs. There is virtually no private sector. With one or two exceptions, no local business employs more than twenty people; a more likely number is two or three employees outside of immediate family members. In total, there are no more than fifty small businesses on the reservation (Pickering 2003). Most households participate in a dynamic mixture of temporary or part-time wage work, home-based enterprise for cash sales, and intracommunity gifts and barter of goods and services. Home-based enterprise on the reservation includes beadworkers, quilters, and seamstresses, shade-tree car mechanics, and sidewalk food-stand operators. A good deal of wage and home-based enterprise activity is undertaken to meet a specific cash need and therefore tends to be short-term and sporadic. Social relationships are used to redistribute goods, food, and cash through ceremonial and community events. Otherwise, household income supplements include retirement pensions, Social Security and Supplemental Security Income (SSI) benefits, food stamps or commodities, and Temporary Assistance to Needy Families (Pickering 2000, 2001).

Three possible sources of business credit for home-based entrepreneurs on the reservation are (1) border-town banks, (2) community-based lending, and (3) the Lakota Fund.[4] Each of these credit alternatives will be analyzed in turn, both in terms of the cultural knowledge and social relationships important to their functioning and in terms of the opportunities and constraints they present to home-based enterprises.

The empirical analysis in this chapter is based on interviews conducted with eighty Oglala Lakota tribal members residing on the Pine Ridge Reservation between April and October 1999. A standard survey instrument was used for each of the interviews. The survey included questions on household characteristics, business and home-based enterprise experience, and credit history. Interview participants were divided into three categories. The first category consisted of a random sample of sixty-two respondents selected from a list of Housing and Urban Development (HUD), A-frame, and trailer housing units on the reservation (*Random Sample*). From the Random Sample, a second category consisted of a subsample of twenty people who were engaged in business activities (*Business Sample*). The Business Sample was examined for ways in which their credit experiences may have differed from the general Random Sample. The third category consisted of eighteen home-based enterprise producers who had received small loans between US$100 and US$1,000 under the Lakota Fund Circle Banking Project (the *Lakota Fund Home-Based Entrepreneurs*), using the lending structure developed by the Grameen Bank in Bangladesh.[5]

Border Town Banks and Credit

There are virtually no banking services on the reservation, an area the size of Connecticut, and only one bank operates a mobile banking unit that drives to the reservation to provide certain banking services on a weekly basis (Adamson 1997). As a result, most residents of Pine Ridge must travel between 40 and 180 miles round-trip to take care of their banking needs. Importantly, any access to formal credit turns on Lakota people entering into banking institutions controlled by non-Indians in reservation border towns. These border towns have a long history of racial tensions and hostility toward Indians (Wagoner 2002). This combination of economic and social conditions has resulted in severe limitations on the access of Lakota households to formal credit markets.

The importance on the reservation of the absence of formal banking is reflected in the access to formal credit of the households studied. Seventy-six percent of the Random Sample households were credit-rationed with respect to producer or consumer credit.[6] Sixty-seven percent of the Lakota Fund home-based entrepreneurs reported being rationed in formal credit markets with respect to business credit. It is also notable that the 33 percent of Lakota Fund home-based entrepreneurs who were not rationed had access to credit predominantly through loans based on direct deposit of a federal check to the bank, creating severe limits on the size of any loan obtained.

Anecdotal evidence suggests that the limits on formal bank credit turn in part on the lack of social relationships between bank officers and the reservation population. This lack of relationships means that information and trust necessary to create formal credit links are also absent. When one businessman was asked why the bank rejected his application, he replied, "[b]asically that it was located on the reservation, our business was located on the reservation. If we would do the same thing off the reservation they would have helped us right away." He even said that "they would fund us a brand-new pickup or trailer house because they can hook onto it and take it, but they would not fund a business that starts out on cement—they cannot take this. Which to me shows they didn't expect us to make our payments." Many respondents shared the feelings of racial and cultural discrimination in relation to border-town banks expressed by this respondent: "The bank wouldn't give me a loan because I'm an Indian. I'm Lakota." Another respondent added, "I think there is a lot of discrimination off the reservation when they go to borrow money at banks." Another respondent shared the sentiment that there was no bank around that was free of the atmosphere of discrimination. "So far, everybody I think has had some kind of bad experience with the bank outside [the reservation]."

Some respondents sensed the pressure on bankers to maintain their social obligations within the border-town community, generating competition between the border towns and the reservation for development dollars. As one reservation business owner explained:

"I got turned down [by the banks] for different reasons. And I can't understand what their reasons are. Well, I already know what their reasons are. If they get us some business down here, it takes business away from them. . . . If you were a banker in a border town, and I came to you and wanted to build a motel, . . . if you give me a loan, the Chamber of Commerce would run you out of town, because the people that come to Pine Ridge to stay, there's no motels or nothing here. So the people that come here to stay naturally go to our bordering towns to stay there, so it takes the business. You give me a loan to build a motel here, the Chamber of Commerce could run you out of town."

Recently, the World Bank and other development organizations have been using the rubric of "social capital" to encourage poor communities to increase their social links outside the community self-consciously as a solution to economic underdevelopment (Woolcock 1998:164–178; Serageldin and Grootaert 2000:54; Portes and Sensenbrenner 1993). One of the underlying assumptions behind this research is that communities are able to forge "external linkages" simply by generating the determination to do so. When a community lacks social relationships with individuals or institutions outside its immediate area, the community is held responsible for that shortcoming and is simply directed to create these beneficial external ties. As Woolcock explains:

"[T]he insights derived from the classical theorists and contemporary studies of urban poverty and ethnic entrepreneurship suggest that business groups in poor communities thus need to forge and maintain linkages transcending their community. . . . [A] community's stock of social capital in the form of [local] integration can be the basis for launching development initiatives, but it must be complemented over time by the construction of new forms of social capital, i.e., linkages to non-community members." (1998:175)

However, while some absence of social relationships between different communities may be inadvertent, in other cases it can only be characterized as deliberate. Cynthia Duncan's research in Appalachia and Mississippi highlights the critical role of exclusionary features of social relationships among local elites in areas of pronounced economic differentiation based on race and class (Duncan 1999).

The Pine Ridge Indian Reservation provides an example of a community with historically constructed exclusion from social relationships in non-Indian border towns, particularly in relation to credit access. In high-poverty areas, the phenomenon of social exclusion is aggravated by justifications for not lending based on such ideas as "statistical discrimination." Isolated instances of bad credit risks are used by bankers to refuse to distinguish one Indian from another, even when such distinctions are continually made for others, such as different economic classes of white applicants. These banks can then claim the costs are too high to make these distinctions, because they lack information to determine the actual credit risks. However, they could obtain that information if they opened up their closed social networks to include Indian people.

Given the presence of credit market imperfections and rationing in formal credit markets, local institutions become important because they can alleviate the rationing and offset the exclusionary character of social networks outside the reservation boundaries. These sources of credit often have informational and cost advantages that allow them to provide the funds not available from banks.

Community-Based Lending: Tiyospayes and Credit

Community sources of credit on the Pine Ridge Reservation are loans from family and friends. Community sources tended to be cheaper for a recipient of funds, since loans from family and friends require little or no interest. Table 9.1 identifies the percentages of each sample that used various forms of formal and informal credit. Three findings emerge from table 9.1. First, few people had credit cards. The absence of credit cards reflects the fact that people on the reservation are not connected with broader markets, generally, and credit markets, specifically. This finding is consistent with our earlier observations regarding rationing of reservation members in formal credit markets.

Second, Random Sample households had greater access to cheaper forms of credit than Lakota Fund home-based entrepreneurs. Random Sample households were more likely to have received a loan from family or friends or

Table 9.1   Informal Sources of Funds

	Random Sample		Lakota Fund
	Full Sample (n=62)	*Business Sample (n=20)*	*Home-based Entrepreneurs (n=18)*
Source of Funds			
Bank Loan	23.5	18	33
Credit Cards	16	15	11
Suppliers	16	25	33
Pawn Shops	24	40	44
Loans From Family & Friends	52	55	28
Aware of Moneylenders*	18	15	17

The numbers in the table are percentages (multiplied by 100). The numbers in the table do not sum to 100 because people were allowed to provide more than one source of credit.
* People were asked if they were aware of people in the community who would lend money to others, not if they had in fact borrowed from a moneylender.

to have received a gift of cash. Lakota Fund home-based entrepreneurs tended to use the more costly forms of credit (pawn shops and suppliers) more often. Obtaining credit from pawn shops depended on owning possessions that would generate enough money to meet the individual's credit needs. Pawn shops provided credit at the highest interest rates reported, followed by suppliers. Most suppliers provided a form of in-store credit or layaway. Generally, one would expect an entrepreneur to seek out her cheapest form of credit. It is notable that the Lakota Fund home-based entrepreneurs were among the poorer residents of the reservation (see endnote 5). The Lakota Fund home-based entrepreneurs' use of these more costly forms of credit suggests that their family and friends generally did not have money to give or lend, perhaps because they were poorer. One Circle Banking Project participant discussed his experience:

> "I try to explain to the younger people now that, you know, life and the participation in business and being successful, you know, is a very serious game. Where if you lose, you know, you've lost completely. But that doesn't mean that you should give up. That if there is something that you want to obtain, that it's possible to obtain it. And that there's always the different, I guess, excuses. You know, I don't have any money. I don't have any abilities in this area. Yet I started from this area from a very poor family. And if I was able to obtain these things and be successful, then the avenues are open for those people."

In the absence of being able to obtain funds from family and friends, the Lakota Fund home-based entrepreneurs turned to pawn shops, input suppliers and, ultimately, the Lakota Fund Circle Banking Project. The Business Sample also tended to use a more costly source of credit; their use of pawn shops was close to that of the Lakota Fund home-based entrepreneurs. These observations regarding Lakota Fund home-based entrepreneurs and the Business Sample suggest that informal markets had not filled the gaps in credit left by formal credit markets for those groups. In the absence of the type of informal lending available to the general population, Lakota Fund home-based entrepreneurs and business people, generally, had to turn to the high-cost sources of funds, at least for part of their borrowing needs.

Third, the high percentage of Random Sample households that obtained loans from family and friends suggests the presence of informal credit markets. The fact that many loans arise among family and friends confirms the observations of Pickering and Mushinski (2001) that the natural unit around which lending might be structured on the reservation is the tiyospaye. The tiyospaye is an extended family unit consisting of relatives by blood, marriage, or social convention and has been the most basic unit of Lakota social organization since long before the Pine Ridge Reservation was established (Pickering 2000:2–3, 8). As Pickering and Mushinski (2001) note, the tiyospaye may be a natural lending unit because it reduces or eliminates the causes of credit market failures. Each individual's social relationships tend to be dominated by tiyospaye relations who reside across the reservation. People feel more comfortable approaching someone for a loan or lending money if they are part of the same tiyospaye. As one Lakota microenterprise producer explained: "If you look at it, the businesses around here are family businesses. Then too, if it was all family, you wouldn't have to pay a middle man, you would all make things and use them for what it cost and then make the money on the outside directly." Informational asymmetries may be absent within the tiyospaye because of members' familiarity with each other. It may reduce monitoring and enforcement costs because of constant contact among members. The importance of the tiyospaye in mitigating market failures is buttressed by the relative absence of moneylenders. Table 9.1 indicates that few of the respondents in the samples reported being aware of moneylenders, let alone borrowing from moneylenders. The effective absence of moneylenders indicates that people who try to lend across tiyospayes may not have significant informational or cost advantages over formal market lenders.

The tiyospaye offers some benefits in terms of an alternative institution for credit. The trust and reliance placed on family members provides a sound method for identifying appropriate credit risks and enforcing repayment. For example, elders within a tiyospaye have great influence over the distribution of resources within the tiyospaye, although that influence is not as great as it was during pre-reservation days. As one Lakota woman involved in the Lakota Fund's Circle Banking Project explained: "From a cultural view, all of our culture is based on the tiyospayes, so to exclude the family is just so totally different from anything we're used to. . . . And if your grandmother was in the Circle, you'd do a lot better with payments, too, since they would know when money was owed and they'd know when you had to make a payment. People wouldn't want to look bad to their elder grandma."

The ongoing nature of information sharing within family groups is also consistent with the ways in which credit is required. Interviews with Lakota Fund home-based entrepreneurs indicated that individual home-based enterprise activity tends to be goal-based. Many people undertake their business activity for a specific purpose, such as making money for an upcoming ceremony. One Lakota woman described how she developed her quilting micro-enterprise: "I started making quilts since 1974, but I didn't sell it or give it then. Then I was putting up a dinner for my sister so I needed quilts for that. But from then on I kept making them, and started selling them about four or five years ago. We needed some stuff, like propane and gas, and we had little ones so we needed Pampers and baby needs." The tiyospaye relationships make funds (up to a limit) available at any time, create a type of joint liability among all members of a tiyospaye, and involve family elders in the decision of whether a given loan is appropriate.

On the other hand, structures based on kinship imply that there is differential access to the informal social institutions within the reservation community, depending on who your relatives are and whether you are respected within your tiyospaye. Not everyone within the Pine Ridge community may have access to the informal institutions structured around tiyospayes. Through a combination of historical disruptions to the traditional residential patterns of Lakota tiyospayes, some residential communities are more closely connected through tiyospaye relationships than others. Initial results from a 2002 random sample of households indicate that 33 percent of Pine Ridge households do not consider themselves part of a tiyospaye.

Furthermore, while the tiyospayes may provide access to nonmarket financial support, the tiyospaye system as a whole does not possess sufficient capital resources currently to meet the credit needs of its members. The extent of this informal credit must be considered. Access to, and use of, informal credit does not mean credit rationing was fully mitigated. None of the community sources of credit were expected to extend more than a few hundred dollars, and more typically US$20 or US$30. As one Lakota woman explained: "I never tried to get a bank loan but I doubt I could. . . . I would borrow and lend say $5 or $10 with people from around here, that's pretty common. Some will even lend up to $400 a month." The fact that the Business Sample, which had access to family and friends, still used pawnshops and suppliers more than Random Sample households suggests that amounts obtained from community-based sources were inadequate. While the social cohesiveness of the local communities may be high enough to provide alternative institutions for credit access, the overall undercapitalization of these networks means that credit access remains limited. There may be an informal structure in place, but that structure still requires external connections to capital resources for additional infusions of capital.

The Lakota Fund

To offset these economic and social barriers to credit on the reservation, the nonprofit Lakota Fund was established in 1986, with help from First Nations Financial Project and Oglala Lakota College, as a completely Lakota-controlled financial institution. With low-cost capital invested by foundations and socially responsible outside investors, the Lakota Fund was able to create a loan fund that combined market principles of risk assessment and repayment with a social understanding of the history, culture, and development needs of Lakota people. The Lakota Fund has provided credit to Lakota home-based entrepreneurs and small-business people through several different programs over the years (Mushinski and Pickering 1996; Pickering and Mushinski 2001). In the early through mid-1990s, the Lakota Fund provided credit to home-based entrepreneurs through its Circle Banking Project. The Circle Banking Project was a form of peer-group lending, modeled on the Grameen Bank, that provided loans between US$100 and US$1,000 to individuals. The project made credit available to groups of four to six individuals who formed groups on their own and undertook certain training. Loans were made sequentially, in six-week increments, first to two members then to two more members and finally to remaining members. Members were jointly liable for all loans made within the group, and if at any time a member was delinquent on payments, no further loans could be made to group members. Interest rates on the home-based enterprise loans through the Circle Banking Project ranged between 15 percent and 18 percent, between the two extremes of high-interest pawnshops and low-interest community-based loans. The Lakota Fund eventually terminated this project for lack of participation (Pickering and Mushinski 2001). Currently the Lakota Fund is providing this same range of small loans to individuals secured with standard or alternative forms of collateral, like beadwork or family heirlooms. The Lakota Fund has also provided individual loans for small businesses with collateral and a series of business-development training courses.

The Lakota Fund is viewed by residents as providing virtually the only source of credit on the reservation. In addition to offsetting the credit rationing arising from informational asymmetries and transaction costs, the Lakota Fund has been able to respond to local social conditions, provide an atmosphere of trust, and view Indian identity positively. The Lakota Fund provides an otherwise unavailable credit alternative on the reservation. In contrast to border-town banks, the Lakota Fund is a local alternative financial institution that, because it functions within the social relationships of the reservation, is able to use informational and cost advantages about actual and potential loan applicants to lend to individuals who cannot access formal credit markets. By using information about local residents that either is not available or is not solicited or analyzed by banks and by having lower monitoring costs, the Lakota Fund is able to reduce some of the problems associated with formal credit market failures. The Lakota Fund has also been able to expand access to credit by servicing loans with collateral not accepted by off-reservation banks. In this context of formal bank rationing, the role of the Lakota Fund has been to fill some of the gaps in business lending.

At the outset, it is notable that, although they faced similar likelihoods of credit rationing as the general reservation population, the Lakota Fund home-based entrepreneurs were able to obtain loans from the Lakota Fund. Eighty-eight percent of the Lakota Fund home-based entrepreneurs who received loans repaid those loans. These loan repayment rates are like those reported in Mushinski and Pickering (1996). This counters the claim that these entrepreneurs lack the ability to repay credit and supports the claim that banks use the combination of statistical discrimination and social networks closed to Indians to justify credit rationing. The Lakota Fund is able to make loans that banks would not make and identify the otherwise rationed borrowers who will repay if provided the opportunity for a loan.

Participants discussed many factors that made the Lakota Fund loan programs critical to their enterprises. The major factor mentioned was that the Lakota Fund provided them with access to a loan. Many participants referred to the Lakota Fund as the only source of credit for a good portion of reservation businesses. One participant commented that "People don't have any other source of funding." The Lakota Fund is also viewed by participants as having important social connections with the Pine Ridge population. Lakota Fund participants feel that better information is exchanged between potential borrowers and the Lakota Fund than with banks because it is a local institution. "I think it's good because [the] Lakota Fund is in a community where everybody knows everybody, so you know, they feel more comfortable going to the Lakota Fund to borrow money." Another participant agreed: "They talk to you, you know what I mean? They plan to stop by, they set up meetings with you, they come, you know? They've always really been friendly and helpful."

Others noted that the Lakota Fund was the only financial institution that understood the special issues confronting businesspeople on the reservation. As one participant explained: "I like that it was here basically. You cannot find a place that will lend you money for anything like that [a new business] other than Lakota Funding. It at least gives you a chance to try what you thought was going to work out."

Also important to participants were the atmosphere and experiences they encountered at the Lakota Fund. As one participant noted: "[at the Lakota Fund] they were very much down to earth and they know the situation on the reservation, and they actually took us, I mean we worked together. They didn't look down on us like the banks did, on all of us." The experiences of discrimination and racial tension associated with banks were absent in discussing the Lakota Fund. As one participant recalled: "It was people that you can talk to and they were more willing to help, and you didn't feel threatened by going and talking to them about what you wanted to do, and, I don't know, it was just easier because I'm Native American and they are too, some of the workers, and it was easy. It was just easy to converse rather than to go here at the local bank. I wouldn't even try going [to the bank] up here." Another participant added that the best part of the Lakota Fund was "that you can get a loan, as an Indian, get a loan."

Another indication of formal credit rationing is the willingness of Lakota Fund loan recipients to pay interest rates that were higher than for bank loans. Even though some participants reported that the interest rates charged by the Lakota Fund were slightly higher than those at banks, they appreciated the chance to obtain a Lakota Fund loan. The rate of interest, which ran from 15 to 18 percent for home-based enterprise loans, did not appear to be a factor in discouraging individuals from applying for loans. The limited significance of the interest rate was most apparent in the number of people who had obtained bank loans but were unaware of the rate of interest they paid to the bank. As one woman who obtained a bank loan explained: "I have no idea [what rate of interest I paid]. That's something I wasn't smart about, watching the interest rates."

A further result of developing relationships with Lakota businesses is that the Lakota Fund is generating important organizational integrity. At the macrolevel of the reservation, institutions like the Lakota Fund, within the social networks of Pine Ridge, are able to develop social links with financial institutions outside the reservation to enhance economic development, where individual attempts to forge such relationships have been rejected. For example, the Lakota Fund has been able to attract socially responsible investors for their lending capital nationally from Boston to San Francisco, providing no more than a 3 percent return for an investment of at least one year. The Lakota Fund is able to bypass the historically constructed exclusion of Indians from social relationships with border-town banks and reach macrolevel synergies through otherwise unexplored social relationships at the national level.

It is important to account for the impact of cultural and social relationships on the efficacy of an institution before introducing the institution to an area. We have elsewhere analyzed the Lakota Fund's attempt to introduce Grameen Bank–type credit groups to the reservation through the Circle Banking Project (Pickering and Mushinski 2001). The Grameen Bank structure was designed to cross family lines; family members were not permitted to be in the same group. A key attribute of the credit groups is joint liability for the loans of other group members. While the incentives created by the structure worked, the Circle Banking Project ultimately failed for lack of participation. We argued that the project failed because it ignored the role of tiyospayes in Lakota culture. People from different tiyospayes have insufficient knowledge of each other and insufficient ability to monitor each other and enforce loan repayment to make them feel comfortable accepting joint liability. As one young Lakota woman explained: "The way I feel about the community as a whole is that there's a lot of people that don't trust others, but for me, I don't go around those people. I just go around the ones I can trust." People from the same tiyospaye, on the other hand, have that knowledge and those abilities.

CONCLUSION

The results in this analysis indicate that formal and informal credit markets in the Pine Ridge Indian Reservation are not deep enough to produce efficient market outcomes. It is no surprise that residents of Pine Ridge have limited access to formal credit markets, such as bank loans. There is a climate of perceived discrimination against Lakota people and reservation businesses by banks. Far from benign social networks harmoniously waiting to make new linkages, the social relationships of border towns developed explicitly with Lakota exclusion in mind. Informal credit markets, while they are present, do not meet the credit needs of home-based entrepreneurs and small-business people. Family and friends meet some credit needs but they are not available to everyone, and the amounts that can be obtained tend to be limited. The insufficiency of informal credit markets indicates that inefficiencies persist. The Lakota Fund is an example of an institution introduced deliberately to fill some of the credit gaps left by formal and informal institutions. The Lakota Fund is able to use local information, experience with the Pine Ridge economy, and training and technical assistance to extend credit to enterprises that would not be considered by banks for formal business loans. There is potential for other local social institutions to play a role in access to credit, but connections with external financial resources are critical.

From a broader perspective, these results reinforce the importance of examining social relationships to understand the functions of both formal and informal economic institutions. In given settings, the absence of social ties between resource-poor communities and resource-controlling communities has been historically structured by powerful political, economic, and social interests (Duncan 1999; Loury 1992). The danger, then, becomes that emphasizing social relationships as the answer to poverty will create a blind spot similar to that first fostered by modernization theory, where local communities are examined in isolation for their role in obstructing economic development. Local cultural cohesion is being portrayed as the culprit for underdevelopment (Woolcock 1998:171–172), while the much greater and more powerful role of regional, national, and international interests in maintaining extractive and predatory relationships to poor peripheries is ignored (Frank 1969; Hechter 1999; Rodney 1974; Tabb 1970; Taylor 1996). The importance of class, race, and ethnicity in explaining economic and social relationships must stay on the research agenda (Biolsi 2001; Duncan 1999; Halperin 1998; Munck 2000). Social relationships are used both to include the group to whom benefits flow and to exclude the groups to whom benefits are consciously denied (Byrne 1999; Mingione 1996).

Furthermore, the mere presence of local informal institutions does not mean that formal market inefficiencies have been mitigated. While the social cohesiveness of a local community may be enough to provide alternative social institutions, the undercapitalization of these networks means their economic development potential is still limited. Poor communities may generate social institutions that help redistribute local resources to those who need them most, but they may also need market interventions to access the level of financial resources necessary to actually improve economic conditions. Economic analysis of local informal markets should include an assessment of the total local financial resources available within the community and the ways in which social exclusion may limit their access to more significant external financial resources (Byrne 1999). Similarly, introduction of new nonmarket institutions must include linkages through those institutions to external financial resources.

NOTES

1. Credit rationing arises when someone is willing to borrow at existing interest rates and lending terms but cannot obtain a loan.

2. See Townsend 1994 for an analysis of the efficiency of informal markets in developing areas. We also note that even if informal markets achieve efficient outcomes, noneconomic (equitable) rationales for external intervention in credit markets may exist.

3. Unemployment rates for the reservation, including discouraged workers, have consistently exceeded 70 percent (Aoki and Chatman 1997). The unemployment rate reported by the Bureau of Indian Affairs in 1999 was 73 percent, although some speculate that it is even higher. Underemployment is also common on the reservation. In the Random Sample, 50 percent of the households reported some wage income, yet 66 percent remained below the poverty threshold.

4. Three additional forms of credit (credit cards, pawn shops, and suppliers) were identified by participants. Those sources are discussed in the section on community-based lending.

5. The table below contains descriptive statistics for the random sample and the Lakota Fund home-based entrepreneurs.

Table 9.2 Mean Values of Socioeconomic Characteristics of Random Sample and Lakota Fund Home-based Entrepreneurs

Socioeconomic Characteristic	Random Sample (n=62)	Lakota Fund Home-based Entrepreneurs (n=18)
Sex (% Female)	63	83
Age	45	49
Number in Household	6.4	6.5
Years of Education	11.6	10.9
Annual Household Income ($)	21564	22061
Annual Household Income Per Capita ($)	5006	4007
Currently Own Business (%)	32	77

6. Credit-rationed households fall into one of several categories (Mushinski 1999). First, households that applied for a loan and were rejected are credit-rationed. Second, households that may have been willing to obtain a loan at existing market rates but did not apply for a loan, either because they did not believe they could get a loan (the probability of receiving a loan offer was too low), the costs of loan application were too high, or they did not have sufficient collateral, are said to be preemptively rationed. Households that accepted alternative forms of credit at rates that are higher than the current interest rate charged by banks may provide further evidence of preemptive rationing. Finally, some households may have applied for a loan and received a lower loan amount than they sought, which is described as quantity rationing.

REFERENCES

Adamson, Rebecca. 1997. Native American Credit Market: Opportunity Knocks, but Relationships Stay. *Journal of Lending and Credit Risk Management* 80(2):32–35.

Aoki, Andrew, and Dan Chatman. 1997. *An Economic Development Policy for the Oglala Nation.* Harvard Project on American Indian Economic Development, April.

Besanko, David, and Anjan Thakor. 1987. Collateral and Rationing: Sorting Equilibria in Monopolistic and Competitive Credit Markets. *International Economic Review* 28(3):671–689.

Besley, Timothy. 1995. Nonmarket Institutions for Credit and Risk Sharing in Low-Income Countries. *Journal of Economic Perspectives* 9(3):115–127.

Besley, Timothy, and Stephen Coate. 1995. Group Lending, Repayment Incentives, and Social Collateral. *Journal of Development Economics* 46(1):1–18.

Bester, Helmut. 1987. The Role of Collateral in Credit Markets with Imperfect Information. *European Economic Review* 31(4):887–899.

Biolsi, Thomas. 2001. *Deadliest Enemies: Law and the Making of Race Relations on and off Rosebud Reservation*. Berkeley and Los Angeles: University of California Press.

Byrne, David. 1999. *Social Exclusion*. Philadelphia: Open University Press.

Carter, Michael R. 1988. Equilibrium Credit Rationing of Small Farm Agriculture. *Journal of Development Economics* 28:83–103.

Duncan, Cynthia M. 1999. *Worlds Apart: Why Poverty Persists in Rural America*. New Haven, Conn.: Yale University Press.

Frank, Andre Gunder. 1969. *Latin America: Underdevelopment or Revolution: Essays on the Development of Underdevelopment and the Immediate Enemy*. New York: Monthly Review Press.

Freixas, Xavier, and Jean-Charles Rochet. 1998. *Microeconomics of Banking*. Cambridge, Mass.: MIT Press.

Granovetter, Mark S. 1973. The Strength of Weak Ties. *American Journal of Sociology* 78(6):1360–1380.

Guinnane, Timothy W. 1994. A Failed Institutional Transplant: Raiffeisen's Credit Cooperatives in Ireland, 1894–1914. *Explorations in Economic History* 31(1):38–61.

Halperin, Rhoda. 1998. *Practicing Community: Class, Culture, and Power in an Urban Neighborhood*. Austin: University of Texas Press.

———. 1988. *Economies across Cultures*. New York: St. Martin's.

Hechter, Michael. 1999 [1975]. *Internal Colonialism*. New Brunswick, N.J.: Transaction Publishers.

Hoff, Karla, and Joseph Stiglitz. 1990. Introduction: Imperfect Information and Rural Credit Markets—Puzzles and Policy Perspectives. *World Bank Economic Review* 4(3):235–250.

Loury, Glenn C. 1992. The Economics of Discrimination: Getting to the Core of the Problem. *Harvard Journal of African American Public Policy* 1:91–110.

Malinowski, Bronislaw. 1984 [1922]. *Argonauts of the Western Pacific.* Prospect Heights, Ill.: Waveland Press.

Mauss, Marcel. 1967 [1925]. *The Gift.* Ian Cunnison, trans. New York: W. W. Norton.

Mingione, Enzo. 1996. Urban Poverty in the Advanced Industrial World: Concepts, Analysis and Debates. In *Urban Poverty and the Underclass: A Reader.* Enzo Mingione, ed. Pp. 3–40. Oxford: Blackwell.

———. 2000. Market and Society: The Social Embeddedment of the Economy. In *Social Economy.* Eric Shragge and Jean-Marc Fontan, eds. Pp. 16–35. Montreal: Black Rose Books.

Mushinski, David. 1999. An Analysis of Offer Functions of Banks and Credit Unions in Guatemala. *Journal of Development Studies* 36(2):87–111.

Mushinski, David, and Kathleen Pickering. 1996. Micro-Enterprise Credit in Indian Country. *Research in Human Capital and Development* 10:147–169.

Nash, Manning. 1967 [1958]. *Machine Age Maya.* Chicago: University of Chicago Press.

Pickering, Kathleen. 2000. *Lakota Culture, World Economy.* Lincoln: University of Nebraska Press.

———. 2001. Legislating Development through Welfare Reform: Indiscernible Jobs, Insurmountable Barriers, and Invisible Agendas on the Pine Ridge and Rosebud Indian Reservations. *Political and Legal Anthropology Review* 24(1):38–52.

———. 2003. Report to the Oglala Oyate Woitancan Empowerment Zone. Kyle, S.D.

Pickering, Kathleen, and David Mushinski. 2001. Cultural Aspects of Credit Institutions: Transplanting the Grameen Bank Credit Group Structure to the Pine Ridge Indian Reservation. *Journal of Economic Issues* 35(2):459–467.

Polanyi, Karl. 1957 [1944]. *The Great Transformation.* Boston: Beacon Press.

Portes, Alejandro, and Julia Sensenbrenner. 1993. Embeddedness and Immigration: Notes on the Social Determinants of Economic Action. *American Journal of Sociology* 98(6):1320–1350.

Radcliffe-Brown, A. R. 1965 [1952]. *Structure and Function in Primitive Society.* New York: Free Press.

Rodney, Walter. 1974. *How Europe Underdeveloped Africa.* Washington, D.C.: Howard University Press.

Serageldin, Ismail, and Christiaan Grootaert. 2000. Defining Social Capital: An Integrating View. In *Social Capital: A Multifaceted Perspective.* Partha Dasgupta and Ismail Serageldin, eds. Pp. 40–58. Washington, D.C.: World Bank.

Sherman, Richard. 1988. *A Study of Traditional and Informal Sector Micro-Enterprise Activity and Its Impact on the Pine Ridge Indian Reservation Economy.* Washington, D.C.: Aspen Institute for Humanistic Studies.

Stiglitz, Joseph. 1990. Peer Monitoring and Credit Markets. *World Bank Economic Review* 4(3):351–366.

———. 2000. Formal and Informal Institutions. In *Social Capital: A Multifaceted Perspective.* Partha Dasgupta and Ismail Serageldin, eds. Pp. 59–68. Washington, D.C.: World Bank.

Stiglitz, Joseph, and Andrew Weiss. 1981. Credit Rationing in Markets with Imperfect Information. *American Economic Review* 71(3):393–410.

Tabb, William K. 1970. *The Political Economy of the Black Ghetto.* New York: W. W. Norton.

Taylor, Peter. 1996. *The Way the Modern World Works.* New York: John Wiley & Sons.

Townsend, Robert M. 1994. Risk and Insurance in Village India. *Econometrica* 62(3):539–591.

Udry, Christopher. 1990. Credit Markets in Northern Nigeria: Credit as Insurance in a Rural Economy. *World Bank Economic Review* 4(3):251–269.

Wagoner, Paula. 2002. *"They Treated Us Just Like Indians": The Worlds of Bennett County, South Dakota.* Lincoln: University of Nebraska Press.

Woolcock, Michael. 1998. Social Capital and Economic Development: Toward a Theoretical Synthesis and Policy Framework. *Theory and Society* 27(2):151–208.—

———. 2001. Microenterprise and Social Capital: A Framework for Theory, Research, and Policy. *Journal of Socio-Economics* 30(2):193–198.

III

CONTEMPORARY VALUABLES AND SYMBOLIC VALUES

10

Inalienable Wealth in North American Households

Eric J. Arnould, Carolyn Folkman Curasi, and Linda L. Price

Henceforth it seems clear that the social cannot be reduced to the sum of possible forms of exchange among humans and therefore cannot originate or be grounded solely in exchange, contract or the symbolic. Beyond the sphere of exchanges lie other domains, another sphere constituted of all that humans imagine they must withhold from exchange, reciprocity, and rivalry, which they must conserve, preserve, and increase.

Maurice Godelier (1999:35)

In this chapter, we turn our attention not to exchange and its objects (things that people buy or things that people give), but to objects outside the limits of exchange—*things that people should not give or sell, but keep—inalienable possessions* (Weiner 1992; Godelier 1999). Relatively familiar examples varying in scale of significance could include collections, family Bibles, religious relics, national archaeological treasures, and strategic gold reserves (Belk 2001; Goux 1991; Weiner 1994). To illustrate the affective power of the desire to keep things out of exchange, imagine citizen reaction if an American president tried to give the original U.S. Constitution as a gift to a foreign leader (Shore 1992).

This chapter's specific purpose is to explore whether and how objects pass from alienable to inalienable status across generations of families situated in contemporary consumer culture. That is, we are interested in the metamorphosis of cherished possessions, those items our informants cherish, into objects that should not be given or sold, but kept within the confines of a kinship structure—inalienable possessions. Our study is situated among middle-class American families and focuses on one category of potentially inalienable wealth: cherished or special possessions. A possible connection between cherished objects, "keepsakes," and inalienable wealth has been broached superficially in previous research. However, the connections remain largely undertheorized (Finch and Mason 2000; Marcoux 2001; Price, Arnould, and Curasi 2000).

In the next sections, we detail the nature of inalienable possessions and their potential role in contemporary families. Following a description of our research activity, we outline our findings and conclude with implications for the exploration of inalienable wealth in contemporary consumer culture. We illustrate similarities between our findings on middle-class American inalienable wealth and discussions of inalienable wealth focused on indigenous peoples. Further, we identify avenues for future research on inalienable wealth in contemporary consumer cultures.

INALIENABLE POSSESSIONS

The growing literature on inalienable possessions reveals a diversity of perspectives. Upon reviewing the literature, we identified six key points about inalienable possessions that are both central to the literature and useful starting points for further inquiry. First, inalienable possessions are powerful. They become priceless, and people hold them out from exchange because they speak to and for an individual's or a group's social identity. In so doing, they affirm felt differences between one person or group and another (Weiner 1992:43). Even if a group is subjugated or enslaved, retention of inalienable objects promises group emancipation and triumph (Godelier 1999). The millennial struggle for control of Middle Eastern holy sites is invested with this kind of drama.

Second, one reason inalienable possessions play a powerful role in legitimating group and individual identity is that their origins are thought to lie "outside the human world, in some sacred, changeless order, and changeless because it is sacred" (Godelier 1999:124; Belk, Wallendorf, and Sherry 1989; Pannell 1994). While Durkheim argued that society is the ultimate source of the sacred, Godelier observes that sacred inalienable objects typically become detached in space and/or time in such a way that, over time, their human origins fade and disappear, to be replaced by "supernatural" powers legitimated through stories and myths (Durkheim 1965; Godelier 1999, Lévi-Strauss 1987). Things that are kept (inalienable) metaphorically transport an individual or group back to another time, to their origins (Godelier 1999:200).

Third, caretakers and guardians fear the loss of inalienable possessions. Loss, whether through forgetting, theft, or market alienation, entails a loss of authority, history, or mythology. Indigenous people describe the loss of an inalienable object as "the most serious evil which could befall a group" (Pannell 1994:28). In a sense, the loss of inalienable objects foreshadows a group's devastation or extinction (Kirsch 2001; Radin 1993). The Lakota people's long struggle to defend their sacred Black Hills from mineral exploitation—a potent symbol of their way of life—is a case in point, but others could be cited (e.g., MacDonald 2001).

Fourth, individuals may possess inalienable objects, but individuals do not own them. Ownership is an alienable construct, entangled with rights to give and sell (Pannell 1994; Radin 1993). Group ancestors and deities retain ownership of inalienable objects and the right to repossess these gifts. Consequently, custodians merely enjoy use rights in inalienable possessions.

Fifth, custodians can and must share with the group the positive effects that emanate from the powers that inalienable possessions contain (Godelier 1999:122). Custodians of inalienable wealth preserve the objects and the knowledge that goes with them. In order to bear or name and socialize a future custodian, caretakers are often exempt from some ordinary social responsibilities and are gifted with reproductive opportunities (Godelier 1999).

Sixth, for an object to remain inalienable, it is only necessary that the social order and reality legitimated by the objects be accepted and shared by the members of the group. At the same time, members of the group share sacred meanings that may resist explicit expression and representation (Godelier 1999). People outside the group may or may not decode some of the public meanings of inalienable wealth.

As the preceding paragraphs hint, inalienable wealth has analytic value in the contexts in which it has been studied. It remains to be seen whether the construct is of analytic value in contemporary Western consumer cultures in which commodity and gift exchange predominate, and social change and fragmentation, cultural heterogeneity, elective identity, and high levels of geographic mobility are characteristic (Giddens 1992; Grodin and Lindlof 1996; Kellner 1992; Smart and Neale 1999).

CONTEMPORARY FAMILIES AND INALIENABLE WEALTH

Several studies claim that transmission of special possessions within families in late-modern consumer culture is significant. One study showed how attics and basements serve as repositories of mnemonic family objects (Korosec-Serfaty 1984). With respect to patterns of personal property kept within the family in England, Finch and Mason (2000:161) observe that their interviewees seemed more engaged emotionally with inherited individual keepsakes, objects retained in memory of an event or giver and usually of no value, than they were with material resources. Many individuals in families they studied displayed a clear stake in the symbolic significance of these items. A third project details the reasons why, and ways in which, special possessions are distributed to descendant kin in middle-class American families (Price, Arnould, and Curasi 2000). This study shows that older people worry about the "biography" of a few special possessions, are concerned that they go to the right person, and hope they will be preserved for future kin. British and American inheritors of keepsakes claim that they are charged with qualities of previous owners (see also Grayson and Shulman 2000; McCracken 1988; Sussman, Cates, and Smith 1970; Tobin 1996; Unruh 1983; Wallendorf and Arnould 1988). Objects may also provide iconic symbols of descendants' relationships with deceased kinsfolk. Finally, keepsakes provide vehicles for animating memories—creating, shaping, and sustaining them (Finch and Mason 2000:172; Grafton Small 1993).

Our review of research on inalienable wealth and late-modern family ties raises the following research questions: Are inherited emblems of family relationships an important source of personal identity, difference, and distinction? Do middle-class Americans seek to collect and bring into the present the history, achievements, and titles of their ancestors? In a context of elective family ties, are emblems of ancestors and kinship destined to return to the alienable domain of gifts and commodities after a single generation? Are they possibly converted to inalienable wealth? Do individuals act as guardians of special objects for future generations? Do guardians use cherished inherited objects to convey values and meanings of significance to their kin? Do Western consumers use inalienable objects as signs of imagined values? Our findings address these empirical questions. Table 10.1 summarizes six points from previous research, our research questions, and some apposite illustrations that anticipate our findings. We believe that study of inalienable wealth within a

Table 10.1 Inalienable Wealth: Theoretical Characteristics, Research Questions, and Illustrations

Characteristics	Our Research Questions	Illustrations From Our Data
Inalienable possessions are powerful because they speak to and for an individual's or a group's social identity and affirm felt differences between one person or group and another (Weiner 1992, 43).	Are inherited emblems of family relationships an important source of personal identity, difference, and distinction?	[Referring to a 102-year-old watch that still "runs perfectly to the second"] That was really a masterpiece kind of thing, and I know when I see my mother wear it that is connecting with her own family . . . and so I think it was not not just a family heirloom as much as it was a symbol of the kind of people they were. They were precise . . . they valued things; they hung onto things and after going through the Depression, they placed a lot of value on something like a fine watch. It probably was one of the few symbols of any kind of maybe, wealth that they might have had (Linnea, 45 years old, referring to June).
Inalienable possessions have legitimating power because their origins are thought to lie "outside the human world, in some sacred, changeless order, and changeless because it is sacred" (Godelier 1999, 124).	Do middle-class Americans seek to collect and bring into the present the history, achievements, and titles of their ancestors?	The Bible, I always remember it being in the family. My grandparents, and then my mother was the oldest daughter so she got it, and then I got it and I will pass it to my oldest daughter. So it's at least four generations right now . . . Because that Bible is so old, and it has all of the births and deaths and marriages. So it is used as a legal register (Della, 93 years old).
Caretakers and guardians fear loss of inalienable possessions because loss places at risk the special knowledge and attributes that define the group (Kirsch 2001, 177).	In a context of elective family ties, are emblems of ancestors and kinship destined to return to the alienable domain of gifts and commodities after a single generation? Are they possibly converted to inalienable wealth?	Yes, I have leather suitcases. I forgot about them until we started talking about them. They were my grandparents. They were leather bound everywhere, um, they are in mint condition with silk lining. They are heavy even when nothing is in them. I'm afraid to even use them, because I'm afraid that they will get stolen. Um, they are all leather bound and I got those when my father passed away, they were my grandparents. . . . They will be passed down through my generation, kids hopefully (Phyllis, 32 years old).

(continued)

Table 10.1 Inalienable Wealth: Theoretical Characteristics, Research Questions, and Illustrations *(continued)*

Characteristics	Our Research Questions	Illustrations From Our Data
People possess inalienable objects, but do not own them. Ancestors and gods retain ownership of inalienable objects, and the right to repossess these gifts. Objects should not be given except for extraordinary reasons (Godelier 1999; Weiner 1992).	Do individuals act as guardians of special objects for future generations?	Ellen: He said for me to save it for George when he gets older. Sam: What does ownership of this mean to you? Ellen: Well it's not really mine. I only have one, but I have a silver dollar too. I guess it's worth some money now. Your Grandpa never wanted to give it to George because he was afraid George would spend it or turn it in. So we just kept it in the box. Papa said George can have it when he dies (Ellen, 74 years old).
What can and must be shared with the group are the positive effects that emanate from the powers contained in these objects (Godelier 1999, p. 122).	Do guardians use cherished inherited objects to convey values and meanings of significance to their kin? If so, how?	Are there any special occasions that you think you would bring out the blankets to share with people? When we have family gatherings at my house, I would love to bring out the quilt to show the family and all sit around and talk about our memories. I feel that would be a very special time to share the quilt (Jan, 31 years old).
The social order and reality legitimated by the objects must be accepted and shared by the members of the group for objects to remain inalienable. While people outside the group may decode some of the public meanings of inalienable wealth, the sacred meanings shared by members of the group resist expression and representation (Godelier 1999).	Do Western consumers use inalienable objects as signs of imagined values?	There are a lot of memories associated with each of these teacups and my daughter would love to hold onto those memories and share them with her children and grandchildren. I realize that the significance of the teacup set from my father will not be the same for someone else but my daughter places a lot of importance on family and the history of our family. These teacups were acquired over a period of approximately forty years, some as gifts and some as purchases of mine. . . . To me they are a reminder of the past and how women used to have tea parties and use teacups such as these. The teacups are very delicate and feminine (Edith, 65 years old, Stanley's mother).

Western consumer culture context will enrich and nuance our conception of this construct (Hebdige 1979; Holt 1997; Mosko 2000).

RESEARCH ACTIVITY

Data Collection

Interviewing for this project began in spring 1997 and continued through spring 2000. Data collection continued until new interviews produced only minor thematic variations from previous interviews. In-depth interviews with thirty-eight informants within fifteen family groups, representing twenty-six intergenerational dyads, make up the primary data set for this project. The first and second authors conducted the interviews, which lasted from one to several hours. Seven informants were interviewed on at least two occasions to address specific questions that arose during the analysis and interpretation stages. We interviewed multiple dyads within a family, providing diverse perspectives on particular possessions. After interviewing generational dyads within a family, as we identified new problems or insights and to resolve questions of fact and interpretation, additional dyads were identified and interviewed (Arnould and Wallendorf 1994). Another set of seventy semistructured interviews representing thirty-five intergenerational dyads spread between males and females of three generations supplemented our primary set of interviews. Trained interviewers conducted these interviews in informants' homes; they ranged between thirty-five and ninety minutes. In about half of these cases, interviewers and informants were blood relations. A small number of telephone interviews were used to contact geographically dispersed family members, and in some cases interviewers traveled to interview informants.

Analysis

As the data collection progressed, we examined the transcribed interviews for emergent categories and patterns. Typical of interpretive methods, additional categories emerged as the investigation progressed, reflecting the increasing complexity of our understanding of the research topic and of the data collected. Analysis focused on understanding common and contrasting structures in the informants' emic representations of practices and meanings associated with cherished possessions and of strategies used to keep objects within the family (Wallendorf and Arnould 1991). Three types of analyses were employed: analyses focused on an informant, between informants within a family, and between informants across our sample of middle-class Americans (Thompson 1997).

Trustworthiness

We incorporated several techniques to ensure the trustworthiness of our results and increase the theoretical generativity of our work (Stewart 1999; Wallendorf and Belk 1989). First, to better understand inalienable wealth creation from the perspective of different family members, we triangulated across informants. Second, trustworthiness was addressed through triangulation across our team of analysts, a team reflecting diversity in gender, research experience, and academic training. Finally, member checks were used to compare our interpretation with that of informants intimately involved in the phenomenon (Wallendorf and Belk 1989; Belk, Sherry, and Wallendorf 1988).

FINDINGS

We begin this section by illustrating that our informants believe that certain objects are inalienable and should be retained within the family for future generations. Next, we consider how the legitimacy of inalienable objects is created and shared across generations. Consistent with previous researchers, we demonstrate the importance of storytelling and ritual use in legitimating inalienable objects within a kinship group. Third, we consider guardianship of inalienable possessions. Guardianship is typically not an ascribed role as in the indigenous cultures examined in other research. Guardian duties uncovered in our research parallel previous findings on this topic (Godelier 1999, Weiner 1992). Fourth, we consider the fragility of inalienable wealth. Contrasting with previous research, our data provide evidence of objects moving from inalienable to alienable owing to a variety of internal (within the group) and external (outside the group) factors.

Things That Should Be Kept

This section shows that our informants believe certain objects are inalienable and should be retained within the family for future generations. In contrast to previous writings on this subject, we illustrate active strategic attempts to move objects from alienable to inalienable and note that the objects themselves are generally not very old—human origins have not faded and disappeared.

> *Well, let's talk about that for a minute. Can you give me an example?* I have all these shells I've been collecting since I started dating your father in 1966. I have them displayed in the wall unit over there in the dining room. They are only

special to me. Maybe a granddaughter or grandson might like them, if I ever have one. *Why are they special to you Mom?* Well they remind me of when I was younger, not that I'm that old 'cause I am still collecting shells, you know. But some of them came from different places that we have been on vacation and things. So they are keepsakes to me, reminders of fun times. The ones I have are all real special, you know. I don't just get regular shells; I look for small, tiny, perfect ones. My collection has all different shells in it. All types. You can have my shell collections, Sam. But if you don't want to display it, you have to promise me that you will take it out on a boat off of the coast of Pensacola and throw them all back in the ocean. In deep water. I mean it, will you do that? If no one wants it, then I want to give them all back to the ocean. I couldn't stand for them to be put in a box or crushed or thrown away in the trash. Hey, I have a better idea! When I am cremated, I want you to put my shells in with me and let them burn up with me. (laughing) Really, do that. Then throw my ashes in the ocean, and the shells and I will be all mixed together. Are you going to write all this down? Oh God, I should shut up.

This conversation between Sheila, age fifty, and her son Sam, the interviewer, is an almost prototypical tale of a mundane object that is in the process of becoming a thing that should be kept as inalienable and, if not kept, should be returned to a supernatural realm. The story, like others reported below, has a classic narrative structure (Riessman 1993). For example, the moral point is that if not cherished by her descendants, her special possessions should be returned to nature, "back to the ocean." During her interview, Sheila describes several objects, each with its own unfolding story, that she would like to become inalienable, kept in the family. She observes, "And I want your children and wife to remember me, and their children, etc. I want to be part of their lives. Someday someone would say, this bracelet came from my Great, Great, Great, Great Grandmother Sheila (laughing). I guess I'm silly, but I am sentimental. I wish I had things from my grandparents, particularly things I could wear like jewelry pieces or rings, etc. That would mean a lot to me."

Sheila is forthright in her desire for symbolic immortality and hopes to accomplish it through objects that substitute for her (Godelier 1999; Tobin 1996; Unruh 1983). Although Sam is not married, Sheila has thought about things he should give his future wife and when (after he's sure she's "a keeper" and for anniversaries) and has thought about his children.

Sheila has only one thing that she would consider a family heirloom. This is a picture of her father with his family when he was about eight years old. She rescued it from one of her mother's drawers (her mother never liked the picture) and now displays it prominently with her new, modern living room set. Ellen, Sheila's mother (age seventy-four), thinks this looks horrible. She mentions the object without any particular fondness, observing:

> Well, I don't know about value, but lately this picture everyone wants, Grandpa's sister, Olympia, asked me about it, and now Holly (Sheila's sister) is mad because they saw it in Sheila's house and she wants it. Holly wants me to take it away from Sheila and give it to her. (laughing) I'm not gonna do that. Hell, she can have it. I said she could have it.

Naturally, Sheila warns Sam (her only child) that he should keep this picture and pass it forward to his children, and so on, and "don't let your Aunt Holly get it!" Sheila, born to Depression-era parents who themselves were born to first-generation immigrants, is typical of many of our informants from this generation. She has few items that have been passed forward to her but is seeking to create an endowment of inalienable wealth for her future lineage. Many of our informants describe an object, observing that it should be kept because it is the only object passed down from a previous generation. It is their only claim to an ancestral past. Margery, age sixty-eight, the second youngest of ten children, observes of her only heirloom: "It is very special. I don't have anything else since there were nine children in the family; this is the only heirloom that I could get."

Our informants' ideas about things that should be kept differ from the findings of other studies of inalienable wealth. Previous research depicts inalienable wealth as detached in space and/or time in such a way that the human origins of the objects fade and then disappear (Godelier 1999:179). From our informants' talk of things that should be kept, we are struck by the paucity of things named, the short time horizons over which objects have become "things to be kept," and the near universality of our informants naming at least one thing that should be kept.

The Social Order and Reality Affirmed by Inalienable Family Objects

Next, we consider how the legitimacy of inalienable objects is created and shared across generations. Our data revealed the importance of storytelling and ritual use in legitimating inalienable objects within a kinship group. Extending previous research, we emphasize the strategic use of storytelling and changes in ritual use that informants exploit to demarcate movement from alienable to inalienable status.

Weiner (1992) and Godelier (1999) note that, to survive as inalienable possessions, objects must affirm a social order and reality that is viewed as legitimate and shared from generation to generation. However, the objects they study seem to have incontrovertible legitimacy within membership groups and were thought to have survived since the groups' origins. Our data access specific ways in which the legitimacy of inalienable wealth is created and affirmed across generations of middle-class American families. Consider Fanny, an only child, now in her seventies, who was given her father's pocket watch, now safely stored "at the bank." Fanny tells us that the minute she received this object, she knew it was something that should be kept within the family, and she hopes to pass it to her oldest grandson. But she also tells us that she would consider selling it because "the new generation don't appreciate anything. And why should I hand it down and it not be as appreciated as I have?" Fanny tells stories that vividly convey her father's strenuous efforts to preserve the watch and pass it forward, and she affirms the transfer of this moral lesson: "I feel like he's part of me there." Despite her strong feelings for the watch and her belief that it should be kept, Fanny, like other informants, fears that the legitimacy of the object will not be affirmed by future generations. Thus, informants often convey the fragile legitimacy of objects and the social order they represent.

In the next sections, we describe storytelling and ritual use, display, and maintenance as central to creating and maintaining inalienable wealth. Both storytelling and ritual use convey the sacred status and power of the object and affirm a social order and reality ideally reproduced by each new generation.

Storytelling

Informants who strategize to create inalienable family possessions from their cherished objects recognize the importance of storytelling. An excellent illustration surrounds a ring that Mrs. Thompson, age seventy-two, hopes will become an inalienable possession. The ring is a gift from Mrs. Thompson's late husband, Jeff, and she tells a detailed, emotional, and romantic story of how she came to have the ring. She plans to pass this to her only daughter, Patricia, age forty-five, with whom she has a close affective relationship, noting, "She has always seen it on me. The ring will always remind her of me after I am gone. To me that is important." Here, she recognizes the legitimating potential of her own contamination of the ring, and the amalgamated stories and meanings that her daughter Patty will bundle with the ring. Telling the story of the object helps Mrs. Thompson to relive an important moment in her own history that coincides with a historical moment in time (the end of World War II) and brings into the present a departed loved one (Price, Arnould, and Curasi 2000). Nevertheless, she tells the story for strategic reasons as well, and it is here that we learn something about the origins of inalienable wealth. She observes with regard to her daughter, "I told her the story a bunch of times, and she always got excited to hear about it, and was very interested with the details." This illustrates the rehearsal of stories that is so important to assure the object endorses a social order and reality affirmed from generation to generation. Mrs. Thompson reveals her aim: "I want the ring to start becoming a family heirloom, and to be passed on to generations. When it's passed down, I want my daughter to tell her daughter, Amanda, the story behind it."

Amanda, age twenty-two, is targeted as the next recipient because Mrs. Thompson and Amanda's older sister "have our differences." However, Amanda and Amanda's older sister, Emily, age twenty-eight, reveal that Emily has been targeted to receive certain prize possessions from her grandmother on her father's side of the family. From Amanda, we learn several interesting things. Unprompted, she reveals her desire to receive the ring and pass it on to her children. A further probe discloses: "My guess would be that I'd pass down the ring to my oldest daughter, assuming I'll get it from my mom. If I have only boys, I'll probably give it to my oldest son's wife. . . . Hopefully it will be something that will become a family heirloom in the future."

Inherited objects, cherished by recipients because they are contaminated with the spirit of their owners, are unlikely to become inalienable without narrative intervention. We encountered several instances when objects' stories had not been told. Not surprisingly, in such cases younger family members either did not know of the cherished possession or lacked significant feelings toward it. Three family dyads (the oldest daughter and mother, the younger daughter and mother, and the son and mother) illustrate this outcome. The failure of transmission occurs despite evident contamination through associ-ation with the objects' originators and presence in families that value inalien-able wealth. Matilda, the mother (age seventy-six), told a story of a cherished seascape painting.

> This picture up here, this painting, my husband and I had gone to an art sale. And I had saved enough money to buy myself a new dryer. And we both saw that picture and fell in love with it. And so we took the money we had saved for a dryer, and bought the picture. (laughs) That was one of the most foolish things we did. . . . It reminded me of home. Because I was born in Pensacola, and there was just something about it, those sand dunes, you know. My husband felt the same way about it. We both just fell in love with that picture. It was really funny, because we don't usually do things frivolous like that. We are very con-servative. But we both just decided that we needed that picture more than we needed a new dryer.

Matilda discusses the painting at length. It represents the contrast between a time when Matilda and her husband's financial status enabled them to make a "frivolous" purchase and the memory of being a teenager during the Great Depression when such financial frivolity was inconceivable. The painting also represents an idyll of youthful freedom and whimsicality lost, as today "they don't even allow you to have fires on the beach."

Both Matilda's daughters and her son were surprised to learn that their mother cherished the painting, and none had heard Matilda's vivid origin story. Here we see an interesting disjuncture between a cherished object that has profound private meanings and a potentially inalienable object that has the capacity to speak for the identity of the family. The oral text bundled with the cherished painting stands in opposition to family values and household tradition. Matilda sees her family as conservative, not frivolous. She would not want this painting to speak for her family's identity.

Possession Use, Display, and Maintenance

Godelier (1999:125) describes his first view of the most sacred inalienable object of the Baruya clan:

> [D]elicately his fingers spread the bark. Finally he opened it [net bag] completely, and I saw lying side by side, a black stone, some long pointed bones, and several flat brown disks. I was unable to say or ask anything. The man had begun to cry,

silently, keeping his gaze averted from what lay before him. He remained in that posture several minutes, . . . and, with the same delicacy and the same precautions, reassembled the packet and wrapped it in the red *ypmoulie.*

Evident here are the care taken to preserve the object and the ritual use and display by the clan's authorized caretaker. Oral texts and especially stories of origin that accompany inalienable objects are central to objects' distinctive value in our data. But as Weiner (1992) insists, along with the stories, objects must be preserved, and rituals of use, display, and maintenance that give these possessions authenticating force must be passed forward.

Our informants provide numerous illustrations of how, as objects move from alienable to inalienable, their display and use is altered to reflect their now sacred status. Josie, eighty-three, describes a sword that belonged to her grandfather, a Civil War veteran. He carried it with him at the battle of Vicksburg. She inherited it when she was only three, because she was "his namesake and his favorite grandchild," and plans to pass it on to her grandson (her son John's son and namesake). Although Josie has stories about the sword, she has no memories of her grandfather with the sword and only vague recollections of him. Nevertheless, she preserves the sword, hides it when she leaves town, and sees it as a proud, distinctive family possession to be kept by future generations. Josie's ritual care of the sword is also noted in our interview with John.

As objects move from alienable to inalienable, caretakers are likely to encase them in protected environments, subject them to ritual use, and limit who handles them to caretakers and initiates into the caretaker role. Maria, age forty-nine, explicitly notes in an interview with her daughter, Claire, that as she came to understand the significance of an object to the family, her own use of that object changed.

Your grandmother gave me the bracelet her mother gave her when she was born. I remember it from when I was little. I always loved it, and Mama would let me wear it around the house if I asked. She gave it to me at my forty-sixth-birthday party. I cried because it meant a lot to me. I always wanted it. . . . She also told me to cherish it and give it to you when the time was right. . . . It's a dress-up bracelet so I only wear it on special occasions. It's funny because when I was younger, when I would wear it when I was little, I would have worn it every day, all day.

Guardianship of Inalienable Possessions

Next, we consider guardianship of inalienable possessions. Weiner (1992:104) remarks:

> Someone must attest to the authentication of a possession and to the history that surrounds it. And even when there are few inalienable possessions, someone must decide about their transmission within or, when necessary, outside the group. Those whose knowledge is honored by others enhance or diminish what an inalienable possession represents.

Middle-class North American guardians preserve the objects and the knowledge that goes with them, name and educate a future custodian, and often take on other ritual responsibilities for inalienable objects. Guardianship is typically not an ascribed role as in the cultures examined in other research. Instead, our informants recognize guardianship and its elective quality as in the following comment from Linnea, age forty-five, claiming and defining the role of "family recorder":

> *Is there anyone in particular you would cherish passing the picture on to?*
> Probably my oldest daughter, Lauren, mostly because she had the most contact. I often think that we tend to have one family member who's maybe a little bit more invested in family things. Sort of like a family recorder. I think I'm that for my family. And I think it's likely to be my oldest.

As in the example above, our results show that the preferred guardian for an inalienable object is generally a same-gender descendant, rather than other-gender descendant or same-gender affine (kin through marriage). Amanda, age twenty-two, speculates that if she inherits her grandmother's ring, she will pass it to her daughter, if she has one, and to a daughter-in-law or granddaughter, if she does not. For her part, Sheila, age fifty, laments that she has no daughters to whom to give her jewelry, hopes for granddaughters, and wants to be sure that a daughter-in-law earns her trust before passing any jewelry her way. These cases are typical.

Weiner (1992) and Godelier (1999) describe the interdependence of men and women in preserving gendered inalienable wealth. In our data, when objects cross gender lines, they are normally held in trust until a future caretaker qualifies for guardianship. For example, twenty-eight-year-old Stanley's mother held his grandfather's watch in trust for him. In his case, entering high school was the rite of passage that qualified him as a guardian. Examples of females keeping objects inherited from males for future male guardians occur often in our data. One case concerns a christening dress that four generations of males in one family have worn. The dress links the men in this family, seamlessly connecting the generations. However, guardianship duties for this possession fall to *daughters-in-law,* who are entrusted to christen their sons in it. Dorothy, seventy-five, received the dress from her mother-in-law, who, in turn, received it from hers. Dorothy christened her two sons in it and prevailed upon her daughter-in-law to christen her first son in it. Because someone outside the family (affine) must keep the object in the family, the object's inalienable status is precarious. Dorothy, separated by kinship and geographical distance from her daughter-in-law, expresses considerable anxiety about the future inalienability of the object, asking "how can we [the older generation] pass this caring about cherished things on?"

Guardians should share sacred powers and other benefits of inalienable wealth among the group—giving while keeping (Godelier 1999; Weiner 1992). Several instances in our data depict ritual obligations to the greater family unit accompanying guardianship of inalienable wealth. Commonly these ritual obligations have to do with "keeping the family history," "keeping the family together," or a combination of these two themes. For example, June and her sister-in-law spent three years compiling genealogical information, plus accompanying pictures, articles, and so on, going back as far as their great, great, great-grandmother in two 800- to 900-page books. June declares: "These will always stay with the family. We hope as their children grow, they will continue to put things into the book for them so they'll have references." Linnea, June's daughter, knows these books are coming to her because her aunt warns her "all the time." She sees these books as capturing the values of her father's side of the family: "It shows what they value. . . [T]hey really kept the family together." Like other inherited objects, these books come with a responsibility to "keep the history of the family" and in that way contribute to realizing this goal.

The Fragility of Inalienable Wealth

We have talked in the preceding sections about objects that have passed from alienable to inalienable—from keepsakes contaminated by a previous owner to things that should be kept within the close confines of the family group. This may appear to be a fairy tale about families honoring ancestors and preserving family history. We have focused on such stories because they help to show how inalienable wealth is created, what it means, and how it is preserved in Western consumer culture. At the same time, we found a general paucity of, and recent origin for, most of our informants' inalienable wealth.

Many of our informants' stories have notes of anxiety, points of tension, and uncertain futures. Frances thanks God that her precious crystal was not broken when she moved; Josie worries that her grandfather's Civil War sword will be stolen and hides it when she is out of town; Melinda tells how the family Spode china was almost sold; and Dorothy worries that distant daughters-in-law will not care about the male inalienable wealth entrusted to their care.

Informants who espouse the view that objects should be kept also offer stories of objects that should have been kept but were not. The fear of loss hovering in stories of objects that have become inalienable resonates with stories of objects intended for inalienability that instead were lost. Ella, age seventy-eight, whose mother died when she was a little girl, retains only a couple of keepsakes. One of those objects, a Chinese bowl, is now on display in her daughter's home. She explains why she has so little from her mother and nothing from her father:

> When my mother died, things just kind of got away. My father rented the house for a while and we went to live with my aunt and uncle, the ones that brought me up afterward. He rented the house furnished, and things got broken. . . . My father remarried and the things he had went to his wife and her family. I have nothing.

Contemporary Families and Inalienable Wealth

Does the character of contemporary middle-class American families uniquely shape inalienable wealth? We believe the answer is yes. For example, Maria (age forty-nine) sees herself as different from her mother, Frances (age seventy-eight), in the way she relates to heirlooms. She explains that this is because families have changed.

> Mother has stuff all over the house. It's like a museum to her. It's very important and she is very proud of every single inherited object she has. They . . . (pause) families were different. They all lived together and saw each other every

day so maybe they had more objects that affected their history. Mother would eat out of the plates and crystal that Mary [her sister] gave her. She has a great piece of her past with her that she can reflect on. *So are you saying heirlooms are not as important to you?* No, I'm saying that I cherish certain heirlooms that mean more to me, while my mother sees them all as equally important.

Maria's comment also hints that there may be practical limits to the number of objects that can be kept as inalienable wealth. Further, geographic dispersion makes portability of inalienable wealth a concern.

Divorce also affects inalienable wealth in contemporary families. In some cases, but not all, divorces lead children to want nothing to do with the inalienable wealth of the severed kin. Richard, age fifty-five, recounts how his mother conspired to keep out of a "second family's" hands, and pass on to him, his father's special possessions:

I acquired it after my father passed away, and after his death at seventy-four, my mother had possession of the wings and the little bars, that she had been keeping for me to pass them on to me after his death so that my adoptive brother would not get his hands on them.

CONCLUSION

This brief chapter summarizes research that examines whether and how objects pass from alienable to inalienable status across generations of families situated in contemporary consumer culture (Curasi, Price, and Arnould n.d.). We sought to extend knowledge about connections between cherished objects and inalienable wealth broached anecdotally in previous research. We specifically aimed to identify practices differentiating alienable and inalienable possessions. In this way, we explored behaviors not previously theorized in Western consumer culture. We hope this investigation will inspire researchers to further explore the construct of inalienable possessions and the domain of inalienability.

We provided and summarized in table 10.1 a template in six points that characterizes inalienable wealth as previously theorized. Our detailed findings generally map to these six points and enable us to affirm the presence and significance of inalienable objects in North American middle-class families. Further, our data show that keepsakes passed from one generation to another differ from individuals' cherished objects.

Inalienable wealth differs from keepsakes by virtue of being actively invested with the properties summarized in table 10.1 (see also Price, Arnould, and Curasi 2000). Our point is not to reify the terms "cherished possessions," "keepsakes," or even "inalienable wealth," but to insist on useful analytical differences between these constructs. Our work is the first to do this systematically.

Limitations and Directions for Future Research

Several obvious methodological limitations constrain the theoretical generativity of certain results and suggest avenues for future research (Stewart 1999). Our results are grounded in several in-depth interview data sets reported here and other related work. These results are descriptive of the phenomenon of inalienable wealth and some of its dynamic qualities in North American consumer culture; for example, the small number of possessions, their banality, the role of guardianships, the role of gender in transmission and guardianship, its temporal fragility, and the like. However, space limitations prevent us from describing how inalienable wealth in North American households differs systematically from inalienable wealth in small-scale societies as described by Annette Weiner, Maurice Godelier, and others. Further, future research could explore the question of the ubiquity of inalienability in the general North American population and variations in how it is constituted across class, ethnic, or regional lines. Our results do not provide an exhaustive catalog of systematic variations in objects; selection choice criteria; legitimating stories; moral themes; habits of storage, use, and display; transmission; and guardianship that should exist. All this too could be pursued in future research.

In this chapter, we investigated a domain of consumption relatively new to consumer studies in anthropology: objects outside the limits of exchange, *things that people should not give or sell, but keep,* objects termed *inalienable possessions* in prior research. Our specific purpose was to explore whether and how objects pass from alienable to inalienable status across generations of families situated in contemporary consumer culture, a possibility raised in previous research (Godelier 1999; Weiner 1994). We believe we have uncovered evidence to support the existence of inalienable wealth, and we have hinted at how it differs in character from inalienable wealth studied in indigenous cultural contexts. Through research in a different social context, we have sought to develop a theoretically enriched construct. In a more extended treatment we have begun to explore how inalienable wealth in North American consumer culture differs from inalienable wealth as described in the ethnographic literature and how it informs the structure of North American kinship (Curasi, Price, and Arnould n.d.) We invite others to pursue this inquiry in other cultural contexts.

NOTE

Authors are listed alphabetically to reflect equal contributions.

REFERENCES

Arnould, Eric J., and Melanie Wallendorf. 1994. Market-Oriented Ethnography: Interpretation Building and Marketing Strategy Formulation. *Journal of Marketing Research* 31(4):484–504.

Belk, Russell W. 2001. *Collecting in a Consumer Society*, London: Routledge.

Belk, Russell W., Melanie Wallendorf, and John F. Sherry Jr. 1989. The Sacred and the Profane in Consumer Behavior: Theodicy on the Odyssey. *Journal of Consumer Research* 16(1):1–38.

Belk, Russell W., John F. Sherry Jr., and Melanie Wallendorf. 1988. A Naturalistic Inquiry into Buyer and Seller Behavior at a Swap Meet. *Journal of Consumer Research* 14(4):449–470.

Curasi, Carolyn Folkman, Linda L. Price, and Eric J. Arnould. n.d. Things That Should be Kept: How Cherished Possessions Become Inalienable Wealth. Department of Marketing, J. Mack Robinson College of Business Administration, Georgia State University.

Durkheim, Emile. 1965 [1912]. *The Elementary Forms of Religious Life*. New York: Free Press.

Finch, Janet, and Jennifer Mason. 2000. *Passing On: Kinship and Inheritance in England*. London: Routledge.

Giddens, Anthony. 1992. *The Transformation of Intimacy*. Cambridge, U.K.: Polity Press.

Godelier, Maurice. 1999 [1996]. *The Enigma of the Gift*. Nora Scott, trans. Chicago: University of Chicago Press.

Goux, Jean-Joseph. 1991. Apropos des trois ronds. In *Lacan avec les philosophes*. Bibliotèque du Collège International de Philosophie, ed. Pp. 173–178. Paris: Albin Michel.

Grafton Small, Robert. 1993. Consumption and Significance: Everyday Life in a Brand-New Second-Hand Bow Tie. *European Journal of Marketing* 27(8):38–45.

Grayson, Kent, and Donald Shulman. 2000. Indexicality and the Verification Function of Irreplaceable Possessions: A Semiotic Analysis. *Journal of Consumer Research* 27(1):17–30.

Grodin, Debra, and Lindlof, Thomas R. 1996. *Constructing the Self in a Mediated World*. Thousand Oaks, Calif.: Sage.

Hebdige, Dick. 1979. *Hiding in the Light: On Images and Things*. New York: Comedia.

Holt, Douglas B. 1997. Poststructuralist Lifestyle Analysis: Conceptualizing the Social Patterning of Consumption in Postmodernity. *Journal of Consumer Research* 23(4):326–350.

Kellner, Douglas. 1992. Popular Culture and the Construction of Postmodern Identities. In *Modernity and Identity*. Scott Lasch and Jonathan Friedman, eds. Pp. 141–177. Oxford: Blackwell.

Korosec-Serfaty, Perla. 1984. The Home from Attic to Cellar. *Journal of Environmental Psychology* 4:303–321.

Kirsch, Stuart. 2001. Lost Worlds: Environmental Disaster, "Culture Loss," and the Law. *Current Anthropology* 42(2):167–199.

Levi-Strauss, Claude. 1987. *Introduction to the Work of Marcel Mauss*. London: Routledge.

MacDonald, Theodore. 2001. Internationalizing Indigenous Community Land Rights: Nicaraguan Indians and the Inter-American Court of Human Rights. Electronic document, www.cs.org/main.htm, accessed February 2001.

Marcoux, Jean-Sébastien. 2001. The "Casser Maison" Ritual: Constructing the Self by Emptying the Home. *Journal of Material Culture* 6(2):213–235.

McCracken, Grant. 1988. *Culture and Consumption*. Bloomington: Indiana University Press.

Mosko, Mark S. 2000. Inalienable Ethnography: Keeping-While-Giving and the Trobriand Case. *Journal of the Royal Anthropological Institute* 6(3):377–396.

Pannell, Sandra. 1994. Mabo and Museums: The Indigenous (Re)-Appropriation of Indigenous Things. *Oceania* 65:18–39.

Price, Linda L., Eric J. Arnould, and Carolyn Folkman Curasi. 2000. Older Consumers' Disposition of Valued Possessions. *Journal of Consumer Research* 27 (September):179–201.

Radin, Margaret. 1993. *Reinterpreting Property.* Chicago: University of Chicago Press.

Riessman, Catherine Kohler. 1993. *Narrative Analysis.* Qualitative Research Methods 30. Newbury Park, Calif.: Sage.

Shore, Bradd. 1992. Take My Sister, Please! *New York Times Book Review,* August 9:8.

Smart, Carol, and Bren Neale. 1999. *Family Fragments.* Cambridge, U.K.: Polity Press.

Sussman, Marvin B., Judith N. Cates, and David T. Smith. 1970. *The Family and Inheritance.* New York: Russell Sage Foundation.

Stewart, Alexander. 1999. *The Ethnographer's Method.* Thousand Oaks, Calif.: Sage.

Thompson, Craig J. 1997. Interpreting Consumers: A Hermeneutical Framework for Deriving Marketing Insights from the Texts of Consumers' Consumption Stories. *Journal of Marketing Research* 34(4):438–455.

Tobin, Sheldon S. 1996. Cherished Possessions: The Meaning of Things. *Generations* 20(3):46–48.

Unruh, David R. 1983. Death and Personal History: Strategies of Identity Preservation. *Social Problems* 30(3):340–351.

Wallendorf, Melanie, and Eric J. Arnould. 1988. "My Favorite Things": A Cross-Cultural Inquiry into Object Attachment, Possessiveness, and Social Linkage. *Journal of Consumer Research* 14(4):531–547.

———. 1991. "We Gather Together": Consumption Rituals of Thanksgiving Day. *Journal of Consumer Research* 18(1):13-31.

Wallendorf, Melanie, and Russell W. Belk. 1989. Assessing Trustworthiness in Naturalistic Consumer Research. In *Interpretive Consumer Research.* Elizabeth Hirschman, ed. Pp. 69–84. Provo, Utah: Association for Consumer Research.

Weiner, Annette B. 1992. *Inalienable Possessions: The Paradox of Keeping-While-Giving.* Berkeley and Los Angeles: University of California Press.

———. 1994. Cultural Difference and the Density of Objects. *American Ethnologist* 21(1):391–403.

11

Virtual Antiquities, Consumption Values, and the Cultural Heritage Economy in a Costa Rican Artisan Community

Jim Weil

The world of art, a sacred island systematically and ostentatiously opposed to the profane, everyday world of production, a sanctuary for gratuitous, disinterested activity in a universe given over to money and self-interest, offers, like theology in a past epoch, an imaginary anthropology obtained by denial of all the negations really brought about by the economy.

Bourdieu (1977:197)

This chapter explores the efforts of one group of Costa Rican artisans to survive and prosper in an increasingly diffuse global marketplace. Beyond taking inputs of raw materials and labor into account, they must pay attention to luxury or "leisure" consumption preferences. Perceptions and strategies of the artisans reflect a struggle to instill in consumers a greater appreciation of commodities, here called Chorotega Revival ceramics, that embody an ancient tradition. Assessments of prospects for the artisans derive from participant observation in the ethnic arts market. The point of departure is a thought-provoking transaction with a gifted artist in a community where ceramic manufacturing skills have passed through the generations since pre-Columbian times. Issues addressed include the conceptualization of *expressive culture* and *consumption values,* the movement toward "virtual" economies based on the social construction of wants ever further removed from fundamental biological needs, and the transformation of a rural Latin American cottage industry over a half-century of intensifying external relations.

Nonnegotiable Values and Prices—A Vignette

"I have to charge you the full price," Carlos Grijalba Acosta said, showing me a beautiful four-footed bowl he had made. It was a replica of a pre-Columbian original pictured in a museum catalog (Snarskis 1983:63). Two animal heads jutted out from the rim, a vulture on one side and a jaguar on the other. Features of the animals and intricate patterns around the bowl were painted in brightly colored clay slips: red, orange, brown, grey, black, and tan (see figure 11.1). It was obvious that this richly evocative piece embodied the refined skills and stylistic conventions of a well-established artisan tradition. Over the preceding decade I had returned several times to the northwestern Costa Rican village of San Vicente for ethnographic fieldwork and never haggled over ceramic purchases.[1] The artisans usually charged less than I was prepared to offer. Carlos knew that I would be visiting and that I wanted examples of his latest work for an exhibit in Minnesota. I immediately assented to his asking price of c/20,000 (colones), equivalent to almost US$60 and half again as much as I ever had paid previously.

Before leaving that day in December of 2001, I selected several other items for purchase. The second to catch my eye was an elegantly shaped and decorated

FIGURE 11.1
Replica ceramic with illustration of prototype in catalog.

FIGURE 11.2
Original ceramic with adaptation
of pre-Columbian designs.

vessel that tapered slightly toward the top and had a pedestal base. Not a replica, it had designs engraved into red, black, orange, grey, and brown bands on a tan underslip: bird and crouching jaguar motifs and braided abstractions—traditional, yet in Carlos's inimitable style. (See figure 11.2.) The price of c/10,000 was relatively high, yet far below the retail standard outside the community. Both of these pieces were of the best quality available, artistically and technically.

FIGURE 11.3
Ocarinas for sale in museum shop.

Then I turned to simpler pieces to purchase for the shop at the Science Museum of Minnesota. Breakage had undercut the profitability of a trial shipment, so I was given the assignment of carrying back ceramics as personal baggage. Four small ocarinas (clay flutes) in animal shapes and a small bowl cost c/1,500 each. Three somewhat larger toucan ocarinas were marked c/2,000 each, but Carlos reduced the price, charging the same c/1,500 for all when he wrote out my receipt. (See figure 11.3.)

I had set aside three ocarinas and a necklace for myself and was now prepared to pay for them separately. But Carlos said these were covered by the purchase price of the pedestal bowl. Then he told me to make another choice from a table with top-of-the-line examples of his work (in the c/5,000 range). When I asked if he was sure he wanted to give me so much extra value, he insisted, again expressing regret for not giving me a special deal on the best pieces. Seeing that I remained a bit bewildered, he explained that he didn't want to overcharge me, but he had to establish the value of his finest products.

As a participant–observer I was acting as consumer and wholesale intermediary in an ongoing marketplace drama. The reflexivity of my ethnographic positioning adds poignancy to the main point I wish to make: increasing physical and social mobility brings people together in exchanges creating broader "regimes of value" than in previous eras with greater segregation of market spheres (Appadurai 1986:4). The relentless acceleration and diversification of trade leaves assumptions about cultural isolation and autonomy less and less tenable. Ramifications of advanced capitalism lead to a quest for wealth accumulation in such nooks and crannies of the global system as the ethnic arts market. As in the work of Eric Wolf (1982) and Sidney Mintz (1985), anthropologists have traced historical processes within a frame of analysis that simultaneously considers local impacts of worldwide influences and reverberations of previously localized goods and practices in widespread destinations.

Ethnographic Context

The rise of international tourism over the past three decades has opened up new economic niches in Costa Rica, primarily in resort areas with jobs in construction and services. San Vicente lies in a village cluster at the foot of a ridge on the hilly Nicoya Peninsula, where the predominantly rural population has struggled with an insufficiency of arable land and inadequate employment opportunities in agrarian wage labor. The boom might have missed this area, except for the presence of a ceramics cottage industry based on nearby sources of fine, colored clays.

As indicated by surface shards and burial sites, San Vicente has been a ceramics center for well over one thousand years. An archaeological zone known as Greater Nicoya covers much of northwestern Costa Rica (including the Nicoya Peninsula) and southwestern Nicaragua (Lange 1984). Although on the southern frontier of Mesoamerica from the foundational Olmec period onward (Sharer 1989:265–266), Greater Nicoya followed a relatively independent developmental trajectory until about twelve hundred years ago. Then successive waves of migration from what is now Mexico brought a more thorough infusion of Mesoamerican iconography and other design elements to local ceramic industries (Healy 1988). Art historians, like Costa Ricans generally, call this area's pre-Columbian cultures "Chorotega"—the name of an indigenous leader at the time of first European contact in the 1520s (Abel-Vidor 1980:163; Scott 1999:105–107).

With Spanish conquest, demographic and social collapse ended production of elegantly shaped and engraved polychromes, but the manufacture of utilitarian ware continued throughout the intervening years. In at least one part of the area, the island of Chira, trade in ceramics continued into the Spanish colonial period (Abel-Vidor 1980:161). We do not know if nonindigenous preferences already led to stylistic change at that time. In the middle of the twentieth century, women continued to make jugs for storing water, pots for boiling beans, and platters for toasting tortillas. The few decorative pieces had simple European folkloric designs. Men did not participate directly in manufacturing but assisted in obtaining raw materials and carrying the finished goods to market in oxcarts (Stone 1950).

Today, many residents remain ambivalent about the ancient heritage. They identify with the Hispanic culture of Costa Rica, while feeling denigrated as peasants (*campesinos*) in a region treated as backward by a modernist society eager to convey a progressive image. Nevertheless, manufacturing ceramics is preferable to the poor returns of agrarian livelihoods. As the world economy privileges and promotes symbolic forms of consumption, replicas and other handmade objects based on pre-Columbian prototypes have become commodities in the ethnic arts market.

Terms of Engagement

What gives value to clay that has been shaped, decorated, and baked? Ceramics called *antiquities* stimulate interest in cultures of the distant past. Not merely old, they evoke and stand for the composite achievements of a society that no longer functions and a way of life that no longer exists. Antiquities markets exist, of course, having a long history intimately associated with colonial ventures. The looting of archaeological sites, once rampant in Costa Rica (Snarskis 1981:18–19), has declined owing to legislation, enforcement, and the emergence of a conservationist ethic shared by most potential sellers and buyers. Contemporary San Vicente ceramics under consideration here are *not* antiquities. The beauty and skill they manifest may suffice to explain their attraction, but a certain aura enhances them. It is this added dimension, a link to peoples and cultures of the past, that supports a market that has grown in tandem with the rise of tourism.[2]

How can material culture that is new but evokes thoughts and feelings attached to ancient objects be characterized? Consider the word *virtual*. Its use as a mere synonym for "almost" misses stronger connotations. It conveys the notion of a substitute that somehow duplicates the essence of "the real." A good replica may even have certain advantages over an original. Antiquities are scarce and their acquisition is usually illegal—hence the virtual may take the place of the unattainable. Antiquities are often damaged, their features eroded—hence the virtual may simulate the pristine.

Why is it useful to think about Chorotega Revival ceramics as *virtual antiquities?* Tourism has become a major component of economic globalization, one facet being the commoditization of cultural heritage. Market interaction creates shared perceptions of *expressive culture*—or, at least, convergence—between the person who makes a ceramic piece in San Vicente and its eventual owner in some North American or European city. Vestiges of colonial encounters persist in negotiations between differently empowered participants, but some consensus emerges through mutual appreciation of ancestral styles and contemporary skills.

Struggling to understand my interactions with Carlos, I pondered the way he set his prices, a process illustrating complexities and subtleties packed into crosscultural exchanges. Fred Myers (2001b:3) gives an overview:

> The conditions of transnationalism under which most people in the world now live have created new and often contradictory . . . values and meanings in ob-

jects—that is, in material culture—as those objects travel in an accelerated fashion through local, national, and international markets and other regimes of value production.

In certain situations, market value has less to do with basic survival through the exchange of goods and services in the immediate area, and more to do with "virtual" needs of lifestyle imagery in far-flung settings. The hypercommercialization of expressive culture during the second half of the twentieth century challenges economic anthropologists to identify new alignments within and between the agency–structure axis and the local–global axis.[3]

The term *virtual* has broader connotations in the current era and can be considered in the context of a reified, ideologically charged, and ultimately "artificial" economy (Carrier and Miller 1998). It offers transitory and vicarious activities (e.g., computer games, theme parks) at lower costs than lived experiences, ultimately creating passive consumers. This model of "virtual reality" derives from and promotes a pervasive market mentality. The perspective of producers like Carlos—at the so-called periphery—may offer a closer view of the underlying political economy than the perspective of consumers—at the so-called center—where disparities between labor values and market values are more likely to be hidden or disguised.

EXPRESSIVE CULTURE AND THE DEVELOPMENT OF THE ETHNIC ARTS MARKET

Continuities and New Departures in the Research Community

Soon after beginning fieldwork in San Vicente in the fall of 1993, I brought a photocopy of an article published in 1950 into the community. Written by Doris Stone, a pioneering Central American archaeologist, it described the ceramics cottage industry at that time in the village cluster that contains San Vicente. When Maribel Sánchez Grijalba recognized her great aunt in a captioned series of photos explaining the step-by-step manufacture of a clay pot, she took the article to show to her mother and grandmother (respectively, the niece and sister of the woman pictured). Others also looked at the illustrations and commented on continuities and changes.

The few decorative ceramics, such as flower vases and fruit bowls, had a simple painted or embossed design. Drawings of distinctive globular figurines caught their attention (Stone 1950:279). "We used those as canteens to carry drinking water when we were working in the fields," Maribel remarked, "and

I still know how to make them." Much to my surprise, she presented me with a figurine several months later at the end of the fieldwork period, a decidedly nontraditional woman in an elegant dancing gown. But most of the utilitarian ceramics depicted in Stone's article have been replaced by cooking pots, water pitchers, and so forth, made in factories from more durable materials. Large concave platters for toasting tortillas are a notable exception, still a specialization of several of the older women. Looking over the various types of ceramics in the article, we did not see any examples of the elaborately shaped and decorated pre-Columbian styles found today, nor did Stone mention their being made at that time. Our discussions of the organization of the industry, drawing on memories of the past and projecting alternative future possibilities, have continued.

Into the 1960s, the cottage industry remained centered on senior women. Skills typically passed from grandmother to granddaughter, with the mother involved but often busy with other household duties. Male relatives continued to help with ancillary tasks. Then, with the rise of tourism, a few of the men began to play a more prominent role in rediscovering the shaping, slip-painting, and engraving techniques of ancestral artisans. Nowadays the division of labor according to gender and age is more complicated (Weil 2001). Many young men prefer to work as "artisan-temps," specializing in painting or engraving decorative designs in workshops run by older women. Women still are more likely than men to shape the pieces. As the industry has grown to employ well over half the community residents, many young wives and husbands share the management of household workshops.

Both Carlos and Maribel were in their early forties when I began research in San Vicente, old enough to remember life there before the rise of tourism and the growth of the ceramics industry. Unlike Carlos, who works alone, Maribel finds supporting roles wherever people collaborate. She has helped in all stages of production in her mother's workshop, whether generating creative ideas or just polishing slips, whether arranging supplies or supervising the tasks of others. She often carries cartons of ceramics to shops in the capital city, thereby retaining profits for the household that otherwise would be lost to intermediaries. Over the years, Maribel has been one of the most active members of the community in promoting ceramics, tourism, and other aspects of development in San Vicente. She has been at the forefront of the waxing and waning initiatives to build an "ecomuseum." My own involvement intensified when she invited me to a planning meeting in 1994 (Weil 1997:23). Maribel and Carlos are first cousins. Although she identifies with the more liberal political party and the Catholic Church and he identifies with the more conservative political party and the Evangelical (Protestant) Church, they regularly "talk shop" together and help each other sell their ceramics. Both have a highly sophisticated understanding of the problems and prospects of the cottage industry.

Art and Authenticity in the Tourist Experience

There is an important category of "commodities made in the third world specifically for first-world consumption" (Miller 1995:153). Within this category, the *ethnic arts market* is one of the lifestyle industries identified as a notable growth sector of recent decades, both economically and as a subject of scholarly attention (Whitten and Whitten 1993; Graburn 1999; cf. Graburn 1976, for an initial formulation and a collection of benchmark studies). As distinct but overlapping domains, both tourism and the ethnic arts market have underwritten the innovative turn to Chorotega Revival ceramics. Artisans in the village of San Vicente sell only a small proportion of their production directly to visitors. Much of their output reaches customers who stop at Guaitil, the adjacent community where the paved access road ends. Most of the rest is purchased by wholesalers and ultimately sold at arts-and-crafts stores in urban or resort areas. Profits are siphoned off by purchasers who take batches outside of the community for sale at roadside stands or shops of their own, or for resale to other retailers.

In pricing, variation in the type and quality of ceramics is highly relevant in efforts to distinguish *consumption values*. Commodities in the ethnic arts market range from casual souvenirs to aesthetic and technical masterpieces. For visitors who come primarily to enjoy the sun and surf, a little ceramic dish—perhaps an ashtray with "Costa Rica" painted in colorful slips—serves as a satisfactory memento. Less-than-perfect execution of form or design may not matter, with low cost (often under c/2,000 [US$6]) a decisive factor in such transactions. A small ocarina in the form of a sea turtle meets the demand of tourists seeking a somewhat more substantial "collectible" from a Costa Rican vacation (in the c/2,000–4,000 range), especially if their adventures include an expedition to watch turtles laying eggs at night on the beach. The country is one of the world's leading centers of ecotourism, so ceramics often draw on prototypes with motifs depicting native fauna.

On the other hand, visitors in quest of a cultural tourism experience can find directions to Guaitil in most of the numerous Costa Rican guidebooks, a few of which also mention San Vicente. They come to watch the ceramics being manufactured in the workshops. Meeting the maker and collecting a fine-art object that represents an ancient tradition can foster a transcendental feeling. Initially, during the 1960s and 1970s, attempts at simple replicas and other pieces closely followed pre-Columbian "Chorotega" stylistic conventions. The mixing and matching of different shapes, motifs, and other design elements, and the emergence of more individualized creativity, soon followed. The layered market resulted, with a continuum of quality and price (cf. Stephen 1991:384–385; Colloredo-Mansfeld 1999:169–173; Chibnik 2000). The microevolution of techniques, fashions, organizational arrangements, and marketing strategies continues.

But are the Chorotega Revival ceramics "authentic"? The extreme view is that if it is not a genuine antiquity, then it is a fake. Except in cases of outright misrepresentation, the cultural status of a replica or near replica is far more complex. Anthropologists have engaged in similar debates over ceramics elsewhere, for instance, in the U.S. southwest (Wade 1985; Deitch 1989; Mullin 2001:132–133; Batkin 1999). The acceptance or rejection of the ceramics of San Vicente as authentic (or genuine) in the terms presented by their makers becomes a kind of litmus test on the eye of the beholder. Chorotega Revival ceramics *are* original pieces, and their significance deepens with reference to prototypes from a previous era. A pre-Columbian replica can stand for itself as an immediate and tangible work of art, but acceptance as a virtual antiquity enhances its aura.[4]

SEMIOTICS OF CONSUMPTION VALUES
"The Turn Toward Consumption" in Economic Anthropology

Developments proceeding under conditions characteristic of global capitalism have reinforced new approaches and methods in economic anthropology (Carrier 1997:5–6; Miller 1997:11–12). In reference to the merging regimes of value mentioned earlier, Appadurai (1986:4) discusses implications of the eclipse of separate "spheres of exchange" identified in an earlier era (by Firth among the Tikopia in Polynesia and by Bohannan among the Tiv in West Africa). In this regard, it has become difficult to ignore expressive culture in economic anthropology. Few would have predicted, for instance, the commoditization of Australian aboriginal art in the global marketplace (Myers 2001a, 2001b:11). Stuart Plattner's (2000) ethnographic research on the avant-garde art market in St. Louis, Missouri, is a contrasting case study.

Thus, the study of Chorotega Revival ceramics in northwestern Costa Rica belongs to a growing research tradition in the economic anthropology of the arts. By the closing decades of the twentieth century in rural Latin America, livelihoods based on foodstuffs and basic raw materials had greatly diminished, as commodity markets favored such "lifestyle" products as ornamental plants, cut flowers, and decorative arts. Ceramic artisans have needed to understand consumption values so that they could track fashions and know what styles tourists would buy. Encroachment by explorers and traders at the remote frontiers of early industrial economies typically brought unwelcome and unneeded goods. Now entrepreneurship at the margins of globalization entails proactive efforts to shape preferences in the metropolitan marketplace.

Assessing theory in economic anthropology at the turn of the twenty-first century, Karen Tranberg Hansen (2002:223) finds that in previous paradigms, "consumption was an epiphenomenon, relegated to the margins of production and distribution." Similarly, Daniel Miller (1995:142) considers the neglect of consumption through the 1970s "extraordinary," relative to research on production and distribution, not only in anthropology but also in the other social sciences and humanities—an exception at the beginning of the twentieth century being Thorstein Veblen's prescient analysis of the economic importance of *conspicuous consumption*.

Following from such other seminal ideas as the cultural centrality of "goods" (Douglas and Isherwood 1979) and "distinction" in taste (Bourdieu 1984), a substantial body of literature on consumption has accumulated in anthropology. This trend is represented by one of the volumes in the Society for Economic Anthropology monograph series, in which the editors conclude:

> In general terms, the study of consumption leads to the examination of daily life on the one hand and of broad systems of stratification on the other; it joins the material world of the production of objects to the ideological world of the evaluation of objects. (Orlove and Rutz 1989:43)[5]

This connection runs through a recent ethnographic study of Ecuadorian artisans by Rudi Colloredo-Mansfeld (1999), *The Native Leisure Class:*

Consumption and Cultural Creativity in the Andes. He reinforces the point that consumption values are an essential component of anthropological research on markets, affecting artisans' own product preferences as well as their assessments of customer choice.

Production Values, Exchange Values, Consumption Values

Attention to the vicissitudes of *value* brings greater coherence to the study of consumption. Maurice Godelier (1972:156) began a lifelong study of cross-cultural economic fundamentals with a conceptual and empirical search for values, especially as a common denominator in comparing capitalism to other social systems. He went on to examine the "embeddedness" of "the economy" in a comprehensive cultural matrix, critically assessing the work of Karl Polanyi (Godelier 1986:179–207). Changes in global political economy led him to revisit Mauss on the theme of exchange, looking for residues of gift giving within the near ubiquity of impersonal market exchange: "Apparently everything, or nearly, is for sale. . . . Ordinary things, precious things, works of art" (Godelier 1999:204). In the form of world capitalism that remained after the communist alternative collapsed, only the individual person is, in principle, not for sale (Godelier 1999:205). While, in important ways, people *do* "sell" and "buy" one another in the marketplace, in another sense they use gift exchange to retain elements of communal relationships. Here lies a point of entry into the cultural heritage economy: encounters between producers and consumers may become part of a quest (all too often abortive) to reproduce communal values.[6]

Godelier (in this volume) says that for human societies the material world is largely, in effect, a mental construction. One need not go that far to recognize that one of the economic drivers of contemporary global capitalism—an area of wiggle room for profit maximization—is *leisure* consumption of goods and services far removed from biological survival. In other words, market investment in quest of *exchange values* is likely to be more successful through responses to the *consumption values* of lifestyle industries (entertainment, recreation, fashion) than to the more basic *use values* in industries serving subsistence needs, or so it would seem to the peasants of San Vicente. Livelihoods based on the sale of agricultural products and wages from agrarian labor become ever less viable, while economic niches in tourism offer more promising opportunities.

When artisans calculate their inputs of time and effort, along with the less tangible value of their skills development—and in San Vicente they do—they find the returns received for manufacturing ceramics and other such crafts to be abysmally low. A detailed quantitative analysis is not possible here, but the main steps in the production process can be listed: obtain raw materials, prepare them, shape the piece, apply and polish an underslip, apply and polish decorative slips (usually), engrave designs into the slips (sometimes), fire and clean the piece. Artisans may choose to carry out the decorative steps carefully or save time by doing them in a perfunctory manner. If they react to an undiscerning and uncaring buyer public, the outcome will be shoddier goods.[7] The question is whether finely made ceramics are worth the effort in terms of remuneration. Some artisans are satisfied with the efficiency of minimal inputs and inexpensive low-quality goods to maximize the volume of production; others care greatly about the aesthetic and technical quality of their work. Women generally bear the brunt of the remunerative squeeze, since they are more likely to engage in artisan production and find their work, as a "spare time" activity, valued less than that of men (Berlo 1991:439–440).

Stephen Gudeman (2001:110–112) explains how a woman in Guatemala had to set her prices below her calculable costs, figuring she would make up losses once her new ceramic designs caught on; but then she had to compete with others who imitated her successful designs. In any case, artisans find they have little control over pricing structures (Jules-Rosette 1984:199). We have seen how, in San Vicente, Carlos struggled to counter this situation by forcing a recognition of higher production values—of his work as an artist—and establishing commensurate prices. His implementation amounted to a kind of "gift wrapping," cushioning the commercial transaction in a personal relationship through which valuable things are not only sold but also given (Godelier 1999 and this volume). His bargaining position in a business dominated by wholesale intermediaries left him few alternatives. Details vary, but many observers of the ethnic arts market will have recognized this pattern of exchange elsewhere.

"Catching the Tourist"

For comparisons of world areas, artistic traditions, and interpretive conventions, several scholars have offered their versions of a kind of ethnological template for classifying artisan products. Graburn (1976:8) arranged his seminal formulation in a six-by-two grid, relating *aesthetic sources* to *intended audiences.* Jules-Rosette (1984:203) diagrams an African market bifurcated between master wood carvings for collectors and galleries and tourist wood carvings for the mass international trade (cf. Chibnik 2000). Clifford (1990:147) applies a "semiotic square" used by Greimas and by Jameson for the "art–culture" system, with a masterpiece–artifact axis and an authentic–inauthentic axis.

There is a longer history of research on the *agency* of artisans and merchants in markets for the ethnic arts of Africa than for those of Latin America. In *Catching the Tourist,* Ulla Wagner (1982:5–8) stressed the difference between the domestic market for textiles in The Gambia and the types of goods and forms of sale that developed for the international tourist market. Sophisticated tie-dyed fabrics were made for local and national consumption, while others, produced with a simpler "marbling" technique and a newly introduced batik process, appealed to foreigners. *The Messages of Tourist Art: An African Semiotic System in Comparative Perspective* by Benetta Jules-Rosette (1984) is an exceptionally comprehensive study, which, among other topics, describes and analyzes the dilemma of creating a market for the less tangible qualities of ethnic arts. Like Godelier, she starts with Mauss and Polanyi in exploring the connection between producer and consumer, comparing intention and meaning at each end of the commodity chain (Jules-Rosette 1984:194–195). She emphasizes the need to "educate" the consumer about both the labor value and the consumption value of artisan products. Beyond the tasks required to produce an object lies the challenge of crafting its meaning. Christopher Steiner (1994, 1995) picks up where Jules-Rosette leaves off, focusing on merchant intermediaries. He traces the long journey of wood carvings from West African villages—where part of the manufacturing process is a treatment that enhances their market value by making them appear "authentically" old—to shops in Europe and North America, where dealers accept them as antiques. Much of the African literature conveys a naïveté among consumers and cynicism on the part of most others, an attitude found already in the 1930s (Lips 1966).

A different theme seems more salient in Latin American research, which often evaluates artisan production less for cultural purity than for socioeconomic impacts on the producers (García Canclini 1993; Nash 1993). The apparent contrast between aesthetic values and production values need not be conflated with the ethnocentric opposition of "modern" to "primitive" culture—an issue that has inspired much polemical writing (Price 1989; Root 1996; Errington 1998). Instead, the artisans of San Vicente engage with tradition as a *resource,* positioning themselves on the modernist side of the divide. They enjoy speculative discussions about the circumstances and worldview shaping cultural production among the pre-Columbian "Chorotega" people. They are open to alternative meanings of the iconography, deferring to archaeologists for interpretations of the Mesoamerican overlay on more ancient and more localized stylistic conventions. They make close replicas for the same reasons that they mix and match stylistic elements or create original designs: a dialectical interplay of their personal aesthetic inspirations and the preferences of purchasers in the marketplace.

San Vicente artisans, whether self-consciously or intuitively, have incorporated these distinctions in their production and marketing strategies. As the industry has grown to employ well over half of the residents in the workforce (Weil 2001:31), those with less developed skills can carry out ancillary tasks or turn out inexpensive but rather crudely made souvenirs. More highly skilled artisans must decide whether and how many customers (more often wholesale than retail) will purchase finely made artistic pieces. Carlos exemplifies those who do not want to compete at the lower-quality end but must devote a proportion of their efforts there while hoping to "catch" discerning customers with their better work.

GLOBALIZATION AND THE HERITAGE ECONOMY: PAST AS PROLOGUE
Precedents, "Ancient" and "Modern"

If markets today cater to a nostalgia for remote cultures (Phillips and Steiner 1999:16), the work of Mary Helms suggests a related sense of mystique among travelers in ancient times. She begins her latest book, *Access to Origins,* by restating her general hypothesis that "in human cosmologies geographical distance corresponds with supernatural distance" (Helms 1998:xi). We might add temporal distance to the formula. Emphasizing the region that contains San Vicente (lower Central America), Helms discusses pre-Columbian exchange of precious objects, whether as gifts or through trade, which offers

> many insights elucidating the role of wealth in enhancing and evidencing aristocratic qualities and identity. . . . [The] examination of methods and circumstances

of acquisition and exchange . . . can cast light upon some of the conditions that also hold potential for eventual aristocratic or chiefly trade. (Helms 1998:166–167)

Who would be today's elites seeking to elevate their status, prestige, and/or wealth by acquiring what Bourdieu (1984) calls the "cultural capital" transmitted by the aura of antiquities? Art dealers and their customers fill this role. On display at the Barakat Gallery in Beverly Hills, for example, I found standing-jaguar vessels and other pieces from the Greater Nicoya culture area at prices ranging beyond $10,000 (see www.barakatgallery.com). Another group consists of archaeologists in the roles of custodians and translators of the past, whether as scientists drawing lessons of economic and political significance from the fate of defunct societies or as humanists celebrating the cultural achievements that had been or might otherwise be forgotten. Mesoamerica, in particular, inspires awe as one of the original centers for the development of a civilization with distinctive innovations in patterns of subsistence, social structure, cosmology, and aesthetic style.

What about nonelites in the current era, characterized by an economy that caters to the common citizen as consumer? Is it too much of a stretch in an intellectual climate of bourgeois hegemony to posit the apotheosis of "the tourist" as avatar of the modern (or postmodern) age, as Dean MacCannell (1989) suggests? If not everyone, then certainly members of large segments of society are sufficiently affluent to travel and gain accoutrements of cosmic control *virtually*.

Whether today's consumption values lead collectors to acquire actual antiquities or pieces that to some extent replicate or evoke antiquity, the connection with ancient peoples will fall far short of full communion. Summing up an attitude prevalent among archaeologists, James Skibo (1999:7) writes that there is

one area of ceramic studies where many researchers still draw the line—artifact meaning. Some archaeologists believe that it is the most important aspect of pottery while others think that it is the one area of pottery studies that may be out-of-bounds using prehistoric data.

As preceding remarks may have implied, this uncertainty should enhance rather than diminish the appeal of virtual antiquities, for their ultimate value to consumers lies in the realm of imagination.

Like antiquities, contemporary ethnographic objects gain market value through an aura of authenticity. Aboriginal Australians have participated in the selective transformation of their sacred designs into fine art (Myers 2001b:11). Many artisan traditions of Mesoamerica have survived or been revived as persisting or new livelihoods, as demonstrated in a set of case studies presented by June Nash (1993). The ceramic artisans of San Vicente share this legacy and are pleased when outsiders covet their creations. The pre-Columbian aura strengthens their competitive position in the marketplace; it simultaneously instills respect for the Chorotega heritage in the context of Costa Rican national society. Although sustainable livelihoods are envisioned rather than actualized, the artisans hope to benefit from the growing "fair trade" movement supported by international marketing cooperatives (Grimes and Milgram 2000).

Imagined Futures for the Cottage Industry in San Vicente

A volume edited by Carrier and Miller (1998), cited earlier, bears the title *Virtualism: A New Political Economy.* The contributors examine the emergence of an "artificial" economy, whereby ordinary people scramble to adapt to a model of economic thought imposed through transnational capitalism and globalization, structural adjustment, and the decline of the public sector. This neoliberal program idealizes and promotes private (some would say *selfish*) initiative, which in the case of Costa Rica is undermining a well-developed civil society. Interactions between international tourists and the present quasi-peasantry in northwestern Costa Rica cannot be understood in terms of earlier anthropological research strategies—and this pertains to economic anthropology in particular. As found also in Ecuador by Colloredo-Mansfeld (2002), neoliberal policies stimulate distinctive forms of competition in artisan villages. The inspirations of the most creative artists are embedded in a persisting communal ethos. Recognizing that a community's reputation in the realm of expressive culture enhances economic opportunities, artisans may be motivated to share their innovations.

Modernization came earlier and less traumatically to rural Costa Ricans than to their counterparts in neighboring countries (cf. Field 1999, on experiences of Nicaraguan ceramic artisans). They have been better positioned to interact with merchants and tourists, often establishing their own contacts in resort areas and the cities. Barriers of knowledge and demeanor separating them from international visitors have not been severe, and the latter find both a friendly welcome and an understanding of what they seek in coming to the village. Homestays have already been institutionalized. Some residents of San Vicente intend to build cabins or open a bed-and-breakfast business for "cultural tourists." Aspirations for upward socioeconomic mobility are being met, in some cases with private telephones and postsecondary educational opportunities. In 2001, after a ten-year struggle, the community obtained funding (from the Inter-American Foundation) to construct a long-planned eco-museum (Weil 1997). But one worrisome possibility is the decline of international travel. People fearing terrorism might turn to "virtual tourism" in megamalls and theme parks to obtain "exotic curios" from remote sweatshop factories without having to leave familiar territory.

Aside from all the adverse impacts of "the West on the rest," the ethnic arts market in San Vicente provides a source of income and valorizes indigenous culture. The spread of global capitalism has brought homogenization of industrial production and mass communications; an ambivalent countermovement celebrates the personal, the local, and the handmade (García Canclini 1993:69–74). As more people get out into the world by means of package charters to resort enclaves, the eagerness of others to go off on their own is intensified. Those who reach San Vicente or other receptive communities may establish person-to-person contacts, even friendships. As consumers they acquire esoteric meanings and artisan goods, which transmit "local knowledge" from the past to new places and to subsequent generations (Geertz 1983). Economic anthropologists, along with practitioners of other ethnographic specializations, are well positioned to document the "traffic" in these things of value (Steiner 1994; Marcus and Myers 1995).

NOTES

Research in San Vicente was funded by a Fulbright Senior Research Award, with additional support from Marquette University, the University of Wisconsin-Milwaukee (Center for Latin America and the Caribbean), and the Science Museum of Minnesota. Residents of San Vicente, members of my family, and numerous colleagues have contributed to the ideas developed here. Comments by the anonymous reviewers were also helpful.

1. Discussions with Kate Hopper, Orrin Shane, and Leslie Spoelstra about their experiences in obtaining ceramics, both as purchases and as gifts, have been especially fruitful.

2. Already in the 1930s, Walter Benjamin (1968) was exploring the potential for a politicized aesthetic to redeem the humanity lost in the commoditized culture of capitalism. In "The Work of Art in the Age of Mechanical Reproduction," he discussed the aura of original works of art that is absent from reproductions. Benjamin has much to tell us about the trajectory that has generated today's tourism industry, especially when it involves a quest for reenchantment, materialized in goods handcrafted by presumed purveyors of ancient traditions. Unlike the aura conveyed through ironic quotation in, say, a Warhol reproduction, San Vicente artisans do not instill a postmodern sensibility (cf. Steiner 1999:89). Related research is accumulating on collecting as a broad form of consumption (Belk 1995) and on tourist collecting in particular (Lee 1999; Batkin 1999; Dubin 2001, see esp. p. 59; Mullin 2001).

3. By "expressive culture" I mean conventionalized manifestations of creativity, sentiment, ethos, and so forth. There is a disturbing futility in the opposition of "culture" to "economics" (or "politics" or . . .) found in much anthropological discourse. Without a conceptualization of culture that subsumes economics, analysis of mutual influences between material and ideational aspects of social life is foreclosed. Precisely the impact of expressive culture (aesthetics) on "hard core" economics is at stake here in the transformation of a ceramic tradition. Elsewhere, I have emphasized access to resources, the organization of work, and community action to promote the artisan industry (Weil 1995, 1997, 2001). As in a village of Sri Lankan ceramic artisans studied by Deborah Winslow (2002:155–156), attention to the "multidimensional local, regional, and national landscapes helps us to understand why they have prospered in recent years and why they have made the choices they have about what to do with their new wealth."

4. *Authenticity* may have objective referents but remains an arbitrary construct, not necessarily intrinsic to any particular object or practice. In "The Genuine Article," Mary Douglas (1994:12–13) borrows the term "autographic" from philosopher Nelson Goodman to indicate objects that, like the San Vicente ceramics, derive their value from historical continuity. Steiner (1999:102) comments on a dilemma: "Original works of art are inauthentic because they do not imitate an agreed-upon style; while objects that imitate the defined styles are also inauthentic because they are not, as it were, originals." Néstor García Canclini (1993:81) puts it aptly: "Every time we read 'Souvenir from Michoacán,' we know that that article was made to be used anywhere but in Michoacán. That formula, supposedly meant to guarantee the authenticity of the object, is a sign of its lack of authenticity." For other pertinent formulations, see Clifford (1990:141), Phillips and Steiner (1999:4, 19), and Graburn (1999).

5. Other anthropologists (e.g., Friedman 1994:16–17; Narotsky 1997:103, 115–117; Smith 2000:139–167) have explicitly distinguished consumption values from production values and explored their enactment in personal lifestyles and cultural identity formation. Richard Wilk (2002:243) evaluates the disciplinary status and practice of "consumer research" as a kind of undertheorized applied anthropology, wondering if consumption has been *over*theorized as an anthropological topic. Nevertheless, this approach to the sale of Chorotega Revival ceramics provides insight into the dialectics of market aesthetics, while contributing to community development initiatives.

6. In San Vicente, my advice and intervention were solicited at times when I would have preferred a more detached observation of decision-making processes. The initiative went in the other direction when my preferences and requests in ceramic purchases influenced choices artisans made about what to produce. Françoise Dussart (1999:193) invoked the "uncertainty principle" (also known as the Heisenberg effect) to describe similar experiences during her research on acrylic painting by aboriginal Australian women.

7. Such pressures increasingly threaten the survival of intricate, elegant, and richly meaningful aesthetic traditions, as in the case of Maya weaving in the Chiapas highlands (Morris 1991:407).

REFERENCES

Abel-Vidor, Suzanne. 1980. The Historical Sources for the Greater Nicoya Archaeological Sub-Area. *Vínculos* 6(1–2):155–186.

Appadurai, Arjun. 1986. Introduction: Commodities and the Politics of Value. In *The Social Life of Things: Commodities in Cultural Perspective*. Arjun Appadurai, ed. Pp. 3–63. New York: Cambridge University Press.

Batkin, Jonathan. 1999. Tourism Is Overrated: Pueblo Pottery and the Early Curio Trade, 1880–1910. In *Unpacking Culture: Art and Commodity in Colonial and Postcolonial Worlds*. Ruth B. Phillips and Christopher B. Steiner, eds. Pp. 282–297. Berkeley and Los Angeles: University of California Press.

Belk, Russell W. 1995. *Collecting in a Consumer Society*. New York: Routledge.

Benjamin, Walter. 1968 [1936]. The Work of Art in the Age of Mechanical Reproduction. In *Illuminations*. Harry Zohn, trans. Hannah Arendt, ed. Pp. 217–251. New York: Schocken Books.

Berlo, Janet Catherine. 1991. Beyond Bricolage: Women and Aesthetic Strategies in Latin American Textiles. In *Textile Traditions of Mesoamerica and the Andes: An Anthology.* Margot Blum Schevill, Janet Catherine Berlo, and Edward B. Dwyer, eds. Pp. 437–479. New York: Garland.

Bourdieu, Pierre 1977 [1972]. *Outline of a Theory of Practice.* New York: Cambridge University Press.

———. 1984 [1979]. *Distinction: A Social Critique of the Judgment of Taste.* Richard Nice, trans. Cambridge, Mass.: Harvard University Press.

Carrier, James G., ed. 1997. *Meanings of the Market: The Free Market in Western Culture.* New York: Berg.

Carrier, James G., and Daniel Miller, eds. 1998. *Virtualism: A New Political Economy.* New York: Berg.

Chibnik, Michael. 2000. The Evolution of Market Niches in Oaxacan Woodcarving. *Ethnology* 39(3):225–242.

Clifford, James. 1990. On Collecting Art and Culture. In *Out There: Marginalization and Contemporary Cultures.* Russell Ferguson, Martha Gever, Trinh T. Minh-ha, and Cornel West, eds. Pp. 141–169. Cambridge, Mass.: MIT Press.

Colloredo-Mansfeld, Rudi. 1999. The Native Leisure Class: Consumption and Cultural Creativity in the Andes. Chicago: University of Chicago Press.

———. 2002. An Ethnography of Neoliberalism: Understanding Competition in Artisan Economies. *Current Anthropology* 43(1):113–137.

Deitch, Lewis I. 1989. The Impact of Tourism on the Arts and Crafts of the Indians of the Southwestern United States. In *Hosts and Guests: The Anthropology of Tourism.* Valene L. Smith, ed. Pp. 223–236. Philadelphia: University of Pennsylvania Press.

Douglas, Mary. 1994. The Genuine Article. In *The Socialness of Things: Essays on the Socio-Semiotics of Objects.* Stephen Harold Riggins, ed. Pp. 9–22. New York: Mouton de Gruyter.

Douglas, Mary, and Baron Isherwood. 1979. *The World of Goods.* New York: Basic Books.

Dubin, Margaret. 2001. *Native America Collected: The Culture of an Art World.* Albuquerque: University of New Mexico Press.

Dussart, Françoise. 1999. What an Acrylic Can Mean: The Meta-Ritualistic Resonances of a Central Desert Painting. In *Art from the Land.* Howard Morphy and Margo Smith Boles, eds. Pp. 193–218. Charlottesville: University of Virginia.

Errington, Shelly. 1998. *The Death of Authentic Primitive Art and Other Tales of Progress.* Berkeley and Los Angeles: University of California Press.

Field, Les W. 1999. *The Grimace of Macho Ratón: Artisans, Identity, and Nation in Late-Twentieth-Century Western Nicaragua.* Durham, NC: Duke University Press.

Friedman, Jonathan, ed. 1994. *Consumption and Identity.* Chur, Switzerland: Harwood Academic Publishers.

García Canclini, Néstor. 1993. *Transforming Modernity: Popular Culture in Mexico.* Lidia Lozano, trans. Austin: University of Texas Press.

Geertz, Clifford. 1983. *Local Knowledge: Further Essays in Interpretive Anthropology.* New York: Basic Books.

Godelier, Maurice. 1972 [1966]. *Rationality and Irrationality in Economics.* Brian Pearce, trans. New York: Monthly Review Press.

———. 1986 [1984]. *The Mental and the Material: Thought, Economy, and Society.* Martin Thom, trans. New York: Verso.

———. 1999 [1996]. *The Enigma of the Gift.* Nora Scott, trans. Chicago: University of Chicago Press.

Graburn, Nelson. 1999. Ethnic and Tourist Arts Revisited. In *Unpacking Culture: Art and Commodity in Colonial and Postcolonial Worlds.* Ruth B. Phillips and Christopher B. Steiner, eds. Pp. 335–353. Berkeley and Los Angeles: University of California Press.

Graburn, Nelson, ed. 1976. *Ethnic and Tourist Arts: Cultural Expressions from the Fourth World.* Berkeley and Los Angeles: University of California Press.

Grimes, Kimberly M., and B. Lynne Milgram, eds. 2000. *Artisans and Cooperatives: Developing Alternative Trade for the Global Economy.* Tucson: University of Arizona Press.

Gudeman, Stephen. 2001. *The Anthropology of Economy.* Malden, Mass.: Basil Blackwell.

Hansen, Karen Tranberg. 2002. Commodity Chains and the International Secondhand Clothing Trade: Salaula and the Work of Consumption in Zambia. In

Theory in Economic Anthropology. Jean Ensminger, ed. Pp. 221–236. Lanham, Md.: Rowman & Littlefield.

Healy, Paul F. 1988. Greater Nicoya and Mesoamerica: Analysis of Selected Ceramics. In *Costa Rican Art and Archaeology: Essays in Honor of Frederick R. Mayer.* Frederic W. Lange, ed. Pp. 293–301. Boulder: University of Colorado Press.

Helms, Mary W. 1998. *Access to Origins: Affines, Ancestors, and Aristocrats.* Austin: University of Texas Press.

Jules-Rosette, Benetta. 1984. *The Messages of Tourist Art: An African Semiotic System in Comparative Perspective.* New York: Plenum Press.

Lange, Frederick W. 1984. The Greater Nicoya Archaeological Subarea. In *The Archaeology of Lower Central America.* Frederick W. Lange and Doris Z. Stone, eds. Pp. 165–194. Albuquerque: University of New Mexico Press.

Lee, Molly. 1999. Tourism and Taste Cultures: Collecting Native Art in Alaska at the Turn of the Twentieth Century. In *Unpacking Culture: Art and Commodity in Colonial and Postcolonial Worlds.* Ruth B. Phillips and Christopher B. Steiner, eds. Pp. 267–281. Berkeley and Los Angeles: University of California Press.

Lips, Julius E. 1966 [1937]. *The Savage Hits Back.* Vincent Benson. trans. New Hyde Park, NY: University Books.

MacCannell, Dean. 1989. *The Tourist: A New Theory of the Leisure Class.* 2nd ed. New York: Schocken Books.

Marcus, George E., and Fred R. Myers, eds. 1995. *The Traffic in Culture: Refiguring Art and Anthropology.* Berkeley and Los Angeles: University of California Press.

Miller, Daniel. 1995. *Capitalism: An Ethnographic Approach.* New York: Berg.

———. 1997. Consumption and Commodities. *Annual Review of Anthropology* 24:141–161.

Mintz, Sidney W. 1985. *Sweetness and Power: The Place of Sugar in Modern History.* New York: Viking.

Morris, Walter F. 1991. The Marketing of Maya Textiles in Highland Chiapas, Mexico. In *Textile Traditiions of Mesoamerica and the Andes: An Anthology.* Margot Blum Schevill, Janet Catherine Berlo, and Edward B. Dwyer, eds. Pp. 403–433. New York: Garland.

Mullin, Molly H. 2001. *Culture in the Marketplace: Gender, Art, and Value in the American Southwest.* Durham, N.C.: Duke University Press.

Myers, Fred R. 2001a. The Wizards of Oz: Nation, State, and the Production of Aboriginal Fine Art. In *The Empire of Things: Regimes of Value and Material Culture.* Fred R. Myers, ed. Pp. 165–204. Santa Fe, N.M.: School of American Research Press.

————, ed. 2001b. *The Empire of Things: Regimes of Value and Material Culture.* Santa Fe, N.M.: School of American Research Press.

Narotzky, Susana. 1997. *New Directions in Economic Anthropology.* Chicago: Pluto Press.

Nash, June, ed. 1993. *Crafts in the World Market: The Impact of Global Exchange on Middle American Artisans.* Albany: State University of New York Press.

Orlove, Benjamin S., and Henry J. Rutz. 1989. Thinking about Consumption: A Social Economy Approach. In *The Social Economy of Consumption.* Henry J. Rutz and Benjamin S. Orlove, eds. Pp.1–57. Lanham, Md.: University Press of America.

Phillips, Ruth B., and Christopher B. Steiner. 1999. Art, Authenticity, and the Baggage of Cultural Encounter. In *Unpacking Culture: Art and Commodity in Colonial and Postcolonial Worlds.* Ruth B. Phillips and Christopher B. Steiner, eds. Pp. 3–19. Berkeley and Los Angeles: University of California Press.

Plattner, Stuart. 2000. Profit Markets and Art Markets. In *Commodities and Globalization: Anthropological Perspectives.* Angelique Haugerud, M. Priscilla Stone, and Peter D. Little, eds. Pp. 113–134. Lanham, Md.: Rowman & Littlefield.

Price, Sally. 1989. *Primitive Art in Civilized Places.* Chicago: University of Chicago Press.

Root, Deborah. 1996. *Cannibal Culture; Art, Appropriation, and the Commodification of Difference.* Boulder, Colo.: Westview Press.

Scott, John F. 1999. *Latin American Art: Ancient to Modern.* Gainesville: University Press of Florida.

Sharer, Robert J. 1989. The Olmec and the Southeast Periphery of Mesoamerica. In *Regional Perspectives on the Olmec.* Robert J. Sharer and David C. Grove, eds. Pp. 247–71. New York: Cambridge University Press.

Skibo, James M. 1999. Pottery and People. In *Pottery and People: A Dynamic Interaction*. James M. Skibo and Gary M. Feinman, eds. Pp. 1–8. Salt Lake City: University of Utah Press.

Smith, M. Estellie. 2000. *Trade and Trade-offs: Using Resources, Making Choices, and Taking Risks*. Prospect Heights, Ill.: Waveland Press.

Snarskis, Michael J. 1981. The Archaeology of Costa Rica. In *Between Continents/Between Seas: Precolumbian Art of Costa Rica*. Elizabeth P. Benson, ed. Pp. 15–84. New York: Harry N. Abrams.

———. 1983. *La cerámica precolombina en Costa Rica*. San José, Costa Rica: Instituto Nacional de Seguros.

Steiner, Christopher B. 1994. *African Art in Transit*. New York: Cambridge University Press.

———. 1995. The Art of the Trade: On the Creation of Value and Authenticity in the African Art Market. In *The Traffic in Culture: Refiguring Art and Anthropology*. George E. Marcus and Fred R. Myers, eds. Pp. 151–165. Berkeley and Los Angeles: University of California Press.

———. 1999. Authenticity, Repetition, and the Aesthetics of Seriality: The Work of Tourist Art in the Age of Mechanical Reproduction. In *Unpacking Culture: Art and Commodity in Colonial and Postcolonial Worlds*. Ruth B. Phillips and Christopher B. Steiner, eds. Pp. 87–103. Berkeley and Los Angeles: University of California Press.

Stephen, Lynn. 1991. Export Markets and Their Effects on Indigenous Craft Production: The Case of the Weavers of Teotitlán del Valle, Mexico. In *Textile Traditions of Mesoamerica and the Andes: An Anthology*. Margot Blum Schevill, Janet Catherine Berlo, and Edward B. Dwyer, eds. Pp. 381–402. New York: Garland.

Stone, Doris Z. 1950. Notes on Present-Day Pottery Making and Its Economy in the Ancient Chorotegan Area. *Middle American Research Records* 1(16):269–280.

Wade, Edwin L. 1985. The Ethnic Art Market in the American Southwest, 1880–1980. In *Objects and Others: Essays on Museums and Material Culture*. George W. Stocking Jr., ed. Pp.167–191. Madison: University of Wisconsin Press.

Wagner, Ulla. 1982. *Catching the Tourist: Women Handicraft Traders in The Gambia*. Stockholm: Department of Anthropology, University of Stockholm.

Weil, Jim. 1995. Changing Sources of Livelihood from the Earth and Sea in Northwestern Costa Rica. *Anthropology of Work Review* 16(1–2):14–23.

———. 1997. An Ecomuseo for San Vicente: Ceramic Artisans and Cultural Tourism in Costa Rica. *Museum Anthropology* 21(2):23–38.

———. 2001. Toward a Model of Changing Social Roles in a Costa Rican Ceramic Artisan Industry. *Anthropology of Work Review* 22(3):27–32.

Whitten, Dorothea S., and Norman E. Whitten Jr., eds. 1993. *Imagery and Creativity: Ethnoaesthetics and Art Worlds in the Americas.* Tucson: University of Arizona Press.

Wilk, Richard. 2002. When Good Theories Go Bad: Theory in Economic Anthropology and Consumer Research. In *Theory in Economic Anthropology.* Jean Ensminger, ed. Pp. 239–251. Lanham, Md.: Rowman & Littlefield.

Winslow, Deborah. 2002. Space, Place, and Economic Anthropology: Locating Potters in a Sri Lankan Landscape. In *Theory in Economic Anthropology.* Jean Ensminger, ed. Pp. 155–181. Lanham, Md.: Rowman & Littlefield.

Wolf, Eric R. 1982. *Europe and the People without History.* Berkeley and Los Angeles: University of California Press.

12

Women's Fashion Magazines: People, Things, and Values

Brian Moeran

Anyone who is a regular reader of women's fashion magazines and interested in the fashion world is likely to find herself puzzling over things that she finds there. Why, for example, are items of clothing named and priced, but hardly shown in fashion photographs? Why are they also occasionally so blurred as to be unrecognizable, even though they are found in a magazine that purports to show its readers the latest fashions? Why will a magazine's cover credits sometimes include the name of a fragrance worn by the cover model when the reader cannot even smell it? Why does a top model get paid US$18,000 for a catwalk show, several million dollars for an advertising campaign, but only US$200 for a fashion magazine cover? Why is a fashion photographer prepared to lose money on a magazine's fashion shoot? And why is it accepted that operating losses by haute couture fashion houses are "in line with management expectations" (Hoover's Online 2000a) and allowed to continue year after year? It is questions like these, together with the problems of cultural or economic irrationality that they pose, that this chapter seeks to illuminate.

The relations between culture and economy, and between anthropology and economics, have formed the foundations of economic anthropology, whose proponents from Weber onward have been concerned to bring moral philosophy and values into the study of economic behavior (cf. Wilk 1996). For some time now, the distinction between "culture" and "economy" has also been exercising the minds of scholars in sociology and cultural studies (e.g., du Gay 1997; Ray and Sayer 1999; Jackson et al. 2000). If there is one thing that has been ingrained in our heads by the latter it is that, while the economy is becoming more culturally inflected, culture is itself becoming more economic in content (Lash and Urry 1994:64). Still, given that this kind of observation was made well over two decades ago by Raymond Williams (1977:136), who wrote that "large scale capitalist economic activity and cultural production are now inseparable," we have not gotten *that* much further in our understandings of just *how* they are inseparable.

Logically, of course, it is impossible for the economic *not* to be social (and cultural), but the important issue of *how much* culture does or does not determine the economy still remains relatively unexplored (Wilk 1996:132). To get around the problem of how symbolic and economic structures articulated with each other, Pierre Bourdieu highlighted the positions, strategies, position-takings and games that social actors played in a particular "field." It seems to me that the concept of field, together with the different social "worlds" (Becker 1982) that it often encompasses (Bourdieu 1993b:34–35), allows us to pry apart the different structural, social, symbolic, and other elements that constitute and complement both the cultural and the economic.

Because economies everywhere are concerned with the production, circulation, representation, and consumption of goods and services, economic anthropology has to address two interrelated sociocultural spheres. One consists of people interacting—by themselves and in the company of others, forming networks, associations, corporations, and other institutions and organizations. Here we are concerned, broadly speaking, with sociology or social anthropology. The other sphere consists of people's relations to the things that they produce, circulate, represent, and consume during the course of their interaction. Here our focus is more on an anthropology of (material) culture.[1] I will illustrate the coexistence of these spheres by discussing women's fashion magazines.

The strictly sociological sphere surrounding the production, circulation, representation, and consumption of things has been well analyzed by Bourdieu (1984, 1986, 1993b) in his extensive work on different forms of cultural production, and by Howard Becker (1982) in his discussion of art worlds. Both have provided us with a means of understanding intricate social forms of economic behavior. By comparison, however, coherent theories in the anthropology of material culture remain relatively undeveloped. It is true that a significant amount of research has been done on, for example, gifts and exchange (e.g., Godelier 1999), or the anthropology of art (e.g., Gell 1998).

Danny Miller (1987), too, has argued that the meanings and values that are embedded in social process are objectified in material culture. Even so, we still have difficulty in explaining in adequate sociological terms such diverse objects as a painting (whether by Picasso or my daughter), compact disc, or fake antique, as well as all kinds of other things, from wine to perfume, by way of stamp collections, vintage cars, a Hollywood blockbuster, or a stoneware vase.

This chapter focuses on the different kinds of values that people bring to bear in their interaction with things. The study of values (these days very often used in the singular) in anthropology has a long history and complex development. But value is used in at least three different senses. One is sociological and applies to "what is ultimately good, proper, or desirable in human life." A second is economic and refers to "the degree to which objects are desired, particularly, as measured by how much others are willing to give up to get them." The third is linguistic and "might be most simply glossed as 'meaningful difference'" (Graeber 2001:1–2).

For some scholars interested in a theory of value(s), the important question has been "why people place so much value on particular objects that are essentially nonutilitarian" (Myers 2001:54). But we might also ask why people give other kinds of value to things that are also utilitarian; so it is the *kind* of values they bring to bear on things that needs careful analysis. To judge from the infuriatingly loose manner in which scholars talk about values, such an approach poses considerable difficulty. For example, in his early discussion of the "structural logic of value," Jean Baudrillard (1981) argues that use, exchange, symbolic exchange, and sign values together constitute a "logic of consumption." But, in passing, he also mentions the following kinds of value: aesthetic, commercial, critical, economic, gestural, statutory, strategic, sumptuary, surplus, symbolic, tactical, and utility. In the recent (and otherwise useful) edited book introduction referred to above, Fred Myers (2001) first distinguishes between quantitative and qualitative values, before going on to mention cash, economic, monetary, utility, and utilitarian values on one hand, and cultural, historical, human, political, social, and sociocultural values on the other.[2]

The work that has been most inspirational to anthropologists interested in pursuing the relation between people, things, and values is the much cited *The Social Life of Things* (Appadurai 1986). Although I will have more to say later about Arjun Appadurai's discussion of value, I intend here to follow his principle that "commodities are things with a particular type of social potential" (Appadurai 1986:6). My interest here is in pursuing relationships among people centering on things, as well as those people's often differing attitudes toward things. Ultimately, my concern is with how things acquire different kinds of values as they move along their "commodity paths" toward a moment of exchange. These values I systematize as a "field" of values.

FASHION MAGAZINES AS COMMODITIES

The first question to address is why I choose to illustrate this discussion by referring to women's fashion magazines.[3] My answer is that women's magazines in general are both cultural products and commodities. As *cultural products,* they circulate in a cultural economy of collective meanings, providing recipes, patterns, narratives, and models of and/or for the reader. As *commodities,* they are products of the print industry and crucial sites for the advertising and sale of commodities (particularly those related to fashion, cosmetics, fragrances, and personal care). Magazines are thus deeply involved in capitalist production and consumption at national, regional, and global levels (Beetham 1996:1–5).

Let us start with fashion magazines as commodities. Within the genre of women's magazines in general, women's fashion magazines form a separate class. In the United States, for example, this class consists of nine titles: *Allure, Elle, Glamour, Harper's Bazaar, InStyle, Mademoiselle, Marie Claire, Vogue,* and *W.* The most popular of these is *Glamour,* with an average paid circulation of 2,139,672 copies. By comparison, *W* sells only 442,358 copies, while *Vogue* sells just over, and *Elle* just under, 1 million copies a month. According to public announcements, total audited sales of fashion magazines come to just over 10 million copies a month.

Readers of these magazines are predominantly women (83.8 percent *InStyle* to 94.8 percent *Mademoiselle*), whose average ages vary between 28.7 *(Allure)* and 37.9 years *(Harper's Bazaar).* From two-thirds (70.5 percent *Harper's Bazaar*) to three-fourths (78.4 percent *Marie Claire*) are employed in some capacity or other. Of these, about one-fourth are in professional or managerial positions (21.9 percent *Mademoiselle* to 31.5 percent *InStyle*). Their median household incomes are between US$49,788 (*Vogue*) and US$67,826 (*InStyle*) (Mediamark Research 2000). Their mean reading time for a fashion magazine is said to be somewhere between fifty-five (*Elle*) and seventy-one (*InStyle*) minutes.

Fashion magazine contents may be divided into fashion, beauty and health, lifestyle, entertainment, technology, issues and culture, and other. In 2000, *Vogue* carried 1,056 pages (57.5 percent) of fashion matter, while *Allure* carried only 243 pages (21.3 percent). These magazines placed correspondingly less or more emphasis on beauty and health (190 pages for *Vogue* vis-à-vis 650 pages for *Allure*). Each magazine tends to differentiate itself from others in its class by devoting more space to particular types of contents. *Marie Claire*, for example, devoted 21 percent of its space to social and cultural issues (vis-à-vis *Allure*'s 2.8 percent); *InStyle* devoted 22.9 percent of its pages to lifestyle topics (vis-à-vis *Allure*'s 0.7 percent).[4]

As in women's and many other kinds of magazines, advertising forms a large percentage of each fashion magazine title's pages and contributes to its overall financial well-being. Full figures are not available, but between January and December 2000, total advertising pages for *Elle* were 2,221; *Vogue* 3,309; *Harper's Bazaar* 1,786; and *W* 2,184 pages. The cost of a full four-color page in the same year was US$75,900 for *Elle* and US$68,680 for *Marie Claire* (with discounts being given for volume purchase of advertising space).[5]

Women's fashion magazines are by no means the same throughout the world. Even though certain titles—such as *Vogue, Harper's Bazaar, Marie Claire,* and *Elle*—are published in different languages all over the world, their contents may vary considerably.[6] Moreover, the publishing field in which fashion magazines are produced, distributed, represented, and consumed is not necessarily the same. For example, in Japan, the class of fashion magazines contains more titles—twenty-three in all. These include such local titles as *Classy, Domani, Ginza, Gli, Grazia, Hi Fashion, Miss, Oggi, Spur, 25 Ans,* and *Vingtaine,* as well as the international titles *Elle, Figaro, Harper's Bazaar, Marie Claire,* and *Vogue.* Circulations are lower and range between 280,000 (*Oggi*) and 105,000 (*Miss*) for the local magazines, and 225,000 (*Vogue Nippon*) and 140,000 (*Harper's Bazaar*) for the international. Total—and, it should be added, unaudited—sales for the class come to approximately 4.5 million copies a month.[7]

There are differences, too, in the readership of women's fashion magazines in Japan. Most readers are aged between 18 and 34, with an average age of approximately 24.5 years. *Elle Japon* readers are younger than readers of the American edition of *Elle;* 87 percent, as opposed to 61.1 percent, are under the age of 34. Fewer (57 percent versus 70.8 percent) are classified as "working women," although the average income (as well as cost of living) of Japanese women is higher. Most of these readers are single; most are employed; and many live at home and thus have a comparatively large amount of discretionary income to spend on fashion, beauty, entertainment, and travel.

Such differences to some extent affect the contents of an international fashion magazine like *Elle,* which, in its Japanese edition, devotes more pages to lifestyle, entertainment, travel, and culture, while still focusing on fashion, beauty, and health in the way that the American edition does. An exact breakdown of these content headings into magazine pages is not available, but most magazines devote about one-third of their contents to fashion, one-third to beauty and health, and the remaining third to the other four topics. Interim database analyses show that an average 237-page issue of *Elle Japon* publishes 53 pages (22.6 percent) of fashion photography, 19 pages (8.1 percent) of beauty and health, and 88 (36.7 percent) pages of textual matter devoted to fashion- and beauty-related news, celebrities, entertainment, travel, social and cultural issues, and so on. Each 336-page issue of American *Elle* publishes 66 pages (19.6 percent) of fashion, 14 pages (4.5 percent) of beauty, and only 63 pages (18.6 percent) of similar textual matter.

Advertising also tends to differ in different national editions of an international magazine and contributes to the contents weighting noted in the previous paragraph: 77 pages (32.6 percent) in *Elle Japon,* but 193 pages (57.3 percent) in the American edition. At the same time, in Japanese fashion magazines, individual one- or two-page advertisements are usually structured in blocks between editorial, fashion, and beauty features rather than run simultaneously with them on opposing pages, as in American fashion titles. The total number of advertising pages carried in 2000 by *Elle Japon* was 1,627, *Marie Claire Japon* 956, and *Vogue Nippon* 928 pages. In the same year, a standard four-color, single-page advertisement cost US$12,000 in *Elle,* US$12,500 in *Marie Claire,* and US$19,583 in *Vogue Nippon.*[8] Although ad rates are thus approximately one-sixth of those in the United States, this correlates with the magazines' lower circulations in Japan.

FASHION MAGAZINES AS CULTURAL PRODUCTS

Let us now turn to fashion magazines as cultural products and look at *Elle* magazine's contents. What values are revealed in the rhetoric of written-clothing used to describe the image-clothing (Barthes 1983:12) in its American and Japanese editions? The language used in fashion magazines serves three purposes. First, it provides a description of what *fashion* is. Second, it adds knowledge to the image that it describes. Third, it emphasizes what is (not) seen. The fact that language emphasizes certain parts of an image (a pattern, for example, a hemline, or material) and not others (a color, collar, or shape) shows that the rhetoric of written-clothing *limits value* (Barthes 1983:15).[9]

Content analysis shows that magazines' primary concern is with *appearance* as a, or the, main focus of interest for readers. Cover headlines in the U.S. edition of *Elle*, for example, focus on fashion and—what is frequently stressed as "American"—beauty. Both fashion and beauty are to a large extent defined in the magazine's pages by *the look* (of summer, the season, Hollywood, and so on). The look may be "sharp," "fresh," "exuberant," or "exotic," but it almost invariably exhibits *attitude*. Attitude itself is expressed by the idea that social life is a *drama* ("a simple, strapless dress takes on a heightened drama"), in which fashion becomes "bold" ("asymmetry makes a bold statement"), "daring" ("daring keyhole cutouts"), and "powerful" ("the power of streamlined neutrals").[10]

A central part of this drama is *sex appeal*, which helps formulate a *style* ("tough and sexy"). Sexiness is found in individual garments ("sexy high-heeled boots"), tailoring ("sexy cuts"), decorative techniques ("sexy crochets"), and colors ("sexy shades of khaki"). It can also be a feeling ("a sexy '70s feel"). Associated words include "flirty," "seductive," "slinky," "sultry," and "animal."

Sexiness is also related to drama in the sense that it incorporates, and is incorporated in, the *celebrity* worlds of entertainment ("glamorous Hollywood-style fur") and royalty ("a gown fit for a czarina"). Image-clothing is thus justified and legitimized by reference to these celebrity worlds. Related to these associations, we find an emphasis on *sophistication* ("a sophisticated blend") and *elegance* ("cool elegance") that mirrors the perceived no-work-and-all-play image of celebrity worlds. The latter image can be seen in such phrases as "real panache," "light and playful," "chic and easy," "funky," "casual," "jaunty," and "eased-up nonchalance."

Although other traits in the language of written-clothing may be found (like "femininity," "romance," "charm," and so on, depending on the season), the most frequently encountered element in the American magazine rhetoric of fashion focuses on *luxury* ("long on luxury") and the neologism "luxe" ("a new lease on luxe"). Rhetorical associations include "opulent," "plush," "sumptuous," "lavish," and so on. Luxury relates to garments ("luscious party dresses"), fabrics ("plush sable"), design ("lavish embroidery"), color ("richness of color"), makeup ("luscious makeup"), and overall feel ("a lush touch of texture"). It is also associated with being *rich* ("strike it rich") and with the trappings of wealth: jewelry ("champagne-colored stones"), gold ("all that glitters"), and treasure ("a treasure trove of simmering sequins"). Together these form *objects of desire.*[11]

This emphasis on luxury is supported by the *price* of every item of image-clothing shown in the magazine.[12] It is also found in supporting editorial coverage of the fashion scene and clearly relates to elegance, sophistication, glamour, and the world of celebrities. All in all, the American edition of *Elle* invites its readers to imagine that they are part of the glamorous drama of the fashion and entertainment worlds, in which sex appeal, sophistication, elegance, luxury, and wealth are paramount virtues defining an "American beauty." It is these same qualities that the magazine sells to advertisers as its "readership" and that advertisers then resell to readers in their advertising campaigns.

A JAPANESE COMPARISON

An international magazine title like *Elle*—with almost three dozen different editions in places as far apart as South Africa and Sweden, Korea and Brazil, and Australia and France—has a worldwide reach. Its publisher ideally aims at producing a global product, with common features, fashion pages, and other editorial content. As part of this package, it offers advertisers attractive discount rates to encourage them to advertise in as many different editions as they wish throughout the world, and so contribute toward its standardized product.

But how much are such business ideals actually achieved in practice? There are all kinds of social and cultural forces that facilitate and/or prevent standardization in the different fields of magazine publication in which *Elle* operates. But one that we can usefully follow here is the rhetoric of written-clothing in Japan, still the world's second-largest economy, where women are known for their high consumption of Western fashion and cosmetics brand goods. This will give us an idea of how cultural considerations come into play and how corporations with global intentions may find themselves struggling to understand and fit into local markets.

The first point revealed by a content analysis of *Elle Japon* is that keywords in the Japanese rhetoric of written-clothing are not focused on attitude as much as on *balance* and *accent*. These are particularly related to the way in which garments are shown and worn, so that the Japanese pay close attention to *form* as they comment critically on both "silhouette" and "line." Unlike that of American *Elle*, *Elle Japon*'s written-clothing is based primarily on technical description and knowledge, and not on image. It pays close attention to *material, cut, detail, technique, color,* and *design*—all of which intimately affect the wearer's senses in one way or another. In short, the rhetoric of written-clothing in Japan is much closer to the language of fashion designers themselves than that found in the American edition of *Elle*.[13]

At the same time, the second point, *femininity* (*onna rashisa*), is a crucial element in Japanese written-clothing and is clearly a vital part of a woman's appearance (cf. Moeran 1995). This femininity is closely aligned to *softness* (*yasashisa*), *quality, elegance* (*yūga*), *high class* (*jōhin*) and a sense of *cleanness* (*senren sareta*). To these should be added other associations found in American magazines: *romance, drama,* and *sexiness.* What is missing, however, is more than a passing allusion to *luxury.* Instead, fashion and femininity are tied into a language of the *senses*—particularly, touch (*tezawari, hadazawari, kanshoku*) and smell (*nioi, kaori*). In short, Japanese written-clothing would seem to be more concerned with an inner intimacy than with an outer world.

This is not to suggest that the rhetoric of written-clothing ignores the social world in which fashion is manufactured, distributed, represented, and consumed. On the contrary, it consciously aims to build up a picture of the *fashion world* and its celebrity names, not just to give provenance to the image-clothing (as in the United States) but also to provide historical and cultural background to fashion labels and their designers. Here Paris becomes the focus of attention as both fashion and cultural centre.

The rhetoric of written-clothing in *Elle Japon,* therefore, suggests that readers should cultivate a femininity that embodies softness, elegance, cleanness, and quality. This can best be brought about by their paying attention to the aesthetics of form. Thus, when deciding what clothes to buy and wear, a woman needs to select carefully the material, cut, color, and design of each item. The fashion—but not entertainment—world is brought into this discussion of femininity, but the rhetoric of written-clothing makes it part of a Japanese woman's educational and cultural knowledge. She views the fashion world detachedly from the outside, unlike the reader of American *Elle,* who is invited to participate in it—if only vicariously. Although ideas of sexiness, romance, and drama are not entirely missing from the language of *Elle Japon,* they are muted and culturally inflected. All ideas of a "brash," American-style beauty, luxury, and overall materiality (symbolized by objects of desire) are absent.

A FIELD OF VALUES

It can be seen from this excursion into a content analysis of the language of written-clothing in two different editions of an international fashion magazine that, although *Elle*'s publisher, Hachette Filipacchi Medias, may be aiming at the *commercial* production of a standardized global commodity, it is not so successful when we take into account the fact that the fashion magazine is also a *cultural* product. Although I have here analyzed only the language of fashion, my research makes it clear that similar differences between American and Japanese editions are to be found in other aspects of the magazine's editorial and advertising matter.

The fact that an apparently standardized global product contains such different features brings me back to the problem of values. After all, while the fashion magazine in question asks American women to identify with money in the form of luxury and wealth and to equate beauty with the kind of sexuality displayed in the world of entertainment, it appeals to its Japanese readers by means of an aesthetic of femininity, in which technical aspects of fashion production are promulgated and knowledge of the fashion world is part of their cultural capital. It is not that sexuality is entirely absent from Japanese readers' worlds; nor is it that American women cannot be feminine. Rather, different emphases exist in different situations in different national contexts. This is where the need for a systematic understanding of a field of values comes in.

In his introduction to *The Social Life of Things,* Appadurai recognizes that changing notions, as well as cultural constructions, of value are extremely important to any discussion of things. He notes that commodities include extremely complex social forms and distributions of knowledge and argues that it is "the *total* trajectory from production through exchange/distribution, to consumption" (1986:3) that we need to study.

Unfortunately, as with so much of his clearly imaginative work, Appadurai gives no examples of how a commodity operates in what he calls a "regime of value." This phrase is evocative and has been much bandied around, but it also embodies several problems—not the least of which is its precise applicability to the production, circulation, and representation, as well as consumption, of things during their "social lives" (Graeber 2001:30–33). Moreover, it has tended to be used qualitatively, in a way that makes it more or less equivalent to "context" (Myers 2001:55).

I have two simple criticisms of the term "regime of value." First, a regime implies some overall controlling mechanism (in the hands of a dominant elite), but it is by no means certain that such a mechanism functions effectively at all stages in a commodity's "career path." Given Bourdieu's (1993a:72, 1993b:163) definition of a "field" as "an independent social universe with its own laws of functioning," consisting of "structured spaces of positions whose properties . . . can be analyzed independently of the characteristics of their occupants," I prefer to talk in terms of a *field* of values.[14] Second, if there were but a single value attached to a commodity, life would be exceedingly simple—and the need for economic anthropology would quietly disappear. This is why we have to talk in terms of a field of plural *values*.

To understand how a field of values operates, we need to know who is bestowing things (commodities, valuables, goods) with what kind of values, when, where, and why. We also have to find out and analyze to what extent these values are contested and negotiated by different specialists or interested parties along a commodity's trajectory from its production to its consumption, by way of its circulation and representation. As we shall see, various people have different inputs, which affect both the commodities represented in fashion magazines and fashion magazines themselves as commodities.

At the production end of the commodity trajectory, *technical values* are extremely important. Those employed in magazine publishing houses make use of and continually develop professional skills that inform their work. Photographers, for example, tend to pride themselves on certain photographic techniques and skills involving cameras, lighting, and film, as well as posing models in such a way as to focus attention on the stitching or drape of a garment. Art directors can talk at great length about the fine variations brought to a magazine page by adoption of different typefaces,[15] or the ways in which grid structures can be used to create aesthetic effects in page layout. Even free-lance writers will have certain criteria about what constitutes a "well-written" article and complain bitterly if, for one reason or another, an editor interferes with the final result. It is interesting in this context that *Elle Japon* invites its readers to take technical values (like material and cut) into account in their appreciation and use of clothes.

As a commodity moves from production to circulation, *social values* come more into play. In creative industries in general, social values are crucial to the successful outcome of a particular product (fashion magazine, gallery exhibition, Hollywood film, and so on). Everybody in the field of fashion magazine publishing—from editors and art directors to photographers and models, by way of agents, stylists, hairdressers, makeup artists, printers, and so on—makes use of networking and personal connections to keep abreast of gossip and information. Such connections also help those in the field become integrated into, and accepted as members of, the social world in which they work. The fact that a photographer can "make" a model encourages liaisons of various kinds between them (like David Bailey and Jean Shrimpton, for example, or Victor Skrebneski and Cindy Crawford). But a model also occasionally "makes" a photographer (as Janice Dickinson did Mike Reinhardt). Alternatively, she can link up with a model agent (as Linda Evangelista did with Gérald Marie) and, via connections with a renowned photographer (in this case, Peter Lindbergh), become famous enough to "make" the agency (Elite) (Gross 1995:28, 190, 356, 456, 481). In all these cases, it is *who* a particular model or photographer is that, as in art, gives the product (a fashion photo-graph or an advertising campaign) a provenance that contributes markedly to the other values outlined here.

Less obvious, but not entirely absent, are the personal attachments that individuals develop with particular objects with which they work. Here senti-ment or affection comes into play, as part of social values. A photographer, for example, may prefer to never be without a particular old and battered camera (her first piece of professional equipment, given her by her father, for exam-ple). If offered a choice, a makeup artist may always opt for a certain kind of mascara or foundation (because that was what his mother or a teenage lover used to wear, and he wishes to remember her).

At various stages in the commodity's trajectory, but most obviously so in its representation (through advertising, public relations, media interest, or specialist criticism), judgment and taste are brought into play. Here *appreciative values* affect the finished product. Such appreciative values can be closely connected with technical values developed by professionals. An art director, for example, knows by training what kind of page layout or color combination works and what does not. A writer with a keen ear cultivates the well-turned phrase. A photographer judges just the right balance of light and shade, or compilation of people and objects, for his photographs. Appreciative values come into play, too, in the selection of a model (blond or brunette, fair or dark skin, waiflike or slender), as well as in decisions about what location to use for a fashion shoot, what kinds and colors of clothes and accessories to dress the model in, and in what combinations. Such aesthetic preferences are then further tweaked in the way a magazine's art director chooses to cut photographs for publication, in their sequence and placement opposite one another, even in the final color shade and border width in which they are printed. Such appreciative values—like the use of a white background for fashion stories in American *Elle*—contribute to a fashion magazine's perceived overall "style."

Appreciation is not limited to such strictly "aesthetic" values. Participants in a social world may imbue an object with other notions such as authenticity, novelty, luxury, and cultural or national identity. All of these forms of appreciation are constantly subject to affirmation, contest, and (re)negotiation by actors involved in "the social life of things." As a result, old forms may be discarded and new values introduced (following, for example, the introduction of new technologies).

Closer to the consumption end of a commodity's trajectory, we find *utility values* at work.[16] Different people may use things in different ways, not always as intended by their producers. Thus, dozens of copies of *Elle* magazine may be stacked upon one another to form legs for a coffee table, where they can never be leafed through again. An empty bottle of perfume can be used to hold wildflowers. A fashion designer may make a model wear a brassiere *over* a blouse, or design a shoe as a hat. Or a hairdresser, in a moment of inspired frustration, may pick up a pair of chopsticks lying nearby atop a half-finished bowl of noodles and use them to keep a model's hair in place. The ways in which such objects are used affects actors' perceptions of them.

This combination of technical, affective, appreciative, use, and social values (what Bourdieu has on different occasions, when discussing people, referred to as social, cultural, and educational capital) parallels, but is not limited to,

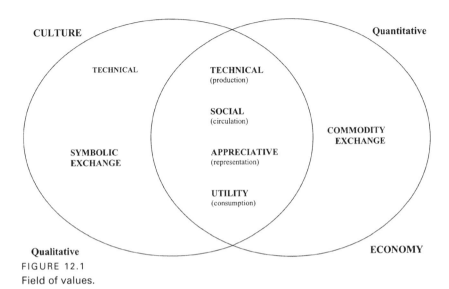

FIGURE 12.1
Field of values.

the production, circulation, representation, and consumption of things (see figure 12.1). Together these values give rise to what may be termed the commodity's *symbolic exchange value* (equivalent to symbolic capital in the realm of human relations). A photograph by Patrick Demarchelier of a pair of jeans designed by Calvin Klein and worn by a topless Kate Moss in the arms of pop singer Marky Mark has a certain cachet that a photograph by you or me of a young woman in a pair of jeans does not. These elements making up symbolic exchange value are, in Myers's (2001) term, qualitative. However, by a strange twist of reasoned calculation, they are converted into a sum of money that enables that particular thing to be exchanged and become "quantitative." This sum of money is an item's *commodity exchange value*. It is the exchange between symbolism and commodity that allows a pair of designer jeans to retail at twice the price of other, less well-known brands.

THE FIELD OF FASHION AND FASHION MAGAZINES

At the beginning of this chapter, I suggested that we see fashion magazines as operating in a particular field (Bourdieu 1993b) of cultural production. This field comprises a number of different social worlds (Becker 1982): fashion (Skov 2000), fashion photography (Aspers 2001), (women's) magazine publishing (Ferguson 1983), advertising (Moeran 1996, 2001), and so on. These social worlds themselves often partially constitute other fields (of, for example, textiles, media, and advertising).

As is the case with fields of cultural production in general, the field of fashion and fashion magazines has its own "social universe having its own traditions, its own laws of functioning and recruitment, and therefore its own history" (Bourdieu 1993a:140). The opposition between the commercial and the noncommercial acts as a fundamental, occasionally disavowed, structuring principle of the field—a principle that then generates many of the judgments made about fashion. The fact that both fashion and fashion magazines are products of "a vast operation of social alchemy" (Bourdieu 1986:137) means that there is often no clear measurement between their cost of production and commercial value. It is this failure to measure valuables (in terms of both objects and people) in monetary terms that I shall consider in the concluding section of this chapter.

The fact that fashion magazines are both sociocultural products and commodities means two things. First, they put forward in their pages an eclectic mixture of written and visual images, in both text and advertising, that upholds a field of values and integrates them into image-clothing as a whole. This is the main means by which magazines attract their audiences. Second, they appeal not to a single set of readers but to several different audiences: to women readers, to advertisers, and to members of the fashion and photography worlds. Publishers print magazines as "cultural products" and sell them to readers. At the same time, they sell the existence of those readers (plus a "pass-along" readership) to corporations interested in advertising their products to women (of the relevant age group). In this latter respect, magazines, together with their readers, are commodities.

What is the relation between advertising and textual matter, between a magazine as commodity and as sociocultural product? First, every magazine uses its cover to advertise and sell itself every time it comes out (McCracken 1993:13–37). In a country like Japan, where subscription rates are customarily very low and a magazine's success depends on newsstand sales, the cover is even more important than it is elsewhere (Moeran 1995:114–120). Fashion magazines, therefore, follow a tried and tested formula that makes it virtually imperative to have a model, celebrity, or star on the cover. These women's faces sell the cover headlines that sell the magazine's contents.

Models also use cover opportunities to advertise themselves in the fashion field. In the fashion-modeling business, being on the front cover of a prestigious fashion magazine is itself prestigious. There is a two-way rubbing-off process between commodity and celebrity that centers on names, with each enhancing the other. Appearance on the cover or in the pages of a well-known fashion magazine also tends to boost a model's career.[17] This means that there is a close structural relationship between models and photographers, since neither can survive without the other. Young women wishing to become models spend a lot of time visiting fashion photographers with their portfolios in the hope that they will be selected for a photo shoot. Photographers, for their part, are always on the lookout for "fresh" or "new" faces to photograph and put into *their* portfolios—which they then take to magazine fashion editors.

When selected for a fashion shoot, neither model nor photographer is paid very much. Indeed, at US$100–200 per published page (Aspers 2001:181),[18] a photographer may lose money if her overheads are too high. What sustains this apparently unsustainable market is advertising. Both model and photographer work for comparatively little in the hope of being selected to do lucrative advertising campaigns. The fashion magazine field thus comprises two different markets—one cultural, the other commercial.[19]

The overlap of the cultural and the commercial that I have outlined in the field of values is thus reduplicated in the social interaction of those who constitute the field of fashion and its magazines. Models, fashion photographers, hairdressers, stylists, designers, and others use their appearance in fashion magazines to promote and sell their work to others in the fashion field. Fashion magazines are the medium by which those in the fashion world show their "artistic talent," "creativity," "beauty," and so on to a mass public, in order to make, sustain, or enhance their names. In other words, magazines as cultural products are enabled and sustained by the fact that they are also commodities. At the same time, the distinction between "culture" and "economy" is actively maintained through social interaction among all actors in the field—actors who calculatedly misrecognize the cultural as "aesthetic" and the economic as a question of "names."

This misrecognition leads to a particular style in the fashion pages presented in the magazines, as editors seek to separate advertising from editorial content. For a start, many pages that set out to provide information on new fashion and beauty products are in effect little more than advertisements for thematically composed garments ("Peasant top, Celine by Michael Kors, US$1,450" or "Shell-trimmed skirt, Rozae Nichols, US$615"). The inclusion of prices on these pages, as well as in bylined commentaries, is important because it marks them out as *not* advertising. Fashion advertisements do not advertise the price of garments shown.[20]

The garments and accessories shown in fashion photographs, however, are loaned free of charge by a fashion house to a magazine and/or photographer with a view to their being used promotionally, since it gets the fashion house free publicity. In some respects, therefore, by saying that a particular camisole costs US$4,620, or a pendant US$12,000, or a pair of slingbacks US$525, a magazine like *Elle* appears somehow to have paid for the privilege of including items produced by Christian Dior, Tiffany, or Manolo Blahnik (even though, of course, it has to hand them back). We thus find two interlocking systems at work in fashion magazine stories: one of commodities-as-gifts, the other of gifts-as-commodities.

Another anomaly arising out of the problematic relationship between advertising and editorial content concerns the actual representation of fashion by magazines. To quote one Swedish fashion editor's instructions to a photographer: "The clothes don't have to be accessible; you may use whatever you want. It does not even have to be clothes; fashion is not just about clothes" (Aspers 2001:179). As a result, items of clothing may be named and priced, but hardly shown, or their photos so blurred that the clothes worn by a model are unrecognizable. Occasionally (as with shoes or tights, for example) products that do not appear at all in a magazine's photos are credited with a designer's name and retail price.

Fashion is a business of contrasts: from haute couture salons in Paris operating at a loss but offering very high-priced, made-to-order, designer originals, to profitable, giant factories mass-producing endless quantities of low-priced apparel. Segmentation occurs in types of apparel (inner- and outerwear, menswear, womenswear, children's wear, and accessories [shoes, handbags, wallets, scarves, gloves, hosiery]), on the one hand; and in terms of the "upstream" production of fibers and textiles, together with their distribution "downstream," on the other. (In each, technical values tend to differ somewhat). The fashion field is highly segmented and overlaps with other fields (in particular, that of textiles [cf. Skov 2000]). It also includes retailers of various kinds, plus those who, like trade journals, fashion magazines, publicists, advertising specialists, fashion consultants, and buying offices, provide information, assistance, and/or advice to producers (Jarnow and Dickerson 1997:3).

There are, in the fashion field, all kinds of organizations that produce the clothing shown and advertised in women's fashion magazines. Many of these corporations are household names. But names do not necessarily correspond to the business organizations that manage them. A second characteristic of the fashion field, therefore, is that its constituent actors are constantly re-forming in new strategic social and organizational alliances. For example, along with fashion houses Celine, Donna Karan, Fendi, Givenchy, Guerlain, Kenzo, Christian Lacroix, and Louis Vuitton, Christian Dior is part of LVMH, the world's largest luxury group, whose brands also include luxury accessories, champagnes and cognacs, watches, retail stores, and so on.[21]

The field is thus dominated by *names* or *brands*. This process of branding takes place at several different levels: things (as with "brand-name" commodities); people (in particular "celebrities," "supermodels," and "stars"); and organizations (Chanel, *Vogue*, Elite Model Agency, and so on) (Moeran 1996:278–280). It is these names (and their associated appreciative values) that dominate the appearance of the field. Besides the—for the most part hidden—organization of fashion houses into business groups, the structure of the fashion field is further obscured by the fact that, through a complicated system of licensing agreements, different companies manufacture different products belonging to a particular brand name. Thus Donna Karan International licenses its name to the likes of Estée Lauder (beauty products), Esprit de Corps (children's apparel), Liz Claiborne (careerwear), Sara Lee (hosiery), and Fossil (watches). For its part, Polo Ralph Lauren licenses its fragrances and skin-care products to L'Oréal, its mens- and womenswear to the Jones Apparel Group, swimwear to Authentic Fitness Products, gloves to Swany, hosiery to Hot Sox, athletic footwear to Reebok International, eyewear to Safilo, jewelry to Carolee, golf bags to Burton Golf, fabric and wallpaper to P. Kauffman, and so on. The company oversees the work of about 180 contracted manufacturers (located mainly in Asia and the United States) and more than thirty licensing partners. It makes nothing itself (Hoover's Online 2000b).

Although several brands may belong to the same group, the brands themselves are kept separate and given independent identities. It is the identity of each fashion house and its products that gives it its competitive edge vis-à-vis its rivals (so that symbolic exchange is used to enable commodity exchange). To this end, each brand (fashion house) employs its creative designers to produce the clothes that will bear the brand's name and attract the attention of fashion aficionados, critics, photographers, and magazines. Like many other fields of cultural production, therefore, the fashion field is marked by two contradictory forces: one a comparatively unstructured world in which fashion designers and other "creatives" work out their ideas and "intuitions" in terms of technical, appreciative, and social values; the other the rational management of business growth by means of sales outlets distributed throughout the world (cf. Skov 2000; Drawbaugh 2001:122–132).

This distinction between creativity and business management partly—but only partly—explains the distinction between two types of fashion: haute couture and prêt-à-porter. Haute couture, practiced by a limited number of primarily European fashion houses that form a syndicate, provides designers with an opportunity to express their "flair," "creativity," "originality," and so on in a range of luxurious and high-priced garments that are occasionally bought (more often loaned, occasionally given) in very small numbers by (and to) the very rich and/or famous. These individualized garments tend to make a loss in their own terms (Storper and Salais 1997:125), but the practice of haute couture continues because it permits a fashion house to establish itself—along with fashion photographers, models, and fashion magazines—as part of a prestige hierarchy in the fashion field. It also permits its designer to establish, maintain, or strengthen a brand identity, or "name." This identity is then used by the fashion house to sell prêt-à-porter (ready-to-wear) merchandise and, importantly, a whole range of accessories and perfumes to a mass market at the lower end of the price range (commodities in which the fashion designer usually plays no creative part). In other words, haute couture symbolically subsidizes and is economically subsidized by prêt-à-porter accessories and fragrance sales—which is why a cover credit may carry the name of a fragrance, as well as the clothing, worn by a model. This is the logic of what Lise Skov (2000), in her study of the Hong Kong fashion world, calls the "name economy" in the field of fashion.[22]

CONCLUSION

This chapter has shown that there are three homologous layers of production that we need to take into account in any discussion of people and things. First, there is the object itself, on which, as I have shown, different actors bring to bear different kinds of values, which together contribute toward the total symbolic and commodity exchange values of that object. Second, there are the individual players or actors involved in the production of the cultural object (fashion garment, fashion photograph, fashion magazine, print advertising campaign). Third, there are the institutions that constitute the fields of fashion and fashion magazine publishing. Together these create, manipulate, and maintain the system of values outlined here, as well as the intricate web of symbolic, cultural, and economic forms of capital analyzed by Pierre Bourdieu (1993b).

NOTES

1. This broad distinction is not intended to deny, of course, that things can be personalized as "people" or that people can become "commodities" (cf. Kopytoff 1986: 64–65).

2. Any perceived systematization here is employed by me, rather than by Myers, who also talks about values that are natural, redemptive, simple, and transcendent.

3. The material presented here derives from an ongoing research project that seeks to compare two international fashion magazines, *Elle* and *Marie Claire,* published in five countries: France, Hong Kong, Japan, the United Kingdom, and the United States. Making use of approximately 500 editions of these and other titles published between 1996 and 2002, the project seeks to discuss the relationship between cultural production, content analysis, and audience reception. Its aim is to discover the extent to which international fashion magazines present a coherent global image of "woman," and how much different country productions of each title need to adapt their structure and contents to local markets (or fields), tastes, and social norms and expectations. I am very grateful to the Danish Research Council for the Humanities (September 2001–December 2002) and the Danish Institute for Advanced Studies in the Humanities (September 2000–August 2001) for enabling this research to take place.

4. There are, however, close affinities between certain titles. For example, quantitative content analysis suggests that *Elle* is a "mini" *Vogue* (which may explain the former's increasing and the latter's declining circulation figures). *Marie Claire,* on the other hand, is remarkably close to *Mademoiselle* in overall ratio of space (though not number of pages) devoted to different topics (which may explain the demise in fall 2002 of the latter title).

5. Source: Publisher's Information Bureau 2000, quoted in *Vogue Marketing* documents.

6. In its Indian edition, for example, *Elle* is somewhat closer in its emphasis on romantic and sexual content to the young women's magazine *Cosmopolitan*.

7. Actual sales (information based on research interviews) are probably closer to two-thirds of this total: 3 million copies.

8. The exchange rate used here is US$1 = ¥120.

9. Barthes (1983:15–16) also claims that written-clothing is "perfectly functional" and does not praise the "aesthetic value" of clothing. As discussed herein, my own research suggests otherwise.

10. As with much else in this part of the discussion, the language of written-clothing is often paralleled in descriptions of beauty and makeup: nails, for example, are "dramatic," and hair is "dynamic." As Jade Jagger says: "Being beautiful gives you a certain amount of power" (quoted in *Elle*, October 1997).

11. The December (Christmas) issue of the American edition of *Elle* regularly carries a feature entitled "Objects of Desire." The cover of the December 1996 edition, for example, advertised "275 Objects of Desire, Luxury, and Style" above cover model Nikki Taylor wearing a silver sequined dress and large bangle earrings. These objects of desire included 35 pairs of shoes, 23 hand and shoulder bags, 7 belts, 10 accessories, 7 beauty/makeup cases, 3 suit/shoe cases, 16 necklaces, 3 bracelets, 57 rings, 11 pieces of miscellaneous jewelry, 14 bottles of perfume, assorted pillows and fabrics, and 4 extremely expensive cars.

12. For example, the byline for the opening page of the fashion reportage *Aquarius Rising* (February 2002) reads: "Printed rayon top, Iceberg, US$212. Stretch shorts, Guess?, US$54. Goatskin coat with sable trim, J. Mendel, US$8,000. Agate necklace, Shelly, US$290. Flower belt, Celine by Michael Kors, US$460. Sandals, Sergio Rossi, US$440."

13. The English-language rhetoric of written-clothing makes heavy use of assonance, puns, clichés, and other verbal games that are almost entirely lacking in Japanese (even though Japanese humor is predominantly based on such linguistic forms in everyday life). This means that the one creates a whole vocabulary of associations ("stripe it rich," "dressed to thrill," "damsel in a dress," "blush hour") that can hardly be translated into the other, so that Japanese to a large extent maintains or creates its own rhetoric of written-clothing. At the same

time, as Japan has during the course of its history borrowed liberally from other languages, Japanese written-clothing tends to include both Western-language (primarily English, but also French) and Japanese words to describe the image-clothing found in magazines (for example, "feminine" and "*onna rashii*").

14. Myers (2001:58) also returns to the work of Pierre Bourdieu and situates "regimes of value" in what he calls "fields of force."

15. I have listened to the French-born art director of the American edition of *Elle* going into raptures over the different typefaces that he uses in the magazine, as well as the techniques used by creative director Gilles Bensimon in his fashion photographs for the magazine.

16. In previous works applying a field of values to advertising (Moeran 1996) and folk art (Moeran 1997), I have used the term "use values." However, to avoid confusion with the Marxist notion of (labor and) use value, I have here resorted to the notion of "utility."

17. There is a certain academic antipathy toward celebrities that reaches its culmination, perhaps, in Delicia Harvey and Lance Strate's (2000:208) discussion of image culture and the supermodel, where the authors suggest gratuitously that the fame of models is "unearned."

18. Informants at *Marie Claire International* in Paris said that a photographer is paid € 150 per fashion page, and twice that amount for a cover. A model is paid € 380 for a page.

19. Aspers (2001:237–248) prefers to call these "aesthetic" and economic markets.

20. Different categories of advertised goods have different rules about price inclusion. In Japan, for example, cosmetics and skin-care products always include their price in advertisements, while fragrances, jewelry, watches, underwear, and some fashion accessories occasionally do so.

21. To further complicate the field, the investment partner of the CEO of LVMH, Bernard Arnault, is Guinness, the U.K. drinks group.

22. I am very grateful to Lise Skov for her long-suffering explanations to me of the workings of the fashion industry and for the many related and intriguing conversations that we have had together over the years. This concluding discussion relies very much on her expertise and I am particularly indebted to her for the idea of "name economy."

REFERENCES

Appadurai, Arjun. 1986. Introduction: Commodities and the Politics of Value. In *The Social Life of Things.* Pp. 1–72. Cambridge, U.K.: Cambridge University Press.

Aspers, Patrik. 2001. *Markets in Fashion: A Phenomenological Approach.* Stockholm: City University Press.

Barthes, Roland. 1983. *The Fashion System.* New York: Hill & Wang.

Baudrillard, Jean. 1981. *For a Critique of the Political Economy of the Signs.* St. Louis, Mo.: Telos Press.

Becker, Howard. 1982. *Art Worlds.* Berkeley and Los Angeles: University of California Press.

Beetham, Margaret. 1996. *A Magazine of her Own? Domesticity and Desire in the Woman's Magazine 1800–1914.* London: Routledge.

Bourdieu, Pierre. 1984. *Distinction: A Social Critique of the Judgment of Taste.* Richard Nice, trans. London: Routledge & Kegan Paul.

———. 1986. The Production of Belief: Contribution to an Economy of Symbolic Goods. In *Media, Culture, and Society: A Critical Reader.* Richard Collins, ed. Pp.131–163. London: Sage.

———. 1993a. *The Field of Cultural Production.* Cambridge, U.K.: Polity.

———. 1993b. *Sociology in Question.* London: Sage.

Drawbaugh, Kevin. 2001. *Brands in the Balance: Meeting the Challenges to Commercial Identity.* London: Reuters/Pearson Education.

du Gay, Paul, ed. 1997. *Production of Culture/Cultures of Production.* London: Sage/Open University.

Ferguson, Marjorie. 1983. *Forever Feminine: Women's Magazines and the Cult of Femininity.* London: Heinemann.

Gell, Alfred. 1998. *Art and Agency: An Anthropological Theory.* Oxford: Oxford University Press.

Godelier, Maurice. 1999. *The Enigma of the Gift.* Nora Scott, trans. Cambridge, U.K.: Polity.

Graeber, David. 2001. *Toward an Anthropological Theory of Value: The False Coin of Our Own Dreams.* New York: Palgrave.

Gross, Michael. 1995. *Model: The Ugly Business of Beautiful Women*. New York: Warner Books.

Harvey, Delicia, and Lance Strate. 2000. Image Culture and the Supermodel. In *Critical Studies in Media Commercialism*. R. Andersen and L. Strate, eds. Pp. 203–213. Oxford: Oxford University Press.

Hoover's OnLine: The Business Information Authority. 2000a. Yves Saint Laurent SA Profile. Electronic document, www.hoovers.com, accessed September 19, 2000.

———. 2000b. Polo Ralph Lauren Corporate Profile. Electronic document, www.hoovers.com, accessed September 20, 2000.

Jackson, Peter, Michelle Lowe, Daniel Miller, and Frank Mort, eds. 2000. *Commercial Cultures: Economies, Practices, Spaces*. Oxford: Berg.

Jarnow, Jeanette, and Kitty Dickerson. 1997. *Inside the Fashion Business*. Upper Saddle River, N.J.: Merrill.

Kopytoff, Igor. 1986. The Cultural Biography of Things: Commoditization as Process. In *The Social Life of Things*. Arjun Appadurai, ed. Pp. 64–91. Cambridge, U.K.: Cambridge University Press.

Lash, Scott, and John Urry. 1994. *Economies of Signs and Space*. London: Sage.

McCracken, Ellen. 1993. *Decoding Women's Magazines: From* Mademoiselle *to* Ms. Basingstoke, U.K.: Macmillan.

Mediamark Research, Inc. 2000. Fall Report. New York: Mediamark Research, Inc.

Miller, Daniel. 1987. *Material Culture and Mass Consumption*. Oxford: Basil Blackwell.

Moeran, Brian. 1995. Reading Japanese in *Katei Gah?:* The Art of Being an Upperclass Woman. In *Women, Media and Consumption in Japan*. L. Skov and B. Moeran, eds. Pp. 111–142. Honolulu: University of Hawai'i Press.

———. 1996. *A Japanese Advertising Agency: An Anthropology of Media and Markets*. Honolulu: University of Hawai'i Press.

———. 1997. *Folk Art Potters of Japan: Beyond an Anthropology of Aesthetics*. Honolulu: University of Hawai'i Press.

———. 2001. The Field of Asian Media Productions. In *Asian Media Productions*. Brian Moeran, ed. Pp.1–35. London: Curzon.

Myers, Fred, ed. 2001. *The Empire of Things.* Santa Fe, N.M.: School of American Research Press; Oxford: James Currey.

Ray, Larry, and Andrew Sayer, eds. 1999. *Culture and Economy after the Cultural Turn.* London: Sage.

Skov, Lise. 2000. Stories of World Fashion and the Hong Kong Fashion World. Ph.D. diss., University of Hong Kong.

Storper, Michael, and Robert Salais. 1997. *Worlds of Production: The Action Frameworks of the Economy.* Cambridge, Mass.: Harvard University Press.

Wilk, Richard. 1996. *Economies and Cultures: Foundations of Economic Anthropology.* Boulder, Colo.: Westview Press.

Williams, Raymond. 1977. *Marxism and Literature.* Oxford: Oxford University Press.

13

Numbered Days, Valued Lives: Statistics, Shopping, Pharmacy, and the Commodification of People

Melanie Rock

On November 19, 1999, Allan Rock, Canada's health minister at the time, declared: "Diabetes costs the Canadian economy an estimated $9 billion per year, and may account for 5 to 14 percent of health care expenditures in Canada."[1] These words formed part of speech to inaugurate the Canadian Diabetes Strategy, an initiative whose stated goals are to monitor and minimize the impact of diabetes.[2] The dollars, in the billions, invoked by Minister Rock to convey the societal impact of diabetes do not disappear. Dollars change hands to cover hospital stays and pharmacological treatment, generating sales and expenditures in equal measures, but for different parties. In addition to such direct costs, diseases may involve indirect costs, such as "lost productivity," that is, potential wages and profits that never materialized. Costing the global impact of a disease, by suggesting ways to increase health and wealth, thus evokes an alternative present and a malleable future.

This chapter analyzes how knowledge about the effects of diabetes may help generate profit, loss, and, thereby, interest in the disease. Many corporations currently construe people with diabetes as a population replete with needs that may be met, at least in part, by exchanging dollars for goods and services. These needs are held to vary according to the sweetness of blood, "type" of diabetes[3] and the presence of "complications,"[4] as well as gender, age, and other characteristics (see Meltzer et al. 1998). Diabetes specialists exhort physicians to treat diabetes "aggressively" because clinical trial results suggest that continual monitoring and tight control over glucose levels will improve and extend lives.

The diabetic body is very much part of this calculus; but what is its status? I will argue that human bodies undergo commodification—yet without being bought, sold, or traded away—when estimating the benefits, costs, and profitability of health-related technologies and services. In the health arena and more generally in Canadian society, human life is often considered sacred, such that human bodies are viewed as valuable things to be preserved and nurtured—that is, kept alive and well.[5] Consistent with the notion that human lives have equal inherent value, a notion enshrined in the Canadian Charter of Rights and Freedoms (1982), human bodies are understood as valuable, malleable, and perishable things that require nurturing to sustain and enhance life. Since many different commodities may be used to sustain and enhance life, health status may engender widespread concern and many financial transactions.

In this light, the present chapter seeks to fuse insights from the anthropology of economic systems with the anthropology of medical systems and the cultural politics of embodiment. To analyze how the profit motive currently combines with health concerns, with the lively tissue and prospects of human existence, this chapter focuses on a particular line of business: the drugstore. More specifically, I investigate why, in the 1990s, Canada's largest drugstore chain construed diabetes as a marketing opportunity. The analysis encompasses the distribution and consumption of pharmaceuticals and other products designed to avert or treat disease, but I also draw attention to how the highly regulated sale of medications routinely intersects with trade in far less prestigious goods, including shampoo, bars of soap, and toilet paper.

This chapter aims to extend an active research agenda in anthropology that draws upon exchange theory to analyze various phenomena that biomedical research and related technologies have helped bring into existence (see, e.g., Hogle 2000; Layne 1999; Lock 2001; Scheper-Hughes 1996). Contributors to this anthropological research agenda have been concerned with the removal, preservation, transfer, and consumption of *body parts,* broadly conceived to include organs and tissues but also minute fragments, even single cells (Sharp 2000). Notably, especially in Western countries, laws and less formal codes regulate the circulation of human organs, tissue, and cells to approximate the ideal of social solidarity through giving, particularly altruistic giving, rather than direct exchange (Mauss 1967; Parry and Bloch 1989; Titmuss 1971).

Anthropological research on organ transplants, in vitro fertilization, and other biomedical treatments that involve the removal of material from human bodies has highlighted variation within and across social arenas in the politics of giving, getting, and keeping. It has sometimes been implied that bodily fragmentation is the key concern with the politics of giving, getting, and keeping in biomedicine and related domains (see Sharp 2000). This position suggests that, to the extent that a human body remains intact (that is, to the extent that people retain all of their "original parts," if not each and every cell with which they were born), persons have elided commodification.

In a bid to foster further reflection about the implications of such a position, the present chapter presents and analyzes a case study in which human bodies undergo a form of commodification in a capitalist system permeated by biomedical technologies and notions, yet without physically undergoing fragmentation. Indeed, in this case study, profits are extracted by marshaling a veritably sacred value ascribed to intact ("healthy") human bodies. Keeping while giving, from the point of view of the people with diabetes who frequent these drugstores, means keeping body and soul together—partly by "giving up" some of their "free time" to shopping for medications and other things that research has shown will probably prolong their lives; keeping while giving, from the point of view of the pharmacists and the drugstore chain with which they are affiliated, means keeping valued customers—partly through "giving away" professional advice (cf. Godelier 1999; Miller 1998).

BACKGROUND TO THE CASE STUDY

Shoppers Drug Mart pharmacists fill approximately 17 percent of all prescriptions and sell about 13 percent of all over-the-counter medications across Canada. The chain operates under the Pharmaprix banner in Quebec in a bid to appeal to that province's Francophone majority. A pharmacist, known as an "associate," owns and operates each store under a license agreement. In return for a share of the profits that varies by store, the chain oversees advertising, promotion, store fixtures, design, merchandising, and accounting. "The system combines entrepreneurial drive and close community ties with the benefits of national scale," according to a recent annual report (Bloom 1999).

During the twentieth century, pharmacists compounded fewer and fewer medicines as an international pharmaceutical industry gained strength. Nevertheless, "the growing complexity of drug therapy, the growth of public concern about iatrogenic disorders, and the recognition that the public needs drug education and counselling has created new social roles for the pharmacist, especially in the area of hospital pharmacy" (Turner 1987:144). Below, I examine the promotion of these new roles for pharmacists in a drugstore chain—a strategy designed to retain the chain's most desired customers.

Pharmacists have a legal monopoly over dispensing an array of pharmaceutical products in many countries, but the "petty bourgeois image of retail pharmacy" has arguably constrained the status of this profession (Turner 1987:144). Presumably, this "general storekeeper" image has also deterred many sociologists and anthropologists from conducting research among pharmacists and on the pharmacy business. Several recent ethnographic studies and review articles by anthropologists scrutinize the manufacture, prescription, and consumption of pharmaceutical products, but not their distribution (see Clarke and Montini 1993; Nichter and Vuckovic 1994; van der Geest, Whyte, and Hardon 1996; Vuckovic 2000; Vuckovic and Nichter 1997). British sociologists have, however, recently revisited the professional status and role of the retail pharmacist; they have highlighted that the power to transform drugs into medicines is vested in pharmacists, and that retail pharmacists have actively sought to enhance their status by formalizing their involvement in the surveillance of prescription and nonprescription medicine sales (Dingwall and Wilson 1995; Harding and Taylor 1997; Hibbert, Bissell, and Ward 2002).

The retail pharmacy business did not figure in my original plans for research into scientific and public knowledge about diabetes. But over the course of field research focused on how, in the 1990s, diabetes gained greater recognition as a public health problem, drugstores became highly visible as sites where a dizzying array of insurance plans, pharmaceutical products, medical devices, and supplies articulate with people whose blood is dangerously sweet. These transactions interlace with the statistical "typing" of people (after Hacking 1986). Biomedical categories such as type 1 or type 2 diabetes establish certain people as being in need of certain medications and supplies, helping to structure the flow of money. In turn, the statistical analysis of sales, profits, and losses helps structure merchandising, advertising, and promotions. Via such statistics, sweet blood gained recognition in the 1990s as an important "business line" in the Canadian drugstore business. Through marketing and promotion campaigns, in turn, drugstore chains contributed to a renewed public understanding of sweet blood as an urgent problem that can be redressed in the here and now.

I first became aware of the role that pharmacists can play in managing diabetes, and fine-tuned awareness in drugstore chains of this role and its utility for marketing purposes, while in Ottawa, Canada's capital, conducting participant-observation research at the 1999 Canadian Diabetes Association Professional Conference. Each registrant received a backpack bearing Shoppers Drug Mart's Healthwatch® logo. When I visited the Shoppers booth in the exhibit hall, the representative on hand (whose title is "disease state manager") told me that the next Diabetes Clinic Day would feature results from a landmark type 2 diabetes clinical trial, namely, that tight blood pressure control as well as tight glucose control can reduce complications and extend lives (see United Kingdom Prospective Diabetes Study Group 1998a, b, c).

To learn more about how and why Shoppers Drug Mart's head office seized upon diabetes as a marketing opportunity,[6] I later conducted a formal extended interview at company headquarters in Toronto with the disease state manager whom I met at the 1999 Canadian Diabetes Association Professional Conference, and I integrated questions about the pharmacy business into more than twenty-five interviews with leading diabetes researchers, clinicians, registered diabetes educators, product representatives, and bureaucrats. I also analyzed more than one hundred company documents, three hundred newspaper articles, one hundred hours' worth of verbatim speeches by politicians and diabetes researchers, the authorized biography of Shoppers Drug Mart's founder (see Rasky 1988), and scores of government documents, independent market research reports, and magazines. I did not, in other words, study a sample of pharmacists in detail. Rather, I investigated the incorporation of public polices along with epidemiologic and demographic data in retail pharmacy management and then analyzed the results of this investigation through the lens of theory in economic anthropology.

PUTTING A DOLLAR VALUE ON HUMAN NEEDS

A taboo on expressing the value of human lives directly in dollars has fueled reliance on a plethora of "end points" and "quality of life" instruments to measure and compare health status in populations (Epstein 1997; Koch 2000; Löwy 2000; Porter 1992; Rock 2000 for discussion). Human life, from this perspective, is sacred and hence should be valued apart from money. Yet monetary flows have been associated with the length and overall quality of human lives. In anthropological terms, the practice of expressing quality of life in relation to dollars, as opposed to in dollars, signals the existence of distinct regimes of value (after Appadurai 1986; Bohannan 1959; Kopytoff 1986).

Anthropologists have historically contrasted commodity with gift exchange in ways that reflect the tendency, since the abolition of slavery in Western countries, to separate monetary value from the value accorded human beings (Bloch and Parry 1989; Miller 1995; Strathern 1996). This distinction—that is, what money can or ought to buy, versus what gifts can or should bring— has infused the political economy tradition and anthropologists' contributions to this tradition. A synthesis of the Marxist understanding of the commodity and the Maussian understanding of gifts that has proved influential in anthropology (see Gregory 1982 and table 13.1) suggests that gifts have an animate character usually not found in commodities. From this perspective, gifts involve and cement personal relationships, while the exchange of commodities remains impersonal. Yet social rank may interweave with commodity consumption: the conversion of commodities into gifts provides a key case in point (Gregory 1982:167–209; see also Miller 1995; Yang 2000). For Gregory, however, commodity exchange—laid bare—comprises a series of vapid transactions that, in the aggregate, set groups of people apart from one another.

Thomas argues that Gregory's distillation of how commodities differ from gifts to exchange revolves around ideal types, which blur in practice: "Precisely because the theoretical contrast is developed with such clarity, the question arises of whether the postulated gift is anything other than the inversion of the commodity" (Thomas 1991:15). This question, in turn, supposes that anthropologists fully grasp the nature of commodification—at least in "the West." Thomas observes that "commonsensical practical knowledge" dictates that, for example, "one does not go into a shop to establish or consolidate a social relationship" (Thomas 1991:8). Yet the case study of interest in this chapter involves

Table 13.1   Gifts versus Commodities

Commodities	Gifts
Alienable	Inalienable
Quantity (Price)	Quality (Rank)
Objects	Subjects

(Thomas 1991, 15; after Gregory 1982)

a network of pharmacist–shopkeepers seeking to establish and consolidate a relationship with certain customers possessed of sweet blood.

I do not defend a particular definition of the commodity, nor of the gift,
in this chapter. Therefore, I do not engage some recent empirical research
and theorizing on the relationship between gift and commodity exchange in
Western and non-Western contexts (e.g., Carrier 1997; Gell 1992; Goddard
2000). Instead, the case study analyzed in this chapter suggests that the
salience of the commodity/gift distinction in economic anthropology, in
Western societies and in many non-Western societies, has led anthropologists
to identify—readily and quite accurately—*certain* biomedical practices, ones
that fragment human bodies, as economic and political phenomena; yet anthropologists have so far not applied theories from economic anthropology to analyze biomedical renderings of human bodies that do not involve the transfer of
body parts or physical dismemberment. To help demonstrate the pertinence of
theory from economic anthropology for understanding the deployment of
biomedical knowledge to keep human bodies alive and intact for as long as
possible, I analyze how a particular company capitalized on some of the qualities that have, in the anthropological literature and more generally in
Western societies, been associated with gift exchange. Put simply, Shoppers
Drug Mart sought to imbue the monetary exchange for goods such as medicines, medical technologies, and medical supplies with traits often associated
with gifts.

The point of departure for this chapter is the analysis of value setting, as
opposed to the commodity/gift distinction. Here I follow Appadurai (1986),
who has argued convincingly that owing to the emphasis on the commodity/
gift distinction in economic anthropology, certain processes that are common
to all transactions have escaped attention. He observes, however, that even
conceptualizing something as exchangeable entails value setting. He refuses to
define "the gift" or "the commodity" and instead offers a definition of a
"commodity situation": the situation in which a thing's exchangeability—
past, present, or future—for some other thing is a socially relevant feature
(Appadurai 1986:13). While Appadurai confines his analysis to the commodification of things, as opposed to people (cf. Kopytoff 1986; Strathern
1992), his insights helped me see that the statistical "typing" of bodies
in biomedicine stems from valuing human life in, simultaneously, categori-
cal and qualified terms. Paradoxically, the sacred value assigned to human

life leads to differentiating among people on the basis of statistics that index the length and overall quality of their lives. Viewed biostatistically, some people seem better off because they are kept alive longer and in better condition.

Putting aside conventional understandings of commodities and gifts in light of Appadurai's (1986) focus on the politics of need and desire, it is clear that the statistical typing of people construes human bodies as malleable, valuable, and interchangeable things. Yet each human body is also unique, particularly from the perspective of the person contained therein (after Kopytoff 1986). This tension between commonality and singularity defies resolution. Nevertheless, the notion that human beings are simultaneously fungible (as members of populations) and idiosyncratic (as individual persons) often seems unremarkable.

That human bodies replace themselves over time, changing as they age, underpins the possibility of shopping for ways to extend and improve on the sacred "gift of life" (cf. Layne 1999). The pharmacy has become a site where Canadians actively weigh the costs and benefits—financial and otherwise—of intensively monitoring and controlling the sweetness of their blood, among many other ominous signs and symptoms. Shoppers Drug Mart has succeeded in charging associations between monetary expenditure and lifeblood to its advantage, which has entailed carefully minimizing any appearance of mercantilism. That is, the company has tried to avoid any suggestion that, while Shoppers Drug Mart benefits from diabetes, people with diabetes do not benefit from Shoppers Drug Mart.

HEALTH INSURANCE IN CANADA

Before we proceed, a few words on the structure of Canada's health care system are in order. Commentators often mistake Canada's health care system for a "socialized" system. In fact, most physicians in Canada are in private practice. Their income depends on the number and type of services they provide. While most physicians in Canada are in private practice, publicly funded health insurance covers all Canadians. The federal government transfers funds to Canada's ten provinces to cover a portion of the costs entailed in delivering health care in clinics and in hospitals, provided that provincial health insurance plans embody five principles: public administration, comprehensiveness, universality, portability, and accessibility.

Provincial health insurance plans in Canada cover all products consumed and services rendered within hospitals, but these plans vary widely in the extent to which they cover pharmaceutical products and medical supplies prescribed for consumption off hospital grounds. Many, but by no means all, Canadians receive coverage for a select range of pharmaceuticals, medical supplies, and services such as dentistry, massage therapy, or counseling through private insurance, typically offered as part of an employee benefits package.

The issue of insurance coverage for pharmaceuticals and the price of these products recurs in charged debates about the future of Canada's health care system, as illustrated by two articles published in the *Globe and Mail*, a nationally circulated newspaper, on consecutive days in 2001. "Six Million Lack Proper Drug Plans, Study Finds," read the headline of the first of these articles (Picard 2001a). The headline of an article published the next day read, "Spending on Drugs Up, Data Say" (Picard 2001b).

For people with diabetes and organizations such as the Canadian Diabetes Association, the cumulative, lifelong financial impact of sickly sweet blood and the availability of insurance coverage to offset these costs are of concern. The capacity to meet diabetes-related needs and the impact of these needs on household budgets vary across Canada with employment status, province of residence, income, and insurance coverage. On average, the Canadian Diabetes Association estimates that someone with diabetes incurs medical costs that are two to five times higher than those of a person without diabetes. Each time people with diabetes test their own blood sugar, which they are advised to do several times a day, the necessary supplies cost about a dollar. In an interview published in the Canadian Diabetes Association's magazine targeting adults with diabetes, the then newly appointed public policy and government relations director, Debra Lynkowski, named as the three most pressing issues in her portfolio government awareness of "the huge financial, emotional, and social costs related to diabetes," "full access to reasonable and adequate insurance coverage," and the "drug review process and pricing" (see *Diabetes Dialogue* 1999).

TARGETING SWEET DEMOGRAPHICS

People do not have to be bought or sold outright for human bodies, in whole or in part, to undergo commodification. Wage labor, for example, commodifies time spent in human bodies while also accommodating a taboo on buying and selling persons. Moreover, entire human populations undergo com-modification when the individual bodies comprising them are construed as amenable to improvement, that is, when it seems possible and even impera-tive to exchange one sort of future for another through the allocation of re-sources, here and now (Rock 2000; cf. Sharp 2000). Below, I aim to contribute to knowledge about how human bodies may constitute repositories of value under capitalism by simply existing or, more specifically, by exhibiting recog-nized needs and the potential for meeting these needs.[7] The analysis trains at-tention on how biomedical knowledge about diabetes interlaces with the evaluation of the productivity and profitability of consumption, with partic-ular concern for bodily action *not* bought and sold as wage labor.

The human body's conversion of food into glucose does not count as labor but underlies the capacity to labor. Two known "modifiable risk factors" for type 2 diabetes, which accounts for 90 percent of all cases, are high body mass and infrequent physical exertion (Black 2002)—both intimately related to "lifestyle," to the patterning of production and consumption. People with all types of diabetes, whose cells cannot absorb glucose from the bloodstream, have dangerously sweet blood. Primary prevention of type 2 diabetes (avert-ing the onset of individual cases) and secondary prevention (averting the on-set of complications in individual cases through timely diagnosis and aggressive treatment) promise to extend the capacity to labor in the course of extending lives. Statistics incorporating lost productivity are often bandied about in rhetoric about diabetes, as illustrated by the speech cited at the out-set of this chapter. Yet in Canada, the possibility of extending and enhancing "life itself" (cf. Foucault 1994; Franklin 2000) receives discursive emphasis,[8] along with the concomitant potential to reduce personal and public health care expenditures (Rock 2003a).

In the 1990s, Shoppers Drug Mart's stress on the pharmacist as a health professional emerged and evolved, reinforcing and exploiting public concern about health, health care, and health care expenditures. The company's focus on diabetes and other select health concerns also entwines with innovations in information technology, the franchise structure of the company, demo-graphic trends, public policies, pressure exerted by competitors, and access to large amounts of capital.

Testifying to the success of Shoppers' emphasis on health and professional ser-vice, in 1999, a self-described "once-sleepy wholesaler" aired a series of television ads specifically designed to wrest away from Shoppers the "moral high ground" (Brent 1999). The advertisements dramatized true stories involving pharmacists supplied by the wholesaler going above and beyond the call of duty. One ad featured a pharmacist climbing over rock slides to deliver medication to a hospital; another featured a pharmacist awakened by an emergency call, opening her store in the dead of night, and delivering supplies to a maternity ward.

But how did Shoppers Drug Mart, a drugstore chain steeped in tobacco profits, manage to gain Canadian pharmacy's "moral high ground"? Imperial Tobaccos was the flagship of Imasco, the conglomerate that owned Shoppers Drug Mart from 1978 until it was dismantled in 1999. In turn, Imperial Tobacco is and was part of the British American Tobacco (BAT) group, whose U.S. subsidiary, Brown and Williamson, plays a villain in the film *The Insider*.[9]

In 1992, Shoppers began distributing fact sheets about each new prescription, billed as Healthwatch® Reminders (Bloom 1995). These PILs, patient information leaflets, are hardly unique to Shoppers Drug Mart, yet they have helped Shoppers Drug Mart build brand-name recognition for its pharmacy services under the Healthwatch® banner (Ralston 2000). With the computerization of prescription claims, pharmacists are positioned to detect potentially harmful drug interactions, as well as efforts to fill the same prescription more than once. Today Shoppers Drug Mart trumpets the health advantages for consumers gained by computerization as part of a comprehensive Healthwatch® System. Yet to a significant extent, Healthwatch© System components other than PILs owe their existence to Wal-Mart.

In 1994, the American discount chain Wal-Mart entered Canada, courtesy of the 1988 Canada-U.S. Free Trade Agreement, with the purchase of more than 120 stores. Wal-Mart pharmacists dispense approximately 5 percent of all prescriptions in Canada. The chain offers low prices on pharmacy products to lure customers. Following Wal-Mart's entry into the Canadian market, other large-surface stores installed pharmacy departments; like Wal-Mart, they began using prescription and over-the-counter drugs as loss leaders. These new players slashed dispensing fees, the fees levied by pharmacists on each prescription drug order that they process. A discount mail-order prescription business also set up shop (Greenwood 1993). Presented with the possibility of obtaining the same prescription drugs for less from new players, consumers took increased notice of dispensing fees, as did third-party insurers, both public and private.

These dynamics played out in the Ontario government's 1996 adoption of a policy to contain pharmaceutical spending under its health insurance plan. Since July 15, 1996, senior citizens and welfare recipients in Ontario pay CAN$2 to fill each prescription, whereas the provincial government used to fully cover their dispensing fees. In response, Wal-Mart promised to absorb each CAN$2 levy. It also slashed its dispensing fees to CAN$4.11; Shoppers Drug Mart and other chain drug stores were charging about three times as much to process prescriptions (Brent 1996a).

"Some retailers will elect to use pharmacy as a traffic builder and treat prescriptions as a commodity to sell more food or soft goods," observed Shoppers' CEO David Bloom at the time (cited in Brent 1996b). But Shoppers also prized health-related purchases for their capacity to draw customers into their stores, necessary to trigger all-important impulse buys. On the day that Ontario's new policy took effect, Shoppers rolled out a new program for Ontario seniors—but not for welfare recipients. Dubbed the Healthwatch® Seniors Club, the program offers a 10 percent discount on its private-label stock, including vitamins, over-the-counter medications, and medical supplies (Brent 1996b).

Wal-Mart, meanwhile, took square aim at employer-sponsored health insurance plans. In exchange for exclusivity, it offered "monitoring and counselling services to ensure maximum cost containment and efficient administration of prescription drug programs" (Brent 1996a). A consultant interviewed for the story noted: "It locks in a whole bunch of people that are affiliated with the partner, and it starts getting the message out that this is the lowest price." He expressed surprise that Shoppers Drug Mart had not adopted this "clever strategy" (cited in Brent 1996a).

In response to fierce new competition, Shoppers reexamined its operations. In 1994, market research among its pharmacists revealed that four medical conditions—diabetes, cardiovascular disease, asthma, and arthritis—generated more regular visits to Shoppers Drug Mart locations than any others. Of these four diseases, managers at Shoppers Drug Mart's central office decided to focus initially on diabetes, partly because of established links with the Juvenile Diabetes Foundation,[10] but also because of its profitability.

Diabetes-related merchandise was identified as a significant "shopfront" category, meaning selling inventory other than prescription drugs, mainly owing to the profit margins on equipment and supplies to monitor blood glucose levels. Shopfront sales had taken on renewed importance in the 1990s with new competitors offering lower dispensing fees on prescriptions and with the reclassification of many prescription drugs to over-the-counter status as provincial governments sought to reduce health care costs. Over-the-counter drugs are not reimbursed under prescription drug plans, which can discourage their purchase, noted the CEO of Shoppers in an annual report to Imasco shareholders (see Bloom 1995).

In September 1994, the Shoppers chain hosted a trade show for its Toronto-area pharmacists, which featured "newfangled" blood glucose monitors designed for patient use.[11] This trade show led Shoppers Drug Mart pharmacists to reflect on how blood glucose monitors and supplies available for purchase in their stores, as well as pharmaceuticals, stand to affect health outcomes. Participants rated the experience highly. In 1995, the company created a new head-office position, the disease state manager, who promptly organized workshops modeled on the Toronto event in locations across Canada.

In 1996, Shoppers Drug Mart intensified the focus on pharmacists' role in diabetes management, with a view to positioning them as active and vital members of the diabetes health care team. Shoppers' disease state manager prepared a resource manual to enhance pharmacists' understanding of diabetes and their role in its control. The company also printed logbooks for distribution to customers, which proved very popular. It turned out that although people with diabetes are supposed to self-monitor the sweetness of their blood at regular intervals, they lacked a ready, steady supply of logbooks in which to record and track their routine blood glucose tests.

In 1998, the "Healthwatch® Diabetes Care Tool Kit" entered a new phase, and the first annual Diabetes Clinic Day took place. By then, Shoppers Drug Mart had developed planning tools and held a "clinic day" to promote better use of asthma medications. "This was the pharmacist coming down from the upper echelon," said the Shoppers Drug Mart disease state manager when reflecting on this event in an interview with me. The "asthma experience" served as a prototype in designating a Canada-wide diabetes clinic day and developing a plan to help guide and reinforce diabetes counseling by Shoppers Drug Mart pharmacists. The diabetes plan incorporates prompts to related information sheets on hypoglycemia, healthy eating, and blood glucose monitoring. Each pharmacist also received a two-sided, laminated card to assist in matching different kinds of customers with blood glucose monitors. Here types of diabetes join stock demographic variables, health insurance coverage, personality, computer skills, "cost consciousness," and the presence of certain physical limitations (such as reduced dexterity and vision impairment) as considerations in the purchase of equipment to monitor the sweetness of blood. In partnership with the Canadian Diabetes Association, Shoppers Drug Mart also developed and distributed a quiz, under the banner "Are you at risk?" to reach customers who had not been diagnosed with diabetes.

Legislation governing health professionals prevents pharmacists from drawing blood. "What could we do without finger pricking that would be of value?" Shoppers Drug Mart central office staff asked. The emphasis on information in the Diabetes Clinic Day emerged in response. The "value-added" component would be knowledge about one's own health, symbolized by a number that situated the individual in a large population. The number would help, and hopefully satisfy, individuals wanting to know: "How do I rate?"

Shoppers' head office has sought to impress upon its pharmacists that many people with diabetes remain underinformed about the disease, to the point that about one-third of all people with type 2 diabetes do not even know that they have this condition (see Harris et al. 1997). By providing educational services in their stores, including appropriate referrals, Shoppers Drug Mart stresses that the pharmacist may positively affect patient outcomes.

To promote commitment among its pharmacists to the prevention of diabetes and its complications, Shoppers Drug Mart publishes a newsletter, *Diabetes and the Pharmacist,* under the Healthwatch® banner. By way of illustration of its contents, the May 1999 version contained information about the Juvenile Diabetes Foundation "Walk for the Cure" fund-raiser; told readers that thirty-nine more of its pharmacists had elected to write the Diabetes Educator Certification Exam under the auspices of the Canadian Diabetes Association; provided information about two clinical trials seeking subjects that "you may wish to tell your patients about"; listed specials on diabetes-related shopfront merchandise that were slated for inclusion in upcoming issues of the national flyer; introduced Regenex®, the recombinant DNA gel that aids the healing of diabetic foot ulcers; highlighted target glucose and lipid levels set out in the *1998 Clinical Practice Guidelines for the Treatment of Diabetes in Canada;* featured a common "patient question" about the use of herbs to control the sweetness of blood, to which a pharmacist with a Ph.D. gave a page-long reply; and, finally, presented evaluation results from the latest Diabetes Clinic Day.

Faced with Wal-Mart and other new competitors, Shoppers Drug Mart wanted to persuade customers to continue doing business with it and individuals and insurers to pay premium prescription dispensing fees for the privilege. The company responded by promoting concern for the health of its customers. Cultivation of the pharmacist–customer relationship took place alongside a very substantial reorganization of the Shoppers Drug Mart network. Until 1997, Shoppers pharmacist–associates did all their own buying from individual vendors and kept their own books. Since 1997, Shoppers Drug Mart has maintained a central accounting system and database, point-of-sale systems, and regional distribution centers linked by satellite to individual stores (Brandao 1997:129). Imasco annual reports from the mid-1990s stress that, in return for the CAN$250-million outlay to realize these changes, billed internally as Vision 97, shareholders could expect greater market share and profitability. Diabetes counseling, which these changes promised to enhance, appeared as a flagship for customer loyalty in Imasco's 1995 annual report:

> In 1995 Shoppers expanded our pharmacists' advisory role by inaugurating a counselling program aimed at patients with chronic diseases. The first disease targeted was diabetes and a system-wide training program enhanced our capacity to help diabetic patients monitor and achieve better control of their blood sugar levels. Private counselling is the fastest growing service area in pharmacy, and Shoppers' health-care advisory function will soon expand to include other diseases such as cardiovascular disease, asthma, and arthritis. This amplified role will be stepped up as Vision 97's streamlining measures free our pharmacists to spend more time with customers. (Bloom 1996:15)

In the end, Shoppers Drug Mart elected to develop a program focused on women's health rather than on arthritis because women of all ages form such a significant portion of the company's customer base: they tend to shop for themselves and for family members. Moreover, the three other main traffic-generating medical conditions—asthma, diabetes, and cardiovascular disease—are all potentially fatal, underscoring the importance of sound management (Ralston 2000).

The establishment of diabetes and other "disease state" management programs from 1996 onward extended and built recognition for the Health-watch® brand:

By focusing on specific disease states such as diabetes, asthma or heart disease, and by fostering a strong connection to Shoppers Drug Mart, we built trust across the board—and not just from people suffering from these diseases. Now we could be seen as managers of health outcomes, reflecting the consumer trend towards self-care. (Ralston 2000)

While the company has historically spent a large part of its advertising budget on television spots, it currently promotes the Healthwatch® brand in magazines as well. For example, it advertises in *Diabetes Dialogue,* the Canadian Diabetes Association's publication for adults, as well as in mainstream magazines. According to a spokesperson, "Healthwatch advertising shows a commitment to pharmacy, thereby increasing its value to the consumer. It has allowed Shoppers to develop a pharmacy brand—an industry first" (Ralston 2000).

Thus, by the mid-1990s, Shoppers Drug Mart aimed to deploy its pharmacists as the vanguard of customer service. Relieved of the minutiae of merchandising and accounting, the pharmacist would be "free" to concentrate on providing services of professional caliber. In doing so, the local pharmacy would embody a "health destination," and while in the stores, customers could attend to other needs as well as impulses. The company and its advertising agency focused on "sweet demographics": people with diabetes and other chronic conditions that generate frequent pharmacy visits, with particular regard for those with higher incomes and insurance for prescriptions.

Annual reports from the late 1990s and 2000 portrayed this renewed focus on professionalism and desirable demographics as a source of competitive advantage. Total sales grew from CAN$3.3 billion in 1995 to CAN$4.3 billion in 1999; total earnings increased from CAN$101 million in 1995 to CAN$277 million in 1999.[12] By 1999, prescriptions, over-the-counter medications, and medical supplies together accounted for 55 percent of total sales. "Nutraceuticals"—vitamins, minerals, herbal remedies, and other dietary supplements—had become more significant and increasingly occupy a demarcated area near the dispensary. After the company installed such kiosks, vitamin sales increased 40 percent (Hanson 1999). A renovation program currently under way aims to facilitate "patient–pharmacist dialogue" and improve the "customer's shopping experience" by introducing waiting areas near dispensaries, semiprivate counseling areas, and private consultation rooms, among other reforms (Bloom 1999:14). Rather than slashing dispensing fees, explained Shoppers'

CEO to investors, "Shoppers Drug Mart's approach is to demonstrate to payers that pharmacy services, properly managed, lead to better patient outcomes and lower overall health-care costs" (Bloom 1999:13). To date, the company has not released any evidence that its approach has led to better outcomes for customers with diabetes or other chronic medical conditions, but by referencing health in advertising, in-store promotions, and pharmacist services, Shoppers Drug Mart has certainly managed to reposition itself most profitably in an altered marketplace.

CONCLUSION

In the late 1980s, some predicted that by the year 2000, pharmacists would become health advisers, such that "you'll have to make an appointment and pay a fee for the consultation as you would with a physician" (Rasky 1988:325). In fact, Shoppers Drug Mart and certain competitors have "freed up" pharmacists to "give away" consultation services on the spot and by appointment, the better to attract and retain choice customers. The development and promotion of "free" Healthwatch® services, such as diabetes education, also help justify the annual franchise fee levied on associate pharmacists. Retail pharmacists receive billing as health professionals, free to "share" their expertise with customers who value their help. The trick of the Healthwatch® brand and related services has been to coat expenditures on disease management and prevention in a reassuring package, one that yields repeat business and a high profit-to-visit ratio.

When I sketched how Shoppers Drug Mart had embraced diabetes education, one interlocutor said, "They [people with diabetes] are cash cows." English-speaking Canadians may not like to imagine themselves as commodifying people, and we do not, at least in the vernacular, talk of human bodies as piggy banks or storehouses (cf. Strathern 1996:517), but we routinely conceive of certain people as "cash cows."

The notion that we might so value human life that health care and health promotion could command, rather than compete for, money and other resources has a romantic ring. Yet if commodification is a universal human phenomenon, the commodification of people would appear inevitable. The commodification of people does not mean that human bodies and body parts always circulate as "commodities" or "gifts," I hasten to add, but rather that they constantly undergo valuation and seem, to varying degrees, replaceable, reproducible, desirable, and amenable to improvement (after Kopytoff 1986; Strathern 1996).

As customers become statistically typed in finer and finer terms (smoker; type 2 diabetic; Internet user), terms that imbricate different people with products, and thus actual and potential profits, retailers and manufacturers truly understand people simultaneously—and interchangeably—as individuals and as populations (pace Foucault 1991). Even though detachment is theoretically characteristic of commodity exchange, the statistical trace left behind by each in-store transaction means that customers and their purchases remain symbolically attached from the company's point of view. Meanwhile, from the customer's point of view, the valorization of professional status and the power vested in pharmacists to convert mere substance into medicines mean that pharmacists and what they sell may also remain symbolically attached.

In the databases currently maintained by drugstore chains, biomedical categories mingle with postal codes, annual incomes, insurance plans, birth dates, and popular perfumes. A recent feature article on the business implications of point-of-sale technologies observed:

> Once upon a time, the person behind the counter knew virtually everything about everybody who walked into the shop. And that's really what today's technology and information gathering is leading up to: a return to one-to-one customer intimacy. (Menzies 2001)

Yet the intimacy achieved through point-of-sale technologies implicates distant statistical analysis, "data mining," rather than direct observation or face-to-face dialogues.

Shoppers Drug Mart's statistically mediated embrace of diabetes underscores that valuation and classification always entail some form of social mediation. The carapace of impersonality afforded by statistics (Porter 1992) permits the valuation of human beings and their lives to occur, for instance, in the guise of "merely" counting cases of diabetes or blood glucose monitors. This form of double counting, weighing the worth of people alongside the cost of supplies, is not necessarily sinister or disadvantageous to those evaluated, but it does take place. The condemnation of commodifying human bodies and body parts within anthropology and more broadly (see Sharp 2000) would appear to conflate commodification (setting value, attributing exchangeability or interchangeability) with inequality. The commodification of people may be inevitable in human societies, but not so the form, conceptualization, and degree of inequality.

NOTES

A doctoral fellowship from the Social Sciences and Humanities Research Council of Canada made this research possible. The Université de Montréal's Groupe de recherche interdisciplinaire en santé awarded a travel grant for me to attend the 2001 Society for Economic Anthropology conference. I was able to revise this material for presentation and publication thanks to support in the form of a postdoctoral fellowship, sponsored by the Canadian Foundation for Health Services Research and the Canadian Institutes for Health Research and held at the Université de Montréal.

1. I share my last name with Allan Rock, but I do not know him personally. Several government officials, researchers, and representatives of lobbying groups asked me, during the course of my field research, whether I am related to this politician—serving notice of just how important personal contacts remain in Canadian politics.

2. These financial estimates were based on dividing counterpart U.S. figures by ten as the American population is approximately ten times larger than Canada's population; homegrown Canadian data of this nature were not available—one of the shortcomings that the Canadian Diabetes Strategy promised to correct.

3. All types of diabetes are diagnosed on the basis of the sweetness of blood (that is, elevated blood glucose levels).

4. People with diabetes are prone to a wide range of health problems, including renal failure, erectile dysfunction, cavities, and gangrene. Compared to people without diabetes, they tend to die at a younger age, notably from cardiovascular disease. For further discussion of the politics of describing and ascribing "risk" in relation to diabetes, see Rock, 2003a.

5. Notably, the death penalty does not exist in Canada.

6. This chapter's concern with how the head office of a drugstore chain identified a particular disease as a marketing opportunity complements research on the identification of disease as a market opportunity in the biotechnology sector (see Fleising 2001).

7. See Povinelli (1993, 2000) for a similar line of inquiry but different problematics.

8. Field research suggests that employers evince concern not only about diabetics' capacity to labor but also about the "burden" placed by diabetes on employee benefit plans. These issues are not, however, openly discussed. They merit additional research.

9. The 1999 film *The Insider* was based on an investigative report (see Brenner 1996). For further information about Brown and Williamson, Imperial Tobacco, and BAT, see Cunningham 1996 and Glantz 1996.

10. In partnership with the Juvenile Diabetes Foundation of Canada, Shoppers Drug Mart has raised funds for diabetes research since the mid-1980s. A board member suggested that corporate donations focus on this charity after his son developed type 1 diabetes.

11. In the wake of clinical trials that found that intensive control over the sweetness of blood improves future prospects, the technological capacity to self-monitor blood glucose greatly increased.

12. The second-largest drugstore chain in Canada, the Jean Coutu group, also reported record earnings during this period.

REFERENCES

Appadurai, Arjun. 1986. Introduction: Commodities and the Politics of Value. In *The Social Life of Things: Commodities in Cultural Perspective*. Arjun Appadurai, ed. Pp. 3–63. Cambridge, U.K.: Cambridge University Press.

Black, Sandra A. 2002. Diabetes, Diversity, and Disparity: What Do We Do with the Evidence? *American Journal of Public Health* 92(4):543–548.

Bloch, Maurice, and Jonathan Parry. 1989. Introduction: Money and the Morality of Exchange. In *Money and the Morality of Exchange*. Jonathan Parry and Maurice Bloch, eds. Pp. 1–32. Cambridge, U.K.: Cambridge University Press.

Bloom, David. 1995. Shoppers Drug Mart / Pharmaprix. In *1994 Imasco Annual Report*. Pp. 16–17. Montreal: Imasco.

———. 1996. Shoppers Drug Mart / Pharmaprix. In *1995 Imasco Annual Report*. Pp. 16–17. Montreal: Imasco.

———. 1999. Shoppers Drug Mart / Pharmaprix. In *1998 Imasco Annual Report*. Pp. 16–17. Montreal: Imasco.

Bohannan, Paul. 1959. The Impact of Money on an African Subsistence Economy. *Journal of Economic History* 19:491–503.

Brandao, Cristina P. 1997. Winning the Tech Wars: The Winners of This Year's Canadian Information Productivity Awards. In *Canadian Business* 70(28):129–130.

Brent, Paul. 1996a. Discounter Wal-Mart Targets Corporate Prescription Plans. In *The Financial Post.* May 3:7.

———. 1996b. Shoppers Fights Back against Price-Cutters. In *The Financial Post.* July 12:12.

———. 1999. "Once-sleepy" Drug Trading Runs Major Campaign: First Big Push in Ten Years. In *National Post.* August 23:C04.

Canada. 1982. Canadian Charter of Rights and Freedoms. Ottawa, Ontario.

Carrier, James G. 1997. *Gifts and Commodities: Exchange and Western Capitalism since 1700.* London: Routledge.

Clarke, Adele, and Theresa Montini. 1993. The Many Faces of RU486: Tales of Situated Knowledges and Technological Contestations. *Science, Technology, and Human Values* 18(1):42–78.

Dingwall, R., and E. Wilson. 1995. Is Pharmacy Really an "Incomplete Profession"? *Perspectives on Social Problems* 7:111–128.

Epstein, Steve. 1997. Activism, Drug Regulation, and the Politics of Therapeutic Evaluation in the AIDS Era: A Case Study of ddC and the "'Surrogate Markers" Debate. *Social Studies of Science* 27(5):691–726.

Fleising, Usher. 2001. In Search of Genohype: A Content Analysis of Biotechnology Company Documents. *New Genetics and Society* 20(1):239–254.

Foucault, Michel. 1991 [1978]. Governmentality. In *The Foucault Effect: Studies in Governmentality with Two Lectures by and an Interview with Michel Foucault.* G. Burchell, C. Gordon, and P. Miller, eds. Pp. 87–104. Chicago: University of Chicago Press.

———. 1994 [1979]. Naissance de la biopolitique. *In* Dits et écrits, vol. 3 (1976–1979). D. Defert, F. Ewald, and J. Lagrange, eds. Pp. 818–825. Paris: Gallimard.

Franklin, Sarah. 2000. Life Itself: Global Nature and the Genetic Imaginary. Department of Sociology, Lancaster University. Electronic document, www.comp.lancs.ac.uk/sociology/soc048sf.html, accessed March 2003.

Gell, Alfred. 1992. Inter-Tribal Commodity Barter and Reproductive Gift-Exchange in Old Melanesia. In *Barter, Exchange, and Value: An Anthropological Approach.*

C. Humphrey and S. Hugh-Jones, eds. Pp. 142–168. Cambridge, U.K.: Cambridge University Press.

Goddard, Michael. 2000. Of Cabbages and Kin: The Value of an Analytic Distinction between Gifts and Commodities. *Critique of Anthropology* 20(2):137–151.

Godelier, Maurice. 1999 [1996]. *The Enigma of the Gift.* Nora Scott, trans. Chicago: University of Chicago Press.

Greenwood, John. 1993. A New Deal on Drugs: Meditrust, Norman Paul's New Drug Mail-Order Business, Is a Bitter Pill to Swallow for Canada's Pharmacy Retailing Giants. In *The Financial Post Magazine.* Pp. 112.

Gregory, Christopher. 1982. *Gifts and Commodities.* London: Academic Press.

Hacking, Ian. 1986. Making Up People. In *Reconstructing Individualism: Autonomy, Individuality, and the Self in Western Thought.* H. C. Heller, M. Sosna, and D. E. Wellbery, eds. Pp. 222–236. Stanford, Calif.: Stanford University Press.

Hanson, Kim. 1999. Natural Remedies Boom: There May Be No Scientific Proof Herbal Remedies Work, but That Hasn't Stopped Family-Run Nutrition House from Building a 60-Store Business. In *National Post.* July17:D5.

Harding, G., and K. Taylor. 1997. Responding to Change: The Case of Community Pharmacy in Great Britain. *Sociology of Health & Illness* 19:547–560.

Harris, M. I., R. C. Eastman, C. C. Cowie, K. M. Flegal, and M. S. Eberhardt. 1997. Comparison of Diabetes Diagnostic Categories in the U.S. Population According to the 1997 American Diabetes Association and 1980–1985 World Health Organization Diagnostic Criteria. *Diabetes Care* 20(12):1859–1862.

Hibbert, Derek, Paul Bissel, and Paul R. Ward. 2002. Consumerism and Professional Work in the Pharmacy. *Sociology of Health and Illness* 24(1):46–65.

Hogle, Linda. 2000. *Recovering the Nation's Body: Cultural Memory, Medicine, and the Politics of Redemption.* New Brunswick, N.J.: Rutgers University Press.

Koch, Tom. 2000. Life Quality vs. the "Quality of Life": Assumptions Underlying Prospective Quality of Life Instruments in Health Care Planning. *Social Science and Medicine* 51(3):419–427.

Kopytoff, Igor. 1986. The Cultural Biography of Things: Commoditization as Process. In *The Social Life of Things: Commodities in Cultural Perspective.* Arjun Appadurai, ed. Pp. 64–91. Cambridge, U.K.: Cambridge University Press.

Layne, Linda, ed. 1999. *Transformative Motherhood: On Giving and Getting in a Consumer Culture.* New York: New York University Press.

Lock, Margaret. 2001. *Twice Dead: Organ Transplants and the Reinvention of Death.* Berkeley and Los Angeles: University of California Press.

Löwy, Ilana. 2000. Trustworthy Knowledge and Desperate Patients: Clinical Tests for New Drugs from Cancer to AIDS. In *Living and Working with the New Medical Technologies: Intersections of Inquiry.* M. Lock, A. Young, and A. Cambrosio, eds. Pp. 49–81. Cambridge, U.K.: Cambridge University Press.

Mauss, Marcel. 1967 [1925]. *The Gift.* I. Cunnison, trans. London: Cohen & West.

Meltzer, S., L. Leiter, D. Daneman, H. C. Gerstein, D. Lau, S. Ludwig, J. F. Yale, B. Zinman, and D. Lillie. 1998. 1998 Clinical Practice Guidelines for the Management of Diabetes in Canada. *Canadian Medical Association Journal* 159 (Suppl. 8):S1–29.

Menzies, David. 2001. Loyalty, At All Costs: It Used to Be Consumers Based Their Choice of Products on Value, Price, and Convenience. Now, Thanks to Company Reward Programs, You Can Add Kickbacks to the List. In *National Post.* Pp. C1, C4. April 21.

Miller, Daniel. 1995. Consumption and Commodities. *Annual Review of Anthropology* 24:141–161.

———. 1998. *A Theory of Shopping.* Ithaca, N.Y.: Cornell University Press.

Nichter, Mark, and Nancy Vuckovic. 1994. Agenda for an Anthropology of Pharmaceutical Practice. *Social Science and Medicine* 39(11):1509–1525.

Parry, Jonathan, and Marc Bloch. 1989. Introduction. In *Morality and Money.* J. Parry and M. Bloch, eds. Pp. 543–548. Cambridge, U.K.: Cambridge University Press.

Picard, André. 2001a. Six Million Lack Proper Drug Plans, Study Finds. In *Globe and Mail.* March 14:A1, A8.

———. 2001b. Spending on Drugs Up, Data Say. In *Globe and Mail.* March 15:A8.

Porter, Theodore. 1992. Objectivity as Standardization: The Rhetoric of Impersonality in Measurement, Statistics, and Cost-Benefit Analysis. *Annals of Scholarship* 9(1):19–59.

Povinelli, Elizabeth A. 1993. *Labor's Lot: The Power, History and Culture of Aboriginal Action.* Chicago: Chicago University Press.

———. 2000. Consuming Geist: Popontology and the Spirit of Capital in Indigenous Australia. *Public Culture* 31(3):501–528.

Q&A with Debra Lynkowski. *Diabetes Dialogue.* 1999. 46:36–37.

Ralston, Jennifer. 2000. Beyond Pill Pushing: How Shoppers Drug Mart Positions Itself above the Pharmacy Fray. In *Marketing Magazine* 105(12):19.

Rasky, Frank. 1988. *Just a Simple Pharmacist: The Story of Murray Koffler, Builder of the Shoppers Drug Mart Empire.* Toronto: McClelland & Stewart.

Rock, Melanie. 2000. Discounted Lives? Weighing Disability When Measuring Health and Ruling on "'Compassionate" Murder. *Social Science and Medicine* 51(3):407–418.

———. 2003a. Deaths, Taxes, and the Midas Touch of Mary Tyler Moore: Accounting for Promises by Politicians to Help Avert and Control Diabetes. *Medical Anthropology Quarterly* 17(2):200–232.

———. 2003b. Sweet Blood and Social Suffering: Rethinking Cause-Effect Relationships in Diabetes, Distress, and Duress. *Medical Anthropology: Cross-Cultural Studies in Health and Illness* 22:131–174.

Scheper-Hughes, Nancy. 1996. The Theft of Life: The Globalization of Organ Stealing Rumours. *Anthropology Today* 12(3):3–11.

Sharp, Lesley. 2000. The Commodification of the Body and Its Parts. *Annual Review of Anthropology* 29:287–328.

Strathern, Marilyn. 1992. Qualified Value: The Perspective of Gift Exchange. *Barter, Exchange, and Value: An Anthropological Approach.* C. Humphrey and S. Hugh-Jones, eds. Pp. 169–191. Cambridge, U.K.: Cambridge University Press.

———. 1996. Cutting the Network. *Journal of the Royal Anthropological Institute* 2(n.s.):517–535.

Thomas, Nicholas. 1991. *Entangled Objects: Exchange, Material Culture, and Colonialism in the Pacific.* Cambridge, Mass.: Harvard University Press.

Titmuss, Richard. 1971. *The Gift Relationship.* London: Allen & Irwin.

Turner, Bryan S. 1987. *Medical Power and Social Knowledge.* London: Sage.

United Kingdom Prospective Diabetes Study Group. 1998a. Effects of Intensive Blood Glucose Control with Metformin on Complications in Overweight Patients with Type 2 Diabetes. *Lancet* 352(9131):854–868.

———. 1998b. Intensive Blood Glucose Control with Sulphonylureas or Insulin Compared with Conventional Treatment and Risk of Complications in Patients with Type 2 Diabetes. *Lancet* 352(9131):837–853.

———. 1998c. Tight Blood Pressure Control and Risk of Macrovascular and Microvascular Complications in Type 2 Diabetes. *British Medical Journal* 317(September):703–713.

van der Geest, Sjaak, Susan Reynolds Whyte, and Anita Hardon. 1996. The Anthropology of Pharmaceuticals: A Biographical Approach. *Annual Review of Anthropology* 25:153–178.

Vuckovic, Nancy. 2000. Fast Relief: Buying Time with Medications. *Medical Anthropology Quarterly* 13(1):51–68.

Vuckovic, Nancy, and Mark Nichter. 1997. Changing Patterns of Pharmaceutical Practice in the United States. *Social Science and Medicine* 44(9):1285–1302.

Yang, Mayfair. 2000. Putting Global Capitalism in Its Place: Economic Hybridity, Bataille, and Ritual Expenditure. *Current Anthropology* 41(4):477–509.

Index

About the Contributors

Eric J. Arnould received a doctorate in social anthropology from the University of Arizona in 1982. He spent over ten years engaged in economic development work in francophone West Africa. He is now professor of marketing at the University of Nebraska, Lincoln. He has taught at the University of South Florida; Odense University in Denmark; California State University, Long Beach; and the University of Colorado, Denver. Dr. Arnould's work often appears in three major U.S. marketing journals, and a variety of social science periodicals and books. His recent work has focused on consumer rituals (holidays, leisure, disposition), service relationships (friendship and betrayal), West African marketing systems, and issues associated with multimethod research.

Duran Bell is professor in the Departments of Economics and Anthropology at the University of California, Irvine. While holding a B.A in economics and a Ph.D. in agricultural economics from U.C. Berkeley, he has devoted himself to research in economic anthropology for the last twenty years, specializing in marriage, marriage payments, sharing, and exchange. Most of his publications in anthropology are available (in PDF format) on his website: http://orion.oac.uci.edu/~dbell. His forthcoming book, *Wealth and Power: Survival in a Time of Global Accumulation)* is being published in Chinese and English.

Carolyn Folkman Curasi is an assistant professor of marketing at the J. Mack Robinson College of Business Administration at Georgia State University. She received her Ph.D. in business administration with a specialization in marketing from the University of South Florida in 1998. Dr. Curasi has been published in scholarly outlets including *The Journal of Consumer Research,* the *Journal of Services Marketing, Anthropology Newsletter, Advances in Consumer Research, The Quarterly Journal of Electronic Commerce,* the *International Journal of Market Research,* and *European Advances in Consumer Research.* Prior to joining the academic community, Dr. Curasi held several executive positions within corporate America.

Colin Danby received a Ph.D. in economics from the University of Massachusetts, Amherst in 1997 and is now associate professor of interdisciplinary arts and sciences at the University of Washington, Bothell. He has written about financial-sector reforms in El Salvador and Mexico, the anthropological literature on gifts, and the work of the Mexican economist Juan Noyola.

Françoise Dussart is an associate professor in the Department of Anthropology and the Women's Studies Program at the University of Connecticut, and the associate director of the Humanities Institute. Trained in France and Australia, her specialties in social anthropology include Australian Aboriginal society and culture (as well as other Fourth World peoples), urban theater culture, iconography and visual systems, various expressions of gender, ritual, and social organization, and ethnicity and nationalism. Dussart's career in anthropology began at the Sorbonne, where she studied the ethnolinguistic nuances of West African naming systems, the culture of street performers in Paris, and the slate factories of southern France. She received her Ph.D. from the Australian National University in 1989 for fieldwork with the Warlpiri, a group of Aborigines living in the Tanami Desert. Since then, she has devoted herself to curatorial efforts involving the acrylic painting of the Warlpiri. She has published extensively on matters of Oceanian art for scholarly journals and the popular press, in French and in English. She has also consulted for numerous museums worldwide, writing catalogs, a monograph, and essays, and assisting in general collection development. Professor Dussart's most current book presents a decade-long study of the issues of kinship, gender, and social identity in the Australian Aboriginal settlement of Yuendumu (*The Politics of Ritual in an Aboriginal Settlement,* 2000). Her most recent fieldwork research project examines the distinct agency of Australian men and women who actively design and carry out governmental policies for Aborigines.

James A. Egan received his Ph.D. in social science from the University of California, Irvine, in 1998, and has conducted ethnographic fieldwork in Yap State within the Federated States of Micronesia since the late 1980s. He is currently a lecturer in the Department of Anthropology at the University of California, Irvine. His continuing research interests include gender, power, kinship, and household economies in Micronesia.

Georgia L. Fox is assistant professor of anthropology in the Department of Anthropology at California State University, Chico (CSU, Chico). Her interest in economic anthropology stems from a background in anthropological archaeology as it pertains to trade, colonization, world systems theory, consumerism, and culture change in the late sixteenth and seventeenth centuries. Her current research areas include the archaeology of colonial port cities of the New World, museum studies, and the conservation of archaeological and ethnographic materials. She serves as codirector of CSU, Chico's Museum of Anthropology and the Museum Studies Program.

Maurice Godelier, an internationally renowned anthropologist, is a specialist on the societies of Oceania. Between 1967 and 1988 his fieldwork focused on the Baruya, a New Guinea Highlands tribe. In addition to his research on Oceania, on the basis of which he has published numerous works and made documentary films, Godelier has also explored a number of essential domains: the role of the *idéel* (mental constructs) in social relations, the distinction between the imaginary and the symbolic, and more recently the distinction between things one gives, things one sells, and things that can be neither given nor sold. He has also devoted an important part of his life to scientific policy making. From 1982 to 1986 he held the position of scientific director at the French National Center of Scientific Research (CNRS), as chairman of the department of the Sciences of Man and Society. He is presently a member of the National Council of Science, and vice president of the National Coordination Board for the Sciences of Man and Society. He has been mandated by the prime minister to take stock of the state of the human and social sciences in France and to promote their development in the framework of the construction of the European Research Space. The CNRS has awarded their Gold Medal for 2001 to Maurice Godelier, *directeur d'études (de classe exceptionnelle)* at *Sociales* at the *Ecole des Hautes Etudes en Sciences Sociales* (EHESS, a prestigious institute for the study of social sciences).

B. Lynne Milgram is associate professor in the Faculty of Liberal Studies at the Ontario College of Art and Design, Toronto, Canada, and adjunct faculty, Faculty of Graduate Studies (Anthropology), York University, Toronto. Her research on gender and development in the Philippines analyzes the cultural politics of social change with regard to "fair trade," women's work in crafts and agriculture, and microfinance initiatives. Her new research explores women's engagement in the secondhand clothing industry and related issues in migration in the northern Philippines. Her recent publications include: "Banking on Bananas, Crediting Crafts: Financing Women's Work in the Philippine Cordillera" (2002) *Atlantis: A Women's Studies Journal* 26 (2):109–118; "Operationalizing Microfinance: Women and Craftwork in Ifugao, Upland Philippines" (2001) *Human Organization* 60 (3):212–224; *Artisans and Cooperatives: Developing Alternative Trade for the Global Economy* (2000) coedited with Kimberly M. Grimes.

Brian Moeran is professor of culture and communication at the Copenhagen Business School. Trained as a social anthropologist, he has published widely on different aspects of Japanese advertising, art, communication, media, and popular culture. Among his books are *Women, Media and Consumption in Japan* (edited with Lise Skov, 1995), *A Japanese Advertising Agency* (1996), *Asian Media Productions* (editor, 2000), and *Advertising Cultures* (edited with Timothy de Waal Malefyt, 2003). He is currently doing comparative research on international fashion magazines in England, France, Hong Kong, Japan, and the United States.

David Mushinski is associate professor with the Department of Economics, Colorado State University. He has a Ph.D in economics from University of Wisconsin, Madison, a J.D. from University of Virginia School of Law, and a B.A. in economics from the College of William and Mary. His research interests include microenterprise and small business access to credit both on and off American Indian reservations, income distributions on American Indian reservations, and American Indian economic development and regional economics.

Beth E. Notar, assistant professor of anthropology at Trinity College in Hartford, Connecticut, received her Ph.D. in anthropology from the University of

Michigan. She has conducted research on tourism and the transition to a market economy in Dali, Yunnan, an ethnic minority region of southwest China. Her current research and teaching interests are in the meanings and uses of money.

Kathleen Pickering is associate professor with the Department of Anthropology, Colorado State University. She has a Ph.D in anthropology from University of Wisconsin, Madison, a J.D. from New York University School of Law, and a B.A. in history from the College of William and Mary. Her research interests focus on political economy and the effects of global economic systems on indigenous communities and local economies, with emphasis on culture change and continuity, economic development, and the socially embedded nature of the economy. Her book *Lakota Culture, World Economy* examines the role of culture, households, and local institutions from the Pine Ridge and Rosebud Indian Reservations in the construction of the world-system, both currently and through history. Before starting graduate school, Pickering worked as a legal services attorney on the Pine Ridge Indian Reservation in South Dakota.

Linda L. Price is the E. J. Faulkner Professor of Agribusiness and Marketing and CBA Agribusiness program director at the University of Nebraska, Lincoln. Dr. Price has published over seventy-five research papers in areas of marketing and consumer behavior. Her research focuses primarily on consumers, and she has coauthored a textbook on global consumer behavior. Price's research concerns the social context of marketplace behaviors and consumers as emotional, imaginative, and creative agents in their decisions and activities. She is listed as one of the top researchers in the field of marketing. Dr. Price is frequently invited to present her work at international conferences and major universities around the world, and she has consulted for a variety of firms varying from small nonprofit organizations to large Fortune 500 businesses. She regularly serves on editorial boards of leading consumer and marketing journals such as *Journal of Marketing, Journal of Public Policy and Marketing,* and *Journal of Consumer Research.*

Melanie Rock received her Ph.D. in anthropology from McGill University in 2002. She is currently an assistant professor in the Department of Community

Health Services at the University of Calgary. Her research interests include commodification, consumption, embodiment, and expertise. Most of her current work focuses on understandings of diabetes and responses to it.

Mahir Şaul teaches in the Department of Anthropology at the University of Illinois, Urbana–Champaign. He conducted most of his ethnographic and historical research in Burkina Faso and the neighboring countries of West Africa. He published articles and book chapters on the organization of farm households, intradomestic relations, rural and urban trade in West Africa, kinship, Islam and traditional religions, ecological history, and precolonial political organization. Most recently, he is the author (with Dr. Patrick Royer) of *West African Challenge to Empire: Culture and History in the Volta-Bani Anticolonial War* (2001).

Jim Weil received his doctorate in anthropology from Columbia University. Before his current research began in Costa Rica in the early 1990s, his projects and publications focused on human ecology, political economy, and the organization of work in Bolivia. His curatorial work at the Science Museum of Minnesota has included the preparation of an exhibit featuring the ceramic artisan cottage industry discussed in this book.

Cynthia Werner is assistant professor of anthropology at Texas A&M University. She has been doing fieldwork in post-Soviet Central Asia, especially Kazakhstan, since 1992. Her research interests in economic anthropology include gift exchange, household networking, market women, and international tourism development. Her current research project examines the social, psychological, and economic impacts of nuclear testing in northern Kazakhstan. Werner is also the coeditor of the *Research in Economic Anthropology* book series (with Norbert Dannhaeuser).